The Brandon Guide for Revising and Editing

Revise with `C` `L` `U` `E` `S` `S` **(pronounced as "clues" for easy memorization).**

`C`oherence: Connect your ideas.

- Are the ideas clearly related?
- Is there a clear pattern of organization (time, space, or emphasis)?
- Is the pattern supported by words that suggest the basis of that organization (time: *now*, *then*, *later*; space: *above*, *below*, *up*, *down*; emphasis: *first*, *second*, *last*)?
- Is coherence improved by the use of transitional terms, pronouns, repetition, and a consistent point of view?

`L`anguage: Use words appropriate for your purpose and audience.

- Is the general style of language usage appropriate (formal or informal) for the purpose and the intended audience?
- Is the tone (language use showing attitude toward material and audience) appropriate?
- Is the word choice (diction) effective? Are the words precise in conveying meaning? Are they fresh and not overused?

`U`nity: Stay on your topic.

- Are the thesis and every topic sentence clear and well stated? Do they indicate both subject and focus?
- Are all points of support clearly related to and subordinate to the topic sentence of each paragraph and to the thesis of the essay?

`E`mphasis: Call attention to your important ideas.

- Are ideas properly placed (especially near the beginning and end) for emphasis?
- Are important words and phrases repeated for emphasis?
- Are there short sentences among long ones to attract attention?

`S`upport: Back up your controlling ideas with evidence and logic.

- Is there adequate material—such as examples, details, quotations, and explanations—to support each topic sentence and thesis?
- Are the points of support placed in the best possible order?

`S`entences: Write correct, effective sentences with structural variety.

- Are the sentences varied in length? Are the beginnings of the sentences varied?
- Are the sentences varied in pattern (simple, compound, complex, and compound-complex)?

Edit with `C` `G` `P` `S` **(pronounced as "see GPS" for easy memorization).**

`C`apitalization

`G`rammar

`P`unctuation

`S`pelling

Writing Process Worksheet

Name _____ **Title** _____ **Due Date** _____

Use the back of this page or separate paper if you need more space.

Assignment   In the space below, write whatever you need to know about your assignment, including information about the topic, audience, pattern of writing, length, whether to include a rough draft or revised drafts, and whether your paper must be typed.

Stage One   **Explore**   Freewrite, brainstorm (list), cluster, or take notes as directed by your instructor.

Stage Two   **Organize**   Write a topic sentence or thesis; label the subject and focus parts.

Write an outline or an outline alternative. For reading-based writing, include references and short quotations with page numbers as support in the outline.

Stage Three   **Write**   On separate paper, write and then revise your paragraph or essay as many times as necessary for **c**oherence, **l**anguage (usage, tone, and diction), **u**nity, **e**mphasis, **s**upport, and **s**entences (**CLUESS**). Read your work aloud to hear and correct any grammatical errors or awkward-sounding sentences.

Edit any problems in fundamentals, such as **c**apitalization, **g**rammar, **p**unctuation, and **s**pelling (**CGPS**).

Thirteenth Edition

Paragraphs and Essays

With Integrated Readings

Lee Brandon

Kelly Brandon

CENGAGE
Learning®

Australia • Brazil • Mexico • Singapore • United Kingdom • United States

CENGAGE
Learning®

***Paragraphs and Essays with Integrated Readings,* Thirteenth Edition**
Lee Brandon, Kelly Brandon

Product Director: Nicole Lloyd

Product Manager: Andrew Rawson

Senior Content Developers: Brooke Foged
and Elizabeth Neustaetter

Associate Content Developer: Jacob Schott

Product Assistant: Julie Bizzotto

Senior Marketing Manager: Necco McKinley

Senior Content Project Manager:
Aimee Bear

Senior Designer: Diana Graham

Manufacturing Planner: Betsy Donaghey

IP Analyst: Ann Hoffman

IP Project Manager: Kathryn Kucharek

Production Service: Cenveo® Publisher
Services

Compositor: Cenveo® Publisher Services

Text Designer: Cenveo® Publisher Services

Cover Designer: Wing-Ip Ngan, Ink Design, Inc.

Cover Image: 145 Wilfried Krecichwost/
Ocean/Corbis

For product information and technology assistance, contact us at
**Cengage Learning Customer & Sales Support,
1-800-354-9706**

For permission to use material from this text or product, submit all
requests online at **www.cengage.com/permissions.**
Further permissions questions can be emailed to
permissionrequest@cengage.com.

Library of Congress Control Number: 2015949967

Student Edition:
ISBN: 978-1-305-65418-1

Loose-leaf Edition:
ISBN: 978-1-305-86593-8

Cengage Learning
20 Channel Center Street
Boston, MA 02210
USA

Cengage Learning is a leading provider of customized learning solutions
with employees residing in nearly 40 different countries and sales in more
than 125 countries around the world. Find your local representative at
www.cengage.com.

Cengage Learning products are represented in Canada by Nelson
Education, Ltd.

To learn more about Cengage Learning Solutions, visit **www.cengage.com.**

Purchase any of our products at your local college store or at our preferred
online store **www.cengagebrain.com.**

Printed in the United States of America
Print Number: 01   Print Year: 2015

Contents

iii

BRANDON BRIDGE

PART 3   WRITING PARAGRAPHS AND ESSAYS: INSTRUCTION, WITH INTEGRATED READING SELECTIONS   107

Chapter 7   Descriptive Narration   109
Moving Through Space and Time

Chapter 8   Exemplification   149

Writing with Examples

BRANDON BRIDGE

BRANDON BRIDGE

Chapter 12 Classification   269
Establishing Groups

Chapter 13   Comparison and Contrast   295
Showing Similarities and Differences

Chapter 14 Definition   327

Clarifying Terms

Chapter 15 Argument   363

Writing to Persuade

Preface

Developed especially for English writing courses one level below freshman composition, *Paragraphs and Essays* has thrived as a textbook since 1968. Its success derives from its emphasis on relentless revision with rigorous editing, integrated reading and writing, fresh and vibrant reading selections, friendly style, and innovative instruction.

Paragraphs and Essays with Integrated Readings, Thirteenth Edition

THE BRANDON BRIDGE

The flexible, adaptable writing strategies and devices described in *Paragraphs and Essays with Integrated Readings* coalesce into a unit of coordinated principles that collectively help students produce well-written statements. These strategies and devices, in essence, serve as a bridge to effective writing. The thirteenth edition features a new icon—the Brandon Bridge—to highlight the five essential features of this transformative instruction: The Writing Process Worksheet, The Brandon Guide for Revising and Editing, The Top 25 Editing Errors, Reading-Based Writing, and Career-Related Writing.

FEATURE ONE: THE WRITING PROCESS WORKSHEET

This form, which walks students through the stages of the writing process, appears on the back of the insert at the front of *Paragraphs and Essays*, on the Instructor Companion Site in Microsoft Word form, and on the Student Companion Site in PDF form. The early chapters of *Paragraphs and Essays* discuss the form in detail, and annotated student examples appear throughout the text. You can ask your students to print or copy the form, or you can download a copy from the Instructor Companion Site and customize it to fit your teaching needs.

FEATURE TWO: THE BRANDON GUIDE FOR REVISING AND EDITING

The Brandon Guide for Revising and Editing includes two acronyms for students to apply in writing and rewriting their paragraphs and essays. The acronym **CLUESS**, pronounced *clues* (**C**oherence, **L**anguage, **U**nity, **E**mphasis, **S**upport, and **S**entences), and the acronym **CGPS**, pronounced *see GPS* (**C**apitalization, **G**rammar, **P**unctuation, and **S**pelling) comprise a comprehensive list of ten of the most important elements in revising and editing. Memorizing the acronyms and instilling the principles associated with them into the student's intuitive, or automatic, approach to revising and editing are the prime objectives of this feature.

Students work with the paragraph-long, mode-specific exercises located at the end of each of the nine chapters devoted to patterns of writing; apply the elements of the Brandon Guide to their writing; and complete the revising, editing, and correction charts that appear on the inside covers and on the companion sites. Students note problems and progress on the Revising and Editing Charts by using abbreviations and symbols from the Correction Chart. Using the charts enables students to review a history of their progress and guides their work on future assignments. The Brandon Guide to Revising and Editing can also be adapted for use as a rubric for in-class peer editing, for cooperative writing activities, and for instructor use.

FEATURE THREE: THE TOP 25 EDITING ERRORS

The Top 25 Editing Errors provides a systematic approach to eradicating twenty-five of the most commonly marked errors on student papers. The Top 25 list, which appears at the beginning of the Handbook chapter, was compiled by a panel of nine veteran instructors at three large community colleges. This feature is supported by ten easily administered, optional exercises. Answers appear in the Annotated Instructor's Edition and in the Instructor's Resource Manual.

FEATURE FOUR: READING-BASED WRITING

Reading-based writing moves students beyond personal narratives to more analytical expression as they write about what they read. Reading-based writing provides substance for compositions and promotes critical thinking. Students engaged in reading-based writing transition more smoothly into English composition and function better in courses across the curriculum.

The typical reading-based writing assignments in *Paragraphs and Essays* require students to read a source, write an analytical reply, and give credit to the originator(s) for borrowed words and ideas. Specific reading-based writing assignments include summaries, reactions, and two-part responses designed to teach students the difference between summaries and reactions. Annotated examples of the three different kinds of reading-based writing appear throughout the book.

FEATURE FIVE: CAREER-RELATED WRITING

This edition includes five chapters with specific examples of patterns of writing used in the workplace:

- 7: Descriptive narration becomes an incident report
- 9: Analysis by division becomes a career review
- 10: Process analysis becomes a set of directions at a workplace
- 13: Comparison and contrast becomes a product, performance, or process evaluation
- 15: Argument becomes a workplace proposal

OTHER FEATURES IN *PARAGRAPHS AND ESSAYS*

- A detailed statement on the first page of Chapters 7 through 15 explains how the featured pattern can be used in cross-curricular, career-related, and workplace writing.
- Fourteen reading selections are new to this edition, including several that are anthologized for the first time in a textbook.
- All readings were selected for cultural and gender balance.
- A restaurant review is used as a model form of analysis by division.
- Nine cartoons amuse while demonstrating patterns of thought.
- A short story highlights cause and effect in human behavior.
- Many suggested writing topics are provided. They include an abundance of reading-based writing topics phrased as prompts, and additional writing topics and prompts grouped as general, cross-curricular, and career-related.
- An ESL unit included in the text provides definitions, rules, and reference that are of special help to writers who are learning English as a second language.

DISTRIBUTION AND PLACEMENT OF CONTENTS IN BRIEF

PART 1 The Writing Process

- Stages of writing: exploring, organizing, writing
- Revising and editing: the Brandon Guide for Revising and Editing, and the Top 25 Editing Errors
- Paragraphs and essays
- Demonstrations, exercises, assignments

PART 2 Linking Reading and Writing

- Reading techniques: underlining, annotating, outlining, taking notes
- Reading-based writing (the major form of text-based writing): summary, reaction, two-part response
- Giving credit for ideas and quotations: basic documentation
- Demonstrations, exercises, assignments

PART 3 Writing Paragraphs and Essays: Instruction, with Integrated Reading Selections

- Forms of discourse: descriptive narration, exemplification, analysis by division, process analysis, cause and effect, classification, comparison and contrast, definition, argument; with recognition that a single form often provides structure for paragraphs and essays but almost never occurs without the presence of other forms
- Examples of career-related writing, with instruction on writing for the workplace
- The nine chapters devoted to patterns of writing have identical formats: functional cartoons, writing instruction, an exercise in finding patterns in photos, two exercises in practicing patterns, model paragraphs and essays by student and professional writers, a student example of writing in stages, a student example of reading-based writing, writing prompts and topics (reading-based, general, cross-curricular, career-related), and a chapter summary

PART 4   Using Sources

- Finding and evaluating sources
- Documenting sources
- Writing a short research paper in ten steps
- Demonstrations and exercises

PART 5   Handbook

- Top 25 Editing Errors
- Rules for Top 25 Editing Errors
- Nine exercises for Top 25 Editing Errors
- Sentence elements
- Sentence patterns
- Sentence combining
- Sentence rhetoric
- Diction
- Punctuation
- Spelling
- ESL instruction

DIGITAL RESOURCES

Aplia

Aplia™ is interactive homework that helps students master the concepts that matter most. It includes dynamic instruction that helps them achieve success and transfer newfound skills to other classes and beyond. Each comprehensive Aplia problem set corresponds to a chapter in the textbook, allowing students to practice the skills they've just learned in a real-world context. The Aplia course for *Paragraphs and Essays* prominently features CLUESS and CGPS revision and editing processes. Scaffolded questions guide students from easily understandable topics to more complicated ideas, and a variety of question types keep the problems fresh and engaging.

Aplia's Grade It Now technology allows students to take multiple unique attempts of specific exercises to help reinforce concepts. Through Aplia's user-friendly grading and performance interface, you are able to quickly and easily track both individual and class-wide student performance, as well as generate and download detailed reports about your students.

The Aplia Diagnostic Assessment identifies specific strengths and weaknesses, allowing students to focus on the concepts that they most need to address. Students work through concepts step-by-step, first practicing the fundamentals and, then, targeting critical thinking skills that ask them to demonstrate their understanding in context.

MindTap

The MindTap course is a fully online, highly personalized learning experience built upon *Paragraphs and Essays*. MindTap combines student learning tools—

an interactive e-book, additional readings, prebuilt flashcards, activities, assessments, and more—into a singular learning path that guides students through their course. Instructors can personalize the experience by customizing authoritative Cengage Learning content and learning tools with their own content in the Learning Path via apps that integrate into the MindTap framework. Engaging assignments powered by Aplia reinforce key concepts and provide students with the practice they need to build fundamental writing and grammar skills.

INSTRUCTIONAL SUPPORT

The Annotated Instructor Edition contains immediate answers and teaching tips for exercises and activities. The Instructor's Guide is located on the Instructor Companion Site, accessed at **login.cengage.com**.

Instructor's Guide

- Tips for new instructors on how to approach the text
- Sample syllabi with suggestions for adaptations for different pedagogies and course lengths
- Answer key to the ten exercises for the Top 25 Editing Errors
- List of readings that are especially effective for reading-based writing
- Reproducible sentence-writing quizzes and answers covering instruction in the Handbook chapter
- Reproducible quizzes on selected readings from Part 3
- Suggestions for effective and time-saving approaches to instruction
- Suggestions for English as a Second Language (ESL) instruction
- Suggestions for teaching basic writers

Instructor Companion Site

The Instructor Companion Site includes these items: A Transition Guide to specify the changes from the previous edition, PowerPoint slides, Instructor's Guide, APA Guide, MLA Guide, Writing Process Worksheet in Word and PDF, Charts page for the Brandon Guide to Revising and Editing, and answers to the nine exercises for the Top 25 Editing Errors.

Student Overview

Connecting Thoughts with Written Statements

BRANDON BRIDGE

You will see this bridge icon frequently in *Paragraphs and Essays* because, like any other bridge, this book connects things. As with a well-functioning bridge linking the banks of a mighty river, this book attempts to provide the principles for connecting thoughts with successful written statements. As, in an engineering sense, there are many kinds of bridges to serve many needs, in writing there are many kinds of bridges for converting thoughts to statements. The photo on the cover of this book depicts a simple floating footbridge in the Mekong River delta in Vietnam. Without doubt, that bridge serves its practical purpose well. It is what it needs to be—and probably more, especially if you have a rich imagination and see beauty in the bridge's colors, textures, and shapes and are inclined to envision lively village folk creatively engaged in the bridge's construction and use. Much of the same can be said literally and often figuratively and about different needs and circumstances for written expression.

This instruction concerns itself with ways to communicate correctly and effectively in written statements. Some observers will tell you that to become a better writer you should practice writing—just sit down and write. Others will say that to become a better writer you should study the principles of writing.

Each view is a half-truth. If you practice without having the knowledge or understanding of the principles of writing correctly and effectively, you'll likely get better only within your own limitations. Moreover, if you practice bad habits, they are likely to become more ingrained and therefore more difficult to correct. For example, in musical performance, if you play the piano with only two fingers, you may learn to play a great "Chopsticks," but Beethoven's "Moonlight Sonata" may remain well beyond your artistic reach. The same can be said about practicing writing without your knowing, or somehow understanding, the principles of writing well. Of course, if you know the principles of writing well and you do not practice them, the principles will probably not become a functional part of your skills.

The solution is in your hands. You are now gazing at instruction with a well-balanced approach, one that combines sound principles with ample writing practice. The sound-principle part of writing will come from instruction in this text and from your professor's teaching. The degree of application of the techniques will be your responsibility.

The Three Core Features in the Brandon Bridge

These three features comprise the core instruction in this book:

1. The Brandon Guide for Revising and Editing (with a Self-Evaluation Chart)

2. The Writing Process Worksheet

3. The Top 25 Editing Errors

These core features are collectively comprehensive and, by nature and design, coordinated so they can almost always be used together. Flexible in their principles, they can be used in all college writing assignments.

THE BRANDON GUIDE FOR REVISING AND EDITING

This first feature is introduced in the form of two acronyms:

- **CLUESS** (pronounced "clues" for easy memorization) represents **C**oherence, **L**anguage, **U**nity, **E**mphasis, **S**upport, and **S**entences for revision, and
- **CGPS** (pronounced "see GPS") represents **C**apitalization, **G**rammar, **P**unctuation, and **S**pelling for editing.

These ten key elements in the acronyms are essential for effective revising and editing. The two acronyms can provide a foundation for self-evaluation and a framework for peer editing, cooperative projects, and student–instructor conferences.

Self-Evaluation Chart for the Brandon Guide

Just inside the front cover, you will see the Self-Evaluation Chart for you to record problems and progress in revising and editing as you apply the Brandon Guide directly to your writing. On the facing page, you'll see an illustrated list of the elements of the acronyms: **CLUESS** and **CGPS**.

- Drawing especially on your instructor's comments on your work, you can use the chart to pencil in matters that need your attention, as well as their location in this book.
- For page numbers of solutions to common writing problems, see the Index at the end of the book.
- As you master a persistent problem, you can place a checkmark, or perhaps a star, alongside it to note an accomplished step in learning to write well.
- Recording notes in the columns will provide you with a history of your progress as a writer.
- If you need more writing space, go to **www.cengagebrain.com** for a printable copy.

Here is a partially completed Self-Evaluation Chart with some brief guidelines for filling out your chart.

CLUESS   Revising Chart

Coherence	Use transitions, p. 29
Language	No overused words, pp. 32–33
Unity	Topic sentence, pp. 33–34
Emphasis	Repeat key words, pp. 34–35
Support	Use examples, pp. 35–37
Sentences	Vary sentence beginning, p. 38

CGPS   Editing Chart

Capitalization	I'm studying biology, English, and math. pp. 39–41
Grammar	Pronoun case: between you and me. pp. 41–43
Punctuation	After she left, I cried. pp. 43–45
Spelling	It's or its? There or their? Recieve or receive? p. 45

THE WRITING PROCESS WORKSHEET

You will find the Writing Process Worksheet on the back of the insert page at the front of this book. As directed by your instructor, print out a copy of the worksheet (available at www.cengagebrain.com) and record details about each of your assignments, such as the due date, topic, audience, length, and form. Using the worksheet will remind you not to overlook key parts of the stages of the writing process (Explore, Organize, and Write), thereby empowering you to take greater responsibility for the quality of your work.

THE TOP 25 EDITING ERRORS

This book contains a special feature called the Top 25 Editing Errors. A panel of nine veteran English instructors from three colleges contributed to the list, which appears at the beginning of the Handbook chapter. It contains the errors most frequently marked on student papers, along with remedies for those errors. Take a look at that section. If any of the items are head-scratchers for you, it would be worthwhile for you to study the entire unit with care.

General Study Tips

1. **Be active and systematic in learning.** Take advantage of your instructor's expertise by being an active participant in class—one who takes notes, asks questions, and contributes to discussion.

   Become dedicated to systematic learning: determine your needs, decide what to do, and do it. Make learning a part of your everyday thinking and behavior.

2. **Read widely.** Samuel Johnson, a great English scholar, once said he didn't want to read anything by people who had written more than they had read. William Faulkner, a Nobel Prize winner in literature, said, "Read, read, read. Read everything—trash, classics, good and bad, and see how writers do it." Read to learn technique, to acquire ideas, to be stimulated to write. Especially read to satisfy your curiosity and receive pleasure. If reading is a main component of your course, approach it as systematically as you do writing. Reading-based writing will offer you opportunities to polish your critical-thinking skills as you compose responses to what you read, much as you do in classes across the curriculum.

3. **Keep a journal.** Keeping a journal may not be required in your particular class; regardless of whether it is required, though, jotting down your observations in a notebook is a good idea. Here are some ideas for daily, or almost daily, journal writing:
   - Summarize, evaluate, or react to reading assignments.
   - Summarize, evaluate, or react to what you see on television and in movies, and to what you read in newspapers, magazines, or online.
   - Describe and narrate situations or events you experience.

- Write about career-related matters you encounter in other courses or on the job.

Your journal entries may read like an intellectual diary, a record of what you are thinking about at certain times. Mainly, keeping a journal will help you understand reading material better, develop more language skills, and think more clearly—as well as become more confident so that you can write more easily. Your entries may also provide subject material for longer, more carefully crafted pieces. Make writing a familiar everyday activity.

4. **Be positive as you look forward.** At the end of this semester, look back to see specifically what you have mastered and checked off your list on your Self-Evaluation Chart. Recognizing your command of effective and correct writing skills will give you a much deserved sense of accomplishment as you look forward.

Best Wishes,
Lee Brandon
Kelly Brandon

PART 1

THE WRITING PROCESS

Think of writing as swimming. If you were a nonswimmer and you jumped into the water without instructions, at best you would swim awkwardly. At worst you would sink. You may face similar dilemmas in writing. If you choose the sink-or-swim method, hope for hidden talent or good luck. A better choice is the writing process, an approach that all writers use to some degree and with modifications for different writing situations. Whether you call it the flow of writing or the writing process, it is all here.

1

The Writing Process: Stage One

Exploring / Experimenting / Gathering Information

 Ideas come from everything.

—ALFRED HITCHCOCK

The Writing Process Defined

The writing process consists of a set of strategies that will help you proceed from idea or purpose to the final statement of a paragraph or an essay. As presented here, the different strategies move from

> **Stage One:** Exploring / Experimenting / Gathering Information
>
> *to*
>
> **Stage Two:** Writing the Controlling Idea / Organizing and Developing Support
>
> *to*
>
> **Stage Three:** Writing / Revising / Editing.

Altogether they represent what is called the **writing process**.

The process of writing is **recursive**, which means "going back and forth." In this respect, writing is like reading. If you do not understand what you have read, you back up and read it again. After you reread the entire passage, you may still go back and reread selectively. The same can be said of your writing. If, for example, you have reached Stage Two and you are working with an outline only to discover that your subject is too broad, you may want to back up and narrow your topic sentence or thesis and then adjust your outline. You may even return to an early cluster of ideas to see how you can use a smaller grouping of them. Revising, in Stage Three, is usually the most recursive part of all. You will go over your material again and again until you are satisfied that you have expressed yourself the best you can.

The Writing Process Worksheet

The blank Writing Process Worksheet, with brief directions for the three stages of the writing process, is designed to be duplicated and completed with each major writing assignment. It gives you clear, consistent guidance and provides your instructor with an easy format for finding and checking information.

The Assignment

Particulars of the assignment, frequently the most neglected parts of a writing project, are often the most important. If you do not know, or later cannot recall, specifically what you are supposed to do, you cannot do satisfactory work. An otherwise excellent composition on a misunderstood assignment may get you a failing grade, a sad situation for both you and your instructor.

As an aid to recalling just what you should write about, the Writing Process Worksheet provides space and guidance for you to note these details: information about the topic, audience, pattern of writing, length of the paper, whether to include a rough draft or revised drafts, whether your paper must be typed, and the date the assignment is due.

At the time your instructor gives that information, it will probably be clear; a few days later, it may not be. By putting your notes on the assignment portion of the worksheet, you remind yourself of what you should do and also indicate to your instructor what you have done.

Your Audience in Personal, Academic, and Career-Related Writing

At the outset of your writing project, you should pause to imagine your likely readers: How much do they know about your topic and how are they related to it? What are their values? Is the purpose of your message mainly to inform, persuade, or entertain your audience? What is the social setting of your message—formal or informal? How well do you and your audience know each other? When you talk, you are likely, consciously or subconsciously, to take those matters into account. The result is that you talk differently to different people for different occasions and purposes. To some extent, you change your speech in tone, vocabulary, and content for family, friendship, work, classroom, party, and public address situations. If you do not acknowledge the immediate social setting you occupy, your communication will suffer. The same can be said of writing. From a casual text message to a close friend, to a thank you letter for a neighbor, to a research paper, to a formal letter of application for your dream job, you need to know your audience, as well as the occasion and purpose of your communication. Good language is what is appropriate language for anything within that range. It should change gracefully as you move through personal, academic, and career-related experiences.

Stage One Strategies

Certain strategies commonly grouped under the heading *prewriting* can help you get started and develop your ideas. These strategies—freewriting, brainstorming, clustering, and gathering information—are very much a part of writing. The understandable desire to skip to the finished statement is what causes the most common student-writer grief: that of not filling the blank sheet or of filling it but not significantly improving on the blankness. The prewriting strategies described in this section will help you attack the blank sheet constructively with imaginative thought, analysis, and experimentation. They can lead to clear, effective communication.

FREEWRITING

Freewriting is an exercise that its originator, Peter Elbow, has called "babbling in print." When you freewrite, you write without stopping, letting your ideas tumble forth. You do not concern yourself unduly with the fundamentals of writing, such as punctuation and spelling. Freewriting is an adventure into your memory and imagination. It is concerned with discovery, invention, and exploration. If you are at a loss for words on your subject, write in a comment such as "I do not know what is coming next" or "blah, blah, blah," and continue when relevant words come. It is important to keep writing. Freewriting immediately eliminates the blank page and thereby helps you break through an emotional barrier, but that is not the only benefit. The words that you sort through in that idea kit will include some you can use. You can then underline or circle those words and even add notes on the side so that the freewriting continues to grow even after its initial spontaneous expression.

The way you proceed depends on the type of assignment: working with a topic of your choice, working from a restricted list of topics, or working with a prescribed topic.

The *topic of your choice* affords you the greatest freedom of exploration. You would probably select a subject that interests you and freewrite about it, allowing your mind to wander among the many parts of that subject, perhaps mixing fact and fantasy, direct experience, and hearsay. A freewriting about music might uncover areas of special interest and knowledge, such as jazz or folk rock, that you would want to pursue further in freewriting or other prewriting strategies.

Working from a *restricted list* requires a more focused freewriting. With the list, you can, of course, experiment with several topics to discover what is most suitable for you. If, for example, "career choice," "career preparation," "career guidance," and "career prospects" are on the restricted list, and you are career-minded, you would probably select one of those topics and freewrite about it. If it works well for you, you would likely proceed with the next step of your prewriting. If you are not satisfied with what you uncover in freewriting, you would explore another item from the restricted list.

When working with a *prescribed topic*, you should focus on it and try to restrict your freewriting to its boundaries. If your topic specifies a division of a subject area, such as "political involvement of your generation," then you would tie those key words to your own information and critical thinking. If the topic asks for, let's say, your reactions to a specific poem, then that poem would give you the framework for your free associations with your own creativity, opinions, and store of experience.

You should learn to use freewriting because it will often serve you well, but you need not use it every time you write. Some very short writing assignments do not call for freewriting. An in-class assignment may not allow time for freewriting, and some writers will find freewriting more useful than others.

Nevertheless, freewriting may become a valuable strategy in your toolbox of techniques. See if it can help you get words on paper, break emotional barriers, generate topics, develop new insights, and explore ideas.

Freewriting can lead to other stages of prewriting and writing, and it can also provide content as you develop your topic.

The following example of freewriting, as well as other writing, revising, and editing examples, is from student Betsy Jackson's work titled "If I Were a Traffic Cop." She selected her topic, bad drivers, from a restricted list. If she had been working with a prescribed topic, she might have been told to concentrate on only one aspect of bad drivers, such as the need for driver education, the need for better laws, or the cost of bad driving. Then she would have done some research. However, she had no such limitation and, therefore, thought about bad drivers broadly in a personal context. After her freewriting, she went back over her work looking for an idea that might be limited enough to use as the basis for a paper. Here is what she wrote:

> Just driving around on streets and freeways can be a scary experience because of all the bad drivers. Whenever I see them, sometimes I just laugh. Sometimes I get mad. Sometimes I get irritated. Sometimes I get scared. It's not just the young drivers or the old drivers it's <u>all kinds</u>. And all types of people no matter what the nationality or the types of vehicles they drive.

All kinds

Drunk drivers

If I were a cop

Tailgaters

Lane changers
Left turners on red
Too fast, too slow
Don't yield

Causes
Effect

Pickup drivers are worse as a group but bad drivers come in all kinds of vehicles. I think someone should do something about them. The worst are the <u>drunk drivers</u>. I don't see them in the morning. But I see them late at night when I'm driving home from work. They should be put away. But a lot of others should be getting serious tickets. Especially the bad ones. <u>Make me a cop</u>—a supercop—a Rambo cop and I'll go after the bad ones. Some of them cause a lot of accidents and get people all mad. Blah. Blah. Blah. Take <u>tailgaters</u> for example. And what about the drivers that go into the emergency lanes on the freeways to pass when there's a jam. And then you've got the <u>lane changers</u> that don't even give signals. And those that just <u>keep going</u> and <u>turn left when</u> the <u>light turns red</u>. Then you've got the ones that drive <u>too fast</u> and <u>too slow</u>. And you've got the ones that <u>don't stop</u> for <u>pedestrians</u>. Blah. Blah. Blah. I guess we all have our pet peeves about bad drivers and everyone would like to be a cop sometimes. I guess if you talked to them some would have reasons. Maybe they're <u>late</u> for work or they are <u>mad</u> about something. Or maybe there's an <u>emergency</u>. Whatever it is, I get concerned when they <u>take *my* life in *their* hands</u>.

After her freewriting session, Jackson examined what she had written for possible ideas to develop for a writing assignment. As she recognized those ideas, she underlined important words and phrases and made a few notes in the margins. By reading only the underlined words in her freewriting, you can understand what is important to Jackson; it was not necessary for her to underline whole sentences.

In addition to putting some words on that dreaded blank sheet of paper, Jackson discovered that she had quite a lot to say about drivers and that she had selected a favorable topic to develop. The entire process took no more than five minutes. Had she found only a few ideas or no promising ideas at all, she might have freewritten on another topic. Although in going back over her work she saw some errors, especially in wording and sentence structure, she did not correct them because the purpose of freewriting is discovery, not revising or editing. Jackson was confident that she could continue with the process of writing a paper as she followed her flow of thought.

EXERCISE 1   Freewriting

Try freewriting on a broad topic such as one of the following:

An event that was important to you in your youth

A concert, a movie, or a television program

The ways you use your computer

Drug use—causes, effects, a friend with a problem

Gang membership—causes, effects, an experience

The benefits of using social media

Ways of disciplining children

Why a person is a hero or role model to you

 A great or terrible party

A bad or good day at school

Why a college education is important

Following the example in Jackson's freewriting, underline and annotate the phrases that may lead to ideas you could explore further.

BRAINSTORMING

Brainstorming features important words and phrases that relate in various ways to your subject area or your specific topic. Brainstorming includes two basic forms: (1) asking and answering questions and (2) listing. These two forms may overlap. For some assignments, writers go directly from listing to outlining or, occasionally, to the rough draft.

Big Six Questions

One effective way to get started is to ask the big six questions about your subject: *Who? What? Where? When? Why? How?* Then let your mind run free as you jot down answers in single entries or lists. Some of the big six questions may not fit, and some may be more important than others, depending on the purposes of your writing. For example, if you were writing about the causes of a situation, the *Why?* question could be more important than the others. If you were concerned with how to do something, the *How?* question would predominate. If you were writing in response to a reading selection, you would confine your thinking to questions appropriately related to the content of that reading selection.

Whatever your focus for the questions is, the result is likely to be numerous ideas that will provide information for continued exploration and development of your topic. Thus your pool of information for writing widens and deepens.

Jackson continued with the topic of bad drivers, and her topic tightened to focus on particular areas.

Who?	Bad drivers; me as a cop
What?	Driving badly, recklessly, unsafely; a cop's job
Where?	On every roadway
When?	All the time

| Why? | Hurried, disrespectful, self-centered, sick, addiction, hostile, irresponsible |
| How? | Lane-changing, driving illegally in emergency lane, not signaling, passing on the shoulder, tailgating, turning left on red, rolling stop, speeding, driving while intoxicated |

Notice that each question is answered in this example, but with some topics some questions may not fit. As Jackson addressed the *Why?* and *How?* questions, her brainstorming produced long lists, suggesting that those areas were strong possibilities for the focus of her paper.

Listing

Simply making a list of words and phrases related to natural divisions of your topic is another effective way to brainstorm, especially if you have a defined topic and a storehouse of information. This strategy is favored by many writers. Being concerned with the bad behavior of drivers, Jackson could have settled on her list under *how*, circled three or four entries for a tentative framework for her short paper, and proceeded to consider each in more depth.

Knowing from the outset that she was concerned mainly with the behavior of drivers, Jackson might have gone directly to making a list indicating what drivers do or how they drive. She then might have selected perhaps four ideas from this list for her framework and circled them for future reference.

(Changing lanes unsafely)
Driving illegally in the emergency lane
Not signaling
Passing on the shoulder
(Tailgating)
(Turning left on red)
Turning right on red without stop
Rolling stop
Speeding
Driving too slow in fast lane
(Driving while intoxicated)
(Driving with handheld cell phone for speaking or texting)
Driving while reading road map
Driving a large truck in car lanes
Dumping trash from car

Even if you do not have a focused topic, you may find a somewhat random listing useful, merely writing phrases as they occur to you. This exploratory activity is similar to freewriting. After you have established such a list, you can sort and group the phrases as you generate your topic and find its natural divisions. Feel free to accept, reject, or insert phrases.

EXERCISE 2   Brainstorming

Further explore the topic you worked with in Exercise 1 by first answering the big six questions and then making a list.

Big Six Questions

Who? _Ryan_

What? _tripped, and fell_

Where? _down the stairs by the library_

When? _yesterday_

Why? _shoes laces untied_

How? _not tying his shoes_

List

crying

bleeding

upset

___

___

___

___

___

___

___

___

CLUSTERING

In **clustering**, double-bubble your topic—that is, write it down in the middle of the page and draw a double circle around it—and then respond to the question "What comes to mind?" Draw a single bubble around other ideas on spokes radiating from the hub that contains the topic. Any bubble can lead to another bubble or to numerous bubbles in the same way. This strategy is sometimes used instead of, or before, making an outline to organize and develop ideas.

The more restricted the topic inside the double bubble, the fewer the number of spokes that will radiate with single bubbles. For example, a topic such as "high school dropouts" would have more spokes than "reasons for dropping out of high school."

Here is Jackson's cluster on the subject of bad drivers. She has drawn dotted lines around subclusters that seem to relate to a workable, unified topic.

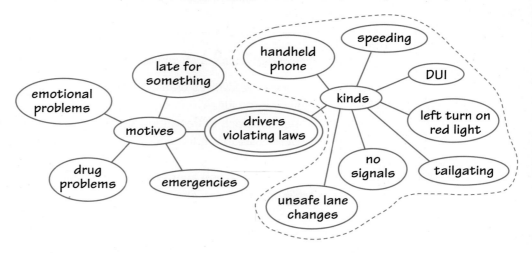

EXERCISE 3   Clustering

Continuing with your topic, develop a cluster of related ideas. Draw dotted lines around subclusters that have potential for focus and more development.

GATHERING INFORMATION

For reading-related writing—especially the kind that requires a close examination of the selection—you will gather information by reading print or electronic sources, making notes, and perhaps outlining or summarizing the text. Of course, you may also want to make notes for other topics to write about as they occur to you. This kind of note taking can be combined with listing and clustering. It can even take the place of them. It can also be used in conjunction with outlining.

Student Betsy Jackson at this point is writing about personal experience. If she wanted to include statistics or an authoritative statement to support her view further, she might do some library research or interview a police officer. In any case, she would take notes.

WRITER'S GUIDELINES   The Writing Process: Stage One

BRANDON BRIDGE

The writing process consists of strategies that will help you proceed from idea or purpose to the final statement of a paragraph or an essay. Throughout all stages of the writing process, you should consider your audience.

Stage One offers four approaches:

1. **Freewriting** consists of writing without stopping, letting ideas tumble forth.

   - Freewriting involves breaking down emotional barriers, generating topics, discovering ideas, and exploring ideas.
   - Your approach to freewriting will depend on whether you work on a topic of your choice (great freedom), a topic from a restricted list (more focused), or an assigned topic (concentration on one idea).
   - You need not use freewriting for all writing experiences. You would probably not use it for very short assignments, in-class assignments with limited time, outline and summary assignments, or assignments on topics you know well.

2. **Brainstorming** is used for quickly developing key words and phrases that relate to your topic. It includes two basic forms: the big six questions and listing.

   - You may ask *Who? What? Where? When? Why?* and *How?* questions about your topic, ignoring questions that do not fit.
   - Or, you may simply list points on likely divisions of your topic, a form that some writers use instead of an outline, especially in timed-writing situations.

3. **Clustering** is a visual way of showing connections and relationships. It is sometimes used with an outline and sometimes in place of one.

   - Start by double-bubbling your topic.
   - Then, in response to the question *What comes to mind?* single-bubble other ideas on spokes radiating from the hub.

4. **Gathering information** can take the form of reading with underlining, annotating, and note taking.

2

The Writing Process: Stage Two

Writing the Controlling Idea / Organizing and Developing Support

Don't write merely to be understood. Write so that you can't possibly be misunderstood.

—ROBERT LOUIS STEVENSON

CHAPTER CONTENTS

BRANDON BRIDGE

The most important advice this book can offer you is *state your controlling idea and support it*. If you have no controlling idea—no topic sentence for a paragraph or thesis for an essay—your writing will be unfocused, and your readers may be confused or bored. But if you organize your material well, so that it supports and develops your controlling idea, you can present your views to your readers with interest, clarity, and persuasion.

Stating the controlling idea and organizing support can be accomplished effectively and systematically. How? This chapter presents several uncomplicated techniques you can use in Stage Two of the writing process.

Defining the Controlling Idea

If you tell a friend you are about to write a paragraph or an essay, be prepared to hear the question "What are you writing about?" If you answer, "Public schools," your friend will probably be satisfied with the answer but not very interested. The problem is that the phrase *public schools* offers no sense of limitation or direction. It just indicates your subject, not what you are going to do with it. *An effective controlling statement, called the **topic sentence** for a paragraph and the **thesis** for an essay, has both a subject **and** a focus.* The **subject** is what you intend to write about. The **focus** is what you intend to do with your subject.

> **Example:** <u>Long homework assignments for children</u> <u>can interrupt family life.</u>
>   subject   focus

In some instances the subject will follow the focus:

> <u>The time has come for a national law legalizing</u>
>   focus
> <u>physician-assisted suicide for the terminally ill.</u>
>   subject

In other instances the subject will divide the focus:

> <u>Four factors establish</u> <u>Elvis Presley</u> <u>as the greatest entertainer of</u>
>   focus   subject   focus
> <u>the twentieth century: appearance, singing ability, style, and influence.</u>

Writing the Controlling Idea as a Topic Sentence or Thesis

The effective controlling idea presents a focus that can be developed with supporting information. The ineffective one is vague, too broad, or too narrow.

Vague: <u>Public schools</u> <u>are great.</u>
                      subject   focus

Better: <u>Public schools</u> <u>do as well academically as private schools,</u>
                      subject   focus
               <u>according to statistics.</u> [made more specific]

Too Broad: <u>Public schools</u> <u>are too crowded.</u>
                      subject   focus

Better: <u>Sellers Elementary School</u> <u>is too crowded.</u> [limiting the
                      subject   focus
               subject to a particular school]

Too Narrow: American public schools were first established in Philadelphia
                                   subject   focus
               in 1779. [only a fact]

Better: The first public schools in America were founded to meet certain
                               subject   focus
               practical needs. [made more specific by indicating aspects]

In writing a sound controlling idea, be sure that you have included both the subject and the focus and that the whole statement is not vague, too broad, or too narrow. Instead, it should be phrased so that it invites development. Such phrasing can usually be achieved by limiting time, place, or aspect. The limitation may apply to the subject (instead of schools in general, a specific school), or it may apply to the focus (you might compare the subject to something else, as in "do as well academically"). You might limit both the subject and the focus.

EXERCISE 1   Evaluating Topic Sentences

In the following controlling ideas, underline and label the subjects (S) and focus (F). Also judge each one as effective (E) or ineffective (I).

Example:

____I____   Basketball is an interesting sport.
                 S   F

_____ **1.** Students who cheat in school may be trying to relieve certain emotional pressures.

_____ **2.** Shakespeare was an Elizabethan writer.

_____ **3.** The quarterback in football and the general of an army are alike in significant ways.

_____ **4.** Animals use color chiefly for protection.

_____ **5.** Portland is a city in Oregon.

_____ **6.** Life in the ocean has distinct realms.

_____ **7.** Rome has had a glorious and tragic history.

_____ **8.** Boston is the capital of Massachusetts.

_____ **9.** The word *macho* has a special meaning to the Hispanic community.

_____ **10.** The history of plastics is exciting.

EXERCISE 2 Evaluating Topic Sentences

In the following controlling ideas, underline and label the subjects (S) and focus (F). Also judge each one as effective (E) or ineffective (I).

_____ 1. An experience in the first grade taught me a valuable lesson about honesty.

_____ 2. The Internet has changed the way many people shop.

_____ 3. President Lincoln was assassinated at the Ford Theater.

_____ 4. The dictionary has an interesting history.

_____ 5. The world is a place of many contrasts.

_____ 6. Rap music can be classified on the basis of the intent of its writers/composers.

_____ 7. Mumbai is one of the most densely populated cities in the world.

_____ 8. What I have seen while working in a fast-food place has made me lose my appetite.

_____ 9. My physical education teacher is called "Coach."

_____ 10. Count Dracula's reputation is based on his exploits as a nocturnal creature.

EXERCISE 3 Writing Topic Sentences

Complete the following entries to make each one a solid topic sentence. Only a subject and part of the focus are provided. The missing part may be more than a single word.

Example: Car salespeople behave differently, depending on _the car they are selling and the kind of customer they are serving._

1. A part-time job can offer _____

2. My school's athletic program should be _____

3. It is almost universally accepted that smoking is _____

4. Students caught cheating should be _____

5. Health care should be _____

6. One of the effects of the rising cost of a college education is _____
_____

7. Offering constructive criticism to a friend who did not ask can _____
_____

8. People who appear on television talk shows are frequently _____

9. The slang of a particular group reveals _____

10. Gestures and facial expressions usually communicate _____

EXERCISE 4   Writing Topic Sentences

Convert each of the following subjects into a topic sentence.

1. Bumper stickers _____

2. Rudeness _____

3. The true character of my neighbor _____

4. Many homeless people _____

5. Being able to use a computer _____

6. Dieting _____

7. The basic forms of jazz and classical music _____

8. Educated citizens _____

9. The required labeling of rock-and-roll albums _____

10. Smoking _____

Your topic sentence or thesis can come from any of several places. You may be able to generate it at Stage One (in your initial freewriting, brainstorming, clustering, or information gathering) or you may be given an assigned topic. In any case, your procedure is the same at this point. You need to work on the statement—just that one sentence—until you have developed an interesting subject and a well-defined focus. The statement may be a bit more mechanical than the one you actually use in your paragraph or essay, but it can easily be reworded once you reach Stage Three of the writing process: writing, revising, and editing.

The controlling idea will probably not pop into your head fully developed. It is more likely to be the result of repeated revisions. Even when you are revising a paper you have written, you may go back and rephrase your topic sentence or thesis. That is part of the back-and-forth (recursive) nature of the writing process.

In the following example, note how Betsy Jackson reworks her controlling idea several times before she settles on a statement that is well focused and able to be developed.

Subject	Focus
Bad drivers	can be found everywhere. (too broad)
Someone	should do something about bad drivers. (vague)
Bad driving	has existed in the United States for more than a century. (too broad)
If I were a traffic cop	I'd crack down on certain types of bad drivers. (workable)

Jackson has limited the subject by reducing it to the hypothetical situation of being a traffic cop. She has limited the focus by dealing with only "certain types of bad drivers," not all bad drivers.

EXERCISE 5   Writing Your Topic Sentence

Using a topic you worked with in the first stage of the writing process, write a topic sentence or thesis. Mark the subject and focus parts.

Organizing Support

You have now studied the first part of the seven-word sentence "State your controlling idea and support it." In the first stage of the writing process, you explored many ideas, experimented with them, and even developed some approaches to writing about them. You may also have gathered information through reading and note taking. The techniques of that first stage have already given you some initial support. The next step is to organize your ideas and information into a paragraph or an essay that is interesting, understandable, and compelling.

Three tools can help you organize your supporting material: listing (a form of brainstorming), clustering, and outlining. You will probably use only one of these organizing tools, depending on course requirements, the assignment, or individual preference. In the continuing demonstration of Jackson's work, each tool is shown.

LISTING

Lists are the simplest and most flexible of the organizing tools. Listing need be nothing more than a column of items presenting support material in a useful sequence (time, space, or importance). As you work with your support material, you can cross out words or move them around on the list. By leaving vertical space between items, you can easily insert new examples and details. Jackson took phrases from the list she had made in Stage One and wrote them below her topic sentence.

<u>If I were a traffic cop,</u> <u>I would crack down on certain types of bad drivers.</u>
       subject   focus

Drunk drivers—most dangerous, top priority, off the road
Tailgaters—hostile, hurried, cause accidents, irritating
Unsafe lane changers—rude, cause accidents
Left-turners on red—reckless, accident prone

CLUSTERING

Chains of circles radiating from a central double-bubbled circle form a cluster that shows the relationship of ideas. In the following example, Jackson has developed part of her Stage One cluster.

<u>If I were a traffic cop,</u> <u>I'd crack down on certain types of bad drivers.</u>
       subject   focus

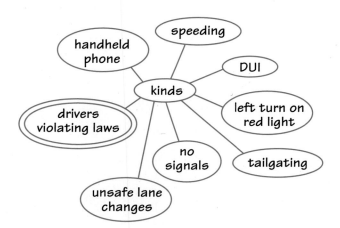

OUTLINING

Outlining is the tool that most people think of in connection with organizing. Because it is flexible and widely used, it will receive the most emphasis in this stage of the writing process. Outlining does basically the same thing that listing and clustering do. Outlining divides the controlling idea into sections of support material, divides those sections further, and establishes sequence.

An outline is a framework that can be used in two ways: (1) It can indicate the plan for a paragraph or an essay you intend to write, and (2) it can show the organization of a passage you are reading. The outline of a reading passage and the outline as a plan for writing are identical in form. If you intend to write a summary of a reading selection, then a single outline might be used for both purposes.

The two main outline forms are the **sentence outline** (each entry is a complete sentence) and the **topic outline** (each entry is a key word or phrase). The topic outline is more common in writing paragraphs and essays.

In the following topic outline, notice first how the parts are arranged on the page: the indentations, the number and letter sequences, the punctuation, and the placement of words. Then read Jackson's outline and see how the ideas in it relate to one another.

Main Idea (will usually be the topic sentence for a paragraph or the thesis for an essay)

    I. Major support
      A. Minor support
        1. Explanation, detail, example
        2. Explanation, detail, example
      B. Minor support
        1. Explanation, detail, example
        2. Explanation, detail, example
   II. Major support
      A. Minor support
        1. Explanation, detail, example
        2. Explanation, detail, example
      B. Minor support
        1. Explanation, detail, example
        2. Explanation, detail, example

Here is Jackson's outline:

<u>If I were a traffic cop,</u> <u>I would crack down on certain types of bad drivers.</u>
        subject   focus

    I. Drunks
   II. Unsafe lane changers
      A. Attitude
        1. Rude
        2. Bullying
      B. Results
        1. Accidents
        2. People irritated
  III. Left-turners on red
      A. Attitude
        1. Self-centered
        2. Putting self above law
      B. Results
        1. Bad collisions
        2. Mass anger
  IV. Tailgaters
      A. Motives
        1. Hostility
        2. Rushed
        3. Impatient
      B. Effects
        1. Accidents
        2. Road fights

The foundation of an effective outline and, hence, of an effective paragraph or essay, is a strong controlling idea. Always begin by writing a sound topic sentence or thesis, one with a specific subject and a well-defined focus. Then divide the focus into parts. The nature of the parts will depend on what you are trying to do in the focus. Just consider the thought process involved. What kinds of material would best support or explain that topic sentence or thesis? How should you organize that material? Should you present a series of examples? A description of a process? A story of human struggle? A combination of methods?

Among the most common forms of dividing and organizing ideas are the following:

- **Narration:** division of time or incident to tell a story

    I. Situation
    II. Conflict
    III. Struggle
    IV. Outcome
    V. Meaning

- **Exemplification:** division into several examples

    I. First example
    II. Second example
    III. Third example

- **Analysis by division:** division into steps telling how something is done

    I. First part
    II. Second part
    III. Third part

- **Process analysis:** division of a unit into parts (for example, a pencil has an eraser, a wooden barrel, and a lead)

    I. Preparation
    II. Steps
        A. Step 1
        B. Step 2
        C. Step 3

- **Cause and effect:** division into causes or effects

    I. Cause (or effect) one
    II. Cause (or effect) two
    III. Cause (or effect) three

EXERCISE 6   Completing Outlines

Fill in the missing parts of the following outlines. It may be helpful to consider, in each case, whether you are dealing with time, examples, causes, effects, parts, or steps. The answers will vary, depending on your individual experiences and views.

1. <u>Borrowing</u> <u>is the mother of trouble.</u>
       subject   focus
   I. Received five credit cards in mail
   II. Saw numerous commercials on television
     A. One about _____
     B. Another about _____
   III. Made purchases with the credit cards
   IV. Two months later _____

2. <u>A successful job interview</u> <u>depends on several factors.</u>
            subject   focus
   I. Good appearance
     A. _____
     B. _____
   II. Behaving properly
   III. Being qualified
     A. Education
     B. _____
   IV. Knowing something about the employer

3. <u>Joe's drug addiction</u> <u>had significant effects on his life.</u>
         subject   focus
   I. Developed mental health problems
     A. _____
     B. _____
   II. Developed _____
   III. Lost his job
   IV. Lost _____

4. <u>A college education</u> <u>is important for several reasons.</u>
         subject   focus
   I. Offers personal enrichment
   II. Fulfills curiosity
   III. Provides contacts that may be satisfying later
   IV. _____

5. An ordinary person can be an environmentalist every day.
       subject   focus
   I. Limit use of internal combustion engines
   II. Avoid using and dumping poisonous chemicals
   III. _____
   IV. _____
       A. Save newspapers
       B. Save _____
       C. _____

6. Cooking spaghetti is not difficult.
       subject   focus
   I. Get pan, water, and pasta
   II. Boil water in pan
   III. _____
   IV. Cook pasta until _____
   V. Remove pasta from pan and rinse the pasta in cold water

7. An excellent doctor must have three qualities.
       subject   focus
   I. _____
   II. _____
   III. _____

8. Some drivers break traffic laws selectively.
       subject   focus
   I. Make rolling stops
   II. _____
   III. _____

EXERCISE 7   Writing Your Outline

Using the subject you converted into a topic sentence or thesis (Exercise 5), compose a topic outline.

WRITER'S GUIDELINES   The Writing Process: Stage Two

BRANDON BRIDGE

1. The most important advice this book can offer you is *state your controlling idea and support it*. If you have no controlling idea—no topic sentence for a paragraph or thesis for an essay—your writing will be unfocused and your readers may be confused or bored. But if you organize your material well, so that it supports and develops your controlling idea, you can present your views to your readers with interest, clarity, and persuasion.

2. An effective controlling statement, called the **topic sentence** for a paragraph and the **thesis** for an essay, has both a subject and a focus. The **subject** is what you intend to write about. The **focus** is what you intend to do with your subject.

   Example: <u>Long homework assignments for children</u> <u>can interrupt family life</u>.

                                 subject   focus

3. Three tools can help you organize your supporting material: listing, clustering, and outlining.
   - Listing presents support material as a column of items in a useful sequence (time, space, or importance).
   - Clustering uses chains of circles radiating from a central double-bubbled circle to show the relationship of ideas.
   - Outlining can be used in two ways: to plan the structure and content of something you intend to write and to reveal the structure and content of something you read.

A typical outline looks like this:

Main Idea (will usually be the topic sentence for the paragraph or the thesis for the essay)

  I. Major support
    A. Minor support
      1. Explanation, detail, example
      2. Explanation, detail, example
    B. Minor support
      1. Explanation, detail, example
      2. Explanation, detail, example
 II. Major support
    A. Minor support
      1. Explanation, detail, example
      2. Explanation, detail, example
    B. Minor support
      1. Explanation, detail, example
      2. Explanation, detail, example

3

The Writing Process: Stage Three

Writing / Revising / Editing

> 66 *By the time I am nearing the end of a story, the first part will have been reread and altered and corrected at least one hundred and fifty times.* 99
>
> —ROALD DAHL

CHAPTER CONTENTS   BRANDON BRIDGE

Writing the First Draft

In Stage Three of the writing process, your work begins to assume its final form. Use your outline, or alternative form of organization, as a guide in composing your paragraph or essay. For college work, your controlling idea should almost always be clearly stated early in the paper. The Roman-numeral parts of the outline will provide the framework for the main ideas of a paragraph assignment or for the topic-sentence ideas in an essay. Supporting information—details, examples, quotations—is likely to be used in approximately the same order as it appears in the outline. Keep in mind that you should not be bound absolutely by the outline. Outlines often need to be redone just as your initial writing needs to be redone.

Most writers do best when they go straight through their first draft without stopping to polish sentences or fix small problems. Try that approach. Using the information in your outline and ideas as they occur to you, go ahead and simply write a paragraph or an essay. Do not be delayed by possible misspelled words, flawed punctuation, or ungraceful sentences. You can repair those problems later.

Whether you write in longhand or on a computer depends on what works better for you. Some writers prefer to do a first draft by hand, mark it up, and then go to the computer. Computers save you time in all aspects of your writing, especially revision. Most professional writers use the computer almost exclusively.

The following paragraph is Betsy Jackson's first draft, which includes some errors in language, spelling, grammar, and punctuation. Notice how the paragraph follows the order of topics in her outline; it also includes some new ideas. Initially she had planned to write only two drafts, but you will see that she writes three—going back and forth while adding and subtracting, correcting and polishing. The third, near the end of this chapter, will be her final draft.

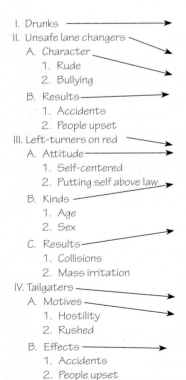

I. Drunks
II. Unsafe lane changers
  A. Character
    1. Rude
    2. Bullying
  B. Results
    1. Accidents
    2. People upset
III. Left-turners on red
  A. Attitude
    1. Self-centered
    2. Putting self above law
  B. Kinds
    1. Age
    2. Sex
  C. Results
    1. Collisions
    2. Mass irritation
IV. Tailgaters
  A. Motives
    1. Hostility
    2. Rushed
  B. Effects
    1. Accidents
    2. People upset

RAMBO TRAFFIC COP

Make me a traffic cop, and I'll crack down on certain types of drivers. First off are the drunks and handheld cell phone users. I'd zap them off the highways right off, and any cop would. But what I'm really talking about is the jerks of the highway. Near the top are the uptight lane changers, for example, this morning when I was driving to school, I saw several. I could of carved at least a couple notches in a vilation pad, and I wasn't even cranky. They cut off people and force their way in, and leave behind upset and hurt people. Then there's the left-turn bullies the ones that keep moving out when the yellow turn to red. They come in all ages and sexes, they can be young or old, male or female. Yesterday, I saw this female in a pick-up barrel right out into the teeth of a red light. She had a baby on board. She had lead in her foot. She had evil in her eye. She was hostile and self-centered. Taking advantage of others. She knew that the facing traffic would probably not pull out and risk a head-on crash. The key word there is probably but many times these people with a green light do move out and colide with the left turn bullies. Third, I'd sap the tailgaters. No one goes fast enough for these guys. I'm not alone in this peeve. One bumper sticker reads, "Stay back. I chew tobacky." And James Bond sprayed cars that chased him. Since the first is dirty and the second is against the law, if I had the clout of a Rambo cop I'd just rack up a lot of tailgater tickets. But there's a lot of road demons out there. Maybe it's good

I'm not a traffic cop, Rambo or otherwise, cause traffic cops are suppose to inforce hundreds of laws. I don't know if I'd have time cause I have my own pet peeves in mind.

If part of the development of your topic seems out of balance or needs more support, subtract or add material as necessary. Do not hesitate about changing the outline. Often going back and forth between the initial draft and the outline will prevent your final work from seeming mechanical. Occasionally, as you discover that you need to expand or diminish a part, it may even be useful to review your Stage One explorations for details and opportunities.

EXERCISE 1   Writing Your Rough Draft

On a separate sheet of paper, use the topic you developed in Stage One and write a rough draft of a paragraph or an essay as directed by your instructor.

The Brandon Guide for Revising and Editing

BRANDON BRIDGE

The term *first draft* suggests quite accurately that there will be other drafts, or versions, of your writing. Only in the most dire situations, such as an in-class examination when you have time for only one draft, should you be satisfied with a single effort. What you do beyond the first draft is called revising and editing. The Brandon Guide for Revising and Editing is a feature composed of two easily remembered acronyms:

- **CLUESS** (pronounced "clues") for revising
- **CGPS** (pronounced "see GPS") for editing

Each letter in these acronyms represents a critical element of effective and correct writing. By considering these simple but comprehensive elements as you revise and edit, you will be making sure you are not overlooking important parts of the writing process. Your practice in exercises and in actual writing assignments will enable you to automatically recall and apply the elements as you compose paragraphs and essays.

Revise with CLUESS

Coherence: Connect your ideas.

Language: Use words appropriate for your purpose and audience.

Unity: Stay on your topic.

Emphasis: Call attention to your important ideas.

Support: Back up your controlling ideas with evidence and logic.

Sentences: Write effective sentences with structural variety.

Edit With

Capitalization

Grammar

Punctuation

Spelling

The Features of the Brandon Guide: Presentation and Practice

Initially, you should concentrate on stating your controlling idea and supporting it as you work with your outline or list. The next phase is revising, also called *rewriting*. The final phase is editing. You will repeatedly go back and forth (a recursive movement) for revising and finally examine your product line by line for editing, all in ways that have been previously explained.

As you complete your writing assignments, CLUESS and CGPS will provide you with order and insight. Later, when practicing with the acronyms for revising and editing, you will, by the end of this semester, be able to develop, polish, and correct your writing routinely with little conscious reference to the guide. This Brandon Guide can also be used as a framework for evaluating the work of your fellow students in classroom peer-review activities, during which your instructor may ask you to apply all features of both acronyms or to focus on only designated features.

Regardless of the assignment or activity, the acronym features need not be addressed in a particular order, though they may be; and at times you may feel compelled to do some of the editing along with the revising—don't always resist, but don't get sidetracked. Of the two acronyms, CLUESS, for revising, is placed first and is followed by CGPS, for editing, according to the common writing sequence going from first draft, to revising, to editing.

REVISING

Revision includes working with organization, content, and language skills. Good writing almost always involves intense, systematic rewriting. The acronym CLUESS is your special memory device that will enable you to memorize the features of effective writing quickly and to use them in enriching and repairing your first draft.

Revise with **C**LUESS (pronounced as "clues" for easy memorization)

Coherence: Connect your ideas.

Coherence is the orderly relationship of ideas, each idea leading smoothly and logically to the next. You must weave your ideas together so skillfully that the reader can easily see how one idea connects to another and to the central thought. This central thought, of course, is expressed in the topic sentence for a paragraph

BRANDON BRIDGE

and in the thesis for an essay. You can achieve coherence efficiently by using the following:

Overall pattern
Transitional terms
Repetition of key words and important ideas
Pronouns
Consistent point of view

Overall Pattern

Several chapters in this book discuss strategies for an overall pattern of organization or order. Three basic patterns prevail: **time** (chronology), **space** (spatial arrangement), and **emphasis** (stress on ideas). Sometimes you will combine patterns. The coherence of each can be strengthened by using transitional words such as the following:

For a *time* pattern: first, then, soon, later, following, after, at that point
For a *space* pattern: up, down, right, left, beyond, behind, above, below
For an *emphasis* pattern: first, second, third, most, more

Transitional Terms

By using transitional terms, you can help your readers move easily from one idea to another. The transitional term in each of the following sentences is italicized.

First, I realized I had to get a job to stay in school.
At the same time, my track coach wanted the team to spend more hours working out.
We were, *after all*, the defending champions.
Finally, I dropped one of my courses.

Following is a list for Narration and another for all patterns. These terms can be used in exercises at the end of this chapter.

Transitional Words

FOR NARRATION (time): **after, before, later, earlier, initially, soon, recently, next, today, tomorrow, yesterday, now, then, until, currently, when, finally, not long after, immediately, (at) first, (at) last, third, previously, in the meantime, meanwhile**

FOR ALL PATTERNS OF WRITING: The <u>HOTSHOT CAT</u> words: <u>h</u>owever, <u>o</u>therwise, <u>t</u>herefore, <u>s</u>imilarly, <u>h</u>ence, <u>o</u>n the other hand, <u>t</u>hen, <u>c</u>onsequently, <u>a</u>lso, <u>t</u>hus

Repetition of Key Words and Important Ideas

Repeat key words and phrases to keep the main subject in the reader's mind and to maintain the continuity necessary for a smooth flow of logical thought. (See the section on Emphasis later in this chapter.)

Pronouns

Pronouns, such as *he, her, them,* and *it,* provide natural connecting links in your writing. Why? Every pronoun refers to an earlier noun (called the **antecedent** of the pronoun) and thus carries the reader back to that earlier thought. Here are some examples.

> I tried to buy *tickets* for the concert, but *they* were all sold.
> Assertive *people* tend to make decisions quickly. However, *they* may not make the wisest decisions.
> *Roger* painted a picture of *his* father's pickup truck. *It* was so good that *his* professor asked *him* to enter *it* in an art show.

Consistent Point of View

Point of view shows the writer's relationship to the material, the subject. It usually does not change within a passage.

If you are conveying personal experience, the point of view will be *first person,* or *I,* which can be either involved (a participant) or detached (an observer).

The *second person, you* and *your,* is usually reserved for how-to writing in college assignments.

If you are presenting something or someone in retrospect, geographical or historical (for example, telling a story about George Washington), the point of view will be *third person,* and the participants will be referred to as *he, she,* and *they.*

Along with the consistency of perspective, you should avoid shifts in number (*she* to *they*) and verb tense (*is* to *was*).

Being consistent in these matters will promote coherence.

Revise with C L UESS

Language: Use words appropriate for your purpose and audience.

BRANDON BRIDGE

In the revision process, the word **language** takes on a special meaning, referring to usage, tone, and diction. If you are writing with a computer, consider using the thesaurus feature, but keep in mind that no two words share precisely the same meaning.

Usage

Usage is the kind of or general style of language we use. All, or almost all, of us operate on the principle of appropriateness. If I used *ain't* as part of my explanations in this textbook, you would be surprised and probably disappointed; you would think about my word choice rather than about what I have to say. Why would you be surprised? Because *ain't* is not appropriate for my audience in this situation. If you write an essay containing slang, you will probably be understood, but if the slang is not appropriate, you will draw unfavorable attention to your message. That does not mean that slang does not have its place—it does. It can be imaginative and colorful. Often, though, it is only a weak substitute for a more precise vocabulary.

Usage is an important part of writing and revising. Judge what is appropriate for your audience and your purpose. What kind of language is expected? What kind of language is best suited for accomplishing your purpose?

Most of the material in the Handbook consists of explanations of standard, mainly formal, English grammar. Using standard verb tenses and pronoun cases will help you write effectively. The Handbook offers clear explanations and examples. As you practice the principles of standard English in your writing and revising, you will master them.

Tone

Have you ever heard someone say, "Don't talk to me in that tone of voice" or "I accepted what she was saying, but I didn't like the tone she used when she told me"? **Tone** in these contexts means that the sound of the speaker's voice and maybe the language choices conveyed disrespect to the listener. The tone could have represented any number of feelings about the subject matter and the audience. Tone can have as many variations as you can have feelings: it can, for example, be sarcastic, humorous, serious, cautionary, respectful, sensitive, objective, groveling, angry, bitter, sentimental, enthusiastic, somber, outraged, or loving.

Let's say you are getting your hair colored. Looking at your reflection in a panoramic mirror bordered with pictures of people with slightly different variations of honey blonde, you see that the hair stylist is going way too light on the color. You could use different tones in giving him or her some timely how-to instructions.

Objective: "If you don't mind, what I meant to say was that I would like my hair color to match the shade in this photograph of Blake Lively from *Gossip Girl*."

Humorous: "I hesitate to make suggestions to someone who is standing over me with a bucket of toxic chemicals, but I really don't want to cross over into the mystical realm of platinum. Could we stick to honey blonde?"

Angry and sarcastic: "Seriously? When I sat down, I said I wanted my hair to look like Blake Lively's in *Gossip Girl*. Apparently, you're a fan of Kim Kardashian's 2015 platinum hair disaster. Do you honestly expect me to go out in public looking like this?"

Respectful and sensitive: "I think you have a lot of talent, and I can see that you are mixing colors with great care, but I would like my hair to be a bit darker than I think you're intending. Do you remember how you colored my sister's hair a few months back? That's a great shade that everyone likes. Could you make my color similar to hers?"

Overbearing: "Damn it. Will you watch what you're doing! I asked for honey blonde, not white."

In speech, feelings and attitudes are represented by inflection, loudness, word choice, and language patterns. In writing, tone is conveyed mainly by word choice and order; it is closely related to style—the variations in the way you write, depending on your purpose. Your purpose is simply to present a particular idea in a particular context to an anticipated audience. It is important to use the tone appropriate for that audience.

Usually your tone will be consistent throughout your presentation, although for the informal essay often assigned in college, occasionally you may choose to begin in a lighthearted, amusing, or ironic tone before switching to a more serious, objective mode, in the same way a speaker may begin his or her presentation with a relevant joke.

Diction

Diction is word choice. If you use good diction, you are finding the best words for a particular purpose in addressing a certain audience. There is some overlap, therefore, between usage and diction. I may look at an area in the subway and present my reaction in the following way:

Poor Diction:

This part of the subway is really a mess. Everywhere I look I can see things people have thrown away, which have fallen through the grates above. Along with the solid items are liquids. On the walls are a hodgepodge of posters and writing. The whole area is very dirty and very unpleasant.

Note how the scene comes to life with better word choice:

Good Diction:

[Before me I saw] an unspeakable mass of congealed oil, puddles of dubious liquid, and a mishmash of old cigarette packets, mutilated and filthy newspapers, and the debris that filtered down from the street above. [The walls were a display of posters]—here a text from the Bible, there a half-naked girl, here a pair of girl's legs walking up the keys of a cash register—all scribbled over with unknown names and well-known obscenities. . . .
(Gilbert Highet, "Subway Station")

The difference between these two passages is obvious. The first is general. Terms such as "very dirty" and "very unpleasant" carry little meaning. The author has not made us see. The word *very* is an empty modifier. The second passage is specific. You can visualize what the writer is saying through the specific diction, the detail. The first is general and, for content, hardly goes beyond a single phrase—mess in the subway.

The following list shows the difference between general and specific words.

General	Specific	More Specific
food	fruit	juicy, ripe peach
mess	litter	candy wrappers, empty cans
drink	soda	Diet Pepsi
odor	kitchen smell	aroma of coffee brewing

Another aspect of diction is freshness and originality of expression. To achieve those distinctions, you should avoid clichés, which are trite, familiar phrases. Consider this sentence:

When the prince married Cinderella, her sisters went green with envy because she was now on easy street, leaving them out in the cold.

Those words were written by a person who does not care about communicating in a clear and an interesting manner. It would be far better to say:

When the prince married Cinderella, her sisters were envious because they had no suitors.

This list shows some clichés to avoid:

young at heart	quick as a flash
rotten to the core	slow but sure
uphill battle	other side of the coin
more than meets the eye	breathless silence
bitter end	acid test
as luck would have it	better late than never
last but not least	six of one, half dozen of the other

Clichés are ready-made expressions. A cliché master manipulates language as if it were a prefabricated building going up, not using any imagination and leaving little opportunity for his or her audience to use theirs. Good diction, however, reflects the writer as an individual and is fresh, original, and clear.

Revise with CL U ESS

BRANDON BRIDGE

U nity: Stay on your topic.

A controlling idea, stated or implied, establishes **unity** in every piece of good writing. It is the central point around which the supporting material revolves. For a paragraph, the elements are the topic sentence and the supporting sentences. For an essay, the elements are the thesis and the supporting developmental paragraphs. All the supporting material should be related to the topic sentence or thesis, and it should all be subordinate to the topic sentence or thesis. Unity can be strengthened and made more apparent if you restate the topic sentence or thesis at the end of the unit and if you repeat key words and phrases from time to time. A good check on unity is to ask yourself if everything in your paragraph or essay is subordinate to and derived from the controlling idea. Make sure that your controlling idea—the topic sentence or thesis—indicates the subject and the focus on that subject.

Example: <u>Detroit</u> <u>is fighting for its economic survival.</u>
                subject   focus

The subject, what you're writing about ("Detroit"), is broad and is often broad enough for a book. The focus, what specific part or parts of your subject you're concentrating on ("is fighting for its economic survival") will be your restricted target area. Anything outside that focus, even if it relates to another aspect of the subject, is outside your topic sentence or thesis and, therefore, creates a problem with unity, regardless of how interesting it might be in itself.

Do not confuse unity and coherence. Coherence involves the clear movement of thought from sentence to sentence or paragraph to paragraph; unity means staying on the topic by staying within the focus. A unified and coherent outline would become incoherent if the parts were scrambled, but the outline technically would still be unified. These qualities of writing go together. You should stay on the topic for unity and make clear connections for coherence.

BRANDON BRIDGE

Revise with CLU**E**SS

Emphasis: Call attention to your important ideas.

Emphasis, a feature of most good writing, helps the reader focus on the main ideas by stressing what is important. Emphasis can be achieved in several ways but mainly through placement of key ideas and through repetition.

Placement of Ideas

The most emphatic part of any passage, whether in a sentence or a book, is usually the last part because we are likely to remember most easily what we read last. The second most emphatic part of a passage is usually the beginning because our mind is relatively uncluttered when we read it. For these reasons, among others, the topic sentence or thesis is usually placed at the beginning of a piece, and it is often restated, or echoed, at the end in a closing statement.

Repetition of Key Words and Important Ideas

Repetition is one of the simplest devices in your writer's toolbox. The words repeated may be single words, phrases, slightly altered sentences, or synonyms. Repetition keeps the dominant subject in the reader's mind and maintains the continuity necessary for a smooth flow of logical thought.

You can use this valuable technique easily. If, as is done in the following example, you are discussing the effects of the school dropout problem, then the word *effect(s)*, along with synonyms such as *result(s)* or *consequence(s)*, and *school dropout(s)*, is likely to be repeated several times. Moreover, phrases giving insight into the issue may be repeated, perhaps with slight variation. Phrases and their repetitions are underlined in this passage:

The causes of the school <u>dropout</u> problem have received much attention recently, but the <u>effects</u> are just as important. One obvious <u>result</u> is that of unemployment or low-paying employment. The student who <u>drops out</u> of school is likely to be <u>dropping</u> into poverty, perhaps even into a lifelong condition. Another <u>effect</u> is juvenile crime. The young person who has no prospects for a good job and no hope all too frequently turns to illegal activities. A third <u>result</u> concerns the psychological well-being of the <u>dropout</u>. Although <u>withdrawing</u> from school seems to offer a quick, viable solution to perceived problems, it almost immediately has <u>consequences</u> for the <u>dropout's</u> self-esteem. Of course, these <u>effects</u> may also be tied to causes, such as drugs, poverty, crime, or psychological problems, but devastating <u>repercussions</u> are there at the far end of the causes-and-effects continuum, and youngsters who are contemplating <u>dropping out</u> should consider them with care.

A word of warning: The effective use of word and phrase repetition should not be confused with an irritating misuse of word repetition. At times we all get stuck on certain words, and the result is a negative response from our audience. Consider this awkward use of repetition:

> She looked at him and frowned. He returned the look and then looked away at a stranger looking for his lost keys.

That's too many *look*'s. Consider this version:

> She looked at him [*or, even better*, She frowned at him]. He glared back and then glanced away at a stranger searching for his lost keys.

The second version preserves the idea of people "looking" by using synonyms. It is more precise and does not grate on the reader's nerves as the first does. But the global use of synonyms, sometimes called *elegant variation*, is widely regarded as the sign of an immature writer, so do not be shy about repeating key words and phrases. Running rampant through your thesaurus in search of longer, more complicated words when you already have simple, direct ones will probably not bring admiring comments from your professor. Reading aloud the passage you write may help you identify problems and make good word choices.

Revise with CLUE S S

BRANDON BRIDGE

Support: Back up your controlling ideas with evidence and logic.

How much **support** as evidence or explanation does a piece of writing need? A good developmental paragraph fulfills its function by developing the topic sentence. An essay is complete when it fulfills its function of developing a thesis. Obviously, you will have to judge what is complete. With some subjects, you will need little supporting and explanatory material. With others, you will need much more.

Paragraphs and essays that describe (creating a word picture) or narrate (give an account of how something occurred) require you to give appropriate details in order to convey ideas. Expository paragraphs analyze or simply explain; their requirements vary depending on what you are trying to communicate and on the nature of the members of your audience—how much do they know about your topic? What are their background, values, and views? And what are you trying to accomplish? An expository or persuasive paragraph or essay may benefit from statements by authorities on your topic, from statistics and from examples. To complicate the matter, these forms—description, narration, exposition, and argumentation—may be combined in any number of ways. Moreover, you may mainly be trying to inform, entertain, or persuade—or combine those. Your best approach is to consider these questions: What am I trying to do? and Who is my audience? Using those questions and your good judgment will usually guide you well. Of course, this book will provide you with abundant instruction for writing with different purposes, for different situations, and for different audiences.

Incompleteness, not overdevelopment, is more common among inexperienced writers. Besides having enough support, be sure the points of support are presented in the best possible sequence.

Consider the following paragraph. Is it complete? Does the writer make the main idea clear and provide adequate support for it? Are the ideas in the right order?

> A cat's tail is a good barometer of its intentions. By various movements of its tail a cat will signal many of its wants. Other movements indicate its attitudes. An excited or aggressively aroused cat will whip its entire tail back and forth.

At first glance, this paragraph seems complete. It begins with a concise topic sentence telling us that a cat's tail is a good barometer of its intentions. It adds information of a general nature in the following two sentences. Then it presents a supporting example about the aggressively aroused cat. But the paragraph is not explicit; there is insufficient supporting material for the opening generalization. The paragraph leaves the reader with too much information to fill in. What are some other ways that cats communicate their intentions with their tails? How do they communicate specific wishes or desires? Is their communication effective? If the passage is to answer these or other questions that may come into the reader's mind, it must present more material to support the beginning generalization. The original paragraph that follows begins with a concise topic sentence that is then supported with particulars. With clarity and simplicity, it describes and explains how cats use body language for an audience made up of readers who are not experts on the behavior of cats.

> A cat's tail is a good barometer of its intentions. An excited or aggressively aroused cat will whip its entire tail back and forth. When I talk to Sam, he holds up his end of the conversation by occasionally flicking the tip of his tail. Mother cats move their tails back and forth to invite their kittens to play. A kitten raises its tail perpendicularly to beg for attention; older cats may do so to beg for food. When your cat holds its tail aloft while crisscrossing in front of you, it is trying to say, "Follow me"—usually to the kitchen, or more precisely, to the refrigerator. Unfortunately, some cats have endangered their tails in refrigerator doors as a consequence.
>
> (Michael W. Fox, "What Is Your Pet Trying to Tell You?")

We can strengthen our understanding of good support by analyzing the structure of this simple model paragraph, putting to use the information we have assimilated to this point in the discussion. The paragraph begins with the highest generalization (the main idea in the topic sentence): "A cat's tail is a good barometer of its intentions." It is followed immediately with six supporting statements and ends with a final sentence. If we place this material in a sequential list, we can easily see the recurrent pattern in the flow of thought from general to particular.

Topic sentence (highest generalization)	A cat's tail is a good barometer of its intentions.
Major support	1. An excited or aggressively aroused cat will whip its entire tail back and forth.
Major support	2. When I talk to Sam, he holds up his end of the conversation by occasionally flicking the tip of his tail.

Major support

3. Mother cats move their tails back and forth to invite their kittens to play.

Major support

4. A kitten raises its tail perpendicularly to beg for attention;

Major support

5. older cats may do so to beg for food.

Major support

6. When your cat holds its tail aloft while crisscrossing in front of you, it is trying to say, "Follow me"—usually to the kitchen, or more precisely, to the refrigerator.

Closing statement

Unfortunately, some cats have endangered their tails in refrigerator doors as a consequence.

Revise with CLUES S

BRANDON BRIDGE

S entences: Write correct, effective sentences with structural variety.

In this revision process, the word *sentences* refers to the effectiveness.

Variety of Sentences

A passage that offers a variety of simple and complicated sentences satisfies the reader, just as various simple and complicated foods go together in a good meal. The writer can introduce variety by including both short and long sentences, by using different sentence patterns, and by beginning sentences in different ways.

Length

In revising, examine your writing to make sure that sentences vary in length. A series of short sentences is likely to make the flow seem choppy and the thoughts disconnected. However, single short sentences often work very well. Because they are uncluttered with supporting points and qualifications, they are often direct and forceful. Consider using short sentences to emphasize points and to introduce ideas. Use longer sentences to provide details or show how ideas are related.

Variety of Sentence Patterns

Good writing includes a variety of sentence patterns. Although there is no limit to the number of sentences you can write, you may be pleased to discover that the conventional English sentence appears in only four basic patterns.

Simple: She did the work well.
Compound: She did the work well, and she was well paid.
Complex: Because she did the work well, she was well paid.
Compound-Complex: Because she did the work well, she was well paid, and she was satisfied.

Each of the four sentence patterns listed has its own purposes and strengths. The simple sentence conveys a single idea. The compound sentence shows, by its structure, that two somewhat equal ideas are connected. The complex sentence shows that one idea is less important than another; that is, it is dependent on, or subordinate to, the idea in the main clause. The compound-complex sentence has the scope of both the compound sentence and the complex sentence.

Variety of Sentence Beginnings

Another way to provide sentence variety is to use different kinds of beginnings. A new beginning may or may not be accompanied by a changed sentence pattern. Among the most common beginnings, other than starting with the subject of the main clause, are those using a prepositional phrase, a dependent clause, or a conjunctive adverb such as *therefore*, *however*, or *in fact*.

- Prepositional phrase (in italics)

  In your fantasy, you are the star.
  Like casino owners, game-show hosts want you to be cheery.

- Dependent clause (in italics)

  When the nighttime Wheel of Fortune *debuted*, the slot was occupied by magazine shows.
  As Pat Sajak noted, viewers often solve the puzzle before the contestants do.

- Conjunctive adverb (in italics)

  Now you know.
  Therefore, you feel happy, excited, and a bit superior.

EDITING

Editing, the final stage of the writing process, involves a careful examination of your work. Look especially for problems with **c**apitalization, **g**rammar, **p**unctuation, and **s**pelling.

Because you can find errors of editing in writing by others more easily than you can find them in your own, computerized checkers of spelling and grammar can be useful. However, checkers will not alert you to words that are correctly spelled but used in the wrong sense (for example, the word *blew* in "the wind blue hard"), and the grammar checker is not infallible, so you should always proofread. It is often helpful to leave the piece for a few hours or a day and then reread it as if it were someone else's work.

Before you submit your writing to your instructor, do what almost all professional writers do before sending their material to the publisher: Read it aloud, to yourself or to a willing audience. Reading material aloud will help you catch the occasional awkwardness of expression, flawed grammar, misplacement of words, overlooked punctuation and capitalization, inappropriate mixing of formal and informal expression, misspelling, and other problems that are easily missed by an author who, sometimes, is too close to his or her work and needs perspective.

Having a system for scrutinizing your work in editing will provide order to your process and ensure that you do not overlook key parts to the correctness of your writing. The Brandon Guide for Revising and Editing provides such an aid. As you move toward that final paragraph or essay, keep in mind that going back and forward for editing is just as important as going back and forward with your revising.

BRANDON BRIDGE

Edit with **C G P S** (pronounced as "see GPS" for easy memorization)

Capitalization

Grammar

Punctuation

Spelling

Sometimes referred to as the mechanics of writing, these elements of editing can be dealt with at any point during your writing, but most writers prefer to address them mainly during the final stages.

The four elements represented in the acronym CGPS provide a useful checklist for your writing. Those elements can be easily memorized by just saying "*see GPS*" a few times.

TOP 25 EDITING ERRORS

This chapter introduces a brief version of editing guidelines as a focus unit. We call the rules collectively the Top 25 Editing Errors.

For the typical student in this class, mastering the rules that provide remedies for these twenty-five most common errors in editing will improve your expertise in writing and boost your confidence. This list was compiled by a panel of nine veteran English professors who have taught collectively at three colleges. The Grammar element in CGPS is covered by seven rules. Each of the other elements is covered by six. Of course, there are far more rules in editing than these, but these rules are the ones that draw the most unfavorable attention from instructors in college paragraph and essay assignments. You already know some of them, but practice will help you sharpen your techniques as you learn the others and make your understanding permanent for all occasions of cross-curricular, career-related, and personal writing.

The brief diagnostic test in this stage will reveal to you which rules you did know, thought you knew, didn't know, or just looked on with much doubt and puzzlement. Concentrating on these twenty-five top troublemakers will give you focus. The rewards of the anticipated mastery will give you energy. Later, you may wonder why you didn't learn these rules earlier.

TOP 6
EDITING
ERRORS

Edit with C **GPS**

Capitalization

Using correct capitalization will serve you well. Capitalization, along with punctuation, makes it possible to easily see where sentences begin and end. Capitalization or the lack of it shows you whether nouns are simple or proper, whether something is a direction or a region, whether a phrase is just a phrase or a title.

In short, good capitalization makes reading easier. Bad capitalization does the opposite. Moreover, bad capitalization, after perhaps a bit of puzzlement, is recognized for what it is and brings unfavorable attention to the written statement.

1. **Error:** Capitalizing words such as math and history.

   Rule: Capitalize any title preceding a name of a school course only if it is named specifically or is derived from a language.

   > **Example:** I like math, Spanish [derived from language] and History 101 [specific course name].

   > **Example:** My favorite subjects are foreign language, math, and history.

2. **Error:** Capitalizing the word school or college.

   Rule: Capitalize the name of a school or college only if it is named specifically.

   > **Example:** I am proud to be attending Santa Ana College [named specifically].

   > **Example:** I am proud to be attending college [not named specifically].

3. **Error:** Capitalizing places, things, and directions that are not proper nouns.

   Rule: Capitalize the names of states, regions, localities, and other geographical areas with specific, formal names, but not directions.

   > **Example:** I live in New York, and was born in Iowa, but most of my relatives are from the South [a region].

   > **Example:** I drove west [a direction] from Kansas.

4. **Error:** Capitalizing words referring to family members as they are related but not using the words instead of names.

   Rule: Capitalize words denoting family relationships when they are used before a name or substituted for a name.

   > **Example:** I am grateful to Grandmother, Mother [words substituted for names], and Aunt [before a name] Julie.

   > **Example:** My mother, my grandmother, and my aunt [denotes only relationships] bought me a car.

5. **Error:** Not capitalizing a title that comes before a name.

   Rule: Capitalize a title coming before a name.

   > **Example:** Professor Soto [before name] teaches math.

   > **Example:** Gilberto Soto, a professor [not before the name], teaches math.

6. Error: Not capitalizing key words in titles.

> **Rule:** Capitalize titles of essays, paragraphs, movies, poems, and songs. However, do not capitalize the short conjunctions and prepositions unless they come at the beginning or the end of the title.
>
> > **Example:** I read *The Last of the Mohicans* [preposition *of* inside title].
> >
> > **Example:** I also read *Of Mice and Men* [preposition *of* at the beginning of the title].

TOP 7
EDITING
ERRORS

Edit with C G PS

Grammar

In the course you are now taking, knowledge of grammar can help you understand your English instructor's comments on your papers and help you make sound choices in your writing. It can also help you understand how language can be used in a variety of ways, freeing you to be more original in phrasing your sentences. In a broad sense, grammar overlaps with sentences in CLUESS for variety as it pertains to sentence patterns, sentence beginnings, and even sentence correctness for fragments, comma splices, and run-ons. For this editing part of your writing, grammar will help you understand such aspects as subject and verb agreement, verb tense, pronoun case, proper modification, and parallel structure. Recognizing grammatical structures will often help you understand punctuation.

1. Error: Using the word *I*, *he*, *she*, or *they* as an object of a preposition.

> **Rule:** Prepositions are words (such as *to*, *at*, *in*, *of*, and *between*) that link their objects to the rest of the sentence in phrases: *to the game*, *at the store*, *in the car*, *of the issue*, and *between us*. The two main errors for objects of prepositions occur when the writer or speaker uses an object incorrectly in these ways: *between you and I* and *to you and I*.
>
> **Solution:** When you have prepositions (such as *between* and *to*) followed by two objects (such as *you and I*), just reverse the objects (*I and you*) and read them aloud and then try substituting *me* for *I*. The readings will reveal that *me* sounds better (more natural) than *I*. The correct forms are *between you and me* and *to you and me*.

2. Error: Changing verb tense without good reason.

> **Rule:** You should seldom change verb tense within a passage you are writing.
>
> > **Example of correct verb tense:** I *left* for work, *drove* several hours in dense traffic, and *arrive* at my workplace late. The third verb, *arrive*, should be set in past tense as *arrived*: I *left* for work, *drove* several hours in dense traffic, and *arrived* at my workplace late.

3. Error: Mistaking *there* or *here* as a subject instead of a filler word, causing a subject–verb agreement problem.

Rule: A sentence filler word is grammatically independent of other words in the sentence; that is, it doesn't have something it refers to or connects with the way parts of speech do. The most common filler words are *there* and *here*. Even though a sentence filler word may precede the verb, it should not be treated as the subject.

> **Example:** There *are* many *problems*. [The verb *are* agrees with the subject *problems*.] Avoid writing, "There's many problems" or "There is many problems."

The words *there* and *here* can also be adverbs; for example, I am *here*, and you are *there*.

4. **Error:** Writing a fragment, which is an incomplete sentence.

   Rule: A sentence signals completeness with structure and punctuation. Structurally a sentence must have a subject and a verb. The subject may be understood and not stated: "Take the dog outside." But a word group can have a subject and a verb and not be a sentence. If I say, "Because they arrived," *they* is a subject and *arrived* is a verb. However, it is not a sentence because of the word *because*, which subordinates the two words that follow. In other words, you could place a period after "Because they arrived," and it would not signal completeness. So if you are not sure whether a word group is a sentence, consider whether it would signal completeness to your audience if you were to say, "Because they arrived." In that case, your audience would expect you to say something else because of the incompleteness of the structure. If you said, "They arrived," they would not necessarily expect more words because the word group is a complete sentence.

5. **Error:** Using *myself* instead of *I* or *me*.

   Rule: *Myself* (also the other *self* words—*himself, herself, themselves, itself*) is called a reflexive pronoun because it reflects back to the use of the word *I*, a personal pronoun.

   > **Example of correct use:** I myself am to blame. NOT: Only myself am to blame.

   > **Example of correct use:** Trixie and I had a great time at the beach. NOT: Trixie and myself had a great time at the beach. Also NOT: Trixie and me had a great time at the beach.

6. **Error:** Needlessly repeating the subject immediately with certain pronouns.

   Rule: Subjects should not be followed immediately with a certain nominative pronoun (*he*, *she*, *they*, *we*, or *it*) as if the subject needs to be repeated.

   > **Example of how to correct a repeated subject:** My father he is too strict. Delete *he* for a correctly phrased sentence: My father is too strict.

7. **Error:** Using double negatives.

   Rule: Avoid double negatives. Words such as *no, not, none, nothing, never, hardly, barely,* and *scarcely* should not be combined.

Double Negative: I do *not* have *no* time for recreation. [incorrect]

Single Negative: I have *no* time for recreation. [correct]

Double Negative: I have *hardly never* lied. [incorrect]

Single Negative: I have *hardly* ever lied. [correct]

TOP 6
EDITING
ERRORS

Edit with CG P S

Punctuation

Good punctuation can make for easy reading. If you want to test that statement, try removing all punctuation from a paragraph and then try to read it swiftly. Punctuation is far more than decoration. It can change the meaning of sentences in many instances and, if wrong, can bring discredit to what you write and, therefore, to you as an educated, thoughtful person. Punctuation can even be the basis for a lawsuit. For an author it can be enjoyable to use because it directs flow and establishes the rhythm of sentences.

1. **Error:** Not placing a comma after a long introductory modifier before the main part of the sentence.

   Rule: A group of four or more words that cannot stand alone at the beginning of a sentence should usually be set off with a comma. This group of words is often a prepositional phrase (beginning with words such as *in*, *at*, *between*, and *over*) or a dependent clause of modification (beginning with words such as *because*, *when*, and *while*).

   Example with correct punctuation: Before the ship sailed [introductory clause], the captain checked the weather report.

   Example with correct punctuation: In the middle of the night [long introductory prepositional phrase], the weather cleared.

2. **Error:** Writing a comma splice—two sentences with only a comma between them.

   Rule: The comma splice consists of independent clauses (actually two sentences) with only a comma between them: The weather was bad, we canceled the picnic.

   Corrections: There are four common ways of correcting a comma splice:

   - Replace the comma between the independent clauses with a period and create two sentences. Begin the second with a capital letter. Example: The weather was bad. We canceled the picnic.
   - Add a coordinating conjunction (FANBOYS—*for*, *and*, *nor*, *but*, *or*, *yet*, or *so*) after the comma. Example: The weather was bad, and we canceled the picnic.
   - Replace the comma with a semicolon, perhaps with a transitional connective as those in HOTSHOT CAT: *however*, *otherwise*, *therefore*, *similarly*, *hence*, *on the other hand*, *then*, *consequently*, *also*, and *thus*. Example without a transitional connective: The weather was bad; we canceled the

picnic. Example with a transitional connective: The weather was bad; therefore, we canceled the picnic.

- Use a subordinating conjunction. Incorrect: The weather was bad, we canceled the picnic. [comma splice]. Correct: *Because* the weather was bad, we canceled the picnic. By inserting the subordinating conjunction *because*, you can transform the first independent clause into a dependent clause and correct the comma splice. Knowing the most common subordinating conjunctions, such as *because*, *after*, *that*, *when*, *although*, *since*, *how*, *than*, *until*, and *before*, will help you in writing sentences and correcting sentence problems.

3. **Error:** Writing a run-on—two sentences with nothing joining them.

   Example of run-on sentence: The weather is bad we canceled the picnic.

   Rule: The run-on differs from the comma splice in only one respect: It has no comma between the independent clauses (actually simple sentences). Therefore, the run-on is simply two independent clauses run together. It can be corrected in the same ways as the comma splices in Error 2 above (see the four bullets), except there are no commas to replace. Use commas and capital letters as needed.

   Correct: The weather was bad. We canceled the picnic.

4. **Error:** Not setting off parenthetical elements.

   Rule: Use commas to set off parenthetical elements such as mild interjections (*oh*, *well*, *yes*, *no*, and others), most conjunctive adverbs, or transitional connectives (*however*, *otherwise*, *therefore*, *similarly*, *hence*, *on the other hand*, and *consequently*, but not *then*, *thus*, *soon*, *now*, and *also*), quotation indicators (*she said*, *he replied*) and special abbreviations (*etc.*, *i.e.*, *e.g.*, and others).

   Examples: *Oh*, what a silly question! [mild interjection]
   It is necessary, *of course*, to leave now. [sentence modifier]
   We left early; *however*, we missed the train anyway. [conjunctive adverb]

5. **Error:** Including quoted passages of a sentence or more without using quotation marks.

   Rule: Use quotations marks to indicate words that are quoted directly, meaning the words were said, written, or thought.

   Incorrect example: Elizabeth Wong wrote, I thought of myself as multicultural.

   Correct example: Elizabeth Wong wrote, "I thought of myself as multicultural."

   [Note that the period is inside the quotation marks. Quotations of more than fifty words would be block indented and not enclosed in quotation marks.]

6. **Error:** Blending paraphrased statements (your own words) with short quotations of less than a sentence without setting the quotations (key words and phrases) off with quotation marks.

Rule: Use quotation marks to blend borrowed words of less than a sentence with words that you have paraphrased (put into your own words).

> **Example of a sentence-long quotation:** Elizabeth Wong wrote: "I thought of myself as multicultural."

> **Example of a blending of a paraphrase and quoted words of less than a sentence:** Wong considered herself "multicultural." [Note that the word *multicultural* is enclosed with quotation marks and that there is no comma after the word *herself*.]

Edit with CGP**S**

Spelling

Spelling correctly makes your writing easier to read and avoids the possible distraction from what you have to say. The distraction of bad spelling can even contribute to the view that your thoughts are less profound than the thoughts of those who do spell well. A relatively small number of words make up a list of the most commonly misspelled words. Six words toward the top of that list are included here. Master them and your misspelling rate will shrink dramatically.

1. **Confusing *you're* with *your*:** *You're* is a contraction of *you are*, as in *"You're* the first to finish." *Your* is a possessive pronoun used as an adjective: *"Your* honesty is admirable." The simplest way to solve the spelling problem with contractions is to avoid using contractions.

2. **Confusing *its* with *it's*:** *It's* is a contraction of *it is*, as in "It's my turn." It's is a possessive pronoun that is an adjective, as in "The dog wagged *its* tail."

3. **Confusing *they're*, *their*, and *there*:** *They're* is a contraction of *they are*, as in *"They're* the winners." *Their* is a possessive pronoun used as an adjective: *"Their* word is *their* bond." *There* is an adverb that can be used in two ways: "Please drive *there* [adverb] and wait." *There* also can be a filler word (commonly called an adverb), as in *"There* is much to be said about politics."

4. **Confusing *affect* with *effect*:**

   affect: Usually a verb meaning "change," as in "Ideas *affect* me."

   effect: Usually a noun meaning "result," as in "That *effect* was surprising."

5. **Confusing *accept* and *except*:**

   accept: A verb meaning "to receive," as in "I *accept* your apology."

   except: A preposition meaning "to exclude," as in "I paid everyone *except* you."

6. **Confusing *than* and *then*.**

   than: A conjunction, as in "He is taller *than* I."

   then: An adverb, as in *"Then* she left town."

Student Demonstration of All Stages of the Writing Process

The Brandon Guide to Revising and Editing is at the heart of the third stage of the writing process. It provides a guided system for shaping, refining, and finishing paragraph and essay assignments. Here we see how Betsy Jackson worked through the entire writing process. In Stage One, she freewrote, brainstormed, listed, and developed a cluster of ideas. In Stage Two, she composed a good topic sentence, developed further a part of her cluster from Stage One, and drew up an outline based on the cluster. Then, in Stage Three, we see one of her early drafts, her revision and editing of that draft, and finally the finished version.

Note that Jackson has used a Writing Process Worksheet, which has been lengthened for you to be able to see all parts of her work. At the front of your book, you will find a full-size blank worksheet, which can be copied, filled in, and submitted with each assignment if your instructor directs you to do so.

BRANDON BRIDGE

Writing Process Worksheet

Name <u>Betsy Jackson</u>   **Title** <u>If I Were a Traffic Cop</u>   **Due Date** <u>Monday, June 4, 8 a.m.</u>

Use the back of this page or separate paper if you need more space.

Assignment

In the space below, write whatever you need to know about your assignment, including information about the topic, audience, pattern of writing, length, whether to include a rough draft or revised drafts, and whether your paper must be typed.

Write a paragraph of 200 to 300 words on a topic from the list—bad drivers. Discuss types for the pattern. Use some examples. Write for readers who have probably shared your experiences. Include this completed worksheet, one or more rough drafts marked for revision, and a typed final paper.

Stage One

Explore Freewrite, brainstorm (list), cluster, or take notes as directed by your instructor.

Freewriting (abbreviated here)

drunks

tailgaters

lane changers

Every day when I drive to school I see bad drivers. Sometimes I'm mad. Sometimes I'm irritated. Sometimes I'm scared. I think someone should do something about them. The <u>drunk drivers</u> are the worst. They should be put away. But a lot of the other should be getting tickets too. Some of the drivers are worse than others. Make me a cop, a supercop, a rambo cop, and I'll go after the worst. Maybe I'd just go after the ones that bother me. Some bad drivers cause a lot of accidents and get people all angry. Take the <u>tailgaters</u> for example. And what about the <u>drivers that go into the emergency lanes</u> on the freeways to pass when there's a jam. And then you've got the <u>lane</u>

no signals

run lights

too fast/slow

all kinds

changers and the <u>people that don't signal</u> and <u>those that keep going and turning left when</u> the <u>light turns red</u>. Then you've got the people that <u>drive too fast</u> and <u>too slow</u>. And you've got the ones that <u>don't stop</u> for <u>pedestrians</u>. <u>All kinds</u> of bad drivers are out there—young, old, male, female, insane, drunk, angry, and rushed.

Brainstorming (Big Six Questions)

Who?	bad drivers; me as a cop
What?	driving badly, recklessly, unsafely; a cop's job
Where?	on every roadway
When?	all the time
Why?	hurried, disrespectful, self-centered, sick, addiction, hostile
How?	lane-changing, driving illegally in emergency lane, not signaling, passing on the shoulder, tailgating, turning left on red, rolling stop, speeding, driving while intoxicated (this became a list for Jackson)

Clustering

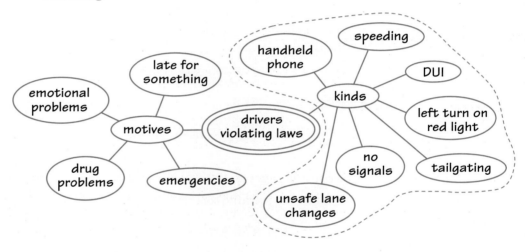

Stage Two

Organize   Write a topic sentence or thesis; label the subject and the focus parts.

<u>If I were a traffic cop</u>, <u>I would crack down on certain types of drivers</u>.
      subject   focus

Write an outline or an outline alternative. For reading-based writing, include references and short quotations with page numbers as support in the outline.

   I. Drunks
  II. Unsafe lane changers
     A. Character
       1. Rude
       2. Bullying
     B. Results
       1. Accidents
       2. People upset

III. Left-turners on red
    A. Attitude
        1. Self-centered
        2. Putting self above law
    B. Kinds
        1. Age
        2. Sex
    C. Results
        1. Collisions
        2. Mass irritation
IV. Tailgaters
    A. Motives
        1. Hostility
        2. Rushed
    B. Effects
        1. Accidents
        2. People upset

Stage Three

Write On separate paper, write and then revise your paragraph or essay as many times as necessary for **c**oherence, **l**anguage (usage, tone, and diction), **u**nity, **e**mphasis, **s**upport, and **s**entences (**CLUESS**). Read your work aloud to hear and correct any grammatical errors or awkward-sounding sentences. (Consider using the Brandon Guide for Revising and Editing.)

Edit any problems in fundamentals, such as **c**apitalization, **g**rammar, **p**unctuation, and **s**pelling (**CGPS**).

Rough Draft: Writing, Revising, Editing

If I Were a Traffic Cop
RAMBO TRAFFIC COP

~~Make me~~ If I were a traffic cop, ~~and~~ I'll I would crack down on certain types of drivers. ~~First~~ My primary target would be off are the drunks. I would zap them ~~off the highways right off~~ arrest immediately, and any cop would. But what ~~I'm~~ I am really ~~talking~~ concerned about ~~is~~ here. the jerks of the highway. Near the top of my hit list are the ~~up-tight~~ unsafe lane changers, ~~for example,~~ This morning when I was driving to school, ~~I saw several.~~ I could ~~of~~ have carved at least a couple of notches in a ~~vilation~~ citation pad, and I ~~wasn't~~ was not even cranky. They cut off ~~people~~ other drivers and force their way in, ~~and leave~~ leaving behind upset and ~~hurt~~ injured people. Then ~~there's~~ there are the left-turn bullies the ones who keep moving out when the yellow turns to red. They come in all ages and sexes, ~~they can be young or old, male or female.~~ Yesterday, I saw this female in a pick-up barrel right out into the teeth of a red light. She had a baby on board~~, She had~~ lead in her foot~~, She had~~ *and* evil

in her eye. She was hostile and self-centered~~,~~ *t*aking advantage of others.

She knew that the facing traffic would probably not pull out and risk a

head-on crash. The key word there is "probably" but many times people with

a green light do move out and colide with the left turn bullies. ~~Third, I'd~~ *Fourth, I would* sap

the tailgaters. No one goes fast enough for ~~these guys.~~ *them.* ~~I'm not alone in this~~ *Many of my fellow drivers agree.*

~~peeve.~~ One bumper sticker reads, "Stay back. I chew tobacky." And James

Bond sprayed *oil on* cars that chased him. Since the first is ~~dirty~~ *unsanitary* and the second

~~is against the law,~~ *illegal* if I had the ~~clout~~ *authority* of a Rambo cop ~~I'd~~ *I would* just ~~rack up~~ *issue* a lot of

tailgater tickets. ~~But there's a lot of road demons out there.~~ *These four types of road demons would feel my wrath.* ~~But~~ *But* Maybe ~~it's~~ *it is* good

~~I'm~~ *I am* not a traffic cop, Rambo or otherwise, *be*cause traffic cops are suppose*d* to

~~i~~*e*nforce hundreds of laws. I ~~don't~~ *do not* know if ~~I'd~~ *I would* have time *be*cause ~~I have my own~~

~~pet peeves in mind.~~ *I would be concentrating on this private list of obnoxious drivers.*

Final Draft

IF I WERE A TRAFFIC COP

Topic sentence
Support

Support

Support (example)

Support

Concluding sentences

<u>If I were a traffic officer in the Rambo mode, I would focus on certain classes of drivers.</u> <u>First are what I call zombies—lumping together the drunken drivers and handheld cell-phone users.</u> They put themselves into a self-centered world, and I would do what I could to get them off the roads. <u>Then the second group would be the zig-zaggers, the impatient, hotheaded lane changers.</u> Often without giving any signals, they zig to the right or zag to the left to fill another air space. They depend on us defensive drivers with good brakes. <u>Third are the bullies that act as if they are colorblind.</u> Actually having good eyesight and thinking only of themselves, they keep rolling well after the yellow light has turned to red. They come in all ages and sexes, and can be young or old, male or female. Yesterday, I saw a female barrel right into the teeth of a red light. She had a baby on board, lead in her foot, and evil in her eye. She was betting that drivers in the facing traffic would not dare make their legal move. <u>Fourth, I would write up what I call bumper huggers, the tailgaters.</u> No one in front goes fast enough for bumper huggers. If I were a Rambo cop, I would be tailgating the tailgaters, ticket pad at the ready. Unfortunately for everyone, there are a lot of demons on the road. <u>Maybe it is good I'm not a traffic cop, Rambo or otherwise, because traffic cops are supposed to enforce all laws. I don't know if I'd have time for laws outside my own pet peeves.</u>

EXERCISE 2   Writing, Revising, and Editing Your Draft

Using the topic chosen in Exercise 1, on separate paper, write, revise, and edit your paragraph or essay to complete Stage Three. Alternatively, you may delay this stage until after you have worked with paragraphs and essays in the next two chapters.

WRITER'S GUIDELINES   The Writing Process: Stage Three

BRANDON BRIDGE

1. Write your first draft, paying close attention to your outline, list, or cluster. Do not concern yourself with perfect spelling, grammar, or punctuation.

2. Consider using the Writing Process Worksheet and the following Brandon Guide for Revising and Editing.

The Brandon Guide for Revising and Editing

Revise with **CLUESS** (pronounced as "clues" for easy memorization).

Coherence: Connect your ideas.

* Are the ideas clearly related?
* Is there a clear pattern of organization (time, space, or emphasis)?
* Is the pattern supported by words that suggest the basis of that organization (time: *now*, *then*, *later*; space: *above*, *below*, *up*, *down*; emphasis: *first*, *second*, *last*)?
* Is coherence improved by the use of transitional terms, pronouns, repetition, and a consistent point of view?

Language: Use words appropriate for your purpose and audience.

* Is the general style of language usage appropriate (formal or informal) for the purpose and the intended audience?
* Is the tone (language use showing attitude toward material and audience) appropriate?
* Is the word choice (diction) effective? Are the words precise in conveying meaning? Are they fresh and not overused?

Unity: Stay on your topic.

* Are the thesis and every topic sentence clear and well stated? Do they indicate both subject and focus?
* Are all points of support clearly related to and subordinate to the topic sentence of each paragraph and to the thesis of the essay?

Emphasis: Call attention to your important ideas.

* Are ideas properly placed (especially near the beginning and end) for emphasis?

- Are important words and phrases repeated for emphasis?
- Are there short sentences among long ones to attract attention?

Support: Back up your controlling ideas with evidence and logic.

- Is there adequate material—such as examples, details, quotations, and explanations—to support each topic sentence and thesis?
- Are the points of support placed in the best possible order?

Sentences: Write correct, effective sentences with structural variety.

- Are the sentences varied in length? Are the beginnings of the sentences varied?
- Are the sentences varied in pattern (simple, compound, complex, and compound-complex)?

Edit with **C G P S** : (pronounced as "see GPS" for easy memorization).

Capitalization

Grammar

Punctuation

Spelling

Practicing the Brandon Guide for Revising and Editing

BRANDON BRIDGE

Written by students in nine patterns, this unit gives you the opportunity to work with CLUESS and CGPS as you learn to sharpen your skills in revising and editing, almost always the two most important phases of writing. The exercises also provide practice in working with support information for different patterns of writing, such as narration, exemplification, cause and effect, and argument.

PATTERN: NARRATION

The Customer Is Always Right
JACK MULLINS

(A) "The customer is always right" is a saying that took on new meaning for me soon after I got my first job back almost twenty years ago. (B) I was a proud attendant in a ~~s~~hell gas station. (C) ~~That was the year when I had a beautiful girlfriend with a new convertible.~~ (D) The manager regularly reminded us workers that we were "Minutemen" and that cheerful, fast service was our primary mission. (E) After all, he was going against the

Situation

trend toward self-service stations that would soon make his business and my job obsolete. (F) I soon developed a basic routine for quick fill-up service—greet the customer, ask how I could help, take off the gas cap, insert the nozzle, start the gas flow, check the oil, clean the windshield, remove the nozzle, collect the money or process the credit card, and thank the customer. (G) At times the unexpected would occur and upset my routine. (H) The "unexpected" on this occasion was a co-worker telling me he couldn't work the next day, meaning I would have to work a double shift. (I) The result

Conflict

was that in my fatigue, after fourteen hours on the job, I skipped one part of my routine: the gas flow had cut off automatically, but I did not remove the nozzle. (J) After I looked at the pump tab, ~~recieved~~ *received* the money, and gave the change. (K) The customer rolled out, (L) *and* I had just turned to walk away when I hear the sound of metal scraping against metal, the snap of the hose,

Struggle

and the gushing of gas. (M) Immediately the manager appeared and shut off

Struggle

the main gas valve. (N) Next the customer was out of his car, pointing to a shallow, two-inch scratch on his paint job—a faded paint job that already had several much larger scratches. (O) The manager apologized, said I was new, and promised "we" would pay when the customer brought in an estimate.

Struggle

(P) After the customer ~~split~~ *left*, the manager explained that "I" would pay out of my wage. (Q) I certainly didn't object. (R) But a few days later, the customer

Struggle

returned with an estimate for three hundred and forty-two dollars. (S) I didn't say ~~nothing~~ *anything*. (T) The manager didn't blink as he wrote out a check.

Outcome

(U) After the man left, the manager said to me, *"It's* ~~Its~~ just public relations."

Meaning

(V) I know you're supposed to ~~suck up~~ *be polite* to clients, but I worked more than a month to pay for the repair. (W) "The customer is always right" may be a necessary slogan for business, but at times the customer may be partly wrong.

EXERCISE 3   Revise and Edit with the Brandon Guide

Revise with `C` `L` `U` `E` `S` `S` **(pronounced as "clues" for easy memorization).**

1. **C**oherence: Connect your ideas. Circle the six connecting words (words such as *at times, next, then, immediately, after*) that begin sentences and make time connections between ideas.
Sentences E, G, M, N, P, U.

2. **L**anguage: Use words appropriate for your purpose and audience. Cross out the two slang words and write your better word choices above them.
Sentences P, V.

3. **U**nity: Stay on your topic. Draw a line through the sentence that is well off the topic.
Sentences C.

4. **E**mphasis: Call attention to your important ideas. Underline the topic sentence and also the closing sentence that echoes key phrasing at the end of the paragraph for both unity and emphasis.
Sentences A, W.

5. **S**upport: Back up your controlling ideas with evidence and logic. In the left margin, annotate this narrative by using these words: *situation* (setting at the beginning), *conflict* (whatever causes problems, stress, or friction), *struggle* (the response(s) to the conflict), *outcome* (the result of the struggle), and *meaning* (significance of the story, or narrative).
See left margin.

6. **S**entences: Write correct, effective sentences with structural variety. Combine sentences K and L by using one of these coordinating conjunctions—*for, and, nor, but, or, yet, so* (FANBOYS)—and by using the proper capitalization and punctuation.

Edit with `C` `G` `P` `S` **(pronounced as "see GPS" for easy memorization).**

7. **C**apitalization: One word that should begin with a capital letter is in lowercase. Cross out the lowercase letter and insert the capital letter above it.
B.

8. **G**rammar: One sentence has a double negative. Cross out the error and write in the correction above it.
S.

9. **P**unctuation: The quotation marks are missing from a quotation near the end of the paragraph. Insert them.
W.

10. **S**pelling: Two words are misspelled. Cross out each misspelled word and write the correct spelling above it.
J, U.

Practice Exercise for the Top 25 Editing Errors

The list of the top twenty-five editing errors was compiled by a panel of nine veteran English professors who have taught collectively at three colleges. Mastering these common editing errors will help you tremendously.

EXERCISE 4 Top 25 Editing Errors: **C** **G** **P** **S**

TOP 25 EDITING ERRORS

Underline the correct answers.

Capitalization

Grammar

Punctuation

Spelling

C   1. My history (professor/Professor) is an expert yodeler.

C   2. My most difficult classes are (Economics/economics) and Math 150.

C   3. The sergeant derisively referred to us as (*college boys/College boys*).

C   4. The settlers were urged to go to the (West/west).

C   5. Your (uncle/Uncle) has the most festive *lederhosen* in the village.

G   6. The location of the treasure is between (you and I/you and me).

G   7. I parked my car, and I (see/saw) a driver back into me.

G   8. (While I stood there listening. /I stood there listening.)

G   9. Three friends and (myself/I) knew the secret of the haunted house.

G   10. You shouldn't (never/ever) store oily rags near a water heater.

P   11. (Before you bait your hook take a deep breath./Before you bait your hook, take a deep breath.)

P   12. (Vikings were in good physical condition, raiding was good exercise./Vikings were in good physical condition. Raiding was good exercise.)

P   13. (Food will be served soon be ready to eat./Food will be served soon. Be ready to eat.)

P   14. (Yertle says, I'm Yertle the Turtle, oh, marvelous me./Yertle says, "I'm Yertle the Turtle, oh, marvelous me.")

P   15. (In *Moby Dick*, the narrator says call me Ishmael./In *Moby Dick*, the narrator says, "Call me Ishmael.")

S   16. (Your/You're) going to be sore after doing two hundred crunches.

S   **17.** (Its/It's) a long way to Timbuktu.

S   **18.** Who will bring (their/there/they're) equipment to the game?

S   **19.** Football players get more attention on campus (then/than) baseball players.

S   **20.** Is it all right if I borrow (your/you're) car for the weekend?

4

Writing the Paragraph

CHAPTER CONTENTS

BRANDON BRIDGE

The Paragraph Defined

Defining the word *paragraph* is no easy task because there are four different kinds of paragraphs, each one having a different purpose:

Introductory: Usually the first paragraph in an essay, it gives the necessary background and indicates the main idea, called the **thesis**.

Developmental: A unit of several sentences, it expands on an idea. This book features the writing of developmental paragraphs.

Transitional: A very brief paragraph, it merely directs the reader from one point in the essay to another.

Concluding: Usually the last paragraph in an essay, it makes the final comment on the topic.

The following paragraph is both a definition and an example of the developmental paragraph.

Topic sentence

Support

Support

Support

Concluding sentence

The developmental paragraph contains three parts: the subject, the topic sentence, and the support. The **subject** is what you will write about. It is likely to be broad and must be focused or qualified for specific focus. The **topic sentence** contains both the subject and the focus—what you will do with the subject. It carries the central idea to which everything else in the paragraph is subordinated. For example, the first sentence of this paragraph is a topic sentence. Even when not stated, the topic sentence as an underlying idea unifies the paragraph. The **support** is the evidence or reasoning by which a topic sentence is developed. It comes in several basic patterns and serves any of the four forms of expression: narration, description, exposition, and argumentation. These forms, which are usually combined in writing, will be presented with both student and professional examples. The **developmental paragraph**, therefore, is a group of sentences, each with the function of supporting a controlling idea called the topic sentence.

Basic Paragraph Patterns

The most important point about a developmental paragraph is that it should state an idea and support it. The support, or development, can take several forms, all of which you already use. It can do the following:

- Give an account (tell a story).
- Describe people, things, or events.
- Explain by analyzing, giving examples, comparing, defining, showing how to do something, or showing causes.
- Argue that something should be done or resisted, that something is true or untrue, or that something is good or bad.

You will not find it difficult to write solid paragraphs once you understand that good writing requires having enough support for main ideas so that your reader can understand how you have arrived at your conclusions.

Usually the developmental paragraph will be indented only one time. However, you will note in your reading that some writers, especially journalists, break a

Figure 4.1
Paragraph Patterns

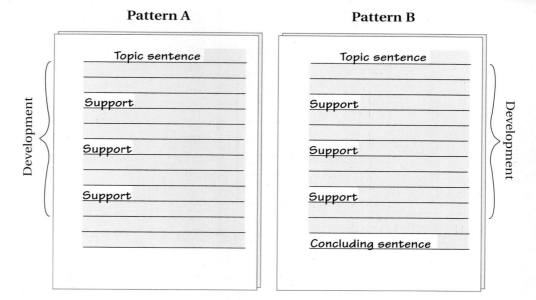

| Pattern A | Pattern B |

paragraph into parts and indent more than once in developing a single idea. That arrangement, called a **paragraph unit**, is fairly common in magazine and newspaper articles (frequently with each sentence indented) but less so in college writing.

Two effective patterns of conventional paragraph structure are shown in Figure 4.1. Pattern A merely states the controlling idea, the topic sentence, and develops it; Pattern B adds a concluding sentence following the development.

Example of Pattern A:

A TIME FOR JUVENILES

Topic sentence

The history of less ancient periods, too, reveals the juvenile character of their chief actors. Many observers have remarked on the smallness of the armor that has come down to us from the Middle Ages. Actually, the men who wore the armor were not grown-ups. They were married at thirteen, were warriors and leaders in their late teens, and senile at thirty-five or forty. Without some familiarity with the juvenile mentality and the aberrations of juvenile delinquency, it would be difficult to make sense of the romanticism, trickery, and savagery that characterized the Middle Ages. Nor did things change markedly in the sixteenth century. Montaigne tells us he hardly ever met a man as old as fifty. In the first half of the sixteenth century, Charles V became Holy Roman Emperor at the age of twenty, Francis I became king of France at twenty-one, and Henry VIII king of England at eighteen.

Support

Support

(Eric Hoffer, "A Time for Juveniles.")

Example of Pattern B:

ADOBE: MUD FOR CASTLES AND HOVELS

Topic sentence

Although adobe is associated with the Southwest, there are few places in the world where some form of adobe has not been used. One of the most easily

Support

Support

Support

Concluding sentence

obtained materials, sun-dried earth blocks have been used for thousands of years. Residential adobe ruins in Egypt predate the great pyramid of Giza. The ruins of Tyre and Nineveh are structurally related to the still-occupied pueblos at Taos and Acoma in New Mexico. One of the seven wonders of the ancient world, the Hanging Gardens of Babylon, was probably built of adobe bricks. The arid lands of the world, where sand and clay are found, and where the sunshine is bountiful, have long histories of earth construction. Because of this construction in highly populated areas such as India, Africa, and the Middle East, about 60 percent of all residential structures in the world today are of adobe.

(James Maurer, "Adobe: Mud for Castles and Hovels.")

EXERCISE 1   Analyzing a Paragraph

Read the following paragraph carefully.

1. Is the paragraph developed in Pattern A (topic sentence/development) or Pattern B (topic sentence/development/concluding sentence)?

2. Identify the parts of the paragraph pattern by underlining and annotating them. Use the two example paragraphs as models.

TYPES OF NIGHTCLUBBERS
Jerry Lopez

Dancers are not the only men who go to nightclubs. Having worked in and attended various clubs, I have come to realize they attract about four different types of guys, who can be grouped by the way they act. First there are the dancers. They are out on the floor most of the night. They are not concerned with their appearance. They usually wear jeans or shorts and a tee shirt. They are there to dance and sweat. Then there are the posers. They go to model and show off their clothes and hair. They won't dance for fear of messing up their appearance or, even worse, sweating! The third group is the scammers. Scammers go to pick up women. They usually stand around and check out the body parts of other people as they pass by. A person close to them can see the lust in their eyes. There are also the boozers or druggies. They can be seen stumbling around, falling down, or lying in some corner where they have passed out. At times I am a member of a fifth group: the observers.

EXERCISE 2   Analyzing a Paragraph

Read the following paragraph carefully.

1. Is the paragraph developed in Pattern A (topic sentence/development) or Pattern B (topic sentence/development/concluding sentence as restated topic sentence)?

2. Identify the parts of the paragraph pattern by underlining and annotating them. Use the two example paragraphs as models.

THE SANTA ANAS
Juanita Rivera

In the Los Angeles Basin, people know why the Santa Anas are called the "devil winds." Sometimes they are only hot and breezy and are just mildly annoying. But we in Los Angeles know they can turn wild. That's when they roar in from the desert, searing hot like the breath of a blast furnace, tumbling over the mountain ranges and streaking down the canyons. Pitilessly they destroy and disrupt. Some trees are stripped of leaves, broken, and toppled. Fires that start in the foothills may become fire storms and bombard the downwind areas with smoke, ash, and burning embers. But even without fire, the winds pick up sand, dirt, and debris and send them toward the ocean as a hot, dry, dirty tide going out. All the time the Santa Anas are relentless, humming, howling, and whining through yards, and rattling and rippling loose shingles. Palm fronds scissor or slap and clatter. Dogs howl and often panic and run away; birds hunker down in wind breaks; and human beings mostly stay inside, wiping up the dust, coughing, and getting grumpy. The devil winds earn their reputation.

The Writing Process and the Paragraph

Learning to write a well-designed developmental paragraph will help you write longer assignments, because the developmental paragraph is often an essay in miniature.

Therefore, you can approach both the developmental paragraph and the essay in the same manner—namely, by working through the three stages of the writing process. In this chapter, we will go through the basic stages and strategies once again. Here is a summary of them:

- *Stage One: Exploring / Experimenting / Gathering Information*.

  Freewrite, brainstorm (answer questions or make lists), cluster, take notes (if doing research or analyzing a reading selection).

- *Stage Two: Writing the Controlling Idea / Organizing and Developing Support*.

  Compose your topic sentence with a subject and a focus.
  Complete an outline or an outline alternative.

- *Stage Three: Writing / Revising / Editing*.

  Write a first draft; then revise and edit as many drafts as necessary to reach the final draft.

Student Demonstration of All Stages of the Writing Process

This example shows how one student, Vera Harris, moved from an idea to a topic sentence to an outline to a paragraph. Harris returned to college while she still had a full-time job as a hairdresser. When her instructor asked her to write a paragraph about types of people she had encountered, she naturally considered her customers for the subject of her paragraph—what she would write about. But she also had a special interest in dogs, and cleverly she was able to include that interest. Although she knew her topic rather well, she worked with some prewriting techniques that allowed her to get her ideas flowing onto paper.

She used the Writing Process Worksheet for guidance, thus also providing her instructor with a record of the development of her work. Her worksheet has been lengthened for you to be able to see her work in its entirety.

BRANDON BRIDGE

Writing Process Worksheet

Name _Vera Harris_   **Title** _Customers Are Like Canines_   **Due Date** _Monday, Nov. 19, 8 a.m._

Use the back of this page or separate paper if you need more space.

Assignment

In the space below, write whatever you need to know about your assignment, including information about the topic, audience, pattern of writing, length, whether to include a rough draft or revised drafts, and whether your paper must be typed.

Write a paragraph of classification in which you group people according to their behavior. Keep your audience in mind as you select words and as you develop your ideas in an appropriate way. Submit this completed Writing Process Worksheet, a rough draft marked for revision, and a typed final draft of about 250 words.

Stage One

Explore   Freewrite, brainstorm (list), cluster, or take notes as directed by your instructor.

Freewriting (partial)

Types of customers

  I have worked in beauty shops for a long time, and I've naturally made a lot of observations about my customers. I could write about what they look like and (how they behave) and how they tip and lots of things. When I first started to work, I guess at first I thought of them as pretty much the same but then I started (to see them as types) mainly as to how they acted and I remember way back then I sometimes thought of how they (reminded me of dogs.) I don't mean that in any bad way but just that human beings have their personalities and their appearances and all and so do dogs.

Both dogs and customers can be grouped

Brainstorming (Big Six Questions)

Who?	my customers
What?	the way they act
Where?	in the beauty salon
When?	for the years I have worked
Why?	their basic nature
How?	behavior sometimes like dogs—hounds, Dobermans, terriers, bulldogs, cockers, poodles, mixed, retrievers, boxers

Brainstorming (Listing)

kinds of dogs
    hounds
    Dobermans
    terriers
    bulldogs
    cockers
    poodles
    mixed
    retrievers
    pit bulls
    boxers

Clustering

Stage Two

Organize   Write a topic sentence or thesis; label the subject and the focus parts.

<u>The customers in the beauty shop where I work</u> <u>remind me of types of dogs</u>
<u>(of which I am fond)</u>.   subject
                focus

Write an outline or an outline alternative. For reading-based writing, include references and short quotations with page numbers as support in the outline.

  I. Poodles (major support)
    A. High-strung (minor support)
    B. Need attention (minor support)
 II. Doberman pinschers (major support)
    A. Demanding (minor support)
    B. Need watching (minor support)
III. Bulldogs (major support)
    A. Act mean (minor support)
    B. Will back down (minor support)

IV. Cocker spaniels (major support)
　A. Lovable (minor support)
　B. Faithful (minor support)
　C. Easy to please (minor support)

Stage Three　　　　**Write**　On separate paper, write and then revise your paragraph or essay as many times as necessary for **c**oherence, **l**anguage (usage, tone, and diction), **u**nity, **e**mphasis, **s**upport, and **s**entences (**CLUESS**). Read your work aloud to hear and correct any grammatical errors or awkward-sounding sentences.

Edit any problems in fundamentals, such as **c**apitalization, **g**rammar, **p**unctuation, and **s**pelling (**CGPS**).

Rough Draft: Writing, Revising, Editing

CUSTOMERS ARE LIKE CANINES
Vera Harris

Language
Punctuation

Over the years while working
~~I have worked~~ in a beauty salon ~~for a long time. There,~~ I have come

Sentences
Punctuation

across almost every kind of salon customer, each with her own unique looks

Because
and personality. I am also a dog lover and have observed numerous dogs

Language

relate them to
with care it is easier to classify these people if I ~~compare them with~~ canine

types—but in a playful rather than a mean way. The first group is made up

Language

and high-strung
of poodles. Poodles are very prissy, with a constant need for attention. Their

Emphasis
Spelling

hair is usually overstyled. They think puffballs in soft colors look great. The

last—
~~next~~ group and largest group is made up of cocker spani*e*ls. The ₵ockers

Omission
Language

and　　　　　*groomed and stroked, but they are easy to please.*
are very lovable the most faithful. They enjoy being ~~pampered.~~ Cockers like

Sentences

to
to see me every week and visit with others. Sometimes I can almost see their

Sentences
Language

s　*OT*
tails wagging. Then come the Doberman pincher*s*, this type scares me the

most. Dobies are hard to please. If one hair goes the wrong way, I will see

expose
their upper lip rise up to ~~show~~ eyeteeth, as if they are snarling. I rarely turn

third　　*members,*
my back while working on this type—a Dobie might bite. The ~~last~~ group the

Punctuation

one does not
bulldogs, are not as mean as Dobies. Bulldogs act mean and tough, but if ~~you~~

Language

~~don't~~ show fear when they get bossy they will back down. This type needs

Punctuation

I am
to feel in charge, even if ~~it's me~~ leading them around on a leash. No matter

Language

what, canines and customers are my best friends.

Final Draft

CUSTOMERS ARE LIKE CANINES
Vera Harris

Topic sentence

Support

Support

Support

Support

Concluding sentence

    Over the years while working in a beauty salon, I have come across almost every kind of salon customer, each with her own unique looks and personality. Because I am also a dog lover and have observed numerous dogs with care, it is easier to classify these people if I relate them to canine types—but in a playful rather than a mean way. The first group is made up of poodles. Poodles are very prissy and high-strung, with a constant need for attention. Their hair is usually overstyled. They think puffballs in soft colors look great. Then come the Doberman pinschers. This type scares me the most. Dobies are hard to please. If one hair goes the wrong way, I will see their upper lip rise up to expose eyeteeth. I rarely turn my back while working on this type—a Dobie might bite. The third group members, the bulldogs, are not as mean as Dobies. Bulldogs act mean and tough, but if one does not show fear when they get bossy, they will back down. This type needs to feel in charge, even if I am leading them around on a leash. The last—and largest—group is made up of cocker spaniels. The cockers are very lovable and the most faithful. They enjoy being groomed and stroked, but they are easy to please. Cockers like to see me every week and to visit with others. Sometimes I can almost see their tails wagging. No matter what, canines and customers are my best friends.

EXERCISE 3   Writing a Paragraph

Select one of the following topic sentences and, on separate paper, write a paragraph based on it.

1. I made that argument at the time, but if I had a second chance, I wouldn't repeat it.

2. It was the worst piece of news I ever had to deliver.

3. I confronted authority and learned from the experience.

4. It was an act of generosity I will never forget.

5. Sometimes there are good reasons for lying.

6. Alcohol addiction has physical, social, and vocational effects.

7. There are several ways to show affection.

8. The job didn't pay well, but it provided me with a good education in balancing my budget, managing my time, and dealing with the public.

9. Teenagers like music for obvious reasons.

10. Homeless people are in their situation for different reasons.

WRITER'S GUIDELINES Writing the Paragraph

BRANDON BRIDGE

1. The **developmental paragraph** is a group of sentences, each with the function of stating or supporting a controlling idea called the **topic sentence**.

2. The developmental paragraph contains three parts: the subject, the topic sentence, and the support.

3. The two main patterns of the developmental paragraph are (A) topic sentence and support, and (B) topic sentence, support, and concluding sentence.

<table>
<tr><td align="center">**Pattern A**</td><td align="center">**Pattern B**</td></tr>
<tr><td>

Topic sentence

Support

Support

Support

</td><td>

Topic sentence

Support

Support

Support

Concluding sentence

</td></tr>
</table>

Development — Development

4. The topic sentence includes what you are writing about—the **subject**—and what you intend to do with that subject—the **focus**.

Being a good parent is more than providing financial support.
    subject   focus

5. The **outline** is a pattern for showing the relationship of ideas. It can be used to reveal the structure and content of something you read or to plan the structure and content of something you intend to write. The following topic outline shows how the parts are arranged on the page as well as how the ideas in it relate to one another.

Main Idea (will usually be the topic sentence for the paragraph or the thesis for the essay)

I. Major support
   A. Minor support
      1. Details (specific information of various kinds)
      2. Details
   B. Minor support
      1. Details
      2. Details

II. Major support
   A. Minor support
   B. Minor support
      1. Details
      2. Details
      3. Details

5

Writing the Essay

 The point of the essay is to change things.

—EDWARD TUFTE

CHAPTER CONTENTS

BRANDON BRIDGE

The Essay Defined in Relation to the Developmental Paragraph

The essay is as difficult to define as the paragraph, but the paragraph definition gives us a framework. Consider this definition: The **developmental paragraph** "is a group of sentences, each with the function of supporting a controlling idea called the topic sentence."

The main parts of the developmental paragraph are the topic sentence (subject and focus), support (evidence and reasoning), and, often, a concluding sentence. Now let's use that framework to define the essay: The **essay** is a group of paragraphs, each with the function of supporting a controlling idea called the thesis.

These are the main parts of the essay:

Introduction: presents the thesis, which states the controlling idea—much like the topic sentence for a paragraph but on a larger scale.
Development: introduces evidence and reasoning—the support.
Transition: points out divisions of the essay (seldom used in the short essay).
Conclusion: provides an appropriate ending—often a restatement of or reflection on the thesis.

Thus, considered structurally, the essay can be an expanded developmental paragraph. That does not mean that all paragraphs can grow to be essays or that all essays can shrink to become paragraphs. For college writing, however, a good understanding of the parallel between well-organized paragraphs and well-organized essays is useful.

As you learn how to write effective paragraphs—with strong topic sentences and strong support—you also learn how to organize an essay. You just expand the process, as shown in Figure 5.1.

Figure 5.1
Paragraph and Essay
Compared

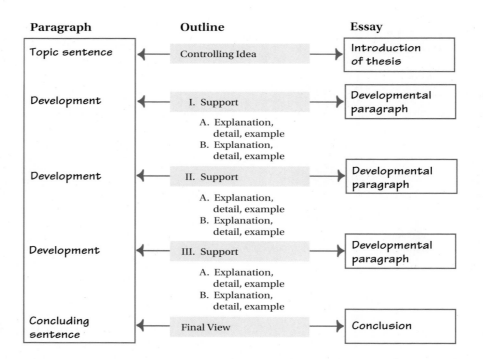

Like the paragraph, the essay may assume different patterns. It may be primarily one form of discourse: narration, description, exposition, or argumentation. It may also be a combination, varying from paragraph to paragraph and even within paragraphs. Regardless of its pattern, the essay will be unified around a central idea, or thesis. The **thesis** is the assertion or controlling purpose. All the other parts of the essay will be subordinate to the thesis and will support it. As with the paragraph, the main point—here, the thesis—will almost certainly be stated, usually in the first paragraph, and again—more often than not—at the end of the essay. The following essay on Elvis illustrates this pattern.

The only difference in concept between the topic sentence and the thesis is one of scope: The topic sentence unifies and controls the content of the paragraph, and the thesis does the same for the essay. Because the essay is longer and more complex than the typical paragraph, the thesis may suggest a broader scope and may more explicitly indicate the parts.

Paragraph:

Short Essay:

GOOD KING ELVIS

A messiah, a jester, a reckless jerk—or a soulful singer from the Deep South—Elvis at different times to different people was all these things. His fans mirror every facet of their idol. "I liked him because of his looks," says Sue Scarborough, forty-nine, of Lexington, Kentucky, as she waits with her husband to tour Graceland. "He didn't put on airs," says Jeff Graff, twenty, of Cleveland, Ohio. "He went out of his way to help people." "I met him in 1960 when I was twelve years old," says Billie Le Jeune of Memphis, who visits Graceland once or twice a month: "He asked me what my favorite subject was." On the pink fieldstone wall outside Graceland, which for years has functioned as an unauthorized bulletin board, the graffiti runs like this: ELVIS IS LOVE; I DID DRUGS WITH ELVIS; and most cryptic of all—ELVIS DIDN'T DESERVE TO BE WHITE.

Topic sentence

Support

Support
Support

Concluding sentence

I. Appearance

II. Helped people

III. Basic goodness

GOOD KING ELVIS

A messiah, a jester, a reckless jerk—or a soulful singer from the Deep South—Elvis at different times to different people was all these things. His fans mirror every facet of their idol. For some fans the attraction is appearance. "I liked him because of his looks," says Sue Scarborough, forty-nine, of Lexington, Kentucky, as she waits with her husband to tour Graceland. She grins good-naturedly at her husband and gives him an affectionate nudge in the ribs when he says, "My wife really likes Elvis, but I'm not jealous because he is dead—I think." Her response tells all: "My husband's a good man at drivin' a truck and fishin' for bass, but no one'll ever paint his picture on velvet."

For others, Elvis was a king with a common touch and humanitarian instincts. "He didn't put on airs," says Jeff Graff, twenty, of Cleveland, Ohio. "He went out of his way to help people." His friend nods his head in agreement. "Elvis must've given away a hundred Cadillacs in his day." Others in line break in to tell stories about the generosity of this good man who once walked among them.

The speakers at Graceland who get the most attention are those who actually met Elvis and have information about his basic goodness.

Introduction

Thesis

Topic sentence

Support

Topic sentence

Support

Topic sentence

"I met him in 1960 when I was twelve years old," says Billie Le Jeune of Memphis, who visits Graceland once or twice a month: "He asked me what my favorite subject was." A few others have stories equally compelling. The crowd listens in awe and envy.

Support

Along with these talkers at Graceland are the writers, who sum up the range of Elvis's qualities. On the pink fieldstone wall outside Graceland, which for years has functioned as an unauthorized bulletin board, the graffiti runs like this: ELVIS IS LOVE; I DID DRUGS WITH ELVIS; and—most cryptic of all—ELVIS DIDN'T DESERVE TO BE WHITE.

Conclusion

Special Paragraphs within the Essay

Because paragraphs of transition (usually running short and having a simple structure) are almost never needed in short essays, we will focus our attention on paragraphs of introduction and conclusion.

INTRODUCTIONS

A good introductory paragraph does many things. It attracts the reader's interest, states or points toward the thesis, and moves the reader smoothly into the body paragraphs, the developmental paragraphs. Here are some introductory methods:

- A direct statement of the thesis
- Background
- Definition of term(s)
- Quotation(s)
- A shocking statement
- Question(s)
- A combination of two or more methods on this list

You should not decide that some of the methods are good and some are bad. Indeed, all are valid, and the most common one is the last, the combination. Use the approach that best fits each essay. Resist the temptation to use the same kind of introduction in every essay you write.

Each of the following statements is an introductory paragraph. The thesis is the same in all of them, yet each uses a different introductory method. Notice the great variety here.

Direct Statement of Thesis: Anyone on the road in any city near midnight on Friday and Saturday is among dangerous people. They are not the product of the witching hour; they are the product of the "happy hour." They are called drunk drivers. These threats to our lives and limbs need to be covered by federal laws with strong punitive provisions.

Subject Focus

Background: In one four-year period in California (2005–2009), 17,942 people were injured and 6,632 were killed by drunk drivers. Each year, the same kinds of figures come in from all our states. The federal govern-ment does virtually nothing. Drunk driving has reached the point of being a national problem of huge proportions. This slaughter of innocent citizens should be stopped by following the lead of many other nations and passing federal legislation with strong punitive provisions.

Subject Focus

Definition: Here is a recipe. Take two thousand pounds of plastic, rubber, and steel, pour in ten gallons of gas, and start the engine. Then take one human being of two hundred pounds of flesh, blood, and bones, pour in two glasses of beer in one hour, and put him or her behind the wheel. Mix the two together, and the result may be a drunken driver ready to cause death and destruction. This problem of drunk driving can and should be covered by federal legislation with strong punitive provisions.

Subject Focus

Quotation: The National Highway Traffic Safety Administration has stated that 50 percent of all fatal accidents involve intoxicated drivers and that "75 percent of those drivers have a Blood Alcohol Content of 0.10 percent or greater." That kind of information is widely known, yet the carnage on the highways continues. This problem of drunk driving should be addressed by a federal law with strong punitive provisions.

Subject Focus

Shocking Statement and Questions: Almost 60,000 Americans were killed in the Vietnam War. What other war kills more than that number every four years? Give up? It is the war with drunk drivers. The war in Vietnam ended more than three decades ago, but our DUI war goes on, and the drunks are winning. This deadly conflict should be covered by a federal law with strong punitive provisions.

Subject Focus

Questions and a Definition: What is a drunk driver? In California it is a person with a blood alcohol content of 0.08 percent or higher who is operating a motor vehicle. What do those drivers do? Every year some of them kill more than 16,000 people nationwide. Those are easy ques-tions. The difficult one is, What can be done? One answer is clear: Drunk drivers should be covered by federal laws with strong punitive provisions.

Subject Focus

All these introductory methods are effective. Some others, however, are inef-fective because they are too vague to carry the thesis or because they carry the thesis in a mechanical way. The mechanical approach may be direct and explicit, but it usually numbs the reader's imagination and interest.

Avoid: The purpose of this essay is to write about the need for strong puni-tive national laws against drunk driving.

Avoid: I will now write a paper about the need for strong punitive national laws against drunk driving.

The length of an introduction can vary, but the typical length for the introduc-tory paragraph of a student essay is three to five sentences. If your introduction is shorter than three, be certain that it conveys all you want to say. If it is longer than five, be certain that it only introduces and does not try to expand on ideas.

That function is reserved for the developmental paragraphs; a long and complicated introduction may make your essay top-heavy.

EXERCISE 1   Writing an Introduction

Select one of the following theses (altering it a bit to suit your own ideas, if you like) and, on separate paper, write at least three introductions for it, using a different method for each one. Underline the thesis in each paragraph, and label the subject and focus parts.

1. Marriages come in different shapes and sizes.
2. Career choices are greatly influenced by a person's background.
3. *Friendship* is just one word, but friends are of different kinds.
4. The spirit of sports has been corrupted by money.
5. Sexual harassment at work often goes unreported for practical reasons.

CONCLUSIONS

Your concluding paragraph should give the reader the feeling that you have said all you want to say about your subject. Like introductory paragraphs, concluding paragraphs are of various types. Here are some effective ways of concluding a paper:

- Conclude with a final paragraph or sentence that is a logical part of the body of the paper; that is, one that functions as part of the support. In the following example, there is no formal conclusion. This form is more common in the published essay than in the student essay.

  One day he hit me. He said he was sorry and even cried, but I could not forgive him. We got a divorce. It took me a while before I could look back and see what the causes really were, but by then it was too late to make any changes.
  (Maria Campos, "A Divorce with Reasons")

- Conclude with a restatement of the thesis in slightly different words, perhaps pointing out its significance or making applications.

  Do not blame it on the referee. Do not even blame it on the fight managers. Put the blame where it belongs—on the prevailing mores that regard prize fighting as a perfectly proper enterprise and vehicle of entertainment. No one doubts that many people enjoy prize fighting and will miss it if it should be thrown out. And that is precisely the point.
  (Norman Cousins, "Who Killed Benny Paret?")

- Conclude with a review of the main points of the discussion—a kind of summary. This is appropriate only if the complexity of the essay makes a summary necessary.

As we have been made all too aware lately in this country, the more energy we conserve now, the more we'll have for the future. The same holds true for skiing. So take the Soft Path of energy conservation as you ski. You will not only be able to make longer nonstop runs, but you will have more energy to burn on the dance floor.

(Carl Wingus, "Conserving Energy as You Ski")

- Conclude with an anecdote related to the thesis.

Over the harsh traffic sounds of motors and horns and blaring radios came the faint whang-whang of a would-be musician with a beat-up guitar and a money-drop hat turned up at his feet. It all reminded me of when I had first experienced the conglomeration of things that now assailed my senses. This jumbled mixture of things both human and nonhuman was, in fact, the reason I had come to live here. Then it was different and exciting. Now it is the reason I am leaving.

(Brian Maxwell, "Leaving Los Angeles")

- Conclude with a quotation related to the thesis.

He [Johnny Cash] had, of course, long since attained a legendary stature few performers ever achieved. Terri Clark, a country songstress two generations removed, captured a sense of it in a statement released Friday. "What really made him stand out, more than the back-beats, the TV shows, the hit records, was how he stood up for the little people, the way he believed in the right things.... He was a beacon for both musical and personal integrity, and he set a bar most of us can only gaze at."

(Dave Tianen, "A Music Legend Fades to Black")

There are also many ineffective ways of concluding an essay. Do not conclude with the following:

- a summary when a summary is unnecessary
- a complaint about the assignment or an apology about the quality of the work
- an afterthought—that is, something you forgot to discuss in the body of the essay
- a tagged conclusion—that is, a sentence beginning with such phrases as *In conclusion*, *To conclude*, *I would like to conclude this discussion*, or *Last but not least*
- a conclusion that raises additional problems that should have been settled during the discussion

The conclusion is an integral part of the essay and is often a reflection of the introduction. If you have trouble with the conclusion, reread your introduction. Then work for a roundness or completeness in the whole paper.

Student Demonstration of All Stages of the Writing Process

Let's see now how one student wrote an essay by working her way through all the stages of the writing process.

Our student writer, Leah, is an inmate at a California prison where, for several years, she was enrolled in a small, low-cost college program. In her English class, her assignment was to write a personal essay of 500 to 800 words. Her instructor suggested she concentrate on a recent development or event at the prison that had changed her life, for better or worse.

Several topics interested her. There was the problem of overcrowding: She lived in an institution built for 900 inmates, and the population was now 2,200. She also considered education. After spending some time in routine prison work and aimless activities, she discovered school and found it highly satisfying. Then there were the accomplishments of her Native American friends at the prison. After years of arguing their case, they had finally obtained permission from the institution to build a sweat lodge for religious purposes, and it was now in operation. That was a subject she knew well, and it was one for which she held the most enthusiasm. She was ready to proceed, knowing that the writing process would provide her with strategies and give her direction.

Leah used the Writing Process Worksheet for guidance, thus also providing her instructor with a record of the development of her work. Her worksheet has been lengthened for you to be able to see parts of her work in their entirety.

BRANDON BRIDGE

Writing Process Worksheet

Name Leah   **Title** Prison Sweat Lodge   **Due Date** Tuesday, April 10, at 1 p.m.

Use the back of this page or separate paper if you need more space.

Assignment

In the space below, write whatever you need to know about your assignment, including information about the topic, audience, pattern of writing, length, whether to include a rough draft or revised drafts, and whether your paper must be typed.

Write a personal essay of 500 to 800 words about some aspect of your prison life that has changed recently. This will be mainly about how something is done; therefore, you will probably organize your discussion by time. Write for a general cross section of the population, one that will probably not have shared the experience you write about. Submit this completed worksheet, a rough draft marked for revision, and a typed final draft.

Stage One

Explore Freewrite, brainstorm (list), cluster, or take notes as directed by your instructor.

Freewriting

• First Leah started freewriting, which enabled her to probe her memory and see which aspects of the subject most interested her. She wrote without stopping, letting her ideas tumble forth in a rich free association on the subject of "sweat lodge."

For several years I have wanted to worship in the way that I did when I was on the reservation. These people here at prison were discriminating against me, I thought. I knew that the other people here could go to the chaplain and to the chapel and they could do so without people complaining or going to any bother. I didn't know why they did not allow me to follow my own religious preference. Then I talked to the other Indian sisters here at prison and they told me that they had been working for many years to get a sweat lodge. I started working with them. It took years of work, but it is worth it for now *we have a sweat lodge* where we can go for our ceremonies. It makes me feel good. I look forward to it. I *have used it once a week for most* of the *last year.* When I am nervous and when things are tense on the prison grounds, I think about the sweat lodge and just thinking about it gives me some peace. Then *when I go there and sweat* for a period of time I seem to feel that I am leaving the prison grounds and I am *at peace* with the universe. It is *a ceremony* that is *important* to me and also to the prison. We even have women who are not Indians who are interested and we teach them about Indian ways and we all learn from what we do. What else is there to say. I could go on and on. That is what I have to say. I love the sweat lodge which we call the sweats. I think it is the most important thing in my life now. I used to be bitter toward the prison for denying me my rights, but now I am even *at peace* with them—most of the time. I remember when we were trying to get approval and … [partial]

Have sweat lodge now

Ceremony important

At peace

Brainstorming (Big Six Questions)

* Leah continued with the subject of the prison sweat lodge, and her topic tightened to focus on particular areas. Although she could have listed the annotations and the words she underlined in her freewriting, she began with the big six questions for her framework.

Who?	American Indian inmates and others
What?	sweat lodge—how it was started—the politics—the ceremonies
Where?	California Institution for Women—off the yard
When?	2009, before, after, long time in planning and building
Why?	spiritual, physical, self-esteem, educational
How?	preparation, steps

Brainstorming (Listing)

* Leah then proceeded to write three useful lists based on her answers to the questions.

Sweat lodge	Ceremony	Result
Problems in building it	Preparation	Relaxed
Reasons	Blankets	Spiritually clean
Fairness	Rocks	Peaceful
Who helped	Fire	
Time to build	Water	
	Tobacco and sweet grass	
	Sweating	
	Passing pipe	
	Tearing down	

Clustering

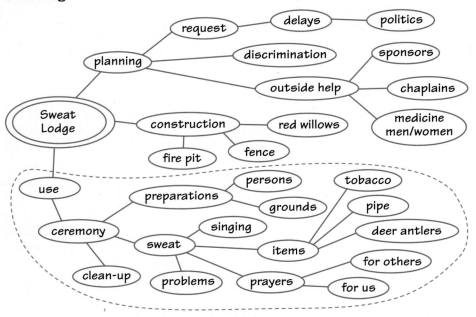

* Notice that after completing her basic cluster, Leah went back and drew a broken boundary around subclusters that offered encouraging areas for focus. Some subclusters, usually with further clustering to provide details, can work as well as an outline for providing structure and content for the development of an essay.

Stage Two

Organize Write a topic sentence or thesis; label the subject and the focus parts.

* After freewriting, brainstorming, and clustering, Leah was ready to focus. She was ready to concentrate on one aspect of her larger topic that could reasonably be developed in an essay of 500 to 800 words. She also wanted to establish a direction for the essay that would target her audience, who knew little about her topic. It would be necessary to explain her topic in detail so that uninformed readers could easily understand. Moreover, she would avoid any Native American words that her audience might not know. Although the sweat lodge was developed in an atmosphere of controversy in which she and others often had to be persuasive, she anticipated that readers of this essay would be open-minded and interested. She would simply inform them about her experience with the sweat lodge, giving a personal perspective. She would also have to avoid using prison slang because this essay was for an assignment in a college writing class.

  Leah made three attempts to write a sentence with both a subject (what she would write about) and a focus (what she would do with her subject). She wanted the focus to be just right, not vague or too broad or too narrow.

I want to explain how we use sweats and why.

Using the prison sweat lodge involves specific practices that contribute to my well-being.

I want to discuss the <u>prison sweat lodge</u>, <u>what we do in the preparation period,</u>
subject
<u>what we do when we were inside for the ceremony, and what we do afterward.</u>
focus

- Her third attempt satisfied her, and the statement became her thesis. Later she would reword it.

Write an outline or an outline alternative. For reading-based writing, include references and short quotations with page numbers as support in the outline.

- Leah's next task was to organize her material. Although she might have used the part of her cluster marked by the dotted lines, she chose the outline form. The outline shows the relationship of ideas, suggests ways to divide the essay according to Leah's thesis, and indicates support. The divisions are Preparation, Ceremony, and Ceremony completion and site restoration. Those items are Leah's Roman-numeral headings.

I. Preparation
    A. Fasting
        1. Duration
        2. Only water
    B. Heat rocks
        1. Thirty to fifty
        2. Build fire
    C. Set up lodge
        1. Permission from sponsor
        2. Cover framework
II. Ceremony
    A. Movement
        1. Going and coming
        2. Passing sacred objects
    B. Establishing attitude
    C. Sweating
    D. Praying and singing
    E. Purification rites
        1. Tobacco ties
        2. Sage
        3. Sweet grass
III. Ceremony completion and site restoration
    A. Personal
        1. Water down
        2. Eat and drink
        3. Change
    B. Site
        1. Remove and store blankets
        2. Move rocks

Stage Three

Write On separate paper, write and then revise your paragraph or essay as many times as necessary for **c**oherence, **l**anguage (usage, tone, and diction), **u**nity, **e**mphasis, **s**upport, and **s**entences (**CLUESS**). Read your work aloud to hear and correct any grammatical errors or awkward-sounding sentences.

Edit any problems in fundamentals, such as **c**apitalization, **g**rammar, **p**unctuation, and **s**pelling (**CGPS**).

- The following is an early draft that shows Leah's revision and editing process using the Brandon Guide for Revising and Editing.

RAZOR WIRE SWEAT LODGE

Rewrite for language

~~I am a~~ [My tribe is] Pomo ~~Indian~~, one ~~tribe~~ of ~~many here~~ [twenty-one represented] on the prison grounds. I have [always] had tremendous interest in my ~~Ancestry~~ [ancestors] and [in] their customs, and the cultures of all Indian tribes. The sacred sweat ceremonies, ~~I've~~ [I have] found to be one

Rewrite for language

of the most interesting. Many women of ~~all~~ [other] races here in the facility have [cultural practices] also taken interest and found ~~peace~~ [other benefits] within themselves from participating in the sweats. I want to discuss the prison sweat lodge, what we do in the preparation period, what we do when ~~we're~~ [we are] inside for the ceremony, and what we do afterward.

Rewrite for stronger topic sentence—unity and emphasis

The first step to sweating [in our prison facility] is the preparation period. Before anyone can sweat there are many requirements ~~in~~ [concerning] what we wear, ~~how we are instructed (depending on how many times we've gone),~~ and how we act. ~~T~~[F]or Twenty-four

Coherence

hours before the sweat we fast. ~~We can only drink~~ [Participants should drink only] water or juices, but if someone has health problems we will excuse them. The lava rocks have to [heat] in the fire approximately three hours before we start sweating. The fire has to

Organize
Be more concise
Support

be built just right in a little house shape. ~~Putting~~ [We put] all the rocks in the middle with the wood standing like a teepee around them; then the paper [is] stuffed between and around the wood. Once ~~there's~~ [there is] a good fire going then we ~~start~~ tend to the sweat lodge itself. Because we have no tarp to put on the sweat lodge, the state has provided us with plenty of blankets. The blankets have to cover the s[w]eat lodge fully. We put at least three layers of blankets on the sweat lodge. We make sure we leave about eight inches of blanket around the bottom of the sweat lodge. ~~Around~~ [By] this time, some women have started

Coherence

making their tobacco ties. These ties are used for ~~putting your~~ [sending] prayer on.

We've got to make sure the sponsor is somewhere by the sweat lodge at all

times. ~~Also about~~ the rock we use thirty to fifty of them it depends on their

size and how many women are sweating that day. Then the women are told

to change into only muu muu; the state provides them also. Then we're read

to go inside. The preparation period is very important ~~and~~ everyone looks

forward to it being over.

  Once everyone is inside the sweat lodge, there are certain things you

must do. ~~The way we enter is~~ first we enter counterclockwise and inside we

~~maintain everything we do~~ counterclockwise. There are four rounds in the

sweat which last about twenty to thirty minutes ~~each~~. We stress that no one

break our circle inside the sweat lodge, but it ~~is possible.~~ Some women ~~can't~~

handle the heat inside we never make them stay. The praying and singing

is in the Sioux language because our outside sponsor is Sioux. Not every-

one has to sing or pray. ~~It's~~ up to ~~them.~~ As someone finishes a prayer ~~they~~

~~say for all their relations~~ then the next person prays. Before ~~anyone even~~

enters the sweat ~~they~~ have to make sure they have peace and good feelings

with all other members. The tobacco ties hang over our heads in the sweat

or around our necks. (Also) we take in sage with us and smudge ourselves

with it. After each round, new hot rocks are brought in. As these rocks are

place in the fire, sweet grass is put on them. ~~All~~ we do inside the sweat lodge

is not only for ourselves, but ~~for~~ our prayers for others. We maintain our-

selves with humility during the whole sweat.

  When the sweat is over, we enter the final phase. We come out and throw

our tobacco ties in the fire pit. The ~~first thing~~ we ~~do is~~ hose ourselves down

with plenty of cold water. The refreshments are opened and someone goes

after food. Once ~~we've~~ eaten and changed our clothes we start taking down

the sweat. The blankets have to be taken off the same way they were put

Coherence

Coherence

Rephrase

Agreement

Be more concise

Verb tense

on and folded up ~~good.~~ ^carefully.^ The leftover wood has to be put away and ~~on both~~

the blankets and the wood ~~we put their covers.~~ ^must be covered.^ Any garbage ~~that's~~ ^that has^ been

left around is thrown in ^to^ the dumpster. Then we lock the gate and bid our

farewells until the next weekend. After ~~it's~~ ^f it is^ all over ~~you really~~ ^we^ feel ~~a sense of~~ ^physically^

refresh~~ness~~ ^ed^ clean and peaceful.

Rewrite

^Using^ The sweat lodge is a custom of most~~ly all~~ Indian tribes. Certain Indian

tribes go about it differently ~~than~~ ^from^ others but once ~~they're~~ ^they are^ all inside everyone

feels of one whole being. All three steps ~~I've~~ ^I have^ gone through are helpful for

a successful sweat ceremony. ~~Many of us members~~ ^Each week we^ look forward to these

ceremonies ~~every week.~~ They help us cope better with the prison system.

Move to end for emphasis

Final Draft

RAZOR WIRE SWEAT LODGE
Leah

My Indian tribe is Pomo, one of twenty-one represented at this prison. I have always had tremendous interest in my ancestors and their customs, and in the cultures of all Indian tribes. The sacred sweat ceremony itself is at the center of my life. Here at prison it has taken on a special meaning. In fact, many women of other races here have also found peace within themselves as a result of participating with me and other Native Americans in the sweats. *Thesis* Each Saturday we have a routine: We make preparations, we sweat, and we conclude with a post-sweat activity.

Topic sentence Before we sweat, we must prepare ourselves and the facility. For twenty-four hours before the sweat, we fast. We do not eat anything and drink only water or juices, but if someone has a health problem, we will excuse her. As for clothing, we wear simple, loose dresses such as the prison-issued muu muus. We bring tobacco ties, sage leaves, sweet grass, and sometimes a pipe. Preparing the facility is more complicated than preparing ourselves. About thirty-five lava rocks must be heated in a fire approximately three hours before we start sweating. The wood for the fire has to be placed in a tepee shape around the pile of rocks and ignited. Once the fire is hot, we tend to the sweat lodge itself. Because we have no tarp to put on the sweat lodge frame, the state provides us with blankets. We use these to cover the lodge fully, draping it with about three layers and leaving an opening to the east. Finally we are ready to go inside. The preparation period is very important, but everyone looks forward to its being over.

Topic sentence From this point on through the ceremony, everything must be done according to rules. First we enter counterclockwise, and once inside we conduct all parts of the ceremony counterclockwise. There are four rounds in the sweat, each of which lasts about twenty to thirty minutes. We stress that no one should break our circle inside the sweat lodge, but it sometimes happens.

Some women cannot handle the steam and the heat, so we never make them stay. Those who do stay are free to participate in the singing and praying or not. The four rounds are similar. For each, six hot rocks are brought in, and six dippers of water are poured onto the rocks. The number six indicates the four directions and the sky and the ground. As someone finishes a prayer (usually in Sioux because our sponsor is a Sioux), she mentions her relatives, for this ceremony is also for others. Then another person follows. As sweet grass burns outside on the fire, we sit in the hot steam and rub sage leaves on our bodies for purification. We maintain ourselves with humility during the whole event.

Topic sentence   <u>When the sweat is over, we enter the final phase.</u> We come out and throw our tobacco ties into the fire pit, and the smoke takes our prayers to the sky. Then we hose ourselves down with plenty of cold water and open the refreshments we brought. Once we have eaten and changed our clothes, we start dismantling the sweat. The blankets have to be taken off the same way they were put up and then folded carefully. The leftover wood has to be put away, and the blankets and wood must be covered. Any garbage that has been left around is thrown into the dumpster. Then we lock the gate to our facility and bid farewell.

Using a sweat lodge is a custom of most Indian tribes. Certain Indian tribes go about it differently from others, but in here when we are together in the lodge, we feel like one whole being. Each week we look forward to this ceremony. It helps us cope better with the prison system. After it is over, we feel physically refreshed, clean, and peaceful.

EXERCISE 2   Completing a Writing Process Worksheet

Select one of the following theses (altering it if you like, even by taking the opposite position) and complete a Writing Process Worksheet at least through Stage Two.

1. The date [marriage, class, game, job] was a disaster [success].

2. I will never forget my first encounter with racial prejudice [cruelty to animals, inhumanity].

3. The kind of music I listen to reflects the kind of person I would like to be.

4. A preoccupation with a single activity or concern throws life out of balance.

5. The importance of student government is often overlooked.

6. A death in the family can teach a person a great deal about life.

7. The way a person drives reveals his or her personality.

8. The way I drive depends on my mood.

9. The way I keep my room [car, house, yard, desk] is a reflection of the way I think [regard life].

10. One of my most embarrassing moments has become, in retrospect, only a humorous recollection.

WRITER'S GUIDELINES   Writing the Essay

BRANDON BRIDGE

1. The **essay** is a group of paragraphs, each with the function of stating or supporting a controlling idea called the **thesis**.

   • The main parts of an essay are the introduction, development, and conclusion.
   • The essay can be considered an amplification of a developmental paragraph.

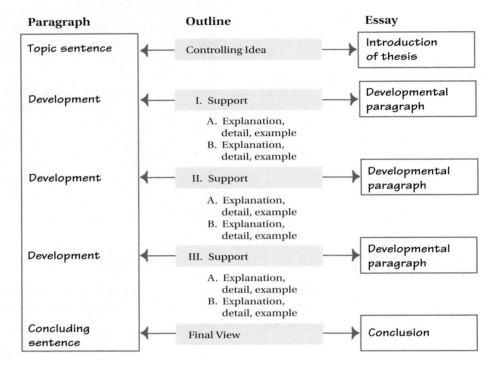

Paragraph	Outline	Essay
Topic sentence	Controlling Idea	Introduction of thesis
Development	I. Support	Developmental paragraph
	A. Explanation, detail, example	
	B. Explanation, detail, example	
Development	II. Support	Developmental paragraph
	A. Explanation, detail, example	
	B. Explanation, detail, example	
Development	III. Support	Developmental paragraph
	A. Explanation, detail, example	
	B. Explanation, detail, example	
Concluding sentence	Final View	Conclusion

2. The **introduction** contains the thesis within a context of comments that give an adequate perspective on the topic. There are many good introductory methods, which include presenting a direct statement of the thesis, background, definition of term(s), quotation(s), a shocking statement, question(s), and a combination of two or more of these methods.

3. The **conclusion** makes a final comment on the development of your thesis. If you do not know how to conclude, reread your introduction for ideas.

4. You can depend on the three stages of the writing process to help you write paragraphs and essays. In the first stage, you are encouraged to explore relevant ideas and perhaps generate a topic sentence or thesis. In the second stage, you move naturally to a precise statement of your topic sentence or thesis and to an organized plan for your support material. Finally, you do the actual writing, revising, and editing of your paragraph or essay. The Brandon Guide for Revising and Editing covers Stage Three of writing. This approach follows the recursive movement of the writing process, going back and forth in a natural flow of writing.

PART 2

LINKING READING AND WRITING

Reading and writing are joined without seam. Reading activates your memory and provides you with substance for writing. Writing helps you examine your ideas and clarify what you have read. Reading and writing often blend as reading-based writing and together are the essence of critical thinking.

6

Reading for Thinking, Discussion, and Writing

 I learned to write by reading the kind of books I wished I'd written.

—BARBARA KINGSOLVER

CHAPTER CONTENTS

BRANDON BRIDGE

Reading-Based Writing

THE WRITING COMPONENT

Reading-based writing was invented to help you fill those intimidating blank pages with thoughtful statements centered on what you have read, broadly called the *text*. *Text* is a term that includes items as diverse as photos, advertisements, online postings, and movies as sources for *text-based writing*, but in this book, we are concerned specifically with writing about reading, hence the term *reading-based writing*.

For instruction in this book, reading-based writing comes in three forms: summary, reaction, and two-part response. In writing a summary, you use your own words to restate the main ideas in what you have read. In writing a reaction, you comment critically on what you have read, while giving credit for the ideas and words you borrow. Then, in composing a two-part response, you write both a summary and a reaction, but you separate them to show your instructors that you know the difference between the two forms.

THE READING COMPONENT

Reading-based writing can also make you a better reader. When you are reading for a writing assignment, you concentrate more because you are thinking about how you will be using the content. When you are writing, your mind reflects back on what you have read, running ideas critically by your windows of experiences and knowledge. Reading-based writing represents the complete *you* as a thinking, feeling person in relation to what you have read. As we have said before, reading-based writing is the essence, or core, of critical thinking.

Reading-Based Writing and Other Approaches in Writing

Reading-based writing will serve you well in classrooms across your campus and also in your career. Of course, *Paragraphs and Essays* presents a range of writing approaches that may or may not make use of reading-based writing, including those called *personal experience*, *individual perspective*, *cross-curricular*, and *career-related*. All of those approaches are presented with instruction, examples, exercises, and suggested topics and prompts. Some approaches overlap, but each has a main thrust with variations imposed by particular writing objectives.

The abundant student and professional reading selections (more than seventy) were selected to stimulate thought and discussion, to provide content for reading-based writing, and to inform writing by strong examples of techniques and forms. Even reading-based writing has its own different forms, and reading itself has its own special techniques. Those techniques and forms are shown here in a concise outline of the instruction that covers the remainder of this chapter:

   I. Reading techniques
      A. Underlining
      B. Annotating
      C. Outlining
      D. Taking notes

Reading Techniques

UNDERLINING

Imagine you are reading a chapter of several pages and you decide to underline and write in the margins. Immediately, the underlining takes you out of the passive, television-watching frame of mind. You are engaged. You are participating. It is now necessary for you to discriminate, to distinguish more important from less important ideas. Perhaps you have thought of underlining as a method designed only to help you with reviewing. That is, when you study the material the next time, you will not have to reread all of it; instead, you can review only the most important—the underlined—parts. However, even while you are underlining, you are benefiting from an imposed concentration because this procedure forces you to think, to focus. Consider the following guidelines for underlining:

1. Underline the main ideas in paragraphs. The most important statement, the topic sentence, is likely to be at the beginning of the paragraph.

2. Underline the support for those main ideas.

3. Underline answers to questions that you bring to the reading assignment. These questions may have come from the end of the chapter, from subheadings that you turn into questions, from your independent concerns about the topic, or from questions posed by your instructor.

4. Underline only the key words. You would seldom underline all the words in a sentence and almost never a whole paragraph.

Does that fit your approach to underlining? Possibly not. Most students, in their enthusiasm to do a good job, overdo underlining.

The trick is to figure out what to underline. You would seldom underline more than about 30 percent of a passage, although the amount would depend on your purpose and the nature of the material. You may want to use a highlighter to mark main ideas, support, and key words. Highlighting and underlining accomplish the same goal, so feel free to choose the method that works best for you. Following the preceding four suggestions will be useful.

ANNOTATING

Annotating, writing notes in the margins, is a practice related to underlining. You can do it independently, although it usually appears in conjunction with underlining to record your understanding and to extend your involvement in reading.

Writing in the margins represents intense involvement because it turns a reader into a writer. If you read material and write something in the margin as a reaction to it, then in a way you have had a conversation with the author. The author has made a statement and you have responded. In fact, you may have added something to the text; therefore, for your purposes, you have become a co-author or collaborator. The comments you make in the margin are of your own choosing according to your interests and the purpose you bring to the reading assignment. Your response in the margin may merely echo the author's ideas, it may question them critically, it may relate them to something else, or it may add to them.

The comments and marks on the following essay will help you understand the connection between writing and reading. Both techniques—underlining to indicate main and supporting ideas and annotating to indicate their importance and relevance to the task at hand—will enhance thinking, reading, and writing.

TOTAL INSTITUTIONS
Seymour Feshbach and Bernard Weiner

Total institution encompasses individual (thesis)

1   A total institution completely encompasses the individual, forming a barrier to the types of social intercourse that occur outside such a setting. Monasteries, jails, homes for the aged, boarding schools, and military academies are a few examples of total institutions.

1. Individual activities in same setting

2   Total institutions have certain common characteristics. First, the individuals in such environments must sleep, play, and work within the same setting. These are generally segmented spheres of activity in the lives of most individuals, but within a total institution one sphere of activity overlaps with others. Second, each phase

2. All life within group

of life takes place in the company of a large group of others. Frequently, sleeping is done in a barracks, food is served in a cafeteria, and so on. In such activities everyone is treated alike and must perform certain essential tasks. Third,

3. Activities tightly scheduled

activities in an institution are tightly scheduled according to a master plan, with set times to rise, to eat, to exercise, and to sleep. These institutional characteristics result in a bureaucratic society, which requires the hiring of other people for surveillance. What often results is a split in the groups within an institution into a large, managed group (inmates) and a small supervisory staff. There tends to be

Managed groups and staff at distance

great social distance between the groups, who perceive each other according to stereotypes and have severely restricted communications.

Two worlds—inside and outside

3   The world of the inmate differs greatly from the outside world. When one enters a total institution, all previous roles, such as father or husband, are disrupted. The individual is further depersonalized by the issuance of a uniform, confiscation of belongings, and gathering of personal information, as well as by more subtle touches like doorless toilets, record keeping, and bedchecks. The effects of an

Personality altered

institutional setting are so all-encompassing that one can meaningfully speak of an "institutional personality": a persistent manner of behaving compliantly and without emotional involvement.

Becomes psychotic, childlike, or depressive

4   Of course, there are individual differences in adaptation to the situation. They can be as extreme as psychosis, childlike regression, and depression or as mild as resigned compliance. Most individuals do adjust and build up a system of satisfactions, such as close friendships and cliques.

Individuals adjust but have trouble later on street

5   But because of these bonds and the fact that the habits needed to function in the outside world have been lost, inmates face great problems upon leaving an institution. A shift from the top of a small society to the bottom of a larger one

(Feshback and Weiner, Personality)

may be further demoralizing.

(S. Feshback and B. Weiner, "Total Institutions," from *Personality*, 1991.)

OUTLINING

After reading, underlining, and annotating the piece, the next step could be outlining. If the piece is well organized, you should be able to reduce it to a simple outline so that you can, at a glance, see the relationship of ideas (sequence, relative importance, and interdependence).

The essay on total institutions can be outlined very easily:

Total Institutions
I. Common characteristics
   A. All activities in the same setting
   B. All phases of life within a larger group
   C. Activities scheduled according to a master plan
      1. Bureaucratic society
      2. Social distance between inmates and staff
II. Adjusting to the world inside
   A. Individual depersonalized
      1. Wears uniform
      2. No personal belongings
      3. No privacy
   B. Adaptation
      1. Negative
         a. Psychosis
         b. Regression
         c. Depression
      2. Positive
III. Problems upon release outside
   A. Adjusting to a different system
   B. Encountering shock of going to the bottom of a new order

EXERCISE 1   Underlining, Annotating, and Outlining

Underline and annotate this passage. Then complete the outline that follows.

EFFECTIVE E-MAIL PRACTICES

1   Use short lines and short paragraphs. A short line length (perhaps 50 to 60 characters) is much easier to read than the 80-character line of most text editors. Similarly, short paragraphs (especially the first and last paragraph) are more inviting to read. Avoid formatting a long message as one solid paragraph.

2   Don't shout. Use all-capital letters only for emphasis or to substitute for italicized text (such as book titles). Do NOT type your entire message in all capitals: It is a text-based form of *shouting* at your reader and is considered rude (not to mention being more difficult to read).

3   Proofread your message before sending it. Do not let the speed and convenience of e-mail lull you into being careless. While an occasional typo or other surface error will probably be overlooked by the reader, excessive errors or sloppy language creates an unprofessional image of the sender.

4   Append previous messages appropriately. Most e-mail systems allow you to append the original message to your reply. Use this feature judiciously. Occasionally, it may be helpful for the reader to see his or her entire message replayed. More often, however, you can save the reader time by establishing the context of the original message in your reply. If necessary, quote pertinent parts of the original message. If the entire original message is needed, treat it as an appendix and insert it at the *end* of your reply—not at the beginning.

5   Use a direct style of writing and think twice; write once. Put your major idea in the first sentence or two. If the message is so sensitive or emotionally laden that a more indirect organization would be appropriate, you should reconsider whether e-mail is the most effective medium for the message. Because it is so easy to respond immediately to a message, you might be tempted to let your emotions take over. Such behavior is called "flaming" and should be avoided. Always assume the message you send will never be destroyed but will be saved permanently in somebody's computer file.

6   Do not neglect your greeting and closing. Downplay the seeming impersonality of computerized mail by starting your message with a friendly salutation, such as "Hi, Amos" or "Dear Mr. Fisher."

7   An effective closing is equally important. Some e-mail programs identify only the e-mail address (for example, "70511.753@compuserve.com") in the message header they transmit. Do not take a chance that your reader will not recognize you. Include your name, e-mail address, and any other appropriate identifying information at the end of your message.

(Adapted from Scot Ober, *Contemporary Business Communication*)

I. Short lines; short paragraphs

    A. _____

    B. _____

II. No shouting
    A. No entire message in capital letters
    B. Causes problems

        1. _____

        2. _____

III. Proofread message before sending
    A. Resist temptation to send without checking
    B. Errors create unprofessional image

IV. Append messages appropriately

    A. _____

    B. Often better to establish context in your message

    C. _____

V. Direct style with deliberation

    A. _____

    B. _____

VI. Greetings and closings

    A. _____

    B. Provide necessary information in closing

       1. _____

       2. _____

       3. _____

TAKING NOTES

Taking notes for reading-based writing in this book consists of underlining and annotating passages in reading selections and jotting down the relevant points for support in your outline as you organize your summary, reaction, or two-part response. While writing, you will use those notes for support as you refer directly to what you have read and use some quotations from it. You will also give credit to the source(s) you are reading, and—if your instructor requires you to do so— you will use documentation, including page numbers and identification of your source(s) for those ideas and words you borrow.

As you carefully and critically read sources in this book, you will naturally underline significant passages (often only a few words at a time) and annotate your reactions to what you read. Those annotations will vary according to your audience, their interests and background, and the nature of your topic. The sooner you settle on a topic and its natural divisions, the better, because only then you will be able to take those relevant notes.

If you already have at least a general topic before you read, you can easily formulate some basic questions to help you focus. Reading some of the prompts before you read the selections will also be useful in helping you concentrate.

Here is an example of a reading-based writing prompt for the essay "Low Wages, High Skills" by Katherine S. Newman. "Transferable skills" are the operative words in organizing the response.

Low Wages, High Skills [title of Newman's essay]

Write a two-part response to the essay. Concentrate your critical thinking on Newman's idea that those who work at Burger Barn have transferable skills. Relate those specific skills to what you have experienced in a low-pay service job. Use direct references to and quotations from the essay. Agree or disagree with Newman. Putting together a simple outline in advance and allowing some writing space between lines will provide you with room to pencil in references and quotes, with page numbers. Then when you write your outline or reaction, you can just incorporate your notes without having to refer back to the reading(s).

Here is an example of how you can place notes inside outlines. It is an excerpt from student Alex Mylonas' reading-based reaction to the short story "The Use of Force" by William Carlos Williams. During his first reading, Mylonas underlined and annotated freely; later he selected phrases as support in his outline, which he submitted with a long paragraph assignment.

I. The surface conflict
   A. Doctor–patient relationship
   B. Physical struggle
      1. Girl won't cooperate
      2. Doctor uses force to examine her throat
II. The inner conflict
   A. Doctor versus himself
      1. Wants to be professional
      2. Loses self-control
         "attractive little thing," p. 333
         "damned little brat," p. 333
      3. Loses sight of objective
         "got beyond reason," p. 334
   B. Emotional (brutal) side wins
      "It was a pleasure to attack her," p. 335
      "blind fury," p. 335

Reading-Based Writing Forms

WRITING A SUMMARY

The **summary**, the purest form of reading-based writing, is a rewritten, shortened version of a source in which you use your own wording to express the main ideas. Learning to summarize effectively will help you in many ways. Summary writing reinforces comprehension skills in reading because it requires you to discriminate among the ideas in the target reading passage. Summaries are usually written in the form of a well-designed paragraph or set of paragraphs. Frequently, they are used in collecting material for research papers and in writing conclusions to essays.

The following rules will guide you in writing effective summaries:

1. Cite the author and title of the text.

2. Reduce the length of the original by about two-thirds, although the exact reduction will vary, depending on the content of the original.

3. Concentrate on the main ideas and include details only infrequently.

4. Change the original wording without changing the idea.

5. Do not evaluate the content or give an opinion in any way (even if you see an error in logic or fact).

6. Do not add ideas (even if you have an abundance of related information).

7. Do not include any personal comments (that is, do not use *I*, referring to self).

8. Use quotations only infrequently. (If you do use quotations, however, enclose them in quotation marks.)

9. Use some author tags ("says York," "according to York," or "the author explains") to remind the reader(s) that you are summarizing the material of another writer.

EXERCISE 2 Evaluating a Summary

Apply the rules of summary writing to the following summary of "Total Institutions." Mark the instances of poor summary writing by using rule numbers from the preceding list.

TOTAL INSTITUTIONS

A total institution completely encompasses the individual. Total institutions have certain common characteristics. Institutions provide the setting for all rest, recreation, and labor. Residents function only within the group. And residents are directed by a highly organized schedule, which, I think, is what they need or they wouldn't be there. There residents are depersonalized by being required to wear a uniform, abandon personal items, and give up privacy. Some adapt in a negative way by developing psychological problems, but most adapt in a positive way by forming relationships with other residents. Several popular movies, such as *The Shawshank Redemption*, show how prison society works. Once outside the total institution, individuals must deal with the problem of relearning old coping habits. They must also withstand the shock of going from the top of a small society to the bottom of a larger one. Society needs these total institutions, especially the jails.

The following is an example of an effective summary.

A SUMMARY OF "TOTAL INSTITUTIONS"
Michael Balleau

In "Total Institutions," Seymour Feshbach and Bernard Weiner explain that a total institution encompasses the lives of its residents, who share three common traits: The residents must do everything in the same place, must do things together, and must do things according to the institution's schedule. The institution takes away the residents' roles they had in society, takes away their appearance by issuing uniforms, takes away their personal property by confiscation, and takes away their privacy by making life communal. The authors say that some residents adapt negatively by developing psychological problems, but most form relationships and new roles within the institution. Upon release, these residents must learn to function in the free world all over again, as they start at the bottom of society. This shift "may be further demoralizing."

WRITING A REACTION

The reaction statement is another kind of reading-based writing, one in which you incorporate your views. Some reactions require evaluation with a critical-thinking emphasis. Some focus on simple discussion of the content presented in the reading and include summary material. Others concentrate on the writer's experience as related directly to the content of the passage.

The following paragraph is student Tanya Morris's reaction statement to "Total Institutions." She could have expanded her ideas to write an essay. Her instructor did not require her to provide page-number locations of her references and quotations.

INSTITUTIONS ALWAYS WIN
Tanya Morris

The short essay "Total Institutions," by Seymour Feshbach and Bernard Weiner, is a study of conflicts in controlled environments. The common characteristics of such places are in personal combat with the individual, in which the resident is stripped of his or her choices and made to "sleep, play, and work within the same setting." The resident who tries to assert his or her uniqueness is controlled by a master plan. That plan is enforced by personnel who become the masters of surveillance, set up social barriers, and maintain control over their underlings. The result is "a bureaucratic society." Cut off from the free world, the resident is in conflict with significant matters of newness—clothes, facilities, regulations, and roles. The authors explain that almost always the institution wins, sometimes converting the resident into a disturbed person or an amiable robot among other inmates. But at some point after that conversion, the institutionalized person may be returned to the free world. There a new conflict arises for the inmate, who goes from "the top of a small society to the bottom of a larger one." The authors of this essay are very clear in showing just how comprehensive these institutions are in waging their war, regardless of the motives, against individuality. After all, they are "total." As such, they should be, whenever possible, avoided.

WRITING A TWO-PART RESPONSE

As you have seen, the reaction response includes a partial summary or is written with the assumption that readers have read the original piece. However, your instructor may prefer that you separate the forms—for example, by presenting a clear, concise summary followed by a reaction. This format is especially useful for critical examination of a text or for problem-solving assignments because it requires you to understand and repeat another's views or experiences before responding. The most comprehensive reading-based writing form, the two-part response also helps you avoid the common problem of writing only a summary of the text when your instructor wants you to both summarize and react.

TOTAL INSTITUTIONS: A SUMMARY
AND A REACTION
Michael Balleau

Part I: Summary

In "Total Institutions," Seymour Feshbach and Bernard Weiner explain that a total institution encompasses the lives of its residents, who share three common traits: The residents must do everything in the same place, must do things together, and must do things according to the institution's schedule. The institution takes away the residents' roles they had in society, takes away their appearance by issuing uniforms, takes away their personal property by confiscation, and takes away their privacy by making life communal. The authors say that some residents adapt negatively by developing psychological problems, but most form relationships and new roles within the institution. Upon release, these residents must learn to function in the free world all over again as they start at the bottom of society. This shift "may be further demoralizing."

Part 2: Reaction [Page-number documentation was not required.]

The basic ideas in "Total Institutions" gave me an insight into the behavior of my older cousin. Let's call him George. He spent almost five years in prison for a white-collar crime he committed at the bank where he worked. Before George was incarcerated, he was an individual, almost to the extreme of being a rebel. When he got out, he was clearly an institutionalized person. Following the pattern of institutionalized behavior laid out in "Total Institutions," George had become a group person without knowing it. Many of "the habits needed to function in the outside world [had] been lost." Even at home after he returned, he had to be around people. He wanted some of us to be with him all the time, and he liked the noise of a radio or television. When we went out, he found it difficult to make decisions, even in buying a simple item, such as a shirt, or ordering food in a restaurant. Once when he was driving, we were stopped by a police officer because his car's taillight was out, and George became transformed into someone who was on automatic pilot in answering questions. It was his "institutional personality." Minutes later, he seemed hostile and had bad, unwarranted things to say about the officer. Altogether, George did five years in prison, and it took him about three more to adjust before he seemed like sort of what he was before. He was certainly never the same. As the authors say, every person reacts differently to "total institutions," and some institutions are more extreme than others, but each one has a profound effect on the resident's individuality.

Kinds of Support for Reading-Based Writing

In your reading-based writing assignments, you are likely to use three methods in developing your ideas: explanations, direct references to the reading selection, and quotations from the reading selection.

- Your explanations will often be expressed in patterns, such as causes and effects, comparison and contrast, definition, and exemplification.

- Your references will point your reader(s) directly toward original ideas in sources. The more specific the references, the more helpful they will be to your readers.
- Your quotations will be words borrowed from sources and credited to those sources. You will use quotation marks around those words, which will appear as sentences or as partial sentences blended with your own words.

Basic Formal Documentation in Reading-Based Writing

Borrowing words or ideas without giving credit to the originator is called **plagiarism** and is not acceptable scholarship, regardless of whether it is intentional. As you use sources from your textbook, your instructor will ask you to document the ideas of others formally or informally. Informally, you will credit a source by title or author's name. Formally, you will indicate the precise location of all the original ideas you have borrowed according to a system.

CITATIONS

Documenting sources for papers based on written material is systematic. Most English instructors use MLA (Modern Language Association) style, the system used in this chapter. Mainly, you need to remember that when using material from a source, you must give enough information so that the reader will recognize it or be able to find it in its original context. Here are the most common principles of documentation that can be used for textbook or other restricted sources, whether the material is quoted, paraphrased (restated), or summarized.

If you use the author's name in introducing a quotation, then usually give only the page number.

> **Example:** Suzanne Britt says that "neat people are bums and clods at heart" (255).

If you use the author's name in introducing a borrowed idea, then usually give only the page number.

> **Example:** Suzanne Britt believes that neat people are weak in character (255).

If you do not use the author's name to introduce a quotation or an idea, then usually give both the author's name and the page number:

> **Example:** Music often helps Alzheimer's patients think more clearly (Weiss 112).

WORKS CITED

Work(s) Cited lists the sources used, meaning those that appear in citations, as shown in the previous section. Each kind of publication has its own order of parts and punctuation.

Here is an example of a Works Cited entry for the previous edition of this book. Note the punctuation between parts and the order of those parts: author's name (last, first), title of composition (quotation marks for a short work, italics for a long work), edition, name of the anthology, editor(s) of the anthology, place of publication, publisher, date of publication, pages on which the selection appears, and medium of publication.

2. Who or what influenced Wong the most?

3. How does she feel about her transformation?

4. Why can't Wong do anything about her transformation?

5. What advice would you give to Wong?

6. What advice do you think the author would give to her daughter?

EXERCISE 4   Suggestions for Reading-Based Writing

Complete one of following reading-based responses.

1. Write a summary of Wong's essay.

2. Write a two-part response composed of labeled summary and reaction parts.

3. In a reaction, analyze the essay as a transformation that Wong experienced. Concentrate on stages of her change, using time as the principle for order, or emphasize how different parts of society—school, neighborhood, and family—influenced her to set aside her culture and adopt another. Resist the temptation to write only a summary.

4. Write a reaction in which you discuss Wong's struggle to be an all-American girl. Explain exactly what happened and, in your estimation, why it happened. Discuss what you have learned by direct experience and by observation. Have you or has someone you know gone through a similar experience of wanting to be part of some other group, such as cultural, ethnic, or social class (from working class to upper middle or upper)? When you were a young teenager, did you sometimes want to divorce your parents? If you discuss your personal experience, do so by relating it to Wong's experience, as you use quotations from and references to her essay.

EXERCISE 5   Three Ways to Use Sources: Quotation, Blending, Paraphrasing

Examples:

Simply and directly introducing the quotation:
Quotation: "At last, I was one of you; I wasn't one of them."
Introducing: Wong said, "At last, I was one of you; I wasn't one of them."

Paraphrasing (rewording):
    Quotation: "The language was a source of embarrassment."
    Paraphrase: She was self-conscious about [or ashamed of] her language.

Blending a short quotation with paraphrase:
    Quotation: "I thought of myself as multicultural."
    Blending: She considered herself "multicultural."

1. Simply and directly introduce this quotation: "Sadly I still am."

2. Paraphrase (reword) this quotation: "Even the people in my culture would cluck and say that I'd do well in life."

3. Change this quotation to a blended paraphrase and short quotation: "When I spoke English, people nodded at me, smiled sweetly, said encouraging words."

EXERCISE 6   Form for Works Cited

Write a Works Cited entry for "The Struggle to Be an All-American Girl" by Elizabeth Wong.

Journal Writing

Your journal entries are likely to be concerned primarily with the relationship between the reading material and you—your life experiences, your views, your imagination. The reading material will give you something of substance to write about, but you will be writing especially for yourself, developing confidence and ease in writing so that writing becomes a comfortable part of your everyday activities, as speaking already is.

These journal entries will be part of your intellectual diary, recording what you are thinking about a certain issue. They will help you understand the reading material; help you develop your writing skills, in uncovering ideas that can be used on other assignments; and help you think more clearly and imaginatively. Because these entries are of a more spontaneous nature than the more structured writing assignments, organization and editing are likely to be of less concern.

Each journal entry should be clearly dated and, if reading related, should specify the title and author of the original piece.

Even if your instructor wants you to concentrate on what you read for your journal writing, he or she might not want you to be restricted to the material in this text. Fortunately, you are surrounded by reading material in newspapers, magazines, and, of course, textbooks from other courses. These topics can serve you well, especially if you want to begin your journal writing now.

Cross-Curricular and Career-Related Writing

This textbook includes cross-curricular and career-related writing topics. These suggestions offer a wide range of subject material to those of you who would like to write about subjects you have encountered across campus, at work, and in your search for a career. Some of that writing may include ideas coming directly from your reading. Those ideas can be documented with a listing of the source, which usually includes the name of the author, title of the work, place of publication, publisher, date, page numbers, and medium of publication. The citations for quotations or specific references can be made in the same fashion as the ones for textbook sources.

WRITER'S GUIDELINES   Reading for Thinking, Discussion, and Writing

BRANDON BRIDGE

1. **Underlining** (or highlighting) helps you to read with discrimination.

   - Underline the main ideas in paragraphs.
   - Underline the support for those ideas.
   - Underline answers to questions that you bring to the reading assignment.
   - Underline only the key words.

2. **Annotating** enables you to actively engage the reading material:

   - Number parts if appropriate.
   - Make comments according to your interests and needs.

3. **Outlining** the passages you read sheds light on the relationship of ideas, including the major divisions of the passage and their relative importance.

4. **Summarizing** helps you concentrate on main ideas. A summary:

   - cites the author and title of the text.
   - is usually shorter than the original by about two-thirds, although the exact reduction will vary depending on the content of the original.
   - concentrates on the main ideas and includes details only infrequently.
   - changes the original wording without changing the idea.
   - does not evaluate the content or give an opinion in any way (even if the original contains an error in logic or fact).
   - does not add ideas (even if the writer of the summary has an abundance of related information).
   - does not include any personal comments by the writer of the summary (therefore, no use of *I*, referring to self).

- seldom contains quotations (although, if it does, only with quotation marks).
- includes some author tags ("says York," "according to York," or "the author explains") to remind the reader(s) that it is a summary of the material of another writer.

5. Two other types of reading-based writing are:

- the reaction, which shows how the reading relates to you, your experiences, and your attitudes; also, it is often a critique of the worth and logic of the piece.
- the two-part response, which includes a summary and a reaction that are separate.

6. Most ideas in reading-based papers are developed through the use of one or more of these three ways:

- explanation
- direct references
- quotations

7. Documenting is giving credit to borrowed ideas and words.

- Informal documentation gives credit to sources as directed by your instructor.
- Formal documentation gives credit to sources according to published guidelines, such as those provided by the MLA (Modern Language Association).

WRITING PARAGRAPHS AND ESSAYS: INSTRUCTION, WITH INTEGRATED READING SELECTIONS

Part 3 discusses—and also demonstrates through reading selections—how our thoughts can be structured as flexible, useful patterns for different purposes. As you write in classes across the campus, notice how many regular writing assignments—especially papers and essay tests— expect you to describe, narrate, analyze (in many forms such as causes and effects, comparison and contrast, and definition), or argue a point. Following the same principles, you may be asked to use similar forms at the workplace as you write incident reports, proposals, evaluations, and recommendations. Although one form may indicate purpose and generally guide organization, it is important to note that written passages are almost always a combination of forms.

7

Descriptive Narration
Moving Through Space and Time

> ❝ *Description begins in the writer's imagination, but should finish in the reader's.* ❞

—STEPHEN KING

CHAPTER CONTENTS   BRANDON BRIDGE

When to Use Descriptive Narration

FOR COLLEGE WRITING ASSIGNMENTS

Descriptive narratives are commonly written in many different college subject areas:

- In English composition classes, you will probably write some paragraphs and essays about your experiences, showing what happened and giving impressions of how things appeared.
- In police science and fire science classes, you may report on scenes and incidents you observed during ride-alongs and visits to stations.
- In classes as varied as sociology, education, ecology, psychology, and music and art appreciation, your reports of what you experienced during field trips and personal visits are likely to be among course requirements.

IN CAREERS AND AT THE WORKPLACE

- At the workplace, you may be called on to write descriptive narratives in incident reports, case studies, employee evaluations, proposals, comparative evaluations of products or services, quality control reports, or testimonials promoting products or services.

DESCRIPTIVE NARRATION IN A CARTOON

At home with the police

Writing Descriptive Narration

As patterns of writing, description and narration are commonly associated. You would almost never describe something without relating it to something else, especially to a story or a narrative. And you would seldom narrate something (tell the story) without including some description. A narrative moves through time; a description usually moves through space. In this chapter the two patterns are linked as descriptive narration. Either one may be emphasized, but the two blend seamlessly. First we will examine their individual principles.

THE NARRATIVE DEFINED

In our everyday lives, we tell stories and invite other people to do so by asking questions such as "What happened at work today?" and "What did you do last weekend?" We are disappointed when the answer is "Nothing much." We may be equally disappointed when a person does not give us enough. After all, we are interested in people's stories and in the people who tell them. We like the narrative.

What is the narrative? *The narrative is an account of an incident or a series of incidents that make up a complete and significant action.* Each narrative has five parts: situation, conflict, struggle, outcome, and meaning.

NARRATIVE PATTERNS

The five narrative patterns are described here as they relate directly to the action.

Situation

Situation is the background for the action. The situation may be described only briefly, or it may even be implied. ("To celebrate my seventeenth birthday, I went to the Department of Motor Vehicles to take my practical test for my driver's license.")

Conflict

Conflict is friction, such as a problem in the surroundings, with another person, or within the individual. The conflict, which is at the heart of each narrative, produces struggle. ("It was raining and my appointment was the last one of the day. The examiner was a serious, weary-looking man who reminded me of a bad boss I once had, and I was nervous.")

Struggle

Struggle, which need not be physical, is the manner of dealing with conflict. The struggle adds action or engagement and generates the plot. ("After grinding on the ignition because the engine was already on, I had trouble finding the windshield wiper control. Next I forgot to signal until after I had pulled away from the curb. As we crept slowly down the rain-glazed street, the examiner told me to take the emergency brake off. All the while, I listened to his pen scratching on his clipboard. 'Pull over and park,' he said solemnly.")

Outcome

Outcome is the result of the struggle. ("After I parked the car, the examiner told me to relax, and then he talked to me about school. When we continued, somehow I did not make any errors, and I got my license.")

Meaning

Meaning is the significance of the story, which may be deeply philosophical or simple, stated or implied. ("Calmness promotes calmness.")

VERB TENSE

Because most narratives relate experience in time order, the verb tense is likely to be the past ("She *walked* into the room") rather than the present ("She *walks* into the room"), although you may use either. An unnecessary change in tense tends to distract or confuse readers.

Two generalizations may be useful as you work with verb tense.

- Writing based on literature is written in the present tense.

    Tom Sawyer *pretends* that painting the fence *is* a special pleasure. His friends *watch* him eagerly. He *talks* and *displays* his joy. They *pay* him to do his work.

- Most historical events and personal experiences are written in the past tense.

    The Battle of Gettysburg *was* the decisive encounter in the Civil War. Although General Lee, the Confederate general in charge of the overall strategy, *was* a wise and an experienced man, he *made* some tactical blunders that *led* to a devastating victory by the Union forces.

    We *walked* down the path to the well-house, attracted by the fragrance of the honeysuckle with which it *was covered*. Someone *was* drawing water and my teacher *placed* my hand under the spout. As the cool stream *gushed* over one hand she *spelled* into the other the word *water*, first slowly, then rapidly.
    (Helen Keller, *The Story of My Life*)

Although Helen Keller chose the conventional past tense for verbs in the last passage, she might have chosen the present tense for a sense of immediacy.

The two main points about tense are the following:

- The generalizations about verb-tense selection (using past for the historical and the personal and using present for fiction) are useful.
- The verb tense in a passage should change only when the shift is needed for clarity and emphasis.

POINT OF VIEW

Point of view shows the writer's relationship to the material and the subject, and it usually does not change within a passage.

If you are conveying personal experience (for example, describing something you saw), the point of view will usually be **first person**, and you will use "I" or "we."

If you are presenting something from a distance—geographical or historical (for example, telling a story about George Washington)—the point of view will usually be **third person**, and the participants will be referred to as "he," "she," and "they."

DIALOGUE

Dialogue is used purposefully in narration to characterize, particularize, and support ideas. It shows us how people talk and think, as individuals or as representatives of society. Not every narrative requires dialogue.

Note in the following paragraph that the snatches of dialogue are brief. The language will ring true to Asian immigrants and to those who have been around Asian immigrants. It is starkly realistic yet sympathetically engaging in context so that we are convinced of its authenticity and drawn into the story. As narrator, the author was present when the utterances in this paragraph were made.

> My brother was even more fanatical than I about speaking English. He was especially hard on my mother, criticizing her, often cruelly, for her pidgin speech—smatterings of Chinese scattered like chop suey in her conversation. "It's not 'What it is,' Mom," he'd say in exasperation. "It's 'What *is* it; what *is* it, what *is* it!'" Sometimes Mom might leave out an occasional "the" or "a," or perhaps a verb of being. He would stop her in mid-sentence: "Say it again, Mom. Say it right." When he tripped over his own tongue, he'd blame it on her: "See, Mom, it's all your fault. You set a bad example."
>
> (Elizabeth Wong, "The Struggle to Be an All-American Girl")

ORDER

The **order** will be essentially time, moving from conflict to meaning. Flashbacks within the sequence are used infrequently in college assignments.

DESCRIPTIVE PATTERNS

Description is the use of words to represent the appearance or nature of something. It is not merely the work of an indifferent camera: Instead, often going beyond sight, it includes details that will convey a good representation. Just what details the writer selects will depend on several factors, especially the type of description and the dominant impression the writer is trying to convey.

Types of Description

Depending on how you wish to treat your subject material, your description is likely to be either objective or subjective.

Objective description presents the subject clearly and directly as it exists outside the realm of emotions. If you are explaining the function of the heart, the characteristics of a computer chip, or the renovation of a manufacturing facility, your description will probably feature specific, impersonal details. Most technical and scientific writing is objective in this sense. It is likely to be practical and utilitarian, making little use of speculation or poetic technique and featuring mainly what can be seen.

Subjective description is also concerned with clarity and it may be direct, but it conveys a feeling about the subject and sets a mood while making a point. Because most expression involves personal views, even when it explains by analysis, subjective description (often called **emotional description**) has a broader range of uses than objective description.

Descriptive passages can be a combination of objective and subjective description; only the larger context of the passage will reveal the main intent. The following description of a baseball begins with objective treatment and then moves to subjective.

Objective treatment moving to subjective treatment

> It weighs just over five ounces and measures between 2.86 and 2.94 inches in diameter. It is made of a composition-cork nucleus encased in two thin layers of rubber, one black and one red, surrounded by 121 yards of tightly wrapped blue-gray wool yarn, 45 yards of white wool yarn, 53 more yards of blue-gray wool yarn, 150 yards of fine cotton yarn, a coat of rubber cement, and a cowhide (formerly horsehide) exterior, which is held together with 216 slightly raised red cotton stitches. Printed certifications, endorsements, and outdoor advertising spherically attest to its authenticity.... Feel the ball, turn it over in your hand; hold it across the seam or the other way, with the seam just to the side of your middle finger. Speculation stirs. You want to get outdoors and throw this spare and sensual object to somebody or, at the very least, watch somebody else throw it. The game has begun.
>
> (Roger Angell, "On the Ball")

The following subjective description, also on the subject of baseball, is designed to move the emotions while informing.

The following details relate to the paradoxes.

Note the emotional appeals, the subjective approach.

> The Babe was a bundle of paradoxes. Somehow one of the most appealing things about him was that he was neither built, nor did he look like, an athlete. He did not even look like a ballplayer. Although he stood six feet two inches and weighed 220 pounds, his body was pear-shaped and even when in tip-top condition he had a bit of a belly. His barrel always seemed too much for his legs, which tapered into a pair of ankles as slender almost as those of a girl. The great head perched upon a pair of round and unathletic shoulders, presented a moon of a face, the feature of which was the flaring nostrils of a nose that was rather like a snout. His voice was deep and hoarse, his speech crude and earthy, his ever-ready laughter a great, rumbling gurgle that arose from the caverns of his middle. He had an eye that was abnormally quick, nerves and muscular reactions to match, a supple wrist, a murderous swing, and a gorgeously truculent, competitive spirit.
>
> (Paul Gallico, "Babe Ruth")

Techniques of Descriptive Writing

As a writer of description, you will need to focus your work to accomplish four specific tasks:

- Emphasize a single point (dominant impression).
- Choose your words with care.
- Establish a perspective from which to describe your subject (point of view).
- Position the details for coherence (order).

Dominant Impression

See if you can find the dominant impression in this description:

> Please help me find my dog. He is a mongrel with the head of a poodle and the body of a wolfhound, and his fur is patchy and dingy-gray. He has only three legs, but despite his arthritis, he uses them pretty well to hobble around and scratch his fleas and mange. His one seeing eye is cloudy, so he runs with his head sideways. His ragged, twisted ears enable him to hear loud sounds, which startle his troubled nervous system and cause him to howl pitifully. If you give him a scrap of food, he will gum it up rapidly and try to wag his broken tail. He answers to the name of Lucky.

Of course, the dominant impression, what is being emphasized, is "misery," or "unlucky," not "lucky." The dominant impression emerges from a pattern of details, often involving repetition of one idea with different particulars. Word choice, which is of paramount importance, depends on your purpose in writing and on your audience.

If you are in a restaurant and you say to your companion, "This food is good," your companion may understand all he or she needs to understand on the subject. After all, your companion can see you sitting there chewing the food, smacking your lips, and wiping the donut glaze off your chin. But if you write that sentence and send it to someone, your reader may be puzzled. Although the reader may know you fairly well, he or she may not know the meaning of "good" (to eat? to purchase for others? to sell?) or of "this food" (What kind? Where is it? How is it special? How is it prepared? What qualities does it have?).

To convey your main concern effectively to readers, you will want to give some sensory impressions. These sensory impressions, collectively called *imagery*, refer to that which can be experienced by the senses—what we can see, smell, taste, hear, and touch. You may use *figures of speech* to convey these sensory impressions; figures of speech involve comparisons of unlike things that, nevertheless, have something in common.

The imagery in this passage is italicized.

Topic sentence
Dominant impression

Image (touch)

Images (sight)   Image (sound)

    Sitting here in Harold's Hefty Burgers at midnight, I am convinced that I am eating the <u>ultimate form of food</u>. The *buns* are *feathery soft* to the touch but *heavy* in the hand and *soggy* inside. As I take a full-mouth, no-nonsense bite, the *melted cheese* and *juices cascade* over my fingers and make little *oil slicks* on the *vinyl table* below. I *chew noisily* and happily like a puppy at a food bowl, stopping occasionally to flush down the *rich, thick taste of spicy*

Image (taste)
Image (smell)
Figure of speech
Note movement
through time   Image (sight)
and space   Image (sound)

animal fat with a *swig* from a *chilled mug of fizzing root beer* that *prickles my nose.* Over at the grill, *the smell of frying onions creeps away* stealthily on *invisible feet* to conquer the neighborhood, turning hundreds of ordinary *citizens* like me into drooling, stomach growling, fast-food addicts, who *trudge* in from the night like the walking dead and *call out* the same order, time after time. "Hefty Burger." "Hefty Burger." "Hefty Burger."

(Dale Scott, "Hefty Burger")

In reading Scott's enthusiastic endorsement of the Hefty Burger, the reader will have no trouble understanding the idea that he liked the food. Through imagery, Scott has involved the reader in what he has seen, smelled, heard, tasted, and touched. He has also used figures of speech, including these examples:

Simile: a comparison using *like* or *as*	"chew noisily and happily like a puppy"
Metaphor: a comparison using word replacement	"feathery [instead of "delicately"] soft"
Personification: an expression giving human characteristics to something not human	"smell of frying onions creeps away stealthily on invisible feet to conquer" [instead of "spreads to entice"]

Subjective description is likely to make more use of imagery, figurative language, and words rich in associations than is objective description. But just as a fine line cannot always be drawn between the objective and the subjective, a fine line cannot always be drawn between word choice in one and in the other. However, we can say with certainty that whatever the type of description, careful word choice will always be important. Consider the following points about word choice (diction), point of view, and order.

Word Choice: General and Specific, Abstract and Concrete

To move from the general to the specific is to move from the whole class or group of items to individual ones, for example:

General	Specific	More Specific
food	hamburger	Hefty Burger
mess	grease	oil slicks on the table
drink	soda	mug of root beer
odor	smell from grill	smell of frying onions

Words are classified as abstract or concrete, depending on what they refer to. **Abstract words** refer to qualities or ideas: *good, ordinary, ultimate, truth, beauty, maturity, love*. **Concrete words** refer to things or a substance; they have reality: *onions, grease, buns, table, food*. Specific concrete words, sometimes called *concrete particulars*, often support generalizations effectively and convince the reader of the accuracy of the description.

Never try to give all the details in a description. Instead, be selective. Pick only those details that you need to project a dominant impression, always taking into account the knowledge and attitudes of your readers. To reintroduce an idea from the beginning of this section, description is not photographic. If you wish to describe a person, select the traits that will project your intended dominant impression. If you wish to describe a landscape, do not give all the details that you might find in a picture; on the contrary, pick the details that support your intended dominant impression. That extremely important dominant impression is directly linked to your purpose. It is created by the judicious choice and arrangement of images, figurative language, and revealing details.

Point of View

Point of view shows the writer's relationship to the subject, thereby establishing the perspective from which the subject is described. It rarely changes within a passage. Two terms usually associated with fiction writing, *first person* and *third person*, also pertain to descriptive writing.

If you want to convey personal experience, your point of view will be *first person*, and you will use "I" or "we." See student Dale Scott's paragraph "Hefty Burger" for an example.

If you want to present something from a detached position, especially from a geographical or historical distance (see "Babe Ruth" and "On the Ball"), your point of view will be *third person*, and you will refer to your subjects by name or by third-person pronouns such as *he*, *she*, *him*, *her*, *it*, *they*, and *them*, without imposing yourself as an *I* person.

Order

The point of view you select may indicate or even dictate the order in which you present descriptive details. If you are describing your immediate surroundings while taking a walk (first person, involved), the descriptive account would naturally develop spatially as well as chronologically—in other words, in both space and time.

Some descriptive pieces—for example, the one on Babe Ruth—may follow an idea progression for emphasis and not move primarily through space or time. Whatever appropriate techniques you use will guide your reader and thereby aid coherence.

All four elements—dominant impression, word choice, point of view, and order—work together in a well-written description.

The dominant impression of the paragraph "On the Ball" is of an object remarkably well designed for its purpose. The point of view is third person, and the order of the description moves from the core of the baseball outward.

The paragraph "Babe Ruth" emphasizes the idea of paradox (something that appears to be a contradiction). The details are presented from a detached point of view (third person) and appear in order from physique to overall appearance to behavior. The details show a person who was not built like an athlete and did not look like an athlete yet was one of the most famous athletes of all time. Collectively those details convey the dominant impression of "Ruth, the paradox."

Scott's "Hefty Burger" can also be evaluated for all four elements:

- *Dominant impression*: good food (images, figurative language, other diction). The reader experiences the incident as the writer did because of the diction.
- *Word choice*: general or specific; abstract or concrete. The general and abstract have been made clear by use of the specific and the concrete. Of course, not

all abstract words need to be tied to the concrete, nor do all general words need to be transformed to the specific. As you describe, use your judgment to decide which words fit your purposes—those needed to enable your audience to understand your ideas and to be persuaded or informed.

- *Point of view*: first person, involved.
- *Order*: chronological (time) for the eating; spatial (space) for the grill and neighborhood.

Transitional Words

Consider using the following transitional words to improve coherence by connecting ideas with ideas, sentences with sentences, and paragraphs with paragraphs.

FOR DESCRIPTION (place): above, over, under, below, nearby, near, across, beyond, among, to the right, to the left, in the background, in the foreground, further, beside, opposite, within sight, out of sight

FOR NARRATION (time): after, before, later, earlier, initially, soon, recently, next, today, tomorrow, yesterday, now, then, until, currently, when, finally, not long after, immediately, (at) first, (at) last, third, previously, in the meantime, meanwhile

FOR ALL PATTERNS OF WRITING: The HOTSHOT CAT words: However, Otherwise, Therefore, Similarly, Hence, On the other hand, Then, Consequently, Also, Thus

CAREER-RELATED WRITING: WORKPLACE REPORTS

At the workplace, numerous reports fit the pattern of narrative writing: trip reports, status reports (from investigation or development of something such as a program or product), or incident reports (one of the most universal types of reports from industry to industry).

In most instances the incident report denotes problems. Something unforeseen has occurred, and it must be documented: an accident, a theft, a disturbance, a dangerous condition, a lost child, an act of vandalism, an equipment failure, or a health emergency other than one caused by an accident. A report on one of these incidents is likely to be written as an important record. It may be the essential information on which law enforcement acts, equipment is replaced, clients are served, safety is assured, security is established, or the physical plant is protected.

These reports are sometimes dictated, but they are more often written by the person most directly related to an incident. Your ability to write an effective report will aid your company and reflect well on you as an intelligent, educated employee. Although the procedure and the form of these incident reports will vary, some principles can be applied to all; these principles follow the basic narrative form.

Situation: Identify the kind of problem.
Conflict: Indicate when and where the problem occurred.

Struggle and outcome: Provide an account of what happened.

Meaning: If appropriate, write a recommendation for what could be done to avoid a repetition of such an incident.

Follow these guidelines in writing an incident report:

- Write in the first person (*I*), for you are the one who is writing the report.
- Start with the date, time, and your reason for involvement.
- If you use the words of anyone reporting on the incident, enclose them in quotation marks and acknowledge the source of those words.
- Use facts, not opinions.
- Do not step outside your work expertise and become a psychologist, philosopher, physician, or moralist. If you do, should this report make its way to a court case, what you say will be discredited.
- Use past tense; you are writing about something that has already happened.
- Use mostly active voice. For example, write, "Mills made the report," not "The report was made by Mills."
- Identify those involved. Drop the titles, such as Mr., Mrs., Dr., and so on. After the first reference to the person in the report, use only the surname or the first initial and the surname.

FINDING PATTERNS IN PHOTOS

EXERCISE 1   An Image-Based Activity for Groups or Individuals

Cheating student

Imagine that you are working on a final examination. Letter grades will be calculated on a curve. You are trying to convey your understanding of the course content to your instructor. Then you look to your left and see a fellow student (the one in the photo) with a cheat card in the palm of his hand. He is part of your competition. His use of the card may mean the difference between your making a lower or higher grade. The final grade may determine whether you can transfer to the university of your choice or not. You look to the front of the room where your instructor sits at his desk, his gaze locked on a stack of bluebook finals he is marking from another class. For a moment you are torn. You have never snitched. You have said publicly you do not believe in snitching. But much is riding on the results of this test. You continue with your work. You finish early. The cheating student is still on task—and still consulting his illegal notes. You use your cell phone camera to take a picture (as shown), in case you need evidence. You are about to submit your test. It is time to do the right thing. But what is the right thing?

Complete the following outline.

Topic Sentence or Thesis: There are occasions when a single event can make people reevaluate a principle they have always upheld, in this case *never snitching*.

    I. Extended example

        A. _____

        B. _____

    II. Example in relation to personal code of conduct

        A. _____

        B. _____

    III. Decision (to snitch or not to snitch)

        A. _____

        B. _____

If your instructor directs you to do so, write a paragraph or short essay based on this imaginary experience.

Practicing Narrative Patterns

Some narratives are more structured than others, but all have the same basic patterns. The parts, especially conflict and struggle, will vary in extent, depending on the circumstances.

EXERCISE 2   Writing Patterns

Fill in the blanks to complete the pattern for the topic "A Random, Unexpected, and Welcome Act of Kindness" or for another topic of your choice. Add descriptive details as needed.

(Situation) I. _____

(Conflict)   II. _____

(Struggle) III. _____

        A. _____

        B. _____

        C. _____

        (Or more) _____

(Outcome) IV. _____

(Meaning) V. _____

EXERCISE 3   Writing Patterns

Fill in the blanks to complete the pattern for the topic "Dealing with an Unpleasant Person at Work" or for another topic of your choice. Add descriptive details as needed.

(Situation) I. _____

(Conflict)   II. _____

(Struggle) III. _____

                 A. _____

                 B. _____

                 C. _____

                     (Or more) _____

(Outcome) IV. _____

(Meaning) V. _____

Practicing Descriptive Patterns

Description, which is almost always used with other patterns, is very important and often neglected. The following exercises feature descriptive writing that supports a dominant impression of colorful action.

EXERCISE 4   Working with Word Choice

Improve the following sentences by supplying specific and concrete words. Use images when they serve your purposes.

Example: The animal was restless and hungry.
The gaunt lion paced about the cage and chewed hungrily on an old shoe.

1. The fans were happy.

2. She was in love.

3. Confusion surrounded him.

4. The traffic was congested.

5. The dessert impressed the diner.

6. The woman liked her date.

7. The salesman was obnoxious.

8. The room was cluttered.

9. His hair was unkempt.

10. The room smelled bad.

EXERCISE 5   Completing Descriptive Patterns

Fill in the blanks. This is a useful procedure for prewriting a descriptive paragraph or essay. Consider using it for your writing assignment in this chapter. Suggested topic: a location on campus, such as a classroom, the cafeteria, the student financial aid office, the stadium, a playing field, a lab, or the parking lot at night.

What is your subject? _____

What is the dominant impression? _____

What is the situation? (Include some movement or action to provide a narrative framework, even if it is only you walking through an area.)

_____

What is the order of details? _____

What details support the dominant impression? (Use listing or clustering.) _____

Listing

1. _____

2. _____

3. _____

4. _____

5. _____

Clustering

Insert your topic in the double bubble and fill in details in the blank single bubbles.

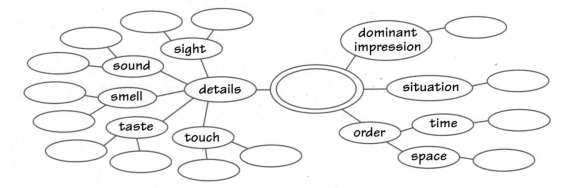

Explain your narrative framework. It need not be complicated.

- Situation _____

- Conflict _____

- Struggle _____

- Outcome _____

- Meaning _____

Readings for Critical Thinking, Discussion, and Writing

READING STRATEGIES AND OBJECTIVES

Underlining and annotating these reading selections will help you answer the questions that follow the selections, discuss the material in class, and prepare for reading-based writing assignments. As you underline and annotate, pay special attention to the author's writing skills, logic, and message, and consider the relevance of the material to your own experiences and values.

PARAGRAPH

Dark Day in the Dust Bowl*

JOHN STEINBECK

In the 1930s, a dust storm descended on the Southwest. The sun disappeared, the chickens went to roost in the middle of the day, a desert invaded the fields, and sand drifted in like snow, in places covering whole houses. Initially, some people, especially those in rural areas, thinking the end of the world was upon them, fled to churches or withdrew into themselves. But then they found the strength to survive, some digging out and digging in, some moving out and moving away. In The Grapes of Wrath, from which this excerpt is taken, John Steinbeck depicts the people in an early stage of confronting this natural disaster.

The people came out of their houses and smelled the hot stinging air and covered their nose from it. And the children came out of their houses, but they did not run or shout as they would have done after a rain. Men stood by their fences and looked at the ruined corn, drying fast now, only a little green showing through the film of dust. The men were silent and did not move often. And the women came out of the houses to stand beside their men—to feel whether this time the men would break. The women studied the men's faces secretly, for the corn could go, as long as something else remained. The children stood nearby, drawing figures in the dust with bare toes, and the children sent exploring senses out to see whether men and women would break. The children peeked at the faces of the men and women, and then drew careful lines in the dust with their toes. Horses came to the watering troughs and nuzzled the water

*Title by editor.

to clear the surface dust. After a while the faces of the watching men lost their bemused perplexity and became hard and angry and resistant. Then the women knew that they were safe and that there was no break. Then they asked, What'll we do? And the men replied, I don't know. But it was all right. The women knew it was all right, and the watching children knew it was all right. Women and children knew deep in themselves that no misfortune was too great to bear if their men were whole. The women went into the houses to their work, and the children began to play, cautiously at first. As the day went forward the sun became less red. It flared down on the dust-blanketed land. The men sat in the doorways of their houses; their hands were busy with sticks and little rocks. The men sat still—thinking—figuring.

EXERCISE 6   Discussion and Critical Thinking

1. Notice how each group looks at something. What do the men look at? What do the women look at? What do the children look at?

2. What is more important, finding a solution to the problem or finding courage to face the problem?

3. Explain how this incident could be a pivotal moment for any person here, but especially for the children.

4. Briefly, what are the situation, the conflict, the struggle, the outcome, and the meaning?

   Situation:

   Conflict:

   Struggle:

   Outcome:

   Meaning:

5. How does descriptive detail heighten the tension? In other words, what is emphasized?

6. What words or phrases suggest the passage of time and give chronological order to this piece?

ESSAYS

Teacher's Protest of Tasteless T-shirt Creates a Teachable Moment*

SANDY BANKS

Sandy Banks is a staff writer for the Los Angeles Times.

1. Garfield High teacher Lynn McGonigle doesn't tend to get worked up about what her students wear to class.

2. But she couldn't ignore two boys in separate classes on different days wearing bright red T-shirts with a giant photo of a buxom, bare-chested young woman in heels, fishnets, and thong. The woman's eyes were covered by a sign that read "hoes" and her body plastered with the slogan "WE ENJOY THEM BUT WE NEVER LOVE THEM."

3. To their teacher, the shirts violated more than the school's dress code.

4. "Heartbreaking," McGonigle called the image and message. She told the boys not to wear the shirts again, but she didn't leave it at that.

5. She visited the Montebello store that sold the shirts and researched the company that made them. "I started thinking about whether they would allow a neo-Nazi message or a racist word," said McGonigle, who's been an English teacher at Garfield for 27 years.

6. "Why would they allow one group of people—women—to be degraded when they wouldn't allow other shirts like that?"

7. McGonigle complained Thursday to mall officials that students and teachers "find these shirts offensive and insulting" and suggested they might boycott the mall. A mall rep agreed they were inappropriate and ordered the shirts pulled from the sales floor.

8. She emailed Street Dreams, the company that created and markets the shirt, and received a mea culpa the same day: "Sorry if we offended you. Yes obviously this shirt was made in bad taste," an email from the company acknowledged. "We are just clearing what's left and this shirt will no longer be available in stores."

9. McGonigle was surprised by the response. "I felt they would laugh at me. I thought if they could make a shirt like that, I'm not a person they would take seriously."

10. But her satisfaction was tempered by the conversation that unfolded when she talked about the T-shirts with her freshman class.

11. "The boys were laughing and being silly," she said. "They mocked the girls a little bit: 'Oh my God. I can't believe you are being so serious. It's just funny.' Some kids were disgruntled that we were even talking about it in class."

12. A few girls raised their hands and acknowledged that the T-shirts bothered them. But several others lined up with the boys, defending the message and the image.

13. It wasn't aimed at girls like them, they said, so why should they be offended?

14. "They're talking about 'hoes,' the girls who put themselves out there [for sex] and don't have any self-respect," one girl said.

15. Those girls' message was as clear as the slogan on the shirts: If you're courting sex, that makes you a hoe. And hoes don't deserve respect.

16. I wrestled with mixed feelings when McGonigle shared her story.

*Sandy Banks, "Teacher's Protest of Tasteless T-shirt Creates a Teachable Moment," September 9, 2014, *LA Times*., Copyright 2015 by Los Angeles Times.

17   Are those unbothered ninth-grade girls affirming a return to old-fashioned morals that value chastity? Are they part of the slut-shaming crowd, desperate to stay on the "good girl" side of the line?

18   Or, as Garfield teacher Monique Ulivi suggests, are teenage girls so accustomed to being labeled and crudely objectified, that a skanky T-shirt doesn't seem worth getting worked up about?

19   "Some felt we'd made an issue of a non-issue," said Ulivi, who talked about the T-shirt flap in her American literature class. She used McGonigle's crusade as a lesson in the power of a single voice to propel change, a theme of the course this fall.

20   "I thought it was a really cool teaching moment," Ulivi said. She may have learned as much as her students.

21   The class discussion made Ulivi think about the messages society sends to young women—even through something as benign as the routine loudspeaker announcement, warning girls to dress modestly in last week's searing heat.

22   "Whenever we talk about the dress code, it's always geared toward girls and what they shouldn't be wearing," she said. No spaghetti straps, no short dresses, nothing that shows too much skin.

23   Yet one of those boys from McGonigle's class had walked around campus all day with the image of a near-naked woman splayed across his chest.

24   Street Dreams' founder Ernest Edwards understands why McGonigle got upset. "It was supposed to be funny and eye-catching, like a parody shirt," he said. "But I know where the teacher was coming from. She felt like we were dogging women."

25   "That's why we pulled the shirt. I don't want anybody to think the brand is about that."

26   The brand reflects a young, urban culture in which a Chris Brown song with the word "hoes" in the title and "bitches" in the chorus sold more than a million copies this year.

27   "Young people don't get hung up on the word," said Edwards, 27. "We perceive it differently."

28   Edwards said he'd like to talk with the teacher and explain his take on youth culture. I think he ought to meet instead with girls from McGonigle's class who can explain why his shirt felt sexist and demeaning.

29   "They spoke up in class," McGonigle said, "even though people were laughing at them."

30   And after class they asked the teacher to help them launch a campus feminist club—one with a name that won't offend and an agenda that embraces everyone.

EXERCISE 7   Vocabulary Highlights

Write a short definition of each word as it is used in the essay. (Paragraph numbers are given in parentheses.) Be prepared to use these words in sentences.

boycott (7)	propel (19)
mea culpa (8)	benign (21)
tempered (10)	splayed (23)
affirming (17)	parody (24)
objectified (18)	agenda (30)

EXERCISE 8   Discussion and Critical Thinking

1. Use phrases or sentences to indicate these parts of this narrative:

   Situation:

   Conflict:

   Struggle:

   Outcome:

   Meaning:

2. How and where does Banks use description in the article?

3. Which of the five kinds of imagery does Banks use?

4. What are the motives of those on both sides of the debate?

5. In paragraph 26 the owner of Sweet Dreams says,

   > The brand reflects a young, urban culture in which a Chris Brown song with the words "hoes" in the title and "bitches" in the chorus sold more than a million copies this year. "Young people don't get hung up on the word," said Edwards, 27. "We perceive it differently."

   Do you agree or disagree? Explain.

6. Do you agree with American literature teacher Monique Ulivi that this was a successful teaching moment? Why or why not?

An American in Mexico*

ALEX ESPINOZA

Alex Espinoza is a freelance writer and a college professor at the University of California at Fresno. He was born in Tijuana, Mexico, and as a child moved to La Puente, California, where he attended elementary and high school. He has degrees from San Bernardino Community College, the University of California at Riverside, and the University of California at Irvine. This essay was first published in Newsweek.

1   When my father came to the United States to work as a day laborer many years ago, he intended to move back to the village in Michoacan where my mother and seven of my siblings lived. He wired my mother money, some of which she used to build a house there in El Ojo de Agua on a parcel of land that has been in her family since before the Mexican revolution. But at some point, my mother had enough of waiting for my father's return. She packed up what little she had and, with her children, traveled to Tijuana to be closer to him and to make visits easier. She stayed in Tijuana for several years—I was born there, the youngest of eleven children. Eventually, we moved to the three-bedroom house outside Los Angeles where I grew up.

2   My childhood was different from the childhood of most of my siblings. I rode my BMX bike through vacant lots, watched cable, and collected "Star Wars" action figures. They climbed mesquite trees, made handmade dolls from old rags, and stole chicken eggs from a neighbor's henhouse to sell for candy. They also shared hardships and misfortunes—hunger, long hours of working in the fields at young ages, the loss of two infant sisters.

3   Their connection to Mexico was close, deep, and also painful, something I simply could not grasp. Growing up, I felt no ties to El Ojo de Agua. I traveled into Mexico with my family as a child a few times, always eager to return to my American life. But as I grew older, I began to want to see the place most of my family called home, the place my siblings had talked about with such complicated feelings. Two years ago, at 33, I finally decided to go. I took my mother along; it had been more than 25 years since she had returned.

4   We flew into Mexico City, where we stayed for one day—strolling through parks and museums and visiting the Basilica of Our Lady of Guadalupe; there we watched the steady flow of devotees making their pilgrimages to the alter on their knees, their hands clasped in prayer. The next day, we traveled by bus to the city of La Piedad, where my uncle picked us up at the depot.

5   After many years in the U.S., my uncle had recently returned home to sell agricultural equipment to local farmers. He employed a maid named Chavela, who lived in one of the nearby villages. Chavela told me that her boyfriend had left for the United States about a month before but that weeks had gone by without news of his whereabouts. She said she hoped to save enough money to be able to go and find him. It made me think of the trip my mother took more than three decades earlier, traveling by train to Tijuana with her children to be near my father.

6   It was threatening to rain the afternoon my uncle drove us out over unpaved roads to the old house. Many of the houses along the main road of the village were empty and dark, with overgrown weeds and broken fences. Now and again, I'd spot one with dim lights illuminating the small windows. Tricycles and toys might be scattered around the front yard, and a column of white smoke threaded out through a hole in the corrugated-metal roof.

7   Gradually, the houses vanished, giving way to tall cornstalks, and we reached the wooden fence marking the entrance to my grandfather's property. We drove up a short distance before stopping and getting out. I spotted a reservoir behind some trees, and the water glistened when the clouds broke enough to allow a few beams of sunlight to touch the surface.

8   The house my mother built was nothing more than four walls made of orange bricks surrounded by thickets of wild shrubs and grass. The windows had no glass, and the front door had been ripped from its hinges. My uncle said that the house was sometimes used as a stable for the livestock that grazed in the hills

not far away. There were broken bottles on the dirt floor, and it smelled of urine and manure.

9   "I lived here," my mother said to me, as if she couldn't believe it herself. "Right here."

10   This was a place that had, over the years, become mythic in my mind. But it was real. I touched the brick walls, and I saw the trees my siblings had climbed, the field where they had worked. The soft mud gave way underneath my shoes. A clean set of my footprints remained.

11   I took pictures, and after the film was developed, I sat on the floor of my apartment back in California and took the photos out. I looked at each one and tried piecing them together, assembling a memory. I really wanted to connect to that land the way my brothers and sisters had—to get a better sense of our shared past. I thought I could understand things like sacrifice, the small traces of ourselves we are forced to leave behind. But all that the pictures showed were indistinguishable sections of walls, windows, and dark doorways.

EXERCISE 9   Vocabulary Highlights

Write a short definition of each word as it is used in the essay. (Paragraph numbers are given in parentheses.) Be prepared to use these words in sentences.

parcel (1)	illuminating (6)
mesquite (2)	reservoir (7)
basilica (4)	grazed (8)
devotees (4)	mythic (10)
clasped (4)	indistinguishable (11)

EXERCISE 10   Discussion and Critical Thinking

1. Alex Espinoza was born a Mexican and became an American. Why did he give his essay the title "An American in Mexico"?

2. Paragraph 2 states the differences of his childhood experiences from most of his siblings. What is implied? Does he feel fortunate, does he feel that he has missed something important, or is it some combination of those feelings? Explain.

3. What was his motive for going to El Ojo de Agua?

4. What does he mean by "complicated feelings"?

5. Why does he include an account of his stop in Mexico City in paragraph 4?

6. What does the story of Chavela represent in Espinoza's essay?

7. In paragraph 10, he says that the place had become mythic in his mind, and now he can touch it. Now that he has visited the setting of the myth, does he believe that he can share the "complicated feelings"?

8. What does he mean by saying, "A clean set of my footprints remained"?

9. Why do the photos he took and later contemplated not help him make the connection he sought?

Not Invulnerable

CHARLES C. ORTIZ

College student and cadet police officer Charles C. Ortiz entered law enforcement with unwarranted confidence and a feeling of invulnerability. Then one calm summer night, only an hour into a routine patrol, eight gunshots put him more in touch with reality.

1   I had always considered myself invulnerable when I was riding in a police unit. I was a knight, a centurion. I was sure that there was nothing I couldn't handle. I had been with the sheriff's department for almost three years, and I was certain that I was ready for anything. Who would have guessed that that mentality would almost cost me my life?

2   On January 16, I was assigned to work 55 Frank, which was a South El Monte crime unit. Because it was my first time working this car, I felt nervous, but at the same time I was also excited. Strangely, although this wasn't my first time in patrol, I still felt somewhat apprehensive. I was sure this night was different, yet I didn't know why.

3   Our shift started pretty slow. All we did for the first three hours was write out traffic citations. Once the traffic began to slacken, we proceeded with our routine patrol checks of the homes and businesses in our area. On a check of Santa Anita Avenue, a man began to flag us down. As we approached him, I noticed he was staggering and yelling at the top of his lungs. He insisted that we take him to jail. Once I had explained his options, he agreed to be taken to our station to begin his sobering-up process. I cuffed him and put him in the back of the unit. This was routine stuff.

4   But as we headed toward the station, a distress call blared over the radio: "Attention, all units in the vicinity of South El Monte. 55 Adam is requesting backup. He has five at gunpoint. All units responding, go Code 3!" Because we were a minute away, we responded. As we took off, my adrenaline started to rise, causing me to feel anxious. Upon arriving at the scene, I grabbed the shotgun, got out of the car, and pointed the shotgun toward the vehicle in question. The first suspect was called out. As he emerged in front of us, he reached into his waistband, pulled out a gun, and pointed it in my direction. In a moment, he fired two shots at me. I hit the ground. At the same time a fear of dying took over my body. I didn't know if I was hit, if I was dying, or what. I was in a state of shock.

5   After I discovered that the shots had missed me and the situation was under control, I rose somewhat slowly. I looked toward the suspect and saw him lying in a pool of blood. He had been shot six times by the deputies at the scene. The other four suspects were arrested for grand theft auto. Even though the incident was secured, I was able to see what "real" fear was. I understood that policing is not a game; it is life-and-death reality. Walking in a cop's shoes is not something that everyone can handle.

6   Facing my most horrible fear has truly shown me how important my life is. It's not something to be taken for granted. I also now know personally what deputies face when they encounter someone who is armed and possibly dangerous. I have found a new sense of respect for all police officers, for I have now experienced law enforcement from their view. Furthermore, I feel a lot older and wiser now. Going into the streets thinking "I'm invulnerable" is the wrong kind of attitude.

EXERCISE 11   Discussion and Critical Thinking

1. Use phrases or sentences to indicate these parts of this narrative:

   Situation:

   Conflict:

   Struggle:

   Outcome:

   Meaning:

2. How does Ortiz use metaphorical language in the first paragraph?

3. What conflicting ideas does the author present in the first two paragraphs that attract reader interest and create suspense?

4. Dramatically what is the effect of the minor conflict in paragraph 3?

5. How does Ortiz's attitude about police work change?

6. To which other parts of the essay does the last line relate?

STUDENT PARAGRAPHS, ESSAY, AND REPORT

Yearning for Love

CHANTRA SHASTRI

Having lived in America for five years, Chantra Shastri asks for freedom—freedom to make a choice in marriage, a choice based on love. In the annotation, the first column indicates images for description and the second indicates the parts of the narrative pattern. The topic sentence and concluding sentences are single-underlined; the descriptive phrases are double-underlined.

Descriptive	Narration	
	Situation	I need not go beyond myself to find examples of love, at least the yearning for love. My home is now America, but I have not left India far
	Conflict	behind. There, in ways still cherished by my traditional family, freedom is based on gender, and I am a female. My parents expect women to cook, clean, and nurture. My parents expect me to marry the man of their choice,
	Struggle	although my brother will have the freedom to choose his own mate. If I disobey, I will no longer be recognized by my parents. It is easy to give in to such a custom; it is difficult to disobey. My parents have always believed as they do. I cannot change them, nor do I want to, but I wish they would accept my difference in this different country. I think my mother under-
Sight		stands. Last week, I saw her crying while she ironed our clothes. When I
Touch		asked her why she was crying, she wiped the warm tears off her thin, soft
Sound		cheeks and pretended not to hear me as she sang. Her singing made me sad because I knew why she had cried, and she knew I knew. I seized the opportunity to say, "I don't want an arranged marriage," but she sang on
Sound		even louder, singing a song of a distant home. In times such as these, like my
Metaphor	Outcome	father, she too covers her ears with the thick dried mud of tradition.
	Meaning	She doesn't want to hear me. It is easier that way.

EXERCISE 12 Discussion and Critical Thinking

1. Why did Shastri's mother cry?

2. What chance does Shastri have to make her own choice?

3. What would you advise Shastri to do?

4. How does the specific example of Shastri's mother crying imply more than it actually says?

When student Mike Kavanagh looked at the assignment to write a paragraph of descriptive narration about something he knew well, he had no trouble in selecting a subject. As a drag racer for sport and prize money, he had built up his car, a 1968 Camaro, to thunder down the track at more than two hundred miles per hour, with all his senses raw to the wind.

His Writing Process Worksheet shows you how his writing evolved from idea to final draft. To conserve space here, the freewriting and the rough draft marked for revision have been omitted. The balance of his worksheet has been lengthened for you to be able to see parts of his work in their entirety.

BRANDON BRIDGE

Writing Process Worksheet

Name Mike Kavanagh   **Title** The Drag   **Due Date** Monday, March 26, 9 a.m.

Use the back of this page or separate paper if you need more space.

Assignment

In the space below, write whatever you need to know about your assignment, including information about the topic, audience, pattern of writing, length, whether to include a rough draft or revised drafts, and whether your paper must be typed.

Write a paragraph of descriptive narration about something you have experienced, an event that occurred in a short period of time, maybe a minute or less. Write so that an uninformed audience can understand what you did, how you did it, and how you felt. About 250 to 300 words. Submit this completed worksheet, a rough draft marked for revision, and a typed final draft.

Stage One

Explore Freewrite, brainstorm (list), cluster, or take notes as directed by your instructor.

Clustering

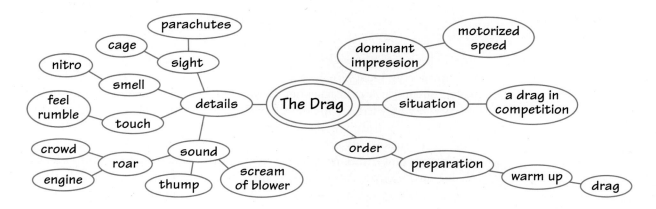

Stage Two

Organize Write a topic sentence or thesis; label the subject and the focus parts.

<u>I</u> <u>climb into the cockpit for my drag.</u>
   subject   focus

Write an outline or an outline alternative. For reading-based writing, include references and short quotations with page numbers as support in the outline.

  I. Preparation
    A. Take position
    B. Strap in
      1. Straps merge
      2. Buckle
 II. Warm up
    A. Fire motor
      1. Feel rumble
      2. Hear blower
      3. Smell nitro
    B. Dry hop tires
III. Drag
    A. Green light
    B. Thrust
    C. Braking
      1. Regular brakes
      2. Parachutes
    D. Success
      1. Scoreboard
      2. Feeling

Stage Three

Write On separate paper, write and then revise your paragraph or essay as many times as necessary for **c**oherence, **l**anguage (usage, tone, and diction), **u**nity, **e**mphasis, **s**upport, and **s**entences (**CLUESS**). Read your work aloud to hear and correct any grammatical errors or awkward-sounding sentences.

Edit any problems in fundamentals, such as **c**apitalization, **g**rammar, **p**unctuation, and **s**pelling (**CGPS**).

Final Draft

The topic sentence and concluding sentence are single-underlined.

THE DRAG
Mike Kavanagh

Descriptive   *Narration*
                 Situation

                 Conflict
                 Struggle

<u>As I climb into the cockpit for my drag, I hear the roar of the crowd and the thundering blasts in the background.</u> Engulfed in an iron cage, I strap myself down. First over the shoulders, then from the waist, and finally from between my legs the straps merge and then buckle at my belly button. This is to ensure my stability in the ironclad, two-hundred-and-thirty-miles-per-hour street rocket. My crew then signals me to fire up the three thousand horsepower motor mounted at my back. With the push of a button, I feel the rumble of the motor, hear the scream of the blower, and smell the distinctive odor of nitro in the air. I then move up to the starting line to dry hop my rear

tires for better traction. I quickly thrust the accelerator pedal to the floor. I am shot forward about two hundred feet. Letting off the accelerator pedal and pulling the brake handle allows me to come to a slow stop. A low, continuous thump from the motor echoes through my head as I reverse back to the starting line. As I creep forward, I stage the beast and wait for the lights to change to green. This feels like an eternity. The lights flicker yellow, yellow, yellow, GREEN! I stab the pedal to the floor. I am flung thirteen hundred and twenty feet faster than I can say my name. When I pull the brake and parachute handles simultaneously, I lunge back from the force of the billowing chutes. I climb out of the jungle gym and look up at the scoreboard, which reads 5.26 seconds at 230.57. There is nothing else like rocketing down the track at 230 m.p.h.

Outcome

Meaning

EXERCISE 13   Discussion and Critical Thinking

1. Is this paragraph mainly descriptive, mainly narrative, or equally balanced?

2. Annotate in the margin and underline at least one image of sound, sight, touch, and smell.

3. Although you probably have not drag raced competitively, you can get a good sense of what it is like to do so by reading this paragraph. What details and what phrasing convince you that the author is writing from experience?

4. What is the dominant impression?

5. List four words of transition used in the first five sentences.

READING-BASED WRITING

Rituals as Comfort Food for the Soul

ADAM RENSKY

Student Adam Rensky selected this assignment from a list: "Write a brief reading-based reaction to a reading selection from your textbook. Demonstrate your understanding of the text by analyzing it and relating it to your experience. Include quotations from and references to the text to convey the author's techniques of description and narration, and use MLA style in providing credit for your citations and in listing the work cited [see Chapter 16]."

1   When I was a child, my father and I used to take walks. Our path never varied: South from our house to make a right turn at the second corner, on past my elementary school, then across from the Youth Center where I had

Boy Scout meetings, by a middle school I would later attend, and down an oak-lined street before turning back on my home street. We did that more than a hundred times. Recently on a nostalgic day, I drove the route to measure what usually seemed a short distance at the time, but was exactly one and a quarter miles.

Topic sentence
Transition

2   <u>Looking back, I now know the walks were as valuable as comfort food, though there was no apparent calculation by my father to make them so.</u> Those were the times when I could say what I wanted to say and ask what I wanted to ask. My father talked about the hardships and fulfillments of growing up in the Hill Country of Texas. I talked about the joys and agonies of a kid growing up right there in the city of Covina, California. Geographical differences, a lot of time, and a lot of cares seemed to blend in stories and questions and answers and peaceful silences, as we walked.

Topic sentence
Transition

Blended quotation
Summary and
interpretation
follow

Quotation

Quotation

Blended quotation

Blended quotation

3   <u>"Closets and Keepsakes" by Willi Coleman carries the same theme, as her memories are brought back by the sight of "a straightening comb" and other relics of the past (101).</u> Her essay is an account of a comforting ritual with her mother. Each week as a child, she sat on the floor, with her head between her mother's knees, and her mother combed her hair and talked with her. That was Coleman's special time. It was as satisfying as comfort food, the childhood treat that somehow still evokes soothing memories when life cries out for relief, as it did long ago. She says, "Our sessions together could halt time, still waters, and predict the future" (101). Both mother and child unburdened their feelings, and the occasion occurred each week at the same time, at the same place, and in the same way. Looking back, she knows that hair care was always secondary to talking—to talking freely. She says, "It never crossed my mind to hold back the hurt, fear, or anger" (102). Her mother, who worked weekdays as a housekeeper for those who were often disrespectful, had plenty of her own problems, but she "talked with ease and listened with undivided attention" (101). Those were special, comforting moments between just mother and child. Coleman "moved away from those Saturday hair sessions, as if from a safe harbor" (102).

Relating text to experience

4   Much has been said about comfort foods, but the fact is that parent-child rituals—just little repeated activities, such as playing board games, changing oil in the car, gardening, playing catch, or shooting baskets—have provided and, at least in recollection, still can provide special comfort too. For Willi Coleman, comfort was sitting on the floor, getting her hair combed and swapping worries, complaints, and stories. For me, it was that mile and a quarter walk, doing the same kind of thing that Willi Coleman did, for the same reasons. It is later that one puts ever-upgrading labels of meaning on experiences such as those.

Work Cited

Coleman, Willi. "Closets and Keepsakes." *Paragraphs and Essays: A Worktext with Readings*. Ed. Lee Brandon. 8th ed. Boston: Houghton, 2001. 101–03. Print.

CAREER-RELATED WRITING

The content of your writing will, of course, depend on your academic and vocational experiences. If you have a job or have worked for pay, you can write narratives about your experiences. Perhaps you are already in the career field of your choice; if so, you could write about a specific event that has given you insight into that field or a reason for your commitment to it. Or perhaps you have already taken college classes relating to your career choices; then you could write a report—incident, progress, or investigative—about something you have witnessed or read about, using a standard form (such as the one that follows) as you practice a kind of writing you will likely use at the workplace.

Incident Report of the Falling Shoppers

DOUGLAS ROSS

As an optional assignment, student Douglas Ross had the choice of writing a narrative about an event that occurred at work, in particular one that was written up as a report or could have been. One event stood out in Ross's mind. He had written an incident report about an accident that occurred in his presence when he worked for a regional market chain. The report had been favorably reviewed by a district manager, and Ross was promoted soon after that time to a full-time senior checker. Here, he re-creates what he reported on that day, composing a form similar to the store template for incident reports.

Employee Report

Form 117-Incident
- ☒ Accident
- ☐ Reported theft
- ☐ Disturbance
- ☐ Dangerous condition
- ☐ Lost child
- ☐ Vandalism
- ☐ Health emergency
- ☐ Other

Business and Location: [Name and address of business omitted by student request]

Time: July 27, 2009, at 09:33 a.m.

Employee Name: Douglas Ross

Situation

Incident Report: At 09:33 a.m. I was working the cash register at Station 3 when I saw an elderly couple approach my empty customer slot from the nearby newspaper, book, and magazine rack. The woman was walking ahead of the man, who carried a small bag of fruit in one hand and a loaf of fresh bakery bread in the other. A younger woman with a shopping cart full of items had also spotted the open slot and headed that way. The wife started

Struggle

walking faster, turned to her husband, said something I couldn't hear, and motioned for him to follow her. He increased his pace and followed. Then

Conflict

he staggered and lost his balance and lunged forward, hitting his wife, who had turned away from him. Thrown off balance, she also lunged forward and struck a display of pastries, knocking it down as she fell to her knees. By this time, her husband had fallen, striking his head on the tile floor.

I came to their aid quickly, helping the woman to her feet. The man rolled over and sat there. I said I would call paramedics. The woman asked the man if he were hurt. He said he would be all right. I got on the phone and called Supervisor Kennedy, who was out at the loading dock. He said I should call paramedics anyway, because the man was still sitting on the floor.

While we were waiting for the paramedics, the man took an oblong loop of stiff plastic binding material from his foot and showed it to me. He explained that it had apparently been left by the magazine rack where it had been used to tie a bundle of newspapers. He said he had stepped on one side of it and, when he did, the other side of it popped up like a small hula hoop and caught his other foot as he was about to take another step. Then he fell and hit his wife, who also fell.

Outcome

The paramedics came and examined the husband and wife, Carl and Ruth Sutton [names changed]. The paramedics asked them about abrasions and pains. They said they needed no further medical care or examination. The paramedics completed a report on the particulars, now attached to this one. Mr. and Mrs. Sutton said they would go to their family doctor.

Supervisor Kennedy took down additional information and gave them his business card. Mrs. Sutton asked me if I had witnessed what happened. I said I saw them fall. She looked at my badge and wrote my name and employee number down in her address book. I gave the loop of plastic binding to Supervisor Kennedy.

Meaning

Recommendation: When stocking the shelves with any items that are bound, the binding should be carefully disposed of. As a further precaution, it would be a good idea to clip the loops of plastic bindings so that no one could trip over them even if they were left on the floor.

Suggested Topics and Prompts for Writing Descriptive Narration

READING-BASED WRITING

Reading-based writing requires you to read critically, write a reply that shows you understand what you have read, and give credit for ideas you borrow and words you quote. The form can be a summary, a reaction, or a two-part response (with separated summary and reaction).

Documentation, in which you give credit for borrowed ideas and words, can be either formal (MLA style) or informal, as directed by your instructor. Definitions of the three forms follow. Any form can be used for any reading selection in this book.

Summary

- The summary is a statement written in response to a reading. It restates only the most important points and uses original wording instead of the author's language. It should not contain added information or personal opinions.

- Because summaries are intended to restate only the main points of a reading, they are typically much shorter than the original text. Often they are approximately a third of the length.

Reaction

- In the reaction, the meaning of what you have read will be central to the topic sentence of your paragraph or to the thesis of your essay.
- Although the reaction is not a personal narrative by itself, it may include personal experience to explain elements of the text. For example, if your source is about driving styles, your own experiences as a driver or an observer of drivers could be relevant in your analysis of the text.
- The reaction may incorporate a summary to convey a broad view of what you have read, but your summary should never be the main part of your reaction.

Two-Part Response

- The two-part response separates the summary from the reaction.
- This form will give you practice in separating your objective summary in the first part from your more personal evaluation, interpretation, or application in the second part, the reaction.

READING-BASED WRITING TOPICS

"Dark Day in the Dust Bowl"

1. Write about how the idea of courage, or of attitude, can influence behavior. Refer to the children, the women, and the men. Use quotations and references.

2. Pretend that you were there as a child, and write about what happens from your (first person) point of view; that is, describe how you feel during the story as you react to how the women and men behave. Include the same details about the effects of the dust; if you use the same phrases, though, enclose those phrases in quotation marks. Be sure to do it as you report from the *I* perspective, such as "I could see that all the mothers were…" You can refer to what was happening to the children by saying, for example, *we* "acted," "watched," "saw," "felt," "started feeling differently," and so on. Discuss the behavior of all three parts of the group: the (other) children, the women, and the men.

3. Write about a time when you or your family felt threatened and then drew strength from the courage of a family member or group leader. Explain how that was different from and similar to the narrative written by Steinbeck. Use quotations and references.

"Teacher's Protest of Tasteless T-shirt Creates a Teachable Moment"

4. Write a summary of the article. Concentrate on representing the main ideas without giving your own opinions. Make sure to use your own words.

5. Write a reaction in which you evaluate the girls' decision to launch a campus feminist club at Garfield High. Why do they decide to launch the club? How could launching the club change the opinions of some of the other students at the school?

6. Write about a time when you tried to change someone else's mind about an important topic or issue. How was your experience different from and similar to McGonigle's?

"An American in Mexico"

7. Write a summary of this essay. Concentrate on the main ideas. Use quotation marks with your quotations. Refer directly to the main ideas in Espinoza's essay.

8. Write a reaction (not the same as just a summary) in which you explain Espinoza's visit. What is he trying to discover or experience? Why is he so concerned with the "complicated feelings" of his siblings? Does he imply that his journey is similar to the pilgrimage of people at the Basilica in Mexico City? How are the photos different from experience? Why aren't they the parts to the puzzle he wants to complete?

9. If you have ever had a similar experience—have come from a migrant family but have not experienced the "home country," with depth—and then traveled there to explore your heritage, then write about an experience and discuss how it was similar to and different from Espinoza's. This topic can also be applied to those whose families had moved within the United States—perhaps from the country to the city—or to a youngster who goes back to the "hills of…" for the summer.

"Not Invulnerable"

10. Using this essay as a model, write a descriptive narration about a time when you or someone you know did something that was dangerous but, through ignorance or preoccupation, approached the event with little or no fear. Consider a rescue or an incident at school, at work, or during recreation. Explain how Ortiz's fear and what he said about fear specifically relate to your experience. Use quotations and references.

11. At the end of Ortiz's essay, he says that the experience made him "feel a lot older and a lot wiser." In a paragraph or an essay, write about a time that made you feel a similar way. What else did you learn from the transformative experience?

"Yearning for Love"

12. Assume that you are a psychologist or the personal-advice columnist for a large newspaper and Shastri has written her paragraph as a letter to you. Realizing that she has a life ahead of her and her family is asking her to choose between independence and family, what would you suggest that she

do? Another possible extension of the issue: What advice would you give Shastri's parents if they wrote to you and said that most American marriages end in divorce and that they, the parents, could make a better decision for a sound marriage for their daughter, one that is more mature and nonemotional, one that is based on what they knew about both Shastri and the young man they had already selected?

"Rituals as Comfort Food for the Soul"

13. Write a reaction in which you discuss your own repeated comforting experience similar to those experiences discussed by Rensky. Include direct references to and quotations from Rensky's essay. Use techniques of descriptive narration as you write about your own comfort sessions—a repeated activity that brought you closer to a parent or another adult by providing you with occasions for talking. Consider activities such as cooking, shooting baskets, playing catch, hiking, shopping, playing board games, gardening, washing the car, driving to and from school, and so on.

GENERAL TOPICS

14. Describe and narrate an exciting moment you have experienced or witnessed. It need not be a sporting event, but it can be.

15. Write a descriptive narration based on a topic sentence such as this: "One experience showed me what _____ [pain, fear, anger, love, sacrifice, dedication, joy, sorrow, shame, pride] was really like."

16. Write a descriptive narration about a fire, a riot, an automobile accident, a rescue, shoplifting, or some other unusual happening you witnessed.

17. Write a descriptive narration that supports (or opposes) the idea of a familiar saying such as one of the following; this will be a paragraph or an essay about one experience, beginning with a conflict, problem, or need you have.

   a. You never know who a friend is until you need one (desperate situation and a friend to the rescue).

   b. Borrowing (maybe using the credit card too much) is the mother of trouble.

   c. A person who marries, dates, or compromises values for money earns it.

   d. The person who lies down with dogs gets up with fleas (bad company).

   e. Never give advice to a friend or, especially, a relative.

   f. Every person has a price.

   g. You get what you pay for (little cost of an item or service but also little quality).

   h. Haste makes waste (an occasion when you should have taken more time).

Objective Description

Give your topic some kind of narrative framework or purpose beyond simply writing a description. As you develop your purpose, consider the knowledge and attitudes of your readers. You might be describing a lung for a biology instructor, a geode for a geology instructor, a painting for an art instructor, or a comet for an astronomy instructor. Or maybe you could pose as the seller of an object, such as a desk, a table, or a bicycle. Describe one of the following topics:

18. A human organ, such as a heart, liver, lung, or kidney

19. A visible part of your body, such as a toe, a finger, an ear, a nose, or an eye

20. A construction, such as a room, desk, chair, commode, or table

21. A mechanism, such as a bicycle, tricycle, wagon, car, motorcycle, can opener, or stapler

Subjective Description

The narrative framework (something happening) is especially useful in providing order and vitality to descriptive writing. Here are three possibilities for you to consider:

22. Personalize a trip to a supermarket, a stadium, an airport, an unusual house, a mall, the beach, a court, a church, a club, a business, the library, or the police station. Describe a simple conflict in one of those places while emphasizing descriptive details.

23. Pick a high point in any event and describe the most important few seconds. Think how a scene can be captured by a video camera and then give focus by applying the dominant-impression principle, using relevant images of sight, sound, taste, touch, and smell. The event might be a ball game, graduation ceremony, wedding ceremony, funeral, dance, concert, family gathering, class meeting, rally, riot, robbery, fight, proposal, or meal. Focus on subject material that you can cover effectively in the passage you write.

24. Pick a moment when you were angry, sad, happy, confused, lost, rattled, afraid, courageous, meek, depressed, or elated. Describe how the total context of the situation contributed to your feeling.

CROSS-CURRICULAR TOPICS

25. Write a paragraph or an essay of descriptive narration about a visit, an observation, or a field trip to a museum, a concert, an institution, or a workplace.

26. Write about a unit of time in which feverish action occurs. You could select a pivotal moment in history (the assassination of a president, a turning point in a battle, the first encounter between two groups of people), in science (the discovery of a process or product), in music (a composer conducting his or her own musical composition), or in art appreciation (a painter finishing a famous painting). Content from other courses will provide most of the framework; your imagination can provide the details. Be inventive, but base your invention on what you know of individuals and the time period. Consult textbooks. Talk to instructors.

CAREER-RELATED TOPICS

27. Write a descriptive narrative account of a work-related encounter between a manager and a worker and briefly explain the significance of the event.

28. Describe a well-furnished, well-functioning office or other work area. Be specific.

29. Describe a computer-related product; give special attention to the dominant trait that gives the product its reputation.

30. Describe a person groomed and attired for a particular job or interview. Be specific in giving details pertaining to the person and in naming the place or situation. Describe yourself from a detached point of view if you like.

WRITER'S GUIDELINES   Descriptive Narration

BRANDON BRIDGE

Narration

1. Include these parts so that you will be sure you have a complete narrative:

   - situation
   - conflict
   - struggle
   - outcome
   - meaning

2. Use these techniques or devices as appropriate:

   - images that appeal to the senses (sight, smell, taste, hearing, touch) and other details to advance action
   - dialogue
   - transitional devices (such as *next, soon, after, later, then, finally, when, following*) to indicate chronological order

3. Give details concerning action.

4. Be consistent with point of view and verb tense.

5. Keep in mind that most narratives written as college assignments will have an expository purpose; that is, they explain a specific idea.

6. Consider working with a short time frame for short writing assignments. The scope would usually be no more than one incident of brief duration for one paragraph. For example, writing about an entire graduation ceremony might be too complicated, but concentrating on the moment when you walked forward to receive the diploma or the moment when the relatives and friends come down on the field could work very well.

Description

In objective description, use direct, practical language appealing mainly to the sense of sight. In subjective description, appeal to the reader's feelings, especially through the use of figurative language and the use of images of sight, sound, smell, taste, and touch. Use concrete, specific words if appropriate.

Apply these questions to your writing:

- What is the subject?
- What is the dominant impression I am trying to convey?
- What details support the dominant impression?
- What is the situation?
- What is the order of the details?
- What is the point of view? (Is it first or third person? involved or objective?)

Consider giving the description a narrative framework. Include some action. Use the writing process.

Incident Report

1. Identify the kind of problem and the location. This may be part of a form provided by your employer.

2. Indicate when the problem occurred.

3. Provide an account of what happened.

4. Write in the first person (*I*); you are the one who is writing the report.

5. Start with the date, time, and your reason for involvement.

6. Include quotation marks if you use the words of anyone reporting on the incident and give the name of the person whose words you use.

7. Use facts, not opinions.

8. Remain objective. Do not step outside your work expertise and become a psychologist, philosopher, physician, or moralist.

9. Use past tense. You are writing about something that has already happened.

10. Use mostly active-voice verbs. For example, write, "Mills wrote the report," not "The report was written by Mills."

11. Identify those involved. Drop the titles, such as Mr., Mrs., Dr., and so on. After the first reference to the person in the report, use only the surname or the first initial and the surname.

12. If appropriate, write a recommendation for what could be done to avoid a repeat of such an incident.

13. **Consider using the Writing Process Worksheet and the Brandon Guide for Revising and Editing for completing your assignment and the Revising and Editing Charts after your assignment is returned.**

Practicing the Brandon Guide for Revising and Editing

PATTERN: DESCRIPTIVE NARRATION

My School Nightmare

ANNA KUANG

(A) My first day in an America school became what I imagined was the worst nightmare of my childhood. (B) At the beginning of my bad dream, my Uncle took me to my classroom and just left. (C) Then my sixth grade teacher talked to me and pointed me to a seat. (D) I pretended I understood what she said. (E) Later, when I saw everyone walk out of the classroom, I followed. (F) I did not realize that the school system in America was different from that in China. (G) In China, the students hardly never change classrooms, the teachers do. (H) Confused, I wondered back to the same classroom again. (I) The teacher looked at my schedule card and led me to another room. (J) Next, I was delivered to another room and once again after that, all the time pretending I knew what was being said. (K) Then noon came. (L) In China, students go home for lunch, so I left to walk to my home, and my nightmare was soon to become worse. (M) As I was leaving the school ground, a security man yelled at me. (N) I didn't know what he was yelling. (O) The principal came out and looked at my schedule card and tried to talk with me. (P) I was frustrated and scared. (Q) I wanted to cry and wake up from the bad dream. (R) My face turned red, and my heart was crying. (S) I hid my tears. (T) Then the principal talked on his cell phone. (U) Almost immediately, a Chinese girl came out of a classroom and talked to me in Chinese. (V) She said we had to stay in school until after the last period and that I should have gone to the office for help when I first arrived. (W) We went to the cafeteria together. (X) At that time, I did not know that she would become my best friend. (Y) I did know, however, she had

awakened me from that school nightmare. (Z) During the next three years,
I gradually learned to look back on that scary experience with a bit of
amusement, because that same school would provide me with some of the
most incredibly awesome memories of my life.

EXERCISE 14   Revise and Edit with the Brandon Guide

Revise with `C` `L` `U` `E` `S` `S` **(pronounce as "clues" for easy memorization).**

1. **Coherence:** Connect your ideas. Circle the ten transitional connective words and phrases that indicate time at the beginning of sentences.

2. **Language:** Use words appropriate for your purpose and audience. Cross out the phrase *most incredibly awesome* in Sentence Z and replace it with a phrase that is more precise and less worn.

3. **Unity:** Stay on your topic. Underline the topic sentence and the closing sentence that unify the paragraphs.

4. **Emphasis:** Call attention to your important ideas. Draw a box around the word and those with similar meanings (used six times) that emphasize a key idea in the paragraph.

5. **Support:** Back up your controlling ideas with evidence and logic. In the left margin, annotate this narrative by using these words: situation, conflict, struggle, outcome, meaning.

6. **Sentences:** Write correct, effective sentences with structural variety. Combine sentences R and S with one of these coordinating conjunctions: *for, and, nor, but, or, yet, so* (FANBOYS). Change the punctuation and capitalization as needed. Mark out any parts that are deleted and write in the changes above them.

Edit with `C` `G` `P` `S` **(pronounce as "see GPS" for easy memorization).**

7. **Capitalization:** One capitalized word should begin with a lowercase letter. Make a line through the capital letter and insert the lowercase letter above it.

8. **Grammar:** One sentence has a double negative. Cross out the negative part and write in the correction above it.

9. **Punctuation:** One word group is a comma splice. Change the comma to a correct punctuation mark.

10. **Spelling:** One word is misspelled. Cross it out and write in the correct spelling above it.

8

Exemplification
Writing with Examples

 The truth of the story lies in the details.

—PAUL AUSTER

CHAPTER CONTENTS   BRANDON BRIDGE

When to Use Exemplification

FOR COLLEGE WRITING ASSIGNMENTS

- In all classes, probably the most common constructive comment on a paper is "Be specific." The problem of vagueness can often be remedied by giving examples. If you write only, "Women were active participants in the War of Independence," you will generalize. But if you add, "Two female heroes were teenager Sybil Ludington, who outraced Paul Revere to warn the colonists in Lexington, and a soldier's wife, Mary Hayes (AKA Molly Pitcher), who not only served soldiers water but also fought beside them," you will provide specific supportive information.
- Across the curriculum, exemplification strengthens sentences, paragraphs, essays, reports, research papers, case studies, and field-trip reports.

IN CAREERS AND AT THE WORKPLACE

- As you look for that initial job in your career field or a better job later on, examples will help you connect commonplace generalizations, as found in most applications, with revealing and vivid accounts of your abilities and accomplishments.
- At the workplace, examples can provide crucial information in incident reports, accident reports, case studies, recommendations, evaluations, support for proposals, and testimonials for products and services.

EXEMPLIFICATION IN A CARTOON

THE QUIGMANS   by Buddy Hickerson

B. Hickerson, copyright Los Angeles Times Syndicate. Reprinted with permission

"So what do you have that's fresh?"

Writing Exemplification

Exemplification means using examples to explain, convince, or amuse. Lending interest and information to writing, exemplification is one of the most common and effective ways of developing ideas. Examples may be developed in a sentence or more, or they may be only phrases or even single words, as in the following sentence: "Children like packaged breakfast foods, such as Wheaties, Cheerios, and Rice Krispies."

CHARACTERISTICS OF GOOD EXAMPLES

As supporting information, the best examples are specific, vivid, and representative. These three qualities are closely linked; collectively, they must support the topic sentence of a paragraph and the thesis of an essay.

You use examples to inform or to convince your reader. Of course, an example by itself does not necessarily prove anything. We know that examples can be found on either side of an argument, even at the extreme edges. Therefore, in addition to providing specific examples so that your reader can follow your argument precisely and vivid examples so that your reader will be interested in what you have to say, you should choose examples that are representative. Representative examples are those that your reader can consider, accept as appropriate, and, in some instances, even match with examples of his or her own. If you are writing about cheating and you give one specific, vivid, and representative example, your reader should be able to say, "That's exactly what happens. I can imagine just how the incident occurred." The reader might even have in mind examples that are similar.

TECHNIQUES FOR FINDING EXAMPLES: LISTING AND CLUSTERING

Writing a good paragraph or essay of exemplification begins, as always, with prewriting. The techniques you use will depend on what you are writing about. If you were writing about cheating at school, you might work effectively with a list, perhaps including a few insights into your topic if you have not already formulated your controlling statement. The following is one such list compiled by student Lara Olivas as she developed her essay later in this chapter; she has circled items she thinks she can use.

Student Cheating

When I copied homework

Looking at a friend's test answers

A student with hand signals

Jake and his electronic system

Time for planned cheating

Those who got caught

(A person who bought a research paper)

Jess, who copied from me

The Internet "Cheaters" source

The two students who exchanged identities

More work than it's worth

More stress than it's worth

The teacher's assistant and his friends

The girl from the biology class

If you are pretty well settled on your subject and you expect to use several different kinds of examples, clustering may work very well for you. Student Garabed Yegavian, whose paragraph appears later in this chapter, first used clustering to explore and then he transferred much of his information to an outline. Yegavian's cluster is shown here.

NUMBER AND ORDER OF EXAMPLES

After you have explored your topic and collected information, you must decide whether to use only one example with a detailed explanation, a few examples with a bit less information, or a cluster of examples. A well-stated topic sentence or thesis will guide you in making this decision. When you are writing about a personal topic, you will probably have far more examples than you can use.

Transitional Words

Consider using the following transitional words to improve coherence by connecting ideas with ideas, sentences with sentences, and paragraphs with paragraphs.

FOR EXEMPLIFICATION: for example, as an example, another example, for instance, such as, including, specifically, especially, in particular, to illustrate, as an illustration, that is, i.e. (meaning *that is*), e.g. (meaning *for example*)

FOR ALL PATTERNS OF WRITING: The HOTSHOT CAT words: However, Otherwise, Therefore, Similarly, Hence, On the other hand, Then, Consequently, Also, Thus

If your example is an incident or a series of incidents, you will probably use time order, reinforcing that arrangement with terms such as *next*, *then*, *soon*, *later*, *last*, and *finally*. If your examples exist in space (maybe in different parts of a room), then you would use space references (*up*, *down*, *left*, *right*, *east*, *west*, *north*, and *south*). Arranging examples by emphasis means going from the most important example to the least important or from the least important to the most important.

FINDING PATTERNS IN PHOTOS

EXERCISE 1   An Image-Based Activity for Groups or Individuals

Chelsea Sektnan/Corbis Wire/Corbis

This photo shows a fried food kiosk at a crowded county fair. Imagine that you are there in the photo. You have decided to explore the fairgrounds. You are searching for a topic in which you can use some specific examples to illustrate a point about the different kinds of food sold at community events. As you stroll, you begin looking at all the different types of food that people are enjoying. In fact, you take out a note pad and begin jotting down different examples. List these examples here:

1. _____   9. _____

2. _____   10. _____

3. _____   11. _____

4. _____   12. _____

5. _____   13. _____

6. _____   14. _____

7. _____   15. _____

8. _____

You now have an idea for writing a paragraph or an essay about your fair. You could use specific examples from your observations to write on this topic: "The fair is very crowded, but fairgoers enjoy a variety of different food options."

If your instructor directs, write a paragraph or an essay in which you use numerous examples from your imaginary exploration of the fairgrounds. If you like,

make some of the examples more specific by giving names to customers and vendors. To be really imaginative, you could briefly interview a few of these imaginary people.

Practicing Patterns of Exemplification

The simple patterns in the following exercise will help you see the relationship between purpose and example(s).

EXERCISE 2   Brainstorming a List of Examples

Make a list of examples that could support the following topic sentence or thesis. Then circle four you might use in writing a paragraph or an essay on that topic. The first item is provided.

Controlling idea: Some people let television watching interfere with their real lives.

Specific occasions where you have observed people watching television instead of doing what they had intended or expected to be doing:

Family gathering on a holiday _____

_____

_____

_____

_____

_____

_____

_____

Readings for Critical Thinking, Discussion, and Writing

READING STRATEGIES AND OBJECTIVES

Underlining and annotating these reading selections will help you answer the questions that follow the selections, discuss the material in class, and prepare for reading-based writing assignments. As you underline and annotate, pay special attention to the author's writing skills, logic, and message, and consider the relevance of the material to your own experiences and values.

PARAGRAPHS

Dropping Way Out*

DAVID LEVINE

Every day, three thousand students give up on high school—for good. They push open the doors and walk out. They turn their backs on school. Drop out, way out. Here we have one of numerous examples of dropout experiences discussed by freelance author David Levine in his essay, "I'm Outta Here."

Think about it. In some ways it seems perfect. Quit school. Just say No—no more pressure, no more stupid rules, no more deadlines, no more uncaring teachers, no more snobby, clique-conscious peers. Nearly every high school student has imagined what it would be like. Beth Kierny did more than imagine. A few months into her senior year at Columbia High School, in East Greenbush, New York, she dropped out of school. Beth is a shy eighteen-year-old with dark, curly hair who hated getting up early for classes. She thought it would be great. She'd just get a job, sleep in later, work at some cool place instead of sitting in boring classes, and lead an easier, more interesting life. But without a diploma, Beth found it difficult to get a job. She had to finally settle for one at the Hessmart gas station a few miles down Route 20. Being the youngest and newest employee, she got stuck working the worst shifts. Often she had to get up even earlier than she had to for school—sometimes she had to be *at work* by 7:00 a.m. Or she'd have to work the midnight shift, which was scary because one never knew if the place might get held up. Or she'd have to work weekends, when her friends were all out partying. The money was terrible—at minimum wage she cleared maybe $90 a week—and she couldn't afford a car, so she had to take cabs to and from work, which cost almost ten bucks a day. That didn't leave much for her share of the $425 a month in rent on [the] small apartment behind the Burger King.

*Title by authors of this book.

EXERCISE 3   Discussion and Critical Thinking

1. What topic is illustrated?

2. What is the message of the essay?

3. Does Levine use one example or many examples? Why?

Everything for a Price

PIERRE BERTON

Taken from The Klondike Fever: The Life and Death of the Last Great Gold Rush, *this paragraph shows that in the frontier town of Dawson, Yukon Territory, Canada, in 1898, almost everything was available—for a price. Born in Dawson, Pierre Berton is a television commentator, a journalist, and the author of four other books.*

You could buy almost anything under the sun during that climactic summer in Dawson City. You could buy clothes and furs, moccasins, and plug hats, shoes and jewelry, fresh grapes, opera glasses, safety pins, and ice cream. You could buy peanuts and pink lemonade, patent-leather shoes, yellow-jacketed novels, cribbage boards, ostrich feathers, and oxen on the brief. You could, if you were so inclined, buy for one hundred dollars the tusk of a prehistoric mammoth, dredged out of the frozen ground by prospectors—or, for twenty-five cents, a slicker coat with a bad cigar thrown in as a premium. You could have your palm read, your picture taken, your back massaged, or your teeth filled with nuggets. You could buy Bibles and sets of Shakespeare and pairs of gold-scales by the hundreds, for these had been standard equipment with almost every man. You could buy rifles by the gross at one dollar each; they were worthless in a town where nobody was allowed to pack a gun. Many men stripped off the barrels to use as pipes for transmitting steam into frozen ground and thawing the soil at the mines, and others bought them by the score and shipped them back Outside at a profit.

EXERCISE 4   Discussion and Critical Thinking

1. Underline the topic sentence of "Everything for a Price."

2. What is the effect of Burton's use of many examples?

3. What aspects of life in frontier Dawson are covered by Berton's selection of examples?

4. What do the examples tell you about the people in Dawson in 1898?

ESSAYS

Small Businesses Use Social Media to Grow*

LAURA PETRECCA

Some small businesses are discovering the benefits of social media.

1   Hamburger chain Smashburger has become a smash hit, growing from three Denver locations in 2007 to 150 outposts nationwide. And while its Angus-beef burgers and unique toppings have helped to propel its success, its secret sauce is social-media outreach.

2   Smashburger offers coupons and trivia contests for its 67,000 Facebook followers, replies to questions and complaints on its Twitter and Facebook profiles, and actively reaches out to bloggers who might write about the new Smashburger restaurants opening in their areas.

3   "The brand was really built on social media and PR strategies," says Jeremy Morgan, senior vice president of marketing and consumer insights. "Social media is an opportunity for us to engage with consumers and have a conversation, which is different than paid media, when you're just shouting through a bullhorn."

4   Wielded wisely, social media can help a growing business boost brand aware-ness, improve customer relations, garner market research, even bolster sales. As the number of people using social media rises, marketing experts say it's essential for even the smallest of companies to consider diving in.

5   "Everybody should take a look at it," says Dan Galbraith, owner of marketing sup-port company Solutionist and a National Small Business Association board member.

6   "Whether they chose to jump into social media or not is a question that only they can answer," he says, but all firms should at least explore how social media could work for them.

7   It just takes a few clicks to potentiality connect with thousands of business con-tacts and customers, he says. In addition to networking, business owners can use social media to glean useful insights by reading comments made by customers, industry experts, even competitors.

8   "There's a lot of good information floating out there," he says.

A time investment

9   It takes dedication to achieve social-media success.

10   "The common misconception about social media is that it's free," says Morgan. "Facebook and Twitter accounts are free, but for small-business owners in particular, time comes at a premium."

11   To keep from feeling overwhelmed, business owners should decide how much time they can dedicate to this burgeoning arena, says Galbraith. Some may need to hire social-media help.

12   Either way, business owners should first set goals, he says. For instance, an owner might want to increase store traffic by 20% by offering coupons via Facebook or another social-media site. Or a business-to-business company could plan to reconnect with 10 former clients and re-establish solid relationships in the next three months.

13   The goals should be clear-cut, but as many business owners have learned, the initial strategies might have to change.

14   "Our social-media education is ongoing and is purely trial and error," says Pawleys Island, S.C., entrepreneur Brian Henry, who started selling pimento cheese with his wife, Sassy, in 2006.

15   In 2009, they used social media to post photos of themselves and their Palmetto Cheese-branded spreads, which blend cheddar cheese, mayonnaise, cream cheese and sweet pimento peppers with spices and ingredients such as jalapeños or bacon.

16   "While this was a great place for us to start, it didn't bring in a lot of followers, because it wasn't creating a dialogue," says Brian.

17   Since then, they've ramped up their digital interactions. They post customer recipes on their Facebook and Twitter profiles, offer trivia contests and T-shirt give-aways, and answer questions on how to buy, store and serve the cheese.

18   As followers increased, so did sales. When the Henrys first began their social-media outreach in 2009, they sold 547,000 containers of Palmetto Cheese. In 2011, they sold 2.1 million.

19   Of course, that sales boost wasn't brought on by social media alone. But the nearly 22,000 people who "like" the Palmetto Cheese Facebook page—and spread word of the brand to their friends—have helped sales. "Once we started truly inter-acting with our customers and created a community, we began to see an increase in interest and customers," Brian says.

Consistency counts

20   While marketing experts advocate joining the social-media conversation, most say that doing it poorly—such as combining personal and professional updates or not posting information consistently—is worse than not doing it at all.

21   "Consumers won't stick around, and you won't get much traction," says Morgan.

22   There are some basic social media tenets to keep in mind, says Sabina Ptacin, co-founder of 'Preneur, which provides tools and resources for small businesses.

23   She first suggests that business owners "baby step it out," to see what feels comfortable to them and is do-able. Those who can't contribute on a daily basis might want to hold off on creating a public profile.

24   "You can't post once a week and think it's going to make an impact," she says. "You need to constantly be contributing, definitely every day."

25   She encourages new entrants to start conversations by posting updates, photos and interesting industry news, as well as questions for followers. The queries can be simple, such as asking for feedback on a new product or for opinions on industry news.

26   "Do not worry if no one responds," she says. "It doesn't mean that no one likes you, or you're bad at Twitter."

27   If the questions are authentic and interesting, they will eventually get replies, she says.

28   And no matter what, don't aggressively push a product or service, she says. That could scare away potential followers.

29   She counsels social-media users to think of it as circulating during a cocktail party.

30   "I always tell people to pretend that they're at a party and (act) how they would behave," she says. "No one wants to talk to the person who is always talking about themselves. . . . They want you to ask them questions and engage in conversations."

EXERCISE 5   Discussion and Critical Thinking

1. Petracca begins with an example. What does the example show?

2. According to Jeremy Morgan, senior vice president of marketing and consumer insights at Smashburger, how is social media different from paid media?

3. What are examples of ways that social media can help a growing business?

4. Morgan explains that social media isn't really free. What is his reasoning?

5. Brian Henry explains how he and his wife use social media to promote their pimento cheese business. What are examples of ways they use social media well?

6. What are examples of ways that Henry and his wife used social media less effectively?

7. Sabina Ptacin, co-founder of 'Preneur, advises that companies should "baby step it out" when they first start using social media. What does she mean by that?

8. Why might aggressively pushing a product scare away potential social media followers?

Who's Cheap?*

ADAIR LARA

Adair Lara is an award-winning newspaper columnist for the San Francisco Chronicle *and the author of five books and dozens of magazine articles. Her best-selling memoir about raising a teenage daughter,* Hold Me Close, Let Me Go, *was published by Random House (2001). Her specialty is writing about her experiences in first-person point of view.*

1   It was our second date, and we had driven one hundred miles up the coast in my car to go abalone-diving. When I stopped to fill the tank at the only gas station in sight, Craig scowled and said, "You shouldn't get gas here. It's a rip-off."

2   But he didn't offer to help pay. And that night, after dinner in a restaurant, he leaned over and whispered intimately, "You get the next one." Though he was sensitive and smart, and looked unnervingly good, Craig was as cheap as a two-dollar watch.

3   This is not an ethical dilemma, you're all shouting. Lose the guy, and fast.

4   Lose the guy? Is this fair? My friend Jill is always heading for the john when the check comes, but I don't hear anybody telling me to lose her. And she's far from the only cheap woman I know. A lot of us make decent money these days, yet I haven't seen women knocking over tables in fights for the lunch tab. In fact, many women with 20/20 vision seem to have trouble distinguishing the check from the salt, pepper, and other tabletop items. But if a guy forgets to chip in for gas or gloats too long over the deal he got on his Nikes, he's had it.

5   Why is this double standard so enduring? One reason is that, while neither sex has a monopoly on imperfection, there *are* such things as flaws that are much more distasteful in one sex than in the other. Women seem especially unpleasant when they get drunk, swear or even insist on pursuing an argument they'll never win. And men seem beneath contempt when they're cheap.

6   These judgments are a holdover from the days when women stayed home and men earned the money. Though that old order has passed, we still associate men with paying for things. And besides, there's just something appealing about generosity. Buying something for someone is, in a sense, taking care of her. The gesture says, "I like you, I want to give you something." If it comes from a man to whom we are about to entrust our hearts, this is a comforting message. We miss it when it's not forthcoming.

7   Then why *not* dump on cheap men?

8   Some men are just skinflints and that's it. My friend Skye broke up with her boyfriend because when they went to the movies he doled out M&Ms to her one at a time. Craig, my date back at the gas station, liked to talk about how he'd bought his car—which in California, where I live, is like buying shoes—as a special present to himself.

9   This kind of cheapness is ingrained; you'll never change it. That guy who parks two miles away to avoid the parking lot fee was once a little boy who saved his birthday money without being told to. Now he's a man who studies the menu and sputters, "Ten dollars for *pasta*?" His stinginess will always grate on you, since he is likely to dole out his feelings as parsimoniously as his dollars.

10   On the other hand, I know a wonderful man, crippled with debts from a former marriage, who had to break up with a woman because she never paid her share, and he was simply running out of money. Though she earned a lot more than he did, she couldn't expand her definition of masculinity to include "sometimes needs to go Dutch treat."

*Adair Lara, "Who's Cheap?" from *San Francisco Chronicle*. By permission.

11   To men, such women seem grasping. One friend of mine, who spends a lot of money on concerts and theater and sailing but not on restaurants he considers overpriced, has evolved a strategy for women who are annoyed at the bohemian places he favors. If his date complains, he offers to donate to the charity of her choice the cost of an evening at her favorite spot. "Some women have bad values," he says, "And if the idea of spending money on a good cause, but not on her, makes her livid, I know she's one of them."

12   I had a bracing encounter with my own values when I told my friend Danny the humorous (I thought) story of a recent date who asked if I wanted a drink after a concert, then led me to the nearest water fountain.

13   Danny gave one of his wry looks. "Let's get this straight," he said, laughing. "As a woman, you are so genetically precious that you deserve attention just because you grace the planet. So, of course, he should buy you drinks. He should also drive the car, open the door, ask you to dance, coax you to bed. And then when you feel properly pampered, you can let out that little whine about how he doesn't treat you as an equal."

14   On second thought, I guess I'd rather buy my own drink.

15   So here's the deal. Before dumping a guy for ordering the sundowner dinner or the house white, better first make sure that you aren't burdening the relationship with outdated ideas of how the sexes should behave. Speaking for myself, I know that if a man looks up from the check and says, "Your share is eleven dollars," part of me remembers that, according to my mother, *my* share was to look charming in my flowered blouse.

16   Wanting the man to pay dies hard. What many of us do now is *offer* to split the check, then let our purses continue to dangle from the chair as we give him time to realize that the only proper response is to whip out his own wallet.

17   Is this a game worth playing? It's up to you, but consider that offering to help pay implies that the check is his responsibility. And this attitude can work both ways. My sister gets angry when her husband offers to help clean the house. "Like it's *my* house!" she snorts.

18   Like it's *his* check.

EXERCISE 6   Vocabulary Highlights

Write a short definition of each word as it is used in the essay. (Paragraph numbers are given in parentheses.) Be prepared to use these words in sentences.

intimately (2)	grate (9)
unnervingly (2)	dole (9)
ethical (3)	parsimoniously (9)
dilemma (3)	bohemian (11)
gloats (4)	genetically (13)

EXERCISE 7   Discussion and Critical Thinking

1. Lara uses examples to explain how she came to a conclusion on who—male, female, or both—should pay on dates. What does she think about the occasion of her second date with Craig when he does not pay for the gas or meal?

2. What examples does Lara use to show that some men are just "skinflints" (paragraph 8)?

3. In your estimation, whose behavior is worse, the one-at-a-time M&Ms guy or the water-fountain guy? Why?

4. In paragraph 9, Lara says that some men have ingrained cheapness and that men who are stingy with money are likely to be stingy with feelings. Do you agree with her generalization? Why or why not?

5. The author seems impressed by the man (in paragraph 11) who says he takes dates to cheap restaurants and if they complain, he offers to give the money he saved to a worthy cause of his date's choice. Then if she does not accept, he assumes she is just interested in having the fine meal for herself. Do you think that is likely a good way to discover his date's value system (as he believes), or is it likely that he has just devised a good way to avoid paying more?

Dreaming Together on the Day of the Dead*

LUIS TORRES

A successful freelance writer, Luis Torres is a wellspring of insight into the Los Angeles Mexican-American culture into which he was born. If his childhood home in the then Chavez Ravine were now resurrected, it would be located in left-center field in Dodger Stadium. His experience of being a reporter in high school during the turmoil of the late '60s introduced him to the field of writing for publication, which would extend to college and after graduation from the University of California at Santa Barbara to his becoming a professor of journalism at California State University, Los Angeles, a position he left for a thirty-year career as a reporter, copywriter, and producer with KNX-1070, a CBS all-news radio station. Meanwhile, he wrote numerous feature articles for the Los Angeles Times and other publications, won a number of regional and national awards for his writing, and was variously involved in the Chicano cultural emergence and development, highlighted at the pop level by his co-producing the first record for Los Lobos, a world-famous, multiple Grammy Award–winning American Chicano rock band from East Los Angeles.

1   Today millions of Mexicans in the republic and millions of Mexican descendants here in the U.S. will observe El Día de los Muertos, the Day of the Dead.

2   I'll observe it in my own quiet, reflective way. And I'll do so while conjuring the memory of a remarkable experience I had a couple of years ago when I spent the night in a cemetery in the ancient southern Mexican city of Oaxaca.

*Luis Torres, "Dreaming Together on the Day of the Dead."

3   That is when I asked an old man named Ramón Hernández López, sitting at the grave of his widow as midnight approached in the campo santo, if he really believed his departed wife would come to him in spirit form and talk with him. He answered, "I cannot say if we will talk together tonight, but I am certain that tonight we will dream together." "*Soñamos juntos esta noche.*"

4   I'll always remember that exchange. It crystallizes for me what Day of the Dead is and represents. In Oaxaca that autumn I was staying with a Zapotec Indian family for whom El Día de los Muertos is the most important holiday observance of the year.

5   Surely, most Americans must find it difficult to understand or appreciate a holiday whose trappings seem rather bizarre and even morbid. Mexicans bake bread in the form of skulls. Decorate altars with candied skulls and flowers. Surround pictures of departed loved ones with food and drink favored by the departed. Even gather at the grave sites of lost family members to "greet" their spirits as they return to this world from the beyond. All this is done in a festive spirit, not in a funereal, somber way. I'm not big on religion, but I am intrigued by ritual, tradition and historical legacy.

6   What Americans don't seem to comprehend is that El Día de los Muertos is not a celebration of death. It's a celebration of life, an acknowledgment that death is inextricably a part of the cycle of life. It's about renewal and connection. It's not a time to cry. It's a time to smile. And an opportunity to embrace life fully, despite the obstacles we face.

7   Scholars remind us that this is an Aztec-rooted ritual that's been observed for thousands of years. When the Spaniards conquered Mexico in the 16th century they attempted to eradicate the ritual. The Spaniards didn't succeed.

8   The Day of the Dead eventually was subsumed into the Catholic calendar as part of the observance of All Saints Day and All Souls Day. It endures today, as the indigenous people endure despite the historical iron fist of genocide and oppression.

9   For Mexican-Americans like me, it remains as a link to our ancestral, indigenous heritage.

10   I'll never forget the remarkable scene in that huge graveyard in Oaxaca a couple of years ago. It was nearly the size of a football field. As midnight approached, almost every grave was illuminated by shimmering candlelight. A haunting surreal glow as far as the eye could see.

11   Families huddled around the graves decorated with *campoxochitl* flowers (Nahuatl for marigolds) as well as small plates of carne asada, tortillas, and glasses of tequila and cigarettes—Delicados and Marlboros. Favorites of the departed. I remember vividly the joy and reverence in the faces of the families who gathered that night.

12   As nonintrusively as I could, I talked with dozens of families about what they were doing and they were pleased to share their feelings.

13   "We do it to honor our ancestors," many told me. "It reminds us that we too will die and that we should not fear that," many others told me. Some said they looked forward to communing with their lost mothers, fathers and other relatives. "We will comfort each other," one young woman told me.

14   That was the night Ramón Hernández López told me, "*Soñamos juntos esta noche.*" We'll dream together tonight.

EXERCISE 8 Vocabulary Highlights

Write a short definition of each word as it is used in the essay. (Paragraph numbers are given in parentheses.) Be prepared to use these words in sentences.

conjuring (2)

crystallizes (4)

morbid (5)

inextricably (6)

eradicate (7)

subsumed (8)

indigenous (8)

surreal (10)

nonintrusively (12)

communing (13)

EXERCISE 9 Discussion and Critical Thinking

1. What is the controlling idea of this essay?

2. What is the setting?

3. Who is the audience for Torres? To whom is he speaking?

4. What kind of support does he use?

5. How does he emphasize his main idea?

6. For Torres, a Mexican-American who is "not big on religion," the Day of the Dead provides "a link to our ancestral, indigenous heritage.... It's about renewal and connection. It's not a time to cry. It's a time to smile. And an opportunity to embrace life fully, despite the obstacles we face." To what extent has this essay given you a clearer understanding of the Day of the Dead? If you observe the tradition of the Day of the Dead, what is your evaluation of the explanation offered by Torres and what would you add to or subtract from his comments? If you do not observe the tradition, what is most significant about what you have learned about the Day of the Dead?

STUDENT PARAGRAPH AND ESSAY

Traveling the World at Home

GARABED YEGAVIAN

An Armenian-American student, Garabed Yegavian has traveled to many countries and encountered many cultures. Living in Southern California, he is constantly reminded that he lives in a global community, but this assignment focused his attention on specific, persuasive examples.

Living in California can be like traveling the world. It is morning! Responding to my alarm clock made in China, I get out of my bed, which was constructed in the United States, and step onto a Persian rug. I'm ready to start my Saturday. I walk to my closet to find my clothes: pants from Indonesia, shirt of fabric from India but made in North Carolina, socks from Mexico, shoes from Italy. For late breakfast I have a bagel and cream cheese. I sit in front of my television to see what is happening in the world today. I flip through the channels—English, Spanish, Chinese—until I get to the local Armenian station for an update. After an hour I'm ready to go. I drive to my Korean friend's garage, where he fills my car with oil refined in a plant down by Long Beach. I pay him with my American dollars, and I'm off for tires. On the way to the tire shop, I stop for some lunch. Zancou's Chicken is the place for me today. I order Armenian-style chicken and a bottle of Perrier water and enjoy my feast. Done with lunch, I motor to the tire shop where an immigrant worker from El Salvador fits American Kelly tires on my car. I drink a small cup of Turkish coffee with the manager and talk about business here in America. After a while, my car is ready, and I leave for a mid-afternoon snack. Where to go? There are just too many choices. I decide to go to a Japanese restaurant near my home. There I eat sushi made with fish caught from the waters off Peru, drink Japanese saki, and reflect on my day's experiences. In miles I had not gone far, but who needs to travel the world when one lives in Southern California?

EXERCISE 10   Discussion and Critical Thinking

1. Underline the topic sentence of the paragraph.

2. Circle each specific example.

3. As Yegavian's community becomes more global, does it become less American, more American, or just a different kind of American? Explain.

4. Do you welcome this kind of change and find it rather exciting, as Yegavian apparently does? Why or why not?

5. This article was written several years ago. To what extent is your environment similar to the one presented in this paragraph? How different was the environment back in your parents' or grandparents' time?

Lara Olivas was asked to write an essay on unproductive student behavior, developing her ideas mainly with examples. Of numerous topics that came to mind, one stood out: cheating. It was a practice she had observed for years and had very briefly experimented with and rejected. Wanting to do something a bit different, she considered all the reasons that cheating is not a good idea and came up with a practical one: Cheating is hard work, and cheaters sometimes work harder at cheating than others do at their work.

Olivas's Writing Process Worksheet shows how her writing evolved from idea to final draft. To conserve space here, the freewriting and the rough drafts marked for revision have been omitted. The balance of her worksheet has been lengthened for you to be able to see her other work in its entirety.

BRANDON BRIDGE

Writing Process Worksheet

Name _Lara Olivas_   **Title** _Cheating Is Not Worth the Bother_   **Due Date** _Wednesday, May 16, 9.00 a.m._

Use the back of this page or separate paper if you need more space.

Assignment

In the space below, write whatever you need to know about your assignment, including information about the topic, audience, pattern of writing, length, whether to include a rough draft or revised drafts, and whether your paper must be typed.

Write a 500- to 750-word essay of exemplification on the topic of unproductive student behavior. Fellow students and the instructor will probably be familiar with your subject but not your examples and your view. Submit this completed worksheet, one or more rough drafts marked for revision, and a typed final draft.

Stage One

Explore Freewrite, brainstorm (list), cluster, or take notes as directed by your instructor.

Listing

STUDENT CHEATING

When I copied homework

Looking at a friend's test answers

A student with hand signals

Jake and his electronic system

Time for planned cheating

Those who got caught

A person who bought a research paper

Jess, who copied from me

The Internet "Cheaters" source

The two students who exchanged identities

(More work than it's worth)

(More stress than it's worth)

The teacher's assistant and his friends

(The girl from the biology class)

Stage Two

Organize Write a topic sentence or thesis; label the subject and the focus parts.

Cheating students often put themselves under more stress than honest students.
     subject   focus

Write an outline or an outline alternative. For reading-based writing, include references and short quotations with page numbers as support in the outline.

   I. Student who bought paper
      A. Had trouble with form
         1. Prewriting
         2. Drafts
      B. Had trouble with quality
      C. Drops class
  II. Student with cheat cards
      A. Had a system
      B. Sometimes under suspicion
      C. Experienced stress

Stage Three

Write On separate paper, write and then revise your paragraph or essay as many times as necessary for **c**oherence, **l**anguage (usage, tone, and diction), **u**nity, **e**mphasis, **s**upport, and **s**entences (**CLUESS**). Read your work aloud to hear and correct any grammatical errors or awkward-sounding sentences.

Edit any problems in fundamentals, such as **c**apitalization, **g**rammar, **p**unctuation, and **s**pelling (**CGPS**).

Final Draft

CHEATING IS NOT WORTH THE BOTHER
Lara Olivas

I knew many students who took college prep classes all the way through high school and never read a book in an English class. They read Cliff's Notes or Monarch Notes, or they copied work from other people who did. But they weren't cheating just in English classes. They had systems of cheating in every class. Cheating became a way of life. They were always conniving and scheming. I am not that pure. I have tried cheating, but I soon rejected it. I did not learn that way, and I lost my self-esteem. I also feared getting caught; and I discovered that most of the time cheating was hard, stressful work. So I never became, like some of my friends, a master cheater, but I did become a master observer of cheaters because students almost always see more than

Thesis

teachers do. <u>What I learned was that cheaters often put themselves under</u> <u>more stress than honest students.</u>

Topic sentence
Specific example

<u>Even the student who pays for school work can become a victim of stress.</u> I remember a student in my junior composition class who needed a research paper, so he found a source and bought one for seventy-five dollars. The first trouble was that he had to submit the work in stages: the topic, the working bibliography, the note cards, the outline, the rough draft, and the final. Therefore, he went to the library and started working backwards. Of course, he couldn't turn in only the bib cards actually used in the paper, and next he had to make out note cards for the material he "would be" documenting, and even make out more. After having all kinds of trouble, he realized that the bought paper was of "A" quality, whereas he had been a "C" student. He went back to his source and was told he should change the sentence structure and so on to make the paper weaker. Finally he dropped the class after spending more time on his paper than I did on mine.

Order by time

Topic sentence
Specific example
Order by time

<u>Then during my senior year, a female student in Biology 2 became another</u> <u>subject for my study in cheating.</u> She was sitting next to me, so I could see everything she did. She kept her cheat cards in her bra. This is the way she did it. On the day of the test, she would wear a loose-fitting blouse or dress. Then when the instructor was not watching, she would hunch her shoulders like a buzzard sleeping and slump so that she could look down the front of her own dress. Sometimes she'd have to fiddle around down there to get the cheat card to pop into place. Her writing was tiny. I know about the writing because one day the teacher left the room, and she just took a card out and used it openly. If the instructor stared at her when she was looking down, she would blow inside her dress as if she were trying to cool off her bosom or something. Then she would smile at the instructor and shake her head and pucker her lips to show how hot it was. Her strategy worked because she did perspire due to the stress. The tests were mainly on muscles and bones and weren't that difficult. She probably worked harder in rigging the cheat cards on her underwear than I did in memorizing information.

Cluster of examples

There were dozens of other examples—the writing on seats, hands, arms, legs, and cuffs; the hand signs, blinks, and coughs; and the plagiarism of all kinds. There were even the classes where cheating would never be caught because some teachers did not watch carefully during the tests, and others didn't read carefully later. But for the most part, the cheaters were the ones who had the most anxiety and often the ones who did the most work—work that was never directed toward learning.

EXERCISE 11   Discussion and Critical Thinking

1. Why did Olivas give up cheating?

2. What evidence is there that the two students she discusses experienced stress?

3. Does Olivas use a large number of specific examples to support her points or does she develop her examples in detail?

4. As Olivas develops her examples in paragraphs, what other pattern of writing emerges?

READING-BASED WRITING

Grading a Professor's Writing

MASON ARNOLD

Student Mason Arnold had an unusual topic. He was asked to write an evaluation of an essay about students who wanted their grade changed. His text was "Making the Grade" by Kurt Wiesenfeld, a professor who reported that for one grading period, about 10 percent of his physics students at Georgia Tech had contacted him after his classes ended, with seemingly trivial, nonacademic arguments for a higher grade. Specifically, Arnold's task was to assign Professor Wiesenfeld a letter grade based mainly on his assertions and the effectiveness of his examples.

1   In writing "Making the Grade," Professor Kurt Wiesenfeld uses three kinds of examples: students with bad values and poor performance, real-world problems, and a culture that allows the unqualified to cause those problems. He is concerned.

Summary with quotation

2   Ten percent of his students are the offenders. He gives examples of visits, phone calls, and e-mails from students who want their grades raised for nonacademic reasons. Although these are the ones who do not work hard or perform well, they try to make the professor feel guilty about their low grades, as they beg and make excuses. He says it is the "disgruntled consumer approach…. If they don't like their grade, they go to the 'return' counter to trade it in for something better" (184).

Interpretation and summary

Quotation
Reference
Question of logic

3   In the same way the students have not been serious and careful about their studies, some people have not been serious and careful at work. In short, they may not be qualified. Wiesenfeld says most of his students are engineering majors, and he is fearful that if they do not get "the answer right" when they are on the job, problems may occur (184). He gives examples of a light tower collapsing, a building beam breaking, and a dorm floor being unlevel (184). He uses these examples to say that those problems could be caused by engineers who were careless students. That may not be the case. He does not know anything about those who were responsible.

Blended quotations and paraphrasing

4   Wiesenfeld traces the blame for loss of respect for education to both individuals and society. He says society is "saturated with surface values" connected with the idea that a degree is something to be traded for a "job, which means money" and that a degree is often treated as more important than an education (185). The students are mainly to blame, but they reflect the view of society. He even says teachers are inconsistent in their grading standards, which is true. But he does not give specific examples, certainly not the kind he finds for the sniveling students and the engineering errors. The fact is that some students try to con their professors because they know from experience and observation that sometimes the con works. There are lots of examples on any campus and in any department.

Evaluation
Critical comment on use of examples

Evaluation as
conclusion

5   For that one shortcoming, I have lowered Professor Kurt Wiesenfeld's grade to a B+. If he e-mails, telephones, or visits to say he would have done better had his classes been smaller and his committee meetings shorter, I will just tell him that for the good of society I will not accept his excuses.

Work Cited

Wiesenfeld, Kurt. "Making the Grade." *From Self to Sources: Essays and Beyond.* Ed. Lee Brandon. Boston: Houghton, 2003. 183–86. Print.

Suggested Topics and Prompts for Writing Exemplification

READING-BASED WRITING

Reading-based writing requires you to read critically, write a reply that shows you understand what you have read, and give credit for ideas you borrow and words you quote. The form can be a summary, a reaction, or a two-part response (with separated summary and reaction).

Documentation, in which you give credit for borrowed ideas and words, can be either formal (MLA style) or informal, as directed by your instructor. Definitions of the three forms follow. Any form can be used for any reading selection in this book.

Summary

- The summary is a statement written in response to a reading. It restates only the most important points and uses original wording instead of the author's language. It should not contain added information or personal opinions.
- Because summaries are intended to restate only the main points of a reading, they are typically much shorter than the original text. Often, they are approximately a third of the length.

Reaction

- In the reaction, the meaning of what you have read will be central to the topic sentence of your paragraph or to the thesis of your essay.
- Although the reaction is not a personal narrative by itself, it may include personal experience to explain elements of the text. For example, if your source is about driving styles, your own experiences as a driver or an observer of drivers could be relevant in your analysis of the text.
- The reaction may incorporate a summary to convey a broad view of what you have read, but your summary should never be the main part of your reaction.

Two-Part Response

- The two-part response separates the summary from the reaction.
- This form will give you practice in separating your objective summary in the first part from your more personal evaluation, interpretation, or application in the second part, the reaction.

READING-BASED WRITING TOPICS

"Dropping Way Out"

1. Write a summary of Levine's essay.

2. Write a reaction to the paragraph. How does Beth Kierny's experience compare to your own understanding of what it would be like to drop out of high school and enter the workforce without a high school diploma?

"Everything for a Price"

3. Write a reaction to the paragraph. Do you live in a community in which you can buy "everything for a price"? Why or why not?

"Small Businesses Use Social Media to Grow"

4. Write a paragraph or an essay in which you relate some of your experiences as a consumer. What suggestions do you have for business owners using paid media or social media to build their brands?

"Who's Cheap?"

5. Write a reading-based paragraph or essay in which you agree or disagree with Lara. Examine her use of numerous examples leading to a conclusion that from now on she will pay her part of the check. Keep in mind that at the end of her essay, Lara knows what she'll say after the meal. She'll say, "I'll pay half," not "Let me pay half." Discuss the difference and whether it matters from your perspective. Consider using some examples from your own experience.

"Dreaming Together on the Day of the Dead"

6. The Day of the Dead is celebrated in different ways in many countries. Even within a country, a state, or a community, there are likely to be a few variations. Some are just a matter of extent. Others bring in different properties even from religions other than Catholic. If you have encountered or studied a different expression of Day of the Dead and have a different set of descriptions and examples, compare and contrast them with the descriptions and examples given by Torres. Use some quotations and references from Torres's essay. As a unifying principle, you might want to incorporate Torres's central idea that Day of the Dead is often misunderstood and is a celebration of life. It is a time for happiness.

7. Torres says, "I'm not big on religion," but he obviously has much respect for and is intrigued by the Day of the Dead. Write a paragraph or an essay of reaction in which you discuss how a person not religious in the traditional sense can, and perhaps should, appreciate the holiday. Use quotations from and references to Torres's essay. An alternate paragraph or essay topic could be one on your feeling that you now understand the Day of the Dead better but still don't care for it.

"Traveling the World at Home"

8. Write a reaction to this paragraph in which you explain why the author's examples are reason for celebration or grief—or something in between. In your view, has the expansion of free trade been mainly good or bad for the American economy and generally for American society? Provide some of your own examples.

"Cheating Is Not Worth the Bother"

9. Write a reaction in which you agree or disagree with Olivas's view that "cheating is not worth the bother." Consider discussing how to compete with cheaters. Evaluate Olivas's examples and incorporate your own examples from personal experience.

"Grading a Professor's Writing"

10. Write a paragraph or an essay of reaction in which you agree or disagree with the views of the professor and then with the criticism of the professor by student Mason Arnold.

GENERAL TOPICS

11. Write a paragraph about something that can be explained or defined by giving an abundance of examples. Consider a garage or yard sale, an antique or thrift store, or a used car lot.

12. Choose or modify one of the following statements as a topic sentence for a paragraph or a thesis for an essay. Support the statement with specific examples.

    a. Television commercials are often amusing [misleading, irritating, sexist, racist, useless, fascinating].

    b. Rap music often carries important messages [makes me sick, brings out the best in people, brings out the worst in people, degrades women, promotes violence, presents reality, appeals to our better instincts, tells funny stories].

    c. Rock groups do not have to be sensational in presentation and appearance to be popular.

    d. A person can be an environmentalist in everyday life.

    e. Many people who consider themselves law-abiding citizens break laws on a selective basis.

    f. People who do not have a satisfying family life will find a family substitute.

    g. Country music appeals to some of our most basic emotions.

CROSS-CURRICULAR TOPIC

13. Use examples to write a paragraph or an essay in the following kinds of assignments.

a. In preparation for an anticipated essay test question in another class, write a paragraph or an essay with an extended example or several specific examples.

b. Reports: Focus on one or more examples as representative of a much larger group, for example, a focused discussion of one work of art in a museum grouping of pieces by style or a study of a particular typical student in a class visit for an education class.

CAREER-RELATED TOPICS

14. Use specific examples to support one of the following statements as applied to business or work.

    a. It's not what you know, it's who you know.

    b. Don't burn your bridges.

    c. Like Legos, business is a matter of connections.

    d. The customer is always right.

    e. A kind word turns away wrath.

15. Discuss how a specific service or product can benefit its users. Use an example or examples.

WRITER'S GUIDELINES   Exemplification

BRANDON BRIDGE

1. Use examples to explain, convince, or amuse.

2. Use examples that are vivid, specific, and representative.

   - Vivid examples attract attention.
   - Specific examples are identifiable.
   - Representative examples are typical and therefore the basis for generalization.

3. Tie your examples clearly to your thesis.

4. Draw your examples from what you have read, heard, and experienced.

5. Brainstorm a list or cluster of possible examples before you write.

6. The order and number of your examples will depend on the purpose stated in your topic sentence or thesis.

7. **Consider using the Writing Process Worksheet and the Brandon Guide for Revising and Editing for completing your assignment and the Revising and Editing Charts after your assignment is returned.**

Practicing the Brandon Guide for Revising and Editing

PATTERN: EXEMPLIFICATION

The Fighting Founding Mothers

MAXINE JOHNSON

(A) People still argue about how well women can fight in military situations, but in the War of Independence more than two hundred years ago, as a matter of historical fact, several women did distinguish themselves for bravery. (B) Paul Revere recieved credit for riding to warn the Patriots in Massachusetts in 1775 that the British were coming on a military move against the Militias at Concord and Lexington. (C) In fact, he did warn some Patriots. (D) Later, he was stopped by the British. (E) Who did get through? (F) Two courageous women did. (G) One being Sybil Ludington, a teen-aged woman. (H) fearlessly rode her horse like a bat out of hell. (I) Another plucky woman became famously known as Molly Pitcher. (J) Her real name was Mary Hayes. (K) During the war, she, like many women, went with her husband to the battlefield. (L) While weapons were firing, she brought the male soldiers pitchers of water (hence her nickname) and helped load the cannon her husband fired. (M) After her husband was shot at the Battle of Monmouth in 1778 she boldly took over the cannon, fought bravely, and carried a desperately wounded man for two miles to safety. (N) Finally, the Patriots won the battle with her help. (O) More than two hundred years ago, these women proved that their gender can be brave and fight as well as men in every sense.

EXERCISE 12   Revise and Edit with the Brandon Guide

Revise with **C L U E S S** (pronounce as "clues" for easy memorization).

1. **C**oherence: Connect your ideas. Circle the five connective words and phrases that appear at the beginning of sentences and refer to time.

2. **L**anguage: Use words appropriate for your purpose and audience. Cross out the one cliché (refers to speed) and replace it with your own fresh expression.

3. **U**nity: Stay on your topic. Underline the topic sentence and the closing sentence. They unify the paragraph.

4. **E**mphasis: Call attention to your important ideas. Draw a box around the key word and its related words that are used for unity and emphasis seven times.

5. **S**upport: Back up your controlling ideas with evidence and logic. In the left margin, write in the word *Example* to label the two examples that are used for support.

6. **S**entences: Write correct, effective sentences with structural variety. Combine sentences C and D by using one of these coordinating conjunctions—*for, and, nor, but, or, yet, so* (FANBOYS)—and by using the proper capitalization and punctuation.

Edit with C G P S (pronounce as "see GPS" for easy memorization).

7. **C**apitalization: One word that should begin with a capital letter is in lower-case. Make a line through that lowercase word and insert the capital letter above it.

8. **G**rammar: One "sentence" is actually a fragment because it does not have a verb. Find it, cross out the word that is posing as a verb, and write a true verb above it.

9. **P**unctuation: One sentence has an adverbial clause, a group of words that has a subject and verb but cannot stand alone, even with a period after it, because it acts as an adverb. Insert a comma after that word group.

10. **S**pelling: One word is misspelled. Cross it out and write the correct spelling above it.

9

Analysis by Division
Examining the Parts

 The noblest pleasure is the joy of understanding.

—LEONARDO DA VINCI

CHAPTER CONTENTS   BRANDON BRIDGE

When to Use Analysis by Division

FOR COLLEGE WRITING ASSIGNMENTS

- If a writing assignment in any class requires that you divide your subject into parts and discuss how the parts relate to make up a unit, then you will turn to analysis by division. The principle is essentially the same regardless of the unit: a short story, a person, an organism, a rock, a painting, or a piece of music.

IN CAREERS AND AT THE WORKPLACE

- Whether you are preparing for a career or are engaged in a career, analysis by division will serve you well as you deal with any unit: requirements to complete your degree (how each one is part of the unit and relates to the other parts), the chain of command at work (each part, or level, with responsibilities and rewards), the job description at the workplace (each aspect separate and all related to a work assignment), the performance review (made up of categories of how you will be [are] evaluated and, perhaps, how you [will] evaluate others).

ANALYSIS BY DIVISION IN A CARTOON

THE QUIGMANS   by **Buddy Hickerson**

Date with a movie critic.

Writing Analysis by Division

PROCEDURE

If you need to explain how something works or exists as a unit, you will write an analysis by division. You will break down a unit (your subject) into its parts and explain how each part functions in relation to the operation or existence of the whole. The most important word here is *unit*. You begin with something that can stand alone or can be regarded separately: a poem, a heart, a painting, a car, a bike, a person, a school, a committee. The following procedure will guide you in writing an analysis by division: Move from subject to principle, to division, to relationship.

Step 1. Begin with something that is a unit (subject).

Step 2. State one principle by which the unit can function.

Step 3. Divide the unit into parts according to that principle.

Step 4. Discuss each of the parts in relation to the unit.

You might apply that procedure to writing about a good boss in the following way:

1.	Unit	Manager
2.	Principle of function	Effective as a leader
3.	Parts based on the principle	Fair, intelligent, stable, competent in the field
4.	Relationship to the unit	Consider each part in relation to the person's effectiveness as a manager.

ORGANIZATION

In an essay of analysis by division, the main parts are likely to be the main points of your outline or main extensions of your cluster. If they are anything else, reconsider your organization. A basic outline of an analysis by division might look like this:

Thesis: To be effective as a leader, a manager needs specific qualities.
  I. Fairness
 II. Intelligence
III. Stability
IV. Competence in the field

SEQUENCE OF PARTS

The order in which you discuss the parts will vary according to the nature of the unit and the way you view it. Here are some possible sequences for organizing the parts of a unit:

- **Time:** The sequence of the parts in your paragraph or essay can be mainly chronological, or time-based (if you are dealing with something that functions on its own, such as a heart, with the parts presented in relation to stages of the function).
- **Space:** If your unit is a visual object, especially if, like a pencil, it does nothing by itself, you may discuss the parts in relation to space. In the example of the

pencil, the parts of the pencil begin at the top with the eraser and end at the bottom with the pencil point.

- **Emphasis:** Because the most emphatic location of any piece of writing is the end (the second most emphatic point is the beginning), consider placing the most significant part of the unit at the end.

Transitional Words

Consider using the following transitional words to improve coherence by connecting ideas with ideas, sentences with sentences, and paragraphs with paragraphs.

FOR ANALYSIS BY DIVISION: Time or numbering: first, second, third, another, last, finally, soon, later, currently, before, along with, another part [section, component]

SPACE: above, below, to the left, to the right, near, beyond, under, next to, in the background, split, divide

EMPHASIS: most important, equally important, central to the, to this end, as a result, taken collectively, with this purpose in mind, working with the, in fact, of course, above all, most of all, especially, primarily, without question

FOR ALL PATTERNS OF WRITING: The HOTSHOT CAT words: However, Otherwise, Therefore, Similarly, Hence, On the other hand, Then, Consequently, Also, Thus

TWO USES OF ANALYSIS BY DIVISION: THE RESTAURANT REVIEW AND THE CAREER REVIEW

From the wide range of uses of analysis by division mentioned in the introduction, two are featured in this chapter: the restaurant review and the career review.

Restaurant Review

Definition

The **restaurant review** is an article of one or more paragraphs that describes three elements: ambiance, service, and food.

- **Ambiance** is the atmosphere, mood, or feeling of a place. For restaurants, it may begin with landscaping and architecture (building style). Ambiance is certainly produced by what is inside, such as the furnishings, seating, style, upkeep, sounds, sights, smells, behavior of other customers, and management style—whatever produces that mood or the feeling, even if it is franchise plastic and elevator music.
- **Service** is mainly concerned with food delivery and those who do it: their attitude, manners, helpfulness, promptness, accuracy, and availability. Self-service or pickup establishments would be judged by similar standards.
- **Food** is the emphasis—its variety, quality, quantity, price, and presentation.

Writing the Review

- Use first person (*I*) as you relate your experience in a particular restaurant or chain.
- If possible, base your evaluation on more than one food item. Here is a low-cost way to do that: Dine with others and ask your companions to order different foods. Then ask them if you can taste (two small bites will suffice) what they are served, thus increasing your experience. Offering to pay a portion of their check may make others more receptive to sharing their food.
- While you are dining, use a simple outline or listing to make sure you have information on ambiance, service, and food. Copy names of foods and prices from the menu. Use quotation marks around any descriptive phrases for items you copy.
- You need not separate comments on ambiance, service, and food or present them in a particular order, but be specific in your details and examples. Use quotation marks for any descriptive phrases you borrow from the menu.

An example of a professional restaurant review, "Chicago in the O.C." appears later in the chapter.

Career Review

The career review is a summary of a career, which you will personalize by relating it to your background, interests, skills, and other relevant work-related matters.

The organization and development of your career review follow the basic procedure for writing an analysis by division as you move from unit to division to development. It is logical, systematic, and highly manageable.

- The unit for an essay is the career field and your quest of that career field.
- The parts of that unit are the parts of the career field and your quest. Those parts can be further subdivided.
- The extent of the dividing may vary, depending on your particular purpose (assignment), the expected audience, and, if applicable, your current involvement in the career field.
- Libraries have an abundance of material that will provide you with career information you can summarize in your review. Your best overall source is probably the *Occupational Outlook Handbook* by the U.S. Department of Labor. It is available in print and online and is ideal for you to summarize selectively for your career review. Updated and published every two years, the handbook covers hundreds of career fields, providing information about earnings, prerequisites of training and education, expected job prospects, job duties, and working conditions. Of course, you should give credit to your source(s) in your list of work(s) cited at the end of your review. This is the online address:

  U.S. Department of Labor. *Occupational Outlook Handbook*. 8 Jan. 2014. Web. <http://www.bls.gov/ooh/>.

- The following main-part outline shows some useful divisions for an essay as a career review. For a shorter essay, just select the main parts that fit the assignment you have in mind. For an even shorter assignment of a paragraph, subdivide one of these Roman-numeral parts for basic organization of your career review, or analysis by division.

Unit: (the career itself)

Divisions: (parts of the unit, the career itself)

   I. My background, interests, and skills

   II. My desired field—an overview

   III. Working conditions, pay, benefits

   IV. Requirements for employment

   V. My step-by-step plan to enter this field

An example of a student career review in the form of an analysis by division appears later in the chapter.

FINDING PATTERNS IN PHOTOS

EXERCISE 1　An Image-Based Activity for Groups or Individuals

Multitasking women climbing ladders to success

Trina Dalziel/Motif/Corbis

The artwork illustrates the incredible effort that many working mothers put forth to achieve their goals. While each person defines success differently, this effort often involves balancing the demands of home life and work life.

Focus on a working mother you know who is juggling different roles. Then select six roles from the left column, rank them according to what you know about the working mother you have in mind, and list those roles on the lines in the right column.

1. Worker   I. _____

2. Entrepreneur   II. _____

3. Parent   III. _____

4. Student   IV. _____

5. Community leader   V. _____

6. Caretaker   VI. _____

7. Volunteer

8. Partner

9. Athlete

10. Advocate

If your instructor directs you to do so, write a paragraph or an essay based on the six roles shown in your outline. Discuss the importance of prioritizing and creating balance.

Consider personalizing this subject if it touches your life or that of someone you know well.

Practicing Patterns of Analysis by Division

In analysis by division, Roman-numeral headings are almost always parts of the unit you are discussing as your subject. Learning to divide the unit into parts will help you move through your assignment quickly and efficiently.

EXERCISE 2   Writing Patterns

Fill in the blanks as if you were organizing material for a paragraph or an essay. Have a specific unit in mind.

1. Unit: friend, relative, hero, or role model
   Principle: that which defines the person
   Name of the person (may be fictitious): _____

   I. _____

   II. _____

   III. _____

   IV. _____

2. Unit: physical object such as a pencil, shoe, baseball, or pair of glasses
   Principle: that which makes the object functional
   Specific name of the unit: _____

   I. _____

   II. _____

   III. _____

   IV. _____

EXERCISE 3   Writing Patterns

Fill in the blanks as if you were organizing material for a paragraph or an essay. Have a specific unit in mind.

1. Unit: movie, television program, or novel
   Principle: that which makes the unit excellent
   Specific name of the unit: _____

   I. _____

   II. _____

   III. _____

   IV. _____

2. Unit: family, relationship, club, or class

   Principle: that which makes the unit excellent

   Specific name of the unit: _____

      I. _____

     II. _____

    III. _____

    IV. _____

Readings for Critical Thinking, Discussion, and Writing

READING STRATEGIES AND OBJECTIVES

Underlining and annotating these reading selections will help you answer the questions that follow the selections, discuss the material in class, and prepare for reading-based writing assignments. As you underline and annotate, pay special attention to the author's writing skills, logic, and message, and consider the relevance of the material to your own experiences and values.

PARAGRAPH

The Zones of the Sea

LEONARD ENGEL

In this paragraph reprinted from The Sea, published by Time-Life Books, the author shows that the sea can be divided into four zones.

The life of the ocean is divided into distinct realms, each with its own group of creatures that feed upon each other and depend on each other in different ways. There is, first of all, the tidal zone, where land and sea meet. Then comes the realm of the shallow seas around the continents, which goes down to about 500 feet. It is in these two zones that the vast majority of marine life occurs. The deep ocean adds two regions, the zone of light and the zone of perpetual darkness. In the clear waters of the western Pacific, light could still be seen at a depth of 1,000 feet through the portholes of the *Trieste* on its seven-mile dive. But for practical purposes the zone of light ends at about 600 feet. Below that level there is too little light to support the growth of the "grass" of the sea—the tiny, single-celled green plants whose ability to form sugar and starch with the aid of sunlight makes them the base of the great food pyramid of the ocean.

EXERCISE 4 Discussion and Critical Thinking

1. What are the four zones of the sea?

2. Is the paragraph organized by space or by time?

3. What characterizes each zone?

4. Draw a cross section of the sea to show the four zones. Make it as elaborate with creatures and plants as you like. Consider using a separate sheet of paper for your drawing. Optional: Include aquatic and other creatures.

ESSAYS

A Partial Remembrance of a Puerto Rican Childhood*

JUDITH ORTIZ COFER

Born in Puerto Rico in 1952, Judith Ortiz Cofer moved with her parents to New Jersey, where she learned a new language and a new culture while in elementary school. Now an author and a university professor, she writes poignantly about her experiences trying to embrace two cultures with different customs and different languages. This essay comes from Silent Dancing: A Partial Remembrance of a Puerto Rican Childhood (1990).

1   My grandmother's house is like a chambered nautilus; it has many rooms, yet it is not a mansion. Its proportions are small and its design simple. It is a house that has grown organically, according to the needs of its inhabitants. To all of us in the family it is known as *la casa de Mamá*. It is the place of our origin; the stage for our memories and dreams of island life.

2   I remember how in my childhood it sat on stilts; this was before it had a downstairs. It rested on its perch like a great blue bird, not a flying sort of bird, more like a nesting hen, but with spread wings. Grandfather had built it soon after their marriage. He was a painter and housebuilder by trade, a poet and meditative man by nature. As each of their eight children were born, new rooms were added. After a few years, the paint did not exactly match, nor the materials, so that there was a chronology to it, like the rings of a tree, and Mamá could tell you the history of each room in her casa, and thus the genealogy of the family along with it.

3   Her room is the heart of the house. Though I have seen it recently, and both woman and room have diminished in size, changed by the new perspective of my eyes, now capable of looking over countertops and tall beds, it

* "A Partial Remembrance of a Puerto Rican Childhood" is reprinted with permission from the publisher of *Silent Dancing: A Partial Remembrance of a Puerto Rican Childhood* by Judith Ortiz Cofer (1999 Arte Publico Press-University of Houston).

is not this picture I carry in my memory of Mamá's casa. Instead, I see her room as a queen's chamber where a small woman loomed large, a throne-room with a massive four-poster bed in its center which stood taller than a child's head. It was on this bed where her own children had been born that the smallest grandchildren were allowed to take naps in the afternoon; here too was where Mamá secluded herself to dispense private advice to her daughters, sitting on the edge of the bed, looking down at whoever sat on the rocker where generations of babies had been sung to sleep. To me she looked like a wise empress right out of the fairy tales I was addicted to reading.

4   Though the room was dominated by the mahogany four-poster, it also contained all of Mamá's symbols of power. On her dresser instead of cosmetics there were jars filled with herbs: *yerba buena*, *yerba mala*, the making of purgatives and teas to which we were all subjected during childhood crises. She had a steaming cup for anyone who could not, or would not, get up to face life on any given day. If the acrid aftertaste of her cures for malingering did not get you out of bed, then it was time to call *el doctor*.

5   And there was the monstrous chifforobe she kept locked with a little golden key she did not hide. This was a test of her dominion over us; though my cousins and I wanted a look inside that massive wardrobe more than anything, we never reached for that little key lying on top of her Bible on the dresser. This was also where she placed her earrings and rosary at night. God's word was her security system. This chifforobe was the place where I imagined she kept jewels, satin slippers, and elegant sequined, silk gowns of heartbreaking fineness. I lusted after those imaginary costumes. I had heard that Mamá had been a great beauty in her youth, and the belle of many balls. My cousins had other ideas as to what she kept in that wooden vault: its secret could be money (Mamá did not hand cash to strangers, banks were out of the question, so there were stories that her mattress was stuffed with dollar bills, and that she buried coins in jars in her garden under rosebushes, or kept them in her inviolate chifforobe); there might be that legendary gun salvaged from the Spanish-American conflict over the Island. We went wild over suspected treasures that we made up simply because children have to fill locked trunks with something wonderful.

6   On the wall above the bed hung a heavy silver crucifix. Christ's agonized head hung directly over Mamá's pillow. I avoided looking at this weapon suspended over where her head would lay; and on the rare occasions when I was allowed to sleep on that bed, I scooted down to the safe middle of the mattress, where her body's impression took me in like a mother's lap. Having taken care of the obligatory religious decoration with a crucifix, Mamá covered the other walls with objects sent to her over the years by her children in the States. *Los Nueva Yores* were represented by, among other things, a postcard of Niagara Falls from her son Hernán, postmarked, Buffalo, N.Y. In a conspicuous gold frame hung a large color photograph of her daughter Nena, her husband and their five children at the entrance to Disneyland in California. From us she had gotten a black lace fan. Father had brought it to her from a tour of duty with the Navy in Europe (on Sundays she would remove it from its hook on the wall to fan herself at Sunday mass). Each year more items were added as the family grew and dispersed, and every object in the room had a story attached to it, a *cuento* which Mamá would bestow on anyone who received the privilege of a day alone with her. It was almost worth pretending to be sick, though the bitter herb purgatives of the body were a big price to pay for the spirit revivals of her story-telling.

EXERCISE 5   Vocabulary Highlights

Write a short definition of each word as it is used in the essay. (Paragraph numbers are given in parentheses.) Be prepared to use the words in sentences.

perspective (3)	inviolate (5)
massive (3)	suspended (6)
dispense (3)	obligatory (6)
acrid (4)	conspicuous (6)
chifforobe (5)	bestow (6)

EXERCISE 6   Discussion and Critical Thinking

1. Ortiz Cofer says her grandmother's house "is like a chambered nautilus" (paragraph 1), a mollusk with a spiral, pearly lined shell with a series of air-filled chambers. Is that figure of speech (simile) a good representation of the house? Why or why not?

2. List at least two other instances in which she uses figures of speech.

3. Why does she consider her grandmother's room the heart of the house?

4. How does her perspective of her grandmother's room change over time?

5. Ortiz Cofer helps you imagine her grandmother's room by describing it in detail. List five specific, concrete visual images she uses in paragraph 6.

Men Are from Mars, Women Are from Venus*

JOHN GRAY

As a writer, marriage counselor, and seminar leader, John Gray specializes in understanding and dealing with gender difference. This excerpt comes from his best-selling book Men Are from Mars, Women Are from Venus *(1992), in which he says men and women are so different they might as well have come from different planets. Like all generalizations, his do not perfectly fit all individuals within groups (genders), but he provides much for you to consider.*

1   The most frequently expressed complaint women have about men is that men don't listen. Either a man completely ignores [a woman] when she speaks to him, or he listens for a few beats, assesses what is bothering her, and then proudly puts on his Mr. Fix-It cap and offers her a solution to make her feel better.

Excerpt from "Mr. Fix-it and the Home Improvement Committee" (pp. 15–23), from Men Are from Mars, Women Are from Venus *by John Gray. Copyright © 1992 by John Gray. Reprinted by permission of HarperCollins Publishers.*

He is confused when she doesn't appreciate this gesture of love. No matter how many times she tells him that he's not listening, he doesn't get it and keeps doing the same thing. She wants empathy, but he thinks she wants solutions.

2   The most frequently expressed complaint men have about women is that women are always trying to change them. When a woman loves a man she feels responsible to assist him in growing and tries to help him improve the way he does things. She forms a home-improvement committee, and he becomes her primary focus. No matter how much he resists her help, she persists—waiting for any opportunity to help him or tell him what to do. She thinks she's nurturing him, while he feels he's being controlled. Instead, he wants her acceptance.

3   These two problems can finally be solved by first understanding why men offer solutions and why women seek to improve. Let's pretend to go back in time, where by observing life on Mars and Venus—before the planets discovered one another or came to Earth—we can gain some insights into men and women.

4   Martians value power, competency, efficiency, and achievement. They are always doing things to prove themselves and develop their power and skills. Their sense of self is defined through their ability to achieve results. They experience fulfillment primarily through success and accomplishment.

5   Everything on Mars is a reflection of these values. Even their dress is designed to reflect their skills and competence. Police officers, soldiers, businessmen, scientists, cab-drivers, technicians, and chefs all wear uniforms or at least hats to reflect their competence and power.

6   They don't read magazines like *Psychology Today, Self*, or *People*. They are more concerned with outdoor activities, like hunting, fishing, and racing cars. They are interested in the news, weather, and sports and couldn't care less about romance novels and self-help books.

7   They are more interested in "objects" and "things" rather than people and feelings. Even today on Earth, while women fantasize about romance, men fantasize about powerful cars, faster computers, gadgets, gizmos, and new more powerful technology. Men are preoccupied with the "things" that can help them express power by creating results and achieving their goals.

8   Achieving goals is very important to a Martian because it is a way for him to prove his competence and thus feel good about himself. And for him to feel good about himself he must achieve these goals by himself. Someone else can't achieve them for him. Martians pride themselves on doing things all by themselves. Autonomy is a symbol of efficiency, power, and competence.

9   Understanding this Martian characteristic can help women understand why men resist so much being corrected or being told what to do. To offer a man unsolicited advice is to presume that he doesn't know what to do or that he can't do it on his own. Men are very touchy about this, because the issue of competence is so very important to them.

10   Because he is handling his problems on his own, a Martian rarely talks about his problems unless he needs expert advice. He reasons: "Why involve someone else when I can do it by myself?" He keeps his problems to himself unless he requires help from another to find a solution. Asking for help when you can do it yourself is perceived as a sign of weakness.

11   However, if he truly does need help, then it is a sign of wisdom to get it. In this case, he will find someone he respects and then talk about his problem. Talking about a problem on Mars is an invitation for advice. Another Martian

feels honored by the opportunity. Automatically he puts on his Mr. Fix-It hat, listens for a while, and then offers some jewels of advice.

12   This Martian custom is one of the reasons men instinctively offer solutions when women talk about problems. When a woman innocently shares upset feelings or explores out loud the problems of her day, a man mistakenly assumes she is looking for some expert advice. He puts on his Mr. Fix-It hat and begins giving advice; this is his way of showing love and of trying to help.

13   He wants to help her feel better by solving her problems. He wants to be useful to her. He feels he can be valued and thus worthy of her love when his abilities are used to solve her problems.

14   Once he has offered a solution, however, and she continues to be upset it becomes increasingly difficult for him to listen because his solution is being rejected and he feels increasingly useless.

15   He has no idea that by just listening with empathy and interest he can be supportive. He does not know that on Venus talking about problems is not an invitation to offer a solution.

16   Venusians have different values. They value love, communication, beauty, and relationships. They spend a lot of time supporting, helping, and nurturing one another. Their sense of self is defined through their feelings and the quality of their relationships. They experience fulfillment through sharing and relating.

17   Everything on Venus reflects these values. Rather than building highways and tall buildings, the Venusians are more concerned with living together in harmony, community, and loving cooperation. Relationships are more important than work and technology. In most ways their world is the opposite of Mars.

18   They do not wear uniforms like the Martians (to reveal their competence). On the contrary, they enjoy wearing a different outfit every day, according to how they are feeling. Personal expression, especially of their feelings, is very important. They may even change outfits several times a day as their mood changes.

19   Communication is of primary importance. To share their personal feelings is much more important than achieving goals and success. Talking and relating to one another is a source of tremendous fulfillment.

20   This is hard for a man to comprehend. He can come close to understanding a woman's experience of sharing and relating by comparing it to the satisfaction he feels when he wins a race, achieves a goal, or solves a problem.

21   Instead of being goal oriented, women are relationship oriented; they are more concerned with expressing their goodness, love, and caring. Two Martians go to lunch to discuss a project or business goal; they have a problem to solve. In addition, Martians view going to a restaurant as an efficient way to approach food: no shopping, no cooking, and no washing dishes. For Venusians, going to lunch is an opportunity to nurture a relationship, for both giving support to and receiving support from a friend. Women's restaurant talk can be very open and intimate, almost like the dialogue that occurs between therapist and patient.

22   On Venus, everyone studies psychology and has at least a master's degree in counseling. They are very involved in personal growth, spirituality, and everything that can nurture life, healing, and growth. Venus is covered with parks, organic gardens, shopping centers, and restaurants.

23   Venusians are very intuitive. They have developed this ability through centuries of anticipating the needs of others. They pride themselves on being considerate of the needs and feelings of others. A sign of great love is to offer help and assistance to another Venusian without being asked.

24   Because proving one's competence is not as important to a Venusian, offering help is not offensive, and needing help is not a sign of weakness. A man,

however, may feel offended because when a woman offers advice he doesn't feel she trusts his ability to do it himself.

25   A woman has no conception of this male sensitivity because for her it is another feather in her hat if someone offers to help her. It makes her feel loved and cherished. But offering help to a man can make him feel incompetent, weak, and even unloved.

26   On Venus it is a sign of caring to give advice and suggestions. Venusians firmly believe that when something is working it can always work better. Their nature is to want to improve things. When they care about someone, they freely point out what can be improved and suggest how to do it. Offering advice and constructive criticism is an act of love.

27   Mars is very different. Martians are more solution oriented. If something is working, their motto is don't change it. Their instinct is to leave it alone if it is working. "Don't fix it unless it is broken" is a common expression.

28   When a woman tries to improve a man, he feels she is trying to fix him. He receives the message that he is broken. She doesn't realize her caring attempts to help him may humiliate him. She mistakenly thinks she is just helping him to grow.

EXERCISE 7   Discussion and Critical Thinking

Although this essay is structured as comparison and contrast, it is organized in a subject-by-subject pattern, and each subject (men and women) is covered separately as an analysis by division. Paragraphs 4 through 15 make up an analysis by division about men, and paragraphs 16 through 28 do the same for women.

1. What are the divisions that make up the nature of men in paragraphs 4 through 15?

2. What are the divisions that make up the nature of women in paragraphs 16 through 28?

3. According to Gray, how do styles in communication affect multiple areas of relationships—values, careers, friendships, activities, family, and so on?

4. Do his views apply equally to different economic and social classes?

5. Is Gray suggesting that men and women should break out of their patterns of thinking and behaving? Explain.

6. Do the people you know fit into these behavioral patterns detailed by Gray? Discuss.

7. What are the shortcomings of Gray's assessment of men and women?

RESTAURANT REVIEW

Chicago in the O.C.

FLOYD GARRISON

Floyd Garrison is a student and freelance writer.

1   Tony's Little Italy in Placentia, CA is one of the best pizza places I know, and the many happy customers there will agree with me. In North Orange County, California, true fans of deep dish–style pizza know Tony's mostly by word of mouth. Tony's is a little restaurant in a small strip mall that looks like any other, but it's not. It's the home of some of the best pizza west of Chicago.

Ambiance

2   I have heard that Tony originally came from Palermo, Italy, but his restaurant is all Chicago. The atmosphere of the place is definitely not fancy, but it really seems like what a pizza store in Chicago would be like. The walls are covered with sports memorabilia from Chicago teams like the Bears and the Cubs, but don't look for anything from the White Sox. Clearly Tony likes only one of the hometown baseball teams. And in case people don't know that he is a Cubs fan, all they have to do is look at the wall which is covered in a giant mural showing a view of the diamond at Wrigley Field as seen from the stands. Banners celebrating winning teams complete with pictures commemorating the Super Bowl team coached by Mike Ditka make this place a shrine to Chicago's sports traditions. The tables and chairs are pretty basic— formica tops with vinyl padded chairs. Two TVs show sporting events most of the time.

Service

3   Service at Tony's is friendly, but this is not a full-service place. People order and pay ahead of time with a beverage bar taking care of the drinks. The restaurant is kept clean, but many customers are simply waiting at tables for their take-out orders—usually pizza—to be ready. And that's the thing about Tony's. The pizza takes a while, sometimes about 45 minutes, but that's okay. This is the best deep dish pizza around, so people are content to have a beer or soda and wait for the mouth-watering delicacy that will eventually be delivered to them.

Food

4   And now, the real point of Tony's—the pizza! This pizza is "bomb"! Nearly two inches thick layered with delicious melted cheese, sauce, and all the best ingredients like pepperoni, sausage, green peppers, and mushrooms. And the

best part just might be the perfectly baked crust. One piece is a meal, but most people can't stop at one piece. Tony's also has delicious Italian submarine sandwiches, pasta dishes, and thin crust pizza, but the thick crust deep dish Chicago style is what it's all about—worth the wait every time. People from Chicago who have visited Tony's know the truth. If you don't have the time to fly to "Chi Town," you gotta drive to Tony's.

EXERCISE 8   Discussion and Critical Thinking

1. Why do you think the reviewer begins by discussing the ambiance?

2. Was this review helpful in explaining the three parts of Tony's Little Italy as a restaurant? Why or why not?

3. What additional information might be useful for potential customers?

STUDENT PARAGRAPH AND ESSAYS

Student Nancy Samuels was faced with writing on the topic of "a personal, popular, or historical hero." She didn't have to go to the library. Right in her household she found her subject—her mother. She writes of an ordinary person who faced a difficult challenge and succeeded, in a situation in which others gave up too easily. You can follow her writing process by studying her Writing Process Worksheet. To conserve space here, the freewriting and the first draft with revisions and editing have been deleted from her submission.

BRANDON BRIDGE

Writing Process Worksheet

Name Nancy Samuels   **Title** More Than Ordinary   **Due Date** Tuesday, May 1, 9:30 a.m.

Use the back of this page or separate paper if you need more space.

Assignment

In the space below, write whatever you need to know about your assignment, including information about the topic, audience, pattern of writing, length, whether to include a rough draft or revised drafts, and whether your paper must be typed.

Write a paragraph of analysis by division about a personal, popular, or historical hero. Name the hero and stress the traits that make that person a hero. Assume that your readers do not know your subject well. Submit this completed worksheet, one or more rough drafts, and a typed final draft.

Stage One

Explore   Freewrite, brainstorm (list), cluster, or take notes as directed by your instructor.

Listing

Unit: Mother
Principle of function: person as hero
    Parts based on the principle:
       optimistic
       persevering
       considerate
       courageous
       tolerant
       self-sacrificing

Stage Two

Organize Write a topic sentence or thesis; label the subject and the focus parts.

<u>My mother</u> is the best example of a hero I can think of.
    subject   focus

Write an outline or an outline alternative. For reading-based writing, include references and short quotations with page numbers as support in the outline.

  I. Optimistic
    A. Would not believe bad news
    B. Consulted several doctors
    C. Had a positive goal

 II. Persevering
    A. Becomes my brother's therapist
    B. Worked with him for three years

III. Courageous
    A. Does not listen to others
    B. Would not accept failure

IV. Self-sacrificing
    A. Concentrating on helping son
    B. Neglected self

Stage Three

Write On separate paper, write and then revise your paragraph or essay as many times as necessary for **c**oherence, **l**anguage (usage, tone, and diction), **u**nity, **e**mphasis, **s**upport, and **s**entences (**CLUESS**). Read your work aloud to hear and correct any grammatical errors or awkward-sounding sentences.

Edit any problems in fundamentals, such as **c**apitalization, **g**rammar, **p**unctuation, and **s**pelling (**CGPS**).

Final Draft

MORE THAN ORDINARY
Nancy Samuels

Topic sentence
(Unit and principle)

My mother is the best example of a hero I can think of. No one will read about her in a book about heroes, but within her small circle of friends, her traits of heroism are well-known. My younger brother is the special beneficiary of her heroism. He was in an accident when he was five years old, and the doctor told us that he would never walk. My mother listened respectfully, but she didn't believe him. She had optimism. She went to another doctor and then another. Finally she found one who prescribed exercises. She worked with my brother for three years. Day after dismal day, she persevered. It wasn't just her working with him that helped my brother. It was her raw courage in the face of failure. My brother worked with her. They both were courageous. We other family members weren't. To us my brother and mother were acting like a couple of people blinded by hope. We thought my mother especially, the leader, was in prolonged denial. But in three years my brother was walking. He won't be an athlete; nevertheless, he gets around. We're proud of him, but we know—and he knows—that without Mother he would never have walked. She sacrificed years of her life for him. Of course, she's not a miracle worker. Most of the time, doctors are right, and some injured people can never walk. But the ones, like my brother, who somewhere have that hidden ability need that special someone like my mother. She's more than ordinary. She's a hero.

(Part) Trait

(Part) Trait

(Part) Trait

Trait

EXERCISE 9   Discussion and Critical Thinking

1. What are the main traits of Samuels's heroic mother?

2. Is she a miracle worker?

3. Will her kind of strength always succeed? Explain.

4. Would she have been heroic if she had not succeeded in helping her son?

READING-BASED WRITING

Elvis Presley: King of the Twentieth Century

EMMETT DAVIS

Emmett Davis faced an assignment in analysis by division in which he would discuss the qualities that made a person successful. He was expected to refer to at least two sources. Davis turned to the early days of rock and roll, his special interest. Almost every source he skimmed, both on the Internet and in his college library's database, contained discussion of Elvis Presley, who became his subject.

1   After having moved a decade into the twenty-first century, we still look back and revise lists of top people of the previous one hundred years. One much-discussed category is the Greatest Performers in Popular Music. Although I have trouble choosing the top person in some categories, in this one I have no problem. Of course, it's Elvis Presley. Four factors stand out and make my choice easy: he was good looking, he could sing, he had style, and he influenced the main world of popular music, which we call "rock 'n' roll."

2   As for his looks, he was darkly handsome, some would say even beautiful, with thick, unruly hair and a sneering smile that appealed to the rebellious side of young people. Dick Clark, producer and host of American Bandstand for four decades, said that youth "copied his style. People imitated his gestures, dressed like him, wanted to be him (or his woman)" (148). Much has been made of the young Elvis and the old Elvis. The young was the person of slender body in a leather jacket. From that image he soon morphed into his spangled outfit phase, a reflection of his ties with country music entertainers but also becoming the model for the glitter look of numerous rock stars. Unfortunately, toward the end of his life, he put on too much weight and favored white bejeweled jump suits.

3   As for singing, he had a powerful, deep voice with a wide range similar to the big voices in rhythm and blues and black gospel music he had listened to and loved as he grew up in Mississippi and Tennessee. Early in his career he was sometimes criticized for not sounding more like traditional crooners. Although it was true that he did howl, wail, and shout in certain arrangements, he could sing religious songs and simple love ballads such as "Teddy Bear" and "Love Me Tender" with great clarity and warmth.

4   When he was on stage, his style was personal, as he shook his hips and belted out songs like "Heartbreak Hotel" and "You Ain't Nothin' But a Hound Dog." While making the guitar respectable, he popularized the driving rhythm of rock. He made music more personal and more aggressive. His body language may look tame today, but in the 1950s, it was revolutionary.

5   Because he was so different and so good, he influenced and inspired others who would become famous artists of rock 'n' roll. Groups like the Beatles and the Rolling Stones gave him credit for his innovations. His influence even extends to academia. In 1995 the University of Mississippi convened an international conference entitled "In Search of Elvis." Professor Vernon Chadwick, who helped organize the conference, said that Elvis "is better known and in many cases more influential than William Faulkner" (Geier 14). Though Chadwick's statement may have upset some of his colleagues, it is well in line with what many of his fans believe.

6   Some fanatical fans believe Elvis is off hiding in the witness protection program and shopping at the K-Marts and WalMarts of the world, but, to me, he's alive in a more important way: he's a legend—he's the Greatest Performer in Popular Music for the Twentieth Century.

Works Cited

Clark, Dick. "Remembering 'Presleymania.'" *Newsweek* 8 June 1998: 148.
    Print.
Geier, Thom. "Eggheads for Elvis." *U.S. News & World Report* 7 Aug. 1995: 14.
    Print.

EXERCISE 10   Discussion and Critical Thinking

1. Which sentence in the first paragraph is the thesis?

2. What is the unit being considered?

3. What is the principle for dividing the unit?

4. Underline the topic sentences that indicate the parts of the unit and, in the margin to the left, use single words to annotate those parts.

5. Emmett Davis has no reservation in picking his "King." Of course, this is all a matter of opinion, but would you argue for another person? If so, who and why?

6. Do you find anything objectionable to the use of the word *King* in referring to the greatest entertainer of the twentieth century?

CAREER-RELATED WRITING: THE CAREER REVIEW

Air Traffic Control as a Career

ROGER MYERS

One of the suggested assignments was to write an essay about a career choice. The entire process would be analyzed. That satisfied the interests of student Roger Myers, who had recently chosen a career field, following several years of vacillation.

1   Since my senior year in high school, I have changed my career goals several times. I was set on being a pilot, an anthropologist, and a teacher. At one time I even made plans to move to Alaska and work in construction and outdoor recreation. After exploring those careers by reading, talking to people in those fields, and taking some courses, I expanded my search and decided on my career for good. Now my short-range and long-range career goals are in place. I intend to be an air traffic controller.

2   I discovered the field when I was taking college aeronautics courses. One was in navigation and communication. On a field trip, we visited a local airport and went up into the control tower to watch landings and take-offs. I was fascinated by the way tower operators directed traffic. I signed up for an introductory course in air traffic control, which included more firsthand observations in the same tower.

Nature of the Work

3   The nature of the work can be reduced to two words: safety and expedition. Safety means simply to keep the aircraft from running into each other. Expedition means to maintain schedules. As every air traveler knows, the two important things are to reach the destination on time and to reach it without getting hurt.

4   There are basically three kinds of air traffic controllers. First there are the control tower operators. They work in a glassed-in cage above the airport. Their main job is to direct aircraft landings and departures. For departures, they direct pilots to taxi from terminals to the runway and finally give permission for take-offs. For arrivals, they receive information from other controllers about incoming flights and give information to pilots, including weather conditions, other traffic in the area, points for reporting in the landing patterns, and permission to land. The landings and the take-offs are coordinated. All of this is done routinely by the operators if the weather is good.

5   If the weather is bad, usually meaning limited visibility, another group of air traffic controllers are engaged: the approach controllers. They are often located in a radar room under the control tower. They use instruments to maintain separation between landing aircraft, guiding pilots on flight paths through low clouds and fog. During good weather they are likely to contact aircraft as they approach the airport and guide them in their descents, finally turning them over to the control tower for movement through the traffic pattern and to a safe landing.

6   A third group of controllers is responsible for enroute flight, monitoring and regulating the upper airspace between airports. There are twenty-one such control centers staffed by about seven hundred controllers. Enroute controllers work in teams using sophisticated radar equipment to maintain vertical and horizontal separation between aircraft. They also warn pilots about bad weather conditions and other potential hazards.

Working Conditions, Benefits, Pay, and Retirement

7   All three kinds of air traffic controllers work a basic 40-hour week and sometimes work overtime. Because the operation of air traffic occurs at all times, controllers work in shifts. Pay varies, depending on the job, but in 2000, the middle 50 percent of controllers made between $62,000 and $101,000. Senior controllers can make almost $150,000. Benefits include 13 to 26 days of vacation and health and life insurance. Because of the mental stress involved in making life-or-death decisions daily, controllers are allowed to retire after working for 25 years, are permitted to retire at the age of 50 with 20 years on the job, and must retire at the age of 56.

Training, Employment, and Job Outlook

8   Air traffic controllers are employed by the Federal Civil Service system. Most controllers go through this procedure: pass a rigorous series of tests, complete the Federal Aeronautics Association Academy for air traffic control, pass another series of examinations, begin work as an apprentice, and gradually

become a certified controller. Continued employment requires yearly physical and performance examinations, as well as periodic drug tests.

9   Individuals with military experience in air traffic control can bypass some of the requirements. They have a major advantage over other applicants because of their occupational knowledge (covered by a large part of the initial examinations) and because they have been certified as air traffic controllers according to basically the same standards used in the civilian field.

10   The job outlook is good, although the competition is keen. Despite recent airline downsizing, the airflight industry continues to thrive and will continue to grow. Even in the worst of times, air traffic controllers are not laid off.

My Final Approach

11   Although I could take the examination for the FAA Academy and probably do well because I have a good basic knowledge of the career field and have passed similar tests for my private pilot's license, I intend to complete two years at my community college and enlist in the United States Air Force. I have talked to recruiters who have assured that I can be guaranteed entrance to the military school for air traffic controllers. In the service, I can learn on the job and, upon being discharged in four years, be in an almost certain position to move into the FAA program. It is possible that I will enjoy military life and remain in the service as an air traffic controller.

Work Cited

United States. Dept. of Labor. *Occupational Outlook Handbook*. 2008–09 Edition. Web. 19 Dec. 2009.

EXERCISE 11   Discussion and Critical Thinking

1. What is the unit for analysis by division?

2. What are the divisions?

3. What is the principle on which the division is based?

4. What paragraph discusses that principle?

5. What double meaning does the last section heading, My Final Approach, carry?

Suggested Topics and Prompts for Writing Analysis by Division

READING-BASED WRITING

Reading-based writing requires you to read critically, write a reply that shows you understand what you have read, and give credit for ideas you borrow and words you quote. The form can be a summary, a reaction, or a two-part response (with separated summary and reaction). Documentation, in which you give credit for borrowed ideas and words, can be either formal (MLA style) or informal, as directed by your instructor. All of the forms of reading-based writing and documentation are discussed with examples in Chapter 6. Definitions of the three forms follow. Any form can be used for any reading selection in this book.

Summary

- The summary is a statement written in response to a reading. It restates only the most important points and uses original wording instead of the author's language. It should not contain added information or personal opinions.
- Because summaries are intended to restate only the main points of a reading, they are typically much shorter than the original text. Often, they are approximately a third of the length.

Reaction

- In the reaction, the meaning of what you have read will be central to the topic sentence of your paragraph or to the thesis of your essay.
- Although the reaction is not a personal narrative by itself, it may include personal experience to explain elements of the text. For example, if your source is about driving styles, your own experiences as a driver or an observer of drivers could be relevant in your analysis of the text.
- The reaction may incorporate a summary to convey a broad view of what you have read, but your summary should never be the main part of your reaction.

Two-Part Response

- The two-part response separates the summary from the reaction.
- This form will give you practice in separating your objective summary in the first part from your more personal evaluation, interpretation, or application in the second part, the reaction.

READING-BASED WRITING TOPICS

"The Zones of the Ocean"

1. Write a summary of "The Zones of the Ocean."

2. Write a paragraph in which you discuss the Earth's layers (crust, mantle, outer core, and inner core). Consider adding a drawing of your own.

"A Partial Remembrance of a Puerto Rican Childhood"

3. Write a summary of "A Partial Remembrance of a Puerto Rican Childhood."

4. Write a two-part response to the essay. Following the summary, write a reaction in which you discuss how Ortiz Cofer makes the house seem alive by personalizing it and by comparing it to a sea creature. Use references and quotations from the essay. Consider extending that discussion by relating Ortiz Cofer's observations to a house you know or remember well. Concentrating on an individual room and the overall layout, you would probably use analysis by division to explain how, over a period of time, that house took on the character of those who lived in it.

"Men Are from Mars, Women Are from Venus"

Although this essay is structured as comparison and contrast, it is organized in a subject-by-subject pattern, and each subject (men and women) is covered separately as an analysis by division. Paragraphs 4 through 15 make up an analysis by division about men, and paragraphs 16 through 28 do the same for women.

5. Select either the first unit (4–15) or the second (16–28) and evaluate it for accuracy. Does Gray oversimplify or stereotype or are his generalizations mostly sound? Do his views correspond with what you know about gender? Do they apply to people at all social levels? Use examples from what you have learned in school and from your experience. Refer to and quote from the essay.

"Chicago in the O.C."

6. Write a two-part response in which you first summarize and then react to Garrison's restaurant review. Be specific. Discuss the parts—ambiance, service, and food—by pointing out the usefulness or the shortcomings or both of his discussion of each part. Refer to the review and use quotations.

"Elvis Presley: King of the Twentieth Century"

7. Write a reaction in which you generally agree or disagree with Emmett Davis's view. Discuss Elvis's qualities: Are these divisions the right ones? Is Elvis the greatest in these ways collectively? Refer directly to the essay and use quotations. Should Davis have discussed Elvis's record sales and movie career?

8. If you believe some other performer is greater than Elvis and deserves to be called the greatest performer of the twentieth century, then write a reaction to argue your point by referring to Davis's essay, by using quotations, and by introducing other factors that should be considered.

GENERAL TOPICS

9. Write a restaurant review in which you divide your evaluation into three parts: ambiance, service, and food. You can even use subtitles for those three parts. You need not pick an expensive or elegant establishment. A fast-food place may do or even your school dining hall, though you may find much more originality and charm in a small, single-owner café. If there is no table service, then evaluate the counter service—the speed of service, the cheerfulness and overall appearance of the attendant, and the accuracy of the order. Pay attention to the cleanliness of the establishment and whether the décor, music in the background, and seating enhance or detract from your dining experience. If the place has a reputation, is that reputation justified? Be specific in your descriptions of all parts, give prices, and use a five-star rating system for each part. For a helpful model on a similar topic, review "Chicago in the O.C."

10. Write a paragraph or an essay about a person you know who has struggled mightily to help himself or herself or to help others and, therefore, deserves the title "hero." Structure your writing around the person's achievements and, especially, traits. For a helpful model on a similar topic, review "More Than Ordinary."

11. Choose one of the following subjects, narrow it to a focused topic, divide it into parts, and analyze it. For example, the general "a wedding ceremony" could be narrowed to the particulars "Jason and Lisa's wedding ceremony."

    a. A machine such as an automobile, a computer, a camera

    b. A city administration, a governmental agency, a school board, a student council

    c. A ceremony—wedding, graduation

    d. A holiday celebration, a pep rally, a sales convention, a religious revival

    e. An offensive team in football (any team in any game)

    f. A family, a relationship, a gang, a club, a sorority, a fraternity

    g. An album, a performance, a song, a singer, an actor, a musical group, a musical instrument

    h. A movie, a television program, a video game

    i. Any well-known person—athlete, politician, criminal, writer

CROSS-CURRICULAR TOPICS

12. Consider the units of material in a class you are taking or have taken. Each unit has its parts: a musical composition in a music appreciation class, a short story in an English class, an organ such as a heart in a biology class, a government in a political science class, a management team in a business class, a family in a sociology class, a painting in an art-history class, a teacher or student in an education class, and so on. Select one unit, consult your textbook(s), talk to your instructor(s), and follow the procedure for writing

an analysis by division. Credit your sources, and use quotation marks around material you borrow.

13. Select a unit from a class and discuss how it can be divided and the reasons for the division. It could be a heart, a brain, or skin in a life science class or a tree trunk in a botany class. (For a good example of a similar topic, see "The Zones of the Sea.") Then illustrate your analysis by division with your own labeled drawing of the unit.

CAREER-RELATED TOPICS

14. Write an analysis by division of your own career field or a career field that interests you. For a paragraph unit, write about one aspect, such as your background and aptitude, an overview of the field, working conditions and benefits, requirements for employment, or your plan for entering the field. For a longer analysis, write about several or all of the parts. For a helpful model on a similar topic, review "Air Traffic Control as a Career."

15. Explain how the parts of a product function as a unit.

16. Explain how each of several qualities of a specific person—such as his or her intelligence, sincerity, education, ability to communicate, manner, attitude, and appearance—makes that individual an effective salesperson, manager, or employee.

17. Explain how the demands or requirements for a particular job represent a comprehensive picture of that job.

18. Explain how the aspects of a particular service (such as friendly, competent, punctual, confidential) work together in a satisfactory manner.

WRITER'S GUIDELINES   Analysis by Division

BRANDON BRIDGE

Almost anything can be analyzed by division—for example, how the parts of the ear work in hearing, how the parts of the eye work in seeing, or how the parts of the heart work in pumping blood throughout the body. Subjects such as these are all approached with the same systematic procedure.

1. This is the procedure.

   Step 1. Begin with something that is a unit.

   Step 2. State the principle by which that unit functions.

   Step 3. Divide the unit into parts according to the principle.

   Step 4. Discuss each of the parts in relation to the unit.

2. This is the way you might apply that procedure to a good boss.

   - Unit   Manager
   - Principle of function   Effective as a leader

- Parts based on the principle   Fair, intelligent, stable, competent in the field
- Relationship to the unit   Consider each part in relation to the person's effectiveness as a manager.

3. This is how a basic outline of analysis by division might look:

Thesis: To be effective as a leader, a manager needs specific qualities.

   I. Fairness

   II. Intelligence

   III. Stability

   IV. Competence in the field

4. The restaurant review will almost certainly use the analysis-by-division pattern.

   - The main parts of a typical review are ambiance, service, and food.
   - The review should contain specific descriptive details, examples, and information from the menu.

5. The career review is another form of analysis by division.

   - The unit is the career quest itself.
   - The parts are the relevant matters that make up the entire quest for a career.
   - The following main-part outline shows some useful divisions for an essay as a career review. For a shorter essay, just select the main parts that fit the assignment you have in mind. For an even shorter assignment of a paragraph, subdivide one of these Roman-numeral parts for basic organization of your career review, or analysis by division.

   Unit: (the career itself)
   Divisions: (parts of the unit, the career itself)

   I. My background, interests, and aptitude

   II. My desired field—an overview

   III. Working conditions, pay, benefits

   IV. Requirements for employment

   V. My step-by-step plan to enter this field

6. Consider using the Writing Process Worksheet and the Brandon Guide for Revising and Editing for completing your assignment and the Revising and Editing Charts after your assignment is returned.

Practicing the Brandon Guide for Revising and Editing

PATTERN: ANALYSIS BY DIVISION

A Summary of "A Big Wheel"

JESSICA RUIZ

(A) In his essay "A Big Wheel," Louis Grossberger explains that *The Wheel Of Fortune* game show has been red hot for years because it has the right parts. (B) He says the idea that holds the parts together is *vicariousness*. (C) Viewers don't exactly identify with the contestants; in their mind, they become the contestants. (D) There is four parts: players, the game, the payoff, and the cast. (E) First, the players are ordinary people. (F) They reveal only a few seconds of information about themselves and then turn to the giant wheel. (G) Viewers begin to identify vicariously with them as game players. (H) Second, the game is a combination of skill and luck. (I) The skill is in solving a word puzzle based on the old hangman's game. (J) Viewers are not told the answer in advance, allowing them to play the game vicariously at home. (K) They may even win and feel superior, even feel they've defeated the actual players. (L) Third, there is a payoff in the game. (M) The contestants call out a letter and spin the wheel. (N) Dollar amounts and prizes are given for correct letter answers. (O) If contestants give an incorrect answer they lose their turn at the wheel. (P) Bad luck occurs when the wheel stops on *Bankrupt* or *Lose a Turn*. (Q) Good luck occurs when the contestant hits special money or prize slots. (R) Fourth, all the while, the cast plays its parts. (S) The good-natured Pat Sajak is the host. (T) He is like a friendly relative. (U) He talks and laughs. (V) He is supported by Vanna White. (W) She is his glitzy partner. (X) She reveals letters in the word puzzles, claps her hands, and does not talk. (Y) Her role is to act like a silent cheerleader for the players and, vicariously, even for the audience. (Z) These four parts function together to make the show successful, and if the audience likes the show, its

part of the success.

EXERCISE 12   Revise and Edit with the Brandon Guide

Revise with **C L U E S S** **(pronounce as "clues" for easy memorization).**

1. **C**oherence: Connect your ideas. Circle the four transitional words that introduce the parts of this analysis by division.

2. **L**anguage: Use words appropriate for your purpose and audience. This summary contains one slang phrase. Cross it out and write in a better word choice.

3. **U**nity: Stay on your topic. Underline the topic sentence and the closing sentence.

4. **E**mphasis: Call attention to your important ideas. Draw a box around the key word and its variation (four altogether) for emphasis and unity.

5. **S**upport: Back up your controlling ideas with evidence and logic. One sentence introduces all three parts of the support. Double-underline it.

6. **S**entences: Write correct, effective sentences with structural variety. Combine sentences V and W by deleting two words and a period and inserting a comma, thereby creating an appositive.

Edit with **C G P S** **(pronounce as "see GPS" for easy memorization).**

7. **C**apitalization: One capitalized word should begin with a lowercase letter. Cross out the lowercase letter and insert a capital letter above it.

8. **G**rammar: One sentence has a subject and verb agreement problem. Cross out the problem verb and insert the correct verb above it.

9. **P**unctuation: One sentence lacks a comma after an introductory adverbial clause (word group that has a subject and verb, acts as an adverb, and cannot stand alone). Insert a comma.

10. **S**pelling: One word is misspelled. Cross it out and write in the correct spelling above it.

10

Process Analysis
Writing About Doing

66 *Writing means sharing. It's part of the human condition to want to share things—thoughts, ideas, opinions.* 99

—PAUL COEHLO

When to Use Process Analysis

FOR COLLEGE WRITING ASSIGNMENTS

Much of your college work appears as process analysis. Instructors and instructional materials, such as this textbook, are explaining how things are done or how things occurred.

- In labs you experiment with processes and learn to perform tasks. To demonstrate your knowledge of what you have learned and your ability to perform tasks, you write paragraphs, essays, and reports, and you take tests.
- Having a systematic pattern for organization for writing these process analyses will enable you to write with efficiency.

IN CAREERS AND AT THE WORKPLACE

Process analysis is central to both career preparation and workplace activities. You learn what to do and how to perform.

- As you work with others, as a member of a team or as a supervisor of new employees, you will need to write memos and directives as process analysis to explain what to do and how something is or was done.
- Whether you do the technical writing or advertising copy, you will need to explain, often in writing, how your products and services are used and how they are beneficial.

PROCESS ANALYSIS IN A CARTOON

THE QUIGMANS   by Buddy Hickerson

"Hold still, it's my first day!"

Writing Process Analysis

If you have any doubt about how frequently we use process analysis, just think about how many times you have heard people say, "How do you do it?" or "How is it done?" Even when you are not hearing those questions, you are posing them yourself when you need to cook a meal, assemble a piece of furniture, troubleshoot technology issues, or figure out how to calculate a tip at a restaurant. In your college classes, you may have to discover how osmosis occurs, how a rock changes form, how blood flows through the heart, how the Central Processing Unit (CPU) of a computer converts data input, or how a bill goes through the legislature.

If you need to explain how to do something or how something was done, you will engage in **process analysis**. You will break down your topic into stages, explaining each so that your reader can duplicate or understand the process.

TWO TYPES OF PROCESS ANALYSIS: DIRECTIVE AND INFORMATIVE

The questions How do I do it? and How is it done? will lead you into two different types of process analysis—directive and informative.

Directive process analysis explains how to do something. As the name suggests, it gives directions for the reader to follow. It says, for example, "Read me, and you can bake a pie [tune up your car, read a book critically, write an essay, take some medicine]." Because it is presented directly to the reader, it usually addresses the reader as "you," or it implies the "you" by saying something such as "First [you] purchase a large pumpkin, and then [you]. . . . " In the same way, this textbook addresses you or implies "you" because it is a long how-to-do-it (directive process analysis) statement.

Informative process analysis explains how something was done by giving data (information). Whereas the directive process analysis tells you what to do in the future, the informative process analysis tells you what has occurred or what is occurring. If it is something in nature, such as the formation of a mountain, you can read and understand the process by which it emerged. In this type of process analysis, you do not tell the reader what to do; therefore, you will seldom use the words *you* or *your*.

WORKING WITH STAGES

Preparation or Background

In the first stage of directive process analysis, list the materials or equipment needed for the process and discuss the necessary setup arrangements. For some topics, this stage will also provide technical terms and definitions. The level of detail provided will depend on both the subject itself and the expected knowledge and experience of the intended audience.

Informative process analysis may begin with background or context rather than with preparation. For example, a statement explaining how blood flows through the heart might begin with a description of the circulatory system.

Steps or Sequence

The actual process will be presented here. Each step or sequence must be explained clearly and directly, and phrased to accommodate the audience. The language, especially in directive process analysis, is likely to be simple and concise. The steps may be accompanied by explanations about why certain procedures are necessary and how not following directions carefully can lead to trouble.

Order

The order will usually be chronological (time based) in some sense. Certain transitional words are commonly used to promote coherence: *first*, *second*, *third*, *then*, *soon*, *now*, *next*, *finally*, *at last*, *therefore*, *consequently*, and—especially for informative process analysis—words used to show the passage of time such as hours, days of the week, and so on.

BASIC FORMS

Consider using this form for the directive process (with topics such as how to cook something or how to fix something).

How to Prepare Spring Rolls

    I. Preparation
       A. Suitable cooking area
       B. Utensils, equipment
       C. Spring roll wrappers
       D. Vegetables, sauce
    II. Steps
       A. Season vegetables
       B. Wrap vegetables
       C. Fold wrappers
       D. Deep-fry rolls
       E. Serve rolls with sauce

Consider using this form for the informative process (with topics such as how a volcano functions or how a battle was won).

How Coal Is Formed

    I. Background or context
       A. Accumulation of land plants
       B. Bacterial action
       C. Muck formation
    II. Sequence
       A. Lignite from pressure
       B. Bituminous from deep burial and heat
       C. Anthracite from metamorphic conditions

COMBINED FORMS

In many cases, it makes sense to use one process or the other. If your aim is to explain how to change a car tire, for example, you would likely use directive process analysis. If your aim is to explain how ozone is formed in the atmosphere, you would use informative process analysis.

There are instances, though, in which it make sense to use both approaches. **Combination process analysis** occurs when directive process analysis and informative process analysis are used together. This often happens when a writer personalizes an account. For example, if I tell you the steps to follow to write a research paper, I am using directive process analysis. However, if I then give you a detailed account of the steps I took to write a particular research paper for a childhood education course I took last semester, I am also using informative process analysis. In this case, you will likely find the directions useful, but the additional information might make the instruction more memorable.

CAREER-RELATED WRITING AS PROCESS ANALYSIS

When you are new on the job, you will be expected first to learn how to execute your job description according to employer expectations, doing work the "company way." Knowing the techniques for process analysis presented here will help you master the workplace subject material more easily. At some point, you will probably be expected to train others. The training you do may require you both to talk and to write. Whatever the method, knowing how to deliver a clear, logical, and correct process analysis will be an asset. Fortunately for you, the two basic organizational patterns of process analysis—directive and informative—are as logical as they are simple.

Process analysis will serve you particularly well in writing memos and guidance sheets, and in giving PowerPoint presentations. In PowerPoint presentations you can treat your outline as an overview as part of your introduction and then you can discuss the specific steps or stages for development. The essay, "Doing a Flame Hair Tattoo," which appears later in the chapter, offers both an outline and a written example of what can be done with a single unit of workplace process.

Transitional Words

Consider using the following transitional words to improve coherence by connecting ideas with ideas, sentences with sentences, and paragraphs with paragraphs.

FOR PROCESS ANALYSIS: Preparation and Background: at the outset, before stages develop, before steps occur, before work begins, as preparation for, in anticipation of, in laying the groundwork

STEPS AND STAGES: first, second, third, another step, next, now, then, at this point, at this stage, at this step, after, at last, finally, subsequently, to begin with, initially, after that, afterward, at the same time, concurrently, meanwhile, soon, during the process, during . . . , in order to, for a minute, for a . . .

FOR ALL PATTERNS OF WRITING: The HOTSHOT CAT words: However, Otherwise, Therefore, Similarly, Hence, On the other hand, Then, Consequently, Also, Thus

USEFUL PREWRITING PROCEDURE

All the strategies of freewriting, brainstorming, and clustering can be useful in writing a process analysis. However, if you already know your subject well, you can simply make two lists, one headed *Preparation* or *Background* and the other *Steps* or *Sequence*. Then jot down ideas for each. After you have finished with your listing, you can delete parts, combine parts, and rearrange parts for better order. That editing of your lists will lead directly to a formal outline you can use in Stage Two of the writing process. Following is an example of listing for the topic of how to prepare spring rolls.

Preparation	**Steps**
stainless steel bowl	slice and mix vegetables
deep-fry pan	add sauce to vegetables
spoon	beat eggs
damp cloth	place wrappers on damp cloth
spring roll wrappers	add 2 to 3 tablespoons of vegetables per wrapper
eggs	fold and seal wrapper with egg
sauce	freeze for later or deep-fry immediately
cabbage	serve with sweet-and-sour sauce
celery	
carrots	
bean sprouts	

FINDING PATTERNS IN PHOTOS

EXERCISE 1   An Image-Based Activity for Groups or Individuals

Imagine you are Valerie in the photo, and you are not a mechanic. Nevertheless, you have calculated you can save a lot of money by switching to self-service in oil changing. You e-mailed a friend with a weird sense of humor and asked her to send you the steps for changing oil. She called and volunteered to do the work. Being an independent person, you said you only want the steps. Later when you heard a noise on your front porch, you investigated and discovered she had quickly come and gone, leaving behind tools, an oil filter, cans of oil, and a list of steps. One problem: She jumbled the order of the steps. You are not amused. Determined to do the work yourself, you look at the items, scratch your head, and begin rearranging the list.

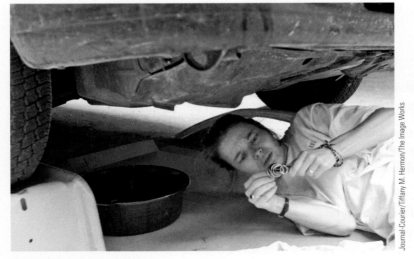

Valerie changes the oil in her car

Journal-Courier/Tiffany M. Hermon/The Image Works

In the following blanks, place the steps from the right-hand column in the correct order. Add steps if you like.

If your instructor requires, use the outline as a framework to write a brief process-analysis paper on changing the oil in your car.

1. _____   A. Dispose of used oil at a recycling center.

2. _____   B. Use wrench to unscrew and remove oil filter.

3. _____   C. Pour oil into crankcase.

4. _____   D. Place catch pan under oil drain plug.

5. _____   E. Drain oil.

6. _____   F. Use wrench to remove oil drain plug.

7. _____   G. Replace oil drain plug.

8. _____   H. Run engine for two minutes.

9. _____   I. Coat oil filter gasket with oil and install oil filter.

10. _____   J. Turn off engine.

11. _____   K. Wait a few minutes to check and adjust oil level.

Practicing Patterns of Process Analysis

A definite pattern underlies a process analysis. In some cases, such as with merchandise assembly instructions, the content reads as mechanically as an outline, and no reader objects. In other presentations, such as your typical college assignments, the writing should be well developed and interesting. Regardless of the form you use or the audience you anticipate, keep in mind that in process analysis the pattern will provide a foundation for the content.

EXERCISE 2   Completing Patterns of Directive Process Analysis

Using directive process analysis, fill in the blanks to complete this pattern for "writing an essay."

I. Preparation (Prewriting)

  A. Understand the assignment.

  B. _____

  C. Write the controlling idea.

  D. _____

II. Steps (Writing)

  A. Draft.

  B. _____

  C. _____

EXERCISE 3   Completing Patterns of Directive Process Analysis

Using directive process analysis, fill in the blanks to complete this pattern for "planting a lawn."

I. Preparation

    A. Obtain tools.

    B. Obtain _____

    C. Obtain _____

    D. Obtain _____

II. Steps

    A. _____

    B. _____

    C. Cultivate soil.

    D. _____

    E. Cover seed with mulch and fertilizer.

    F. _____

EXERCISE 4   Completing Patterns of Informative Process Analysis

Using informative process analysis, fill in the blanks to complete this pattern. Use a topic from a subject you are studying or have studied and explain some phenomenon such as how a volcano, a hurricane, a tidal wave, cell division, tree growth, a common cold, a sunburn, a blister, a headache, chapped lips, land erosion, quicksand, computer crash, asthma, fossil, fog, or the like occurs.

I. Background

    A. _____

    B. _____

    C. _____

II. Sequence

    A. _____

    B. _____

    C. _____

    D. _____

EXERCISE 5   Completing Patterns of Informative Process Analysis

Using informative process analysis, fill in the blanks to complete this pattern. Use a topic from a subject you are studying or have studied and explain some phenomenon such as how a tornado, dust storm, riptide, osmosis, human growth, flu, termite damage, skin cancer, tooth cavity, baldness, wrinkling, airplane flight, rise and fall of tides, rainbow, radar, rust on metal, egg hatching, egg fertilization, HIV, frog croaking, cricket chirping, or the like occurs.

I. Background

    A. _____

    B. _____

    C. _____

II. Sequence

    A. _____

    B. _____

    C. _____

    D. _____

Readings for Critical Thinking, Discussion, and Writing

READING STRATEGIES AND OBJECTIVES

Underlining and annotating these reading selections will help you answer the questions that follow the selections, discuss the material in class, and prepare for reading-based writing assignments. As you underline and annotate, pay special attention to the author's writing skills, logic, and message, and consider the relevance of the material to your own experiences and values. In text, a horizontal line shows the point at which the preparation (materials, setup, explaining words, and so on) ends and the steps begin. The steps are numbered in the margin.

PARAGRAPHS

How to Sharpen a Knife

FLORENCE H. PETTIT

The simplest tasks are often the most poorly done because we assume that we know how to do them and do not seek instruction. Here Florence H. Pettit explains how to sharpen a knife properly, and what we learn suggests that we could probably take lessons on performing any number of everyday chores.

If you have never done any whittling or wood carving before, the first skill to learn is how to sharpen your knife. You may be surprised to learn that even a brand-new knife needs sharpening. Knives are never sold honed (finely sharpened), although some gouges and chisels are. It is essential to learn the firm stroke on the stone that will keep your blades sharp. The sharpening stone must be fixed in place on the table, so that it will not move around. You can do this by placing a rubber inner tube or a thin piece of foam rubber under it. Or you can tack four strips of wood, if you have a rough worktable, to frame the stone and hold it in place. Put a generous puddle of oil on the stone—this will soon disappear into the surface of a new stone, and you will need to keep adding more oil. Press the knife blade flat against the stone in the puddle of oil, using your index finger. Whichever way the cutting edge of the knife faces is the side of the blade that should get a little more pressure. Move the blade around three or four times in a narrow oval about the size of your fingernail, going *counterclockwise* when the sharp edge is facing right. Now turn the blade over in the same spot on the stone, press hard, and move it around the small oval *clockwise*, with more pressure on the cutting edge that faces left. Repeat the ovals, flipping the knife blade over six or seven times, and applying lighter pressure to the blade the last two times. Wipe the blade clean with a piece of rag or tissue and rub it flat on the piece of leather strop at least twice on each side. Stroke *away* from the cutting edge to remove the little burr of metal that may be left on the blade.

EXERCISE 6   Discussion and Critical Thinking

1. What type of process analysis (informative or directive) does Pettit use?

2. Is Pettit trying to inform or persuade?

3. What is the prevailing tone (objective, humorous, reverent, argumentative, cautionary, playful, ironic, ridiculing) of this selection?

Survival in the World of Zombies

JERZY KOVAC

Student Jerzy Kovac responds to the following prompt: "Imagine you are writing an action movie. Your main character is in a life-or-death situation. Explain to your character what he or she will have to know and do in order to survive."

Wake Up! While you were asleep last night, some strange illness started to affect the population of your town, at least it appears to be an illness. As you rub the sleepy sand from your eyes and lurch toward your kitchen window to get a good look at the new day, the world seems to be a little different—a little off. One thing is for sure. Your neighbor, Mr. Johanson, is not acting as he usually does. Instead of saying his usual crisp "Good Morning," as he walks his dog, Bridget, he moans like a homesick Labrador, "Ahoooooo!" and runs up and down your street in pajamas with his face smeared with ketchup—or is it blood? Either way, things are getting pretty weird, and they are getting weirder. When you turn on the news, footage of mobs of disheveled and vacant-eyed people wandering aimlessly through your town streets rolls for minutes on end. Okay, think hard, and make yourself some coffee so that you can think better. What do you think is happening? That's right, my friend. It's the end of the world, at least the end of the world you are used to living in. You now are a human in a world of zombies. And, of course, zombies are human beings whose brains have been infected with some noxious virus that kills them but then allows them to come back as mindless eating machines whose favorite food is **you**—your brain, especially. Now you have to take steps if you want to survive. Round up food, guns, ammo, and try to get to a place without zombies. Mr. Johanson is definitely a zombie, so your neighborhood is no good. Better get in your car and start driving. Forget about traffic laws; there are no laws anymore. Get to the country away from those darn creatures. If you get bitten, you will be infected, too, and then you will become one of them. Maybe you'll enter a real-life flash-mob marathon, or maybe you'll crash an actual zombie party.

EXERCISE 7   Discussion and Critical Thinking

1. Who is the intended audience?

2. Underline the steps Kovac tells his main character to take.

3. What's the consequence of disregarding the instructions?

ESSAYS

How Nairobi Got Its Ad-Hoc Bus System on Google Maps*

SHARA TONN

Shara Tonn explains how researchers came together to create a much-needed map of the non-formal bus system in Nairobi, Kenya.

1   Painted with the faces of celebrities like Bob Marley and Tupac Shakur, and furnished with disco balls that lurch and twinkle as they weave through traffic, the thousands of matatus on the roads in Nairobi are bright and loud. Blaring music and honking their way through congestion, these mini-buses are the main mass transit network in the Kenyan capital, and 70 percent of the population uses them to get around. They're cheap and convenient, filling the public transit void. But the system is chaotic.

2   Individual matatu buses and routes are privately owned and operated, which means schedules and ticket prices can change at the whim of whoever's in charge. Even finding the right stop can be tricky. You just kind of have to … know. If you choose the wrong line, you could waste half a day on an already long trip. Since most routes run through the city center before going back out, the roads—not designed for the megacity that Nairobi has become—are flooded with matatu congestion. One or two accidents on the main thoroughfares can shut down traffic for hours.

*Shara Tonn/Wired; © Conde Nast.

3   The situation makes it difficult for riders, who could save time if they knew about better routes, and challenging for major transit projects meant to improve city life. A recent highway project in Nairobi didn't plan for the matatus, and the informal highway stops they make are dangerous, adding traffic that the planners didn't anticipate. A full picture of the matatu system would be useful, to say the least.

4   That picture now exists: In a collaboration called Digital Matatus, researchers from MIT, Columbia University, and the University of Nairobi along with the design firm Groupshot released a map of the entire matatu system last year—a first for a non-formal transit system. And on Wednesday, it became the first informal network to be launched on Google Maps. Just as New York commuters can plot their subway routes on the service, residents of Nairobi can now jack into the matatu system on their smartphones.

5   "Hats off to Digital Matatus and Google for doing this," says Robert Cervero, a professor of city and regional planning at the University of California, Berkeley. "This is a very important pilot test demonstration and if the data can be put to good use designing better systems, it can have tremendous benefits."

6   The idea to map the matatus began in 2012 when Sarah Williams and Jacqueline Klopp, two researchers working on land use projects in Nairobi, connected with Groupshot co-founder Adam White. "Adam and I started talking about the problem of working on sustainable transportation," says Klopp, an associate research scholar at the Columbia Center for Sustainable Urban Development. "There were all these transportation projects going on, but there was no basic data about the existing transit system in Nairobi."

7   The annals of the city government held some matatu data, but not much. Digital Matatus found records for about 75 percent of the routes, but they only included the start and end points, making it impossible to know how the buses navigated through the city. So armed with smartphones, ten university students spent four months riding the matatus, noting the name and location of each stop in a purpose-built app, which also used GPS to track the route. In dangerous neighborhoods, they followed behind the brightly painted buses in private cars.

8   By the end, the students recorded almost 3,000 stops on more than 130 routes. Next, all that data needed to be put in a usable format—specifically, a global standard called the General Transit Feed Specification (GTFS), which is compatible with open-source software used to make routing apps like Google Maps. But GTFS, developed in 2005, is geared towards formal transit systems, ones with fixed times and schedules.

9   That's when Digital Matatus connected with Google Maps. Along with the rest of the robust GTFS community, Google agreed to update the global standard to make room for flexible transit networks with constantly changing schedules, routes, and stops. Nairobi was a perfect test bed. "In our efforts to expand public transportation on Google Maps, it was a good place to go next because there were people eager and willing to work on it," said Mara Harris, a Google rep.

10   In the meantime, the Digital Matatus team turned to the project of visualizing the entire matatu system in one map. When they plotted the GPS coordinates in their software, they generated a neuron-like mass of overlapping routes and colors. Separating and structuring that mass into a formal subway-style map, designers at the MIT Civic Data Design Lab gave each of the main corridors going through the city center a different color, with well-known landmarks such as the Karura Forest and Ngong Road Forest anchoring the map in the city. A little over a year after starting the project, Digital Matatus released the Nairobi Matatu Routes paper map and the free GTFS transit data in January 2014.

11   City officials, who had been passively attending project meetings throughout, finally made it their official transit map. And, crucially, they also started using it as a guide for their evolving mass rapid transit proposals. The strength of an ad-hoc system like the matatus is that over time—over many traffic jams and missed appointments—trial-and-error driving can lead to more efficient, emergent routes.

12   The tech community pumped out five routing apps for smartphones and old-school feature phones as well as one payment app that calculated actual ticket fares in an effort to combat price fluctuations. Matatu drivers began planning more routes to underserved areas and alternative routes to avoid congestion. And citizens were shocked to see all the routes on the map, said Williams. They could find more efficient routes that they didn't even know existed. "There were interesting observations from women, especially, who said 'This is really valuable because at night, I want to make sure I'm on the right matatu,'" said Klopp. "'I don't want to get on the wrong one where I don't feel safe.'"

13   Launching the matatu routes in Google emphasizes the need to study the informal transit networks that shuttle masses of people around in sub-Saharan Africa, southeast Asia, and south Asia. "You're saying this is part of the system," said Klopp. And since the GTFS data structure and the Nairobi data are open source, Digital Matatus gives other groups in Mexico City, Manila, Dhaka, China, and elsewhere a plan to collect and disseminate data on their transit. The collaboration has already received requests from around the world to map their cities.

14   Digital Matatus has also started talks with four more cities in Africa—Kampala, Accra, Lusaka, and Maputo—to use the same methods to map their informal mass transit systems. "So many of our problems in developing cities where you have extreme poverty and awful environmental conditions—they're always tied in some way to the transport sector," said Cervero. "It's very chaotic and unmanaged, so this is a huge first step towards enhancing those services."

15   People in Nairobi still use the paper maps because the matatu routes have not changed since their release, and the ultimate goal is a formal transit system with set maps, times, and prices. But hopefully "formal" will still mean you enjoy your commute with twinkling disco balls and a good beat.

EXERCISE 8   Discussion and Critical Thinking

1. Is this directive or informative process analysis? Explain.

2. What background information does Tonn provide? Why was the map needed?

3. Who created the map?

4. List the steps they took to create the map.

5. How might the map help people in other parts of the world?

Attitude*

GARRISON KEILLOR

Author, humorist, and storyteller, Garrison Keillor is best known as host of A Prairie Home Companion *straight from Lake Wobegon, long featured on National Public Radio. In this essay, first published in* The New Yorker, *he tells us how to play slow-pitch softball with "attitude."*

1   Long ago I passed the point in life when major-league ballplayers begin to be younger than yourself. Now all of them are, except for a few aging trigenarians and a couple of quadros who don't get around on the fastball as well as they used to and who sit out the second games of doubleheaders. However, despite my age (thirty-nine), I am still active and have a lot of interests. One of them is slow-pitch softball, a game that lets me go through the motions of baseball without getting beaned or having to run too hard. I play on a pretty casual team, one that drinks beer on the bench and substitutes freely. If a player's wife or girlfriend wants to play, we give her a glove and send her out to right field, no questions asked, and if she lets a pop fly drop six feet in front of her, nobody agonizes over it.

2   Except me. This year. For the first time in my life, just as I am entering the dark twilight of my slow-pitch career, I find myself taking the game seriously. It isn't the bonehead play that bothers me especially—the pop fly that drops untouched, the slow roller juggled and the ball then heaved ten feet over the first baseman's head and into the next diamond, the routine singles that go through outfielders' legs for doubles and triples with gloves flung after them. No, it isn't our stone-glove fielding or pussyfoot baserunning or limp-wristed hitting that gives me fits, though these have put us on the short end of some mighty ridiculous scores this summer. It's our attitude.

3   Bottom of the ninth, down 18–3, two outs, a man on first and a woman on third, and our third baseman strikes out. *Strikes out!* In slow-pitch, not even your grandmother strikes out, but this guy does, and after his third strike—a wild swing at a ball that bounces on the plate—he topples over in the dirt and lies flat on his back, laughing. *Laughing!*

4   Same game, earlier. They have the bases loaded. A weak grounder is hit toward our second baseperson. The runners are running. She picks up the ball, and she looks at them. She looks at first, at second, at home. We yell, "Throw it! Throw it!" and she throws it, underhand, at the pitcher, who has turned and run to back up the catcher. The ball rolls across the third-base line and under the bench.

*Reprinted with the permission of Scribner, a Division of Simon & Schuster, Inc. and Prairie Home Productions, LLC, from "Attitude" *The New Yorker*, August 27, 1979, as included in HAPPY TO BE HERE by Garrison Keillor. Copyright © 1979 by Garrison Keillor. All rights reserved.

Three runs score. The batter, a fatso, chugs into second. The other team hoots and hollers, and what does she do? She shrugs and smiles ("Oh, silly me"); after all, it's only a game. Like the aforementioned strikeout artist, she treats her error as a joke. They have forgiven themselves instantly, which is unforgivable. It is *we* who should forgive them, who can say, "It's all right, it's only a game." They are supposed to throw up their hands and kick the dirt and hang their heads, as if this boner, even if it is their sixteenth of the afternoon—*this* is the one that really and truly breaks their hearts.

5   That attitude sweetens the game for everyone. The sinner feels sweet remorse. The fatso feels some sense of accomplishment; this is no bunch of rumdums he forced into an error but a team with some class. We, the sinner's teammates, feel momentary anger at her—dumb! dumb play!—but then, seeing her grief, we sympathize with her in our hearts (any one of us might have made that mistake or one worse), and we yell encouragement, including the shortstop, who, moments before, dropped an easy throw for a force at second. "That's all right! Come on! We got 'em!" we yell. "Shake it off! These turkeys can't hit!" This makes us all feel good, even though the turkeys now lead us by ten runs. We're getting clobbered, but we have a winning attitude.

6   Let me say this about attitude: Each player is responsible for his or her own attitude, and to a considerable degree you can *create* a good attitude by doing certain little things on the field. These are certain little things that ballplayers do in the Bigs, and we ought to be doing them in the Slows.

7   **1.** When going up to bat, don't step right into the batter's box as if it were an elevator. The box is your turf, your stage. Take possession of it slowly and deliberately, starting with a lot of back-bending, knee-stretching, and torso-revolving in the on-deck circle. Then, approaching the box, stop outside it and tap the dirt off your spikes with your bat. You don't have spikes, you have sneakers, of course, but the significance of the tapping is the same. Then, upon entering the box, spit on the ground. It's a way of saying, "This here is mine. This is where I get my hits."

8   **2.** Spit frequently. Spit at all crucial moments. Spit correctly. Spit should be *blown*, not ptuied weakly with the lips, which often results in dribble. Spitting should convey forcefulness of purpose, concentration, pride. Spit down, not in the direction of others. Spit in the glove and on the fingers, especially after making a real knucklehead play; it's a way of saying, "I dropped the ball because my glove was dry."

9   **3.** At bat and in the field, pick up dirt. Rub dirt in the fingers (especially after spitting on them). Toss dirt, as if testing the wind for velocity and direction. Smooth the dirt. Be involved with dirt. If no dirt is available (e.g., in the outfield), pluck tufts of grass. Fielders should be grooming their areas constantly between plays, flicking away tiny sticks and bits of gravel.

10   **4.** Take your time. Tie your laces. Confer with your teammates about possible situations that may arise and conceivable options in dealing with them. Extend the game. Three errors on three consecutive plays can be humiliating if the plays occur within the space of a couple of minutes, but if each error is separated from the next by extensive conferences on the mound, lace-tying, glove adjustments, and arguing close calls (if any), the effect on morale is minimized.

11   **5.** Talk. Not just an occasional "Let's get a hit now" but continuous rhythmic chatter, a flow of syllables: "Hey babe hey babe c'mon babe good stick now hey babe long tater take him downtown babe . . . hey good eye good eye."

12   Infield chatter is harder to maintain. Since the slow-pitch pitch is required to be a soft underhand lob, infielders hesitate to say, "Smoke him babe hey low heat hey throw it on the black babe chuck it in there back him up babe no hit no hit." Say it anyway.

13   **6.** One final rule, perhaps the most important of all: When your team is up and has made the third out, the batter and the players who were left on base do not come back to the bench for their gloves. *They remain on the field, and their teammates bring their gloves out to them*. This requires some organization and discipline, but it pays off big in morale. It says, "Although we're getting our pants knocked off, still we must conserve our energy."

14   Imagine that you have bobbled two fly balls in this rout and now you have just tried to stretch a single into a double and have been easily thrown out sliding into second base, where the base runner ahead of you had stopped. It was the third out and a dumb play, and your opponents smirk at you as they run off the field. You are the goat, a lonely and tragic figure sitting in the dirt. You curse yourself, jerking your head sharply forward. You stand up and kick the base. How miserable! How degrading! Your utter shame, though brief, bears silent testimony to the worthiness of your teammates, whom you have let down, and they appreciate it. They call out to you now as they take the field, and as the second baseman runs to his position he says, "Let's get 'em now," and tosses you your glove. Lowering your head, you trot slowly out to right. There you do some deep knee bends. You pick grass. You find a pebble and fling it into foul territory. As the first batter comes to the plate, you check the sun. You get set in your stance, poised to fly. Feet spread, hands on hips, you bend slightly at the waist and spit the expert spit of a veteran ballplayer—a player who has known the agony of defeat but who always bounces back, a player who has lost a stride on the base paths but can still make the big play.

15   This is *ball*, ladies and gentlemen. This is what it's all about.

EXERCISE 9   Discussion and Critical Thinking

1. Is the process-analysis part of this essay informative or directive?

2. What is the source of "attitude," as Keillor would like to see it demonstrated on his slow-pitch team?

3. Why does he skip over the preparation stage?

4. Keillor provides us with six steps. Are the steps to be performed in a particular order?

5. In what other sports is attitude important? Give some examples of attitude-building rituals in other sports.

6. What attitude-building behavior is used by people outside sports: at school, at work, at worship, on the road?

7. What is the tone of this essay and what does Keillor expect readers to do?

CAREER-RELATED WRITING

A Successful Interview*

C. EDWARD GOOD AND WILLIAM FITZPATRICK

Freelance authors C. Edward Good and William Fitzpatrick describe the interview as systematic. To be successful in an interview, a person being interviewed must understand the system. In this way, the interviewee will not only follow what is going on and anticipate questions but also, in some instances, be able to control the flow of the interview.

1   Facing the interview might make you apprehensive, but there is no reason to fear it. It is your real opportunity to get face to face with your product's potential buyer and bring to bear all of your personal selling skills. If you go into the situation with confidence based on preparation and not on ego, you are more likely to come out a winner. Take the time to prepare properly. The interview has been your goal thus far in the job search, so it is your stepping stone to future success. Be positive, be enthusiastic, and rely on your experience in communicating with people.

The Interview

The interviewer will probably take the following steps with you:

2   *Establish Rapport.*   The interviewer's responsibility is to put you at ease, both physically and emotionally. The more relaxed you are, the more you will trust the interviewer and open up to him or her. Skilled interviewers will not put you in front of a desk. They will put the chair beside the desk so there are no barriers between you or will not use a desk at all. Initial conversation will be about trivial matters such as the weather, parking, or any subject to get you talking.

3   *Determine Your Qualifications.*   The interviewer has to find out as early as possible if you are technically qualified (on the surface) for the job. Time is valuable, and an interviewer can't waste it on unqualified candidates. The determination is made by a review of the application and your résumé. This can turn into a simple yes and no session as the interviewer matches your qualifications against the requirements for the position. During this phase, information is gathered to develop questions later on in the conversation. This technique is called *blueprinting.*

4   *Explain the Company and the Job.*   At this point in the interview, the interviewer will try to get you excited about wanting to work for the company. He or she generally will cover job responsibilities and company benefits to interest you even further.

*C. Edward Good and William Fitzpatrick, "A Successful Interview," 1993. By permission.

5   *Determine Your Suitability*.   The interviewer now has to determine if you are the best candidate. In many cases this is a subjective judgment based upon impressions of your conduct and your ability to handle the questions posed to you. In this part of the interview you will be asked situational questions, which may or may not be directly related to your future duties. The interviewer may even ask some startling questions to get your response. The technique used is to ask open-ended questions (those that require more than a one-word answer) during this phase, rather than close-ended questions (those that only require a simple yes or no).

6   *Conclusion*.   Now it is the interviewer's responsibility to review the major points you covered during the interview and get you out of the office in a timely manner. The interviewer should ensure all of your questions have been answered and will generally let you know what the next step is and when a decision will be made.

7   As you can see, an interview is a planned and controlled process. As stated, a trained and skilled interviewer will guide you through the steps and will know exactly how to keep you on track. The managers in the second and subsequent interviews may not follow a planned agenda and may even have trouble staying on track themselves. If you understand what is happening, you can take control. The rules for the interview are based on one theory only. If you were called, you probably are qualified for the job. Your task is to show the company you are the best qualified of the candidates who are competing. Here are some suggestions for doing that.

8   *Always Be Positive*. Losers dwell on past losses, winners dwell on future successes. Don't worry about where you have been, worry about where you're going. Make sure your accomplishments are related to your capabilities.

9   *Listen, Listen, Listen*. Throughout the interview, concentrate to be sure you're really listening to what the interviewer has to say. It looks very bad when you ask a question the interviewer just answered.

10   *State Your Qualifications, Not Your Drawbacks*.   Tell them what you can do; let them wonder about what you can't do.

11   *Ask Questions*.   Be sure to ask intelligent, well-thought-out questions that indicate you are trying to find out what you can do for the company. Base any statements on proven experience, not dreams and hopes.

12   *Watch Out for Close-Ended Questions*.   Be wary of interviewers who ask close-ended questions. They probably don't know what they are doing. If you begin to hear a series of questions that require only a yes or no, the other candidates are probably hearing the same questions. If the interviewer asks three candidates the same question and all he gets are three no answers, he or she won't be able to distinguish among the three. If all the answers are the same, the interviewer can't make an intelligent choice. Your strategy, then, is to turn these close-ended questions into open-ended ones so you can put a few intelligent sentences together. In this way, you will distinguish yourself from the other yes and no candidates.

13   *Stay Focused*.   Concentrate on the conversation at hand. Don't get off on extraneous matters that have nothing to do with the job or your qualifications.

14   *Don't Get Personal*.   Keep personal issues out of the interview. Never confide in an interviewer no matter how relaxed and comfortable you feel. If you feel the urge to bare your soul, your feelings should tell you the interviewer is very skilled and followed the first step of the interview extremely well.

15   *Rehearse.*   Plan some answers to obvious questions. Why did you leave your previous position? Why did you choose your academic major? What are your training and experience going to do for the company?

16   *Maintain Eye Contact.* If you can't look interviewers in the eye, they won't believe your answer. Further, there are no answers written on the ceiling, so if you get in a bind, don't look up for divine guidance. The answer is not on the ceiling. It's in your head.

17   *Pause a Moment.*   Take a moment before each answer to consider what you will say. Don't answer the question in a rush, but reflect a moment to get it straight.

18   *Take Notes.*   If you plan on taking notes, ask first. Some people are uncomfortable when their words are written down. Do not attempt to record the conversation.

19   *Multiple Interviewers.*   If you are interviewed by more than one person, answer all of them equally. Begin with the questioner, let your eyes go to each of the others as you continue your answer, and finally come back to the original questioner. Each of them will then feel you are speaking to him or her alone.

20   *Don't Drink, Don't Smoke.*   In fact, don't ingest anything at all. Although it is polite to accept a proffered cup of coffee or a soft drink, it is not polite to spill it in your lap. You will be nervous, so don't take the chance. Remember, they are merely trying to establish rapport. Besides, you can't maintain eye contact while drinking or eating.

21   *Likely Open-Ended Questions.*   What follows are some properly formulated open-ended questions you may hear later. Get used to the format and prepare answers. Keep them down to a couple of sentences, not paragraphs.

1. In your relationship with your previous supervisor, would you mind giving an example of how you were alike or not alike?
2. How would you define success?
3. Would you demonstrate some methods you would use to cause a marginal employee to rise to his or her full potential?
4. How can a team atmosphere improve your personal effectiveness?
5. If you were a problem, how would you solve yourself?

After the Interview

22   When the interview concludes, don't linger, but don't run out the door, either. If the interviewers haven't indicated when a decision will be reached, ask them. This will give them the impression that you might have other offers you are considering. After you return home, write an email to thank each of the people who interviewed you. It is important that the message reach the interviewers by the next day. You hope that soon after they receive it they will be comparing your letter of application and résumé with those of other candidates. At that time you would have provided at least three documents for them to consider along with your performance during the interview. That personal touch of sending the thank you note could very well help, and it will certainly make you sure that you have done all you could to establish a competitive edge.

EXERCISE 10   Discussion and Critical Thinking

1. Is this essay informative or directive?

2. What are the major steps that an interviewer is likely to follow?

3. Are the suggestions presented in any sequence that need be followed?

4. Is the interview process discussed here formal or informal or a combination?

5. How does this "planned and controlled process" (paragraph 7) compare with interviews you have participated in?

6. What principles of good email practice should you follow for this occasion?

READING-BASED WRITING

A Summary of "How Low-Balling Works on Your Mind"

LARRY GARDNER

The assignment for student Larry Gardner was to write a summary of a selection, "How Low-Balling Works on Your Mind." He was directed to annotate the preparation and steps and to italicize the transitional words.

Preparation

Steps

1

2

3

4

In "How Low-Balling Works on Your Mind," Sharon S. Brehm discusses what she says may be "the most unscrupulous of all compliance techniques" (199). Low-balling can be used in many undertakings, but it is used mostly in selling. In selling automobiles, the salesperson *first* wins the customer over by agreeing to a good price for a vehicle. The ball thrown is a high pitch, a good one to hit. The customer is pleased and begins thinking of ownership. *Then* the salesperson comes back and throws the low ball: the sales manager says that the price is not enough because of the vehicle's special feature(s) and that the sale can be made only if the price is increased. *Next* the salesperson expresses regret and claims to be on the customer's side. *Finally* the customer, already emotionally committed to the deal and maybe identifying with the seemingly supportive salesperson, accepts whatever the sales manager said or a negotiated higher price. The customer has been low-balled.

Work Cited

Brehm, Sharon S. "How Low-Balling Works on Your Mind." *Social Psychology*. 5th ed. Boston: Houghton, 2002. 237–38. Print.

A CAREER-RELATED ESSAY WITH ALL STAGES

Student Tina Sergio was mainly interested in the law program, but in her English class she had an opportunity to write on a topic from another discipline at her school, cosmetology. With that, a school field of study and her work experience came together, and she wrote about the preparation for and the steps of an exotic, creative process she occasionally performs at her workplace to the considerable satisfaction of herself and her clients.

BRANDON BRIDGE

Writing Process Worksheet

Name _Tina Sergio_   **Title** _Doing a Flame Hair Tattoo_   **Due Date** _Thursday, March 8, 11 a.m._

Use the back of this page or separate paper if you need more space.

Assignment

In the space below, write whatever you need to know about your assignment, including information about the topic, audience, pattern of writing, length, whether to include a rough draft or revised drafts, and whether your paper must be typed.

Write a process-analysis essay about a procedure you have done at a workplace. Your audience will be those who may be familiar with your topic but have not performed the procedure. It may be helpful to imagine that you have just been promoted and your replacement needs to be instructed, in writing, about the performance of a specific task. Include the preparation stage and the steps. Use one or more illustrations. Submit a completed Writing Process Worksheet and a typed final draft with a marked first draft. Because you are already familiar with your topic, you may skip the Stage One part of the worksheet.

Stage One

Explore   Freewrite, brainstorm (list), cluster, or take notes as directed by your instructor.

This section was omitted because of the student's familiarity with her topic.

Stage Two

Organize   Write a topic sentence or thesis; label the subject and the focus parts.

<u>Doing the Flame Hair Tattoo well</u> <u>requires careful preparation and specific</u>
            subject   focus
<u>steps</u>.

Write an outline or an outline alternative. For reading-based writing, include references and short questions with page numbers as support in the outline.

I. Preparation
    A. Consult with the customer about the Flame Hair Tattoo.
    B. Gather materials.
    C. Gather tools.
II. Steps
    A. Make stencil designs, still consulting with the customer.
    B. Pre-cut the customer's hair.
    C. Perform the bleach procedure.
        1. Mix the bleach.
        2. Apply the bleach with a brush.
        3. Monitor the chemical processing of the bleach.
    D. Dye the customer's bleached hair.
        1. Mix the colors.
        2. Brush in the colors.
        3. Monitor the chemical processing of the colors.
    E. Admire the unique creation: the Flame Hair Tattoo.

Stage Three

Write   On separate paper, write and then revise your paragraph or essay as many times as necessary for **c**oherence, **l**anguage (usage, tone, and diction), **u**nity, **e**mphasis, **s**upport, and **s**entences (**CLUESS**). Read your work aloud to hear and correct any grammatical errors or awkward-sounding sentences.

Edit any problems in fundamentals, such as **c**apitalization, **g**rammar, **p**unctuation, and **s**pelling (**CGPS**).

This essay is annotated, with underlines for transitional words.

Final Draft

DOING A FLAME HAIR TATTOO
Tina Sergio

1   As a hair stylist for several years, I have seen many styles emerge, become popular, and then disappear. Sometimes they resurface again with variations, sort of like men's neckties. Their popularity may be national, regional, or local. They may be trends or just fads. One of my creations is the Flame Hair Tattoo. It is like a tattoo because it is permanently set in the hair, at least until the hair grows or is rebleached and redyed. Doing this design well requires careful preparation and specific steps. Keep in mind that this is a procedure I use, as a cosmetologist, in a hair styling salon. Because it deals with some strong chemicals, I do not recommend that inexperienced persons attempt it in their home.

I. Preparation
  A. Willing customer

2   Preparation is extremely important because once I start, I cannot afford to delay the sequence of steps. <u>First</u>, of course, I need a customer. Often now, it is a person who has been referred after having seen one of my creations on the street. Let us say this person (with dark hair) asks me for a hair

tattoo. I start by showing some photographs of satisfied clients, then explain what I can do, and give the price. <u>After</u> we agree on a style and particular colors, I need to make sure I have a large, flexible piece of thin cardboard, an X-acto knife, a drawing pencil, a paper plate, shampoo, towels, cream bleach, cream developer, a 1-inch-wide and a small paintbrush, tints in shades of the intended flames, scissors, and clippers with a number 2 attachment. All of these items are at my disposal in my fully equipped beauty salon. The customer is sitting in an adjustable chair.

3   The sequence <u>begins</u>. My <u>first step</u> is to prepare stencils that will become a wall of flames extending around the client's head and licking at the top. As the client watches and I explain what I am doing, I draw outlines of flames for stencils on my piece of cardboard. <u>At that point</u> the client can still make minor changes in the shading and design. <u>Then</u> I cut out the stencils with the X-acto knife, tracing the lines I have drawn on the cardboard, as shown in Figure 10.1. The annotations indicate the approximate locations of colors that will be added.

4   <u>Next, before starting</u> the bleaching process, I clip and buzz the hair to no more than 1/8 inch with the scissors and number 2 clippers. <u>After</u> making sure the cut hair is whisked or blown off the client's head, I am ready for the bleach. I mix a cream bleach first with equal parts of 20 volume cream developer and then with equal scoops of a powdered bleach. I stir this mixture until no lumps are left and it has a consistency of mayonnaise. The consistency is important, for if it is too runny, it might leave its own blurry design.

5   <u>Now</u> is the time to apply the bleach, but before applying it, I ask an assistant to hold each stencil firmly in place as I work. Using the larger

B. Obtain materials
C. Obtain tools

II. Steps
A. Make stencils

B. Pre-cut hair
C. Perform bleach procedure

1. Mix bleach

2. Apply bleach

Figure 10.1
One Flame

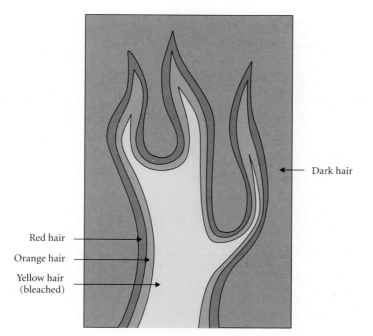

Dark hair

Red hair

Orange hair

Yellow hair
(bleached)

3. Process bleach

brush, I apply bleach generously to the open areas of each stencil, making sure all the edges are covered to produce a flame image before it is removed. <u>After completing</u> the last stencil, I reapply the bleach carefully with the larger brush, making sure that each part of the band of flames appears in flowing, even lines. With the application of bleach completed, I cover the treated hair with a plastic bag and let the chemicals process for an hour or until the bleached portions reach a pale yellow color. <u>Once the hair has processed</u>, I rinse out the bleach and gently shampoo the hair one time. <u>After towel drying</u> the hair, I am ready to start the coloring process.

D. Dye hair

1. Mix colors
2. Brush in colors

6   The first step of the coloring process is to select and display the colors. I use semi-permanent dyes of the brand Fudge. <u>After deciding</u> which colors to use, I squeeze each onto a paper plate in separate piles, sometimes mixing them, just as an artist might in painting with oils. Next, using the small paintbrush, I <u>first</u> outline and <u>then</u> fill in the flames, always going from light colors to dark. I make much use of a hand mirror so the client knows what I am doing as I work. By stages, I add the yellows, oranges, and reds—whatever the design calls for as I figuratively set his or her hair on fire.

3. Process colors

7   With the colors in place, processing takes at least thirty minutes. <u>After that time</u> is up, I wash the hair with shampoo one more time. The Flame Hair Tattoo is finished. The client's head is "permanently" ablaze with flames from temple to temple, moving upward from the hairline and across the top of the head.

E. Admire the creation

8   This style is not for everyone, but those who like the Flame Hair Tattoo wear it with pride and pleasure. They are having fun. I regard my hair tattoos in much the same way. No two designs are exactly the same. Each hair color and head conformation is a different medium and a new challenge for my craft and art.

EXERCISE 11   Discussion and Critical Thinking

1. In what way is this essay a directive process analysis?

2. Why might Sergio's essay also be considered an informative process analysis?

3. Underline the thesis.

4. Draw a line between the preparation and the steps.

Suggested Topics and Prompts for Writing Process Analysis

READING-BASED WRITING

Reading-based writing requires you to read critically, write a reply that shows you understand what you have read, and give credit for ideas you borrow and words you quote. The form can be a summary, a reaction, or a two-part response (with separated summary and reaction). Documentation, in which you give credit for borrowed ideas and words, can be either formal (MLA style) or informal, as directed by your instructor. Definitions of the three forms follow. Any form can be used for any reading selection in this book.

Summary

- The summary is a statement written in response to a reading. It restates only the most important points and uses original wording instead of the author's language. It should not contain added information or personal opinions.
- Because summaries are intended to restate only the main points of a reading, they are typically much shorter than the original text. Often, they are approximately a third of the length.

Reaction

- In the reaction, the meaning of what you have read will be central to the topic sentence of your paragraph or to the thesis of your essay.
- Although the reaction is not a personal narrative by itself, it may include personal experience to explain elements of the text. For example, if your source is about driving styles, your own experiences as a driver or an observer of drivers could be relevant in your analysis of the text.
- The reaction may incorporate a summary to convey a broad view of what you have read, but your summary should never be the main part of your reaction.

Two-Part Response

- The two-part response separates the summary from the reaction.
- This form will give you practice in separating your objective summary in the first part from your more personal evaluation, interpretation, or application in the second part, the reaction.

READING-BASED WRITING TOPICS

"How to Sharpen a Knife"

1. Pretending that you are the author and that you have an audience that wants only the basic information, change this paragraph to a concise outline or to a summary that includes only the preparation and the steps.

"Survival in the World of Zombies"

2. Write a reaction to Kovac's paragraph. How clear are his instructions? How could he revise his paragraph to make it more effective?

"How Nairobi Got Its Ad-Hoc Bus System on Google Maps"

3. Write a two-part response to the essay. In your reaction, discuss which step in the researchers' process is most impressive to you and why.

"Attitude"

4. Write a summary of this essay.
5. Write a reaction in which you focus on Keillor's intent in writing this essay. Explain whether he is just trying to be funny or whether he is serious about the game and the behavior of his fellow players. Discuss his choice of words and his use of examples, as well as the overall content. Refer directly to the essay and use quotations.
6. Write a reaction in which you apply Keillor's idea about taking his game "seriously" to another sport, thereby discussing how to perform certain tasks, customs, or rituals in your sport in the "proper" way. Use some references to and quotations from the essay in explaining how your approach is similar to that of Keillor.

"A Successful Interview"

7. Using the interview process discussed in this essay, describe an interview you experienced as either an interviewer or an interviewee. Refer to and quote from this essay.

8. With your classmates (perhaps in groups of five), prepare for a practice interview, conduct the interview, and write about the results of this activity. Refer to and quote from this essay.

   a. Create and define an imaginary company or decide on a company you are all familiar with, such as Walmart, JCPenney, or Sears.

   b. Divide the class into three groups: those who are interviewing; those who are being interviewed (looking for a job); and those who are watching, taking notes, and advising other groups.

   c. All groups prepare for mock interviews: deciding on job specifications (duties, pay, benefits, etc.), phrasing questions, and anticipating questions.

   d. Rehearse.

   e. Conduct interviews.

   f. Take notes.

   g. Write an informative process analysis based on a particular interview and related to the procedure described in the essay. Discuss the background and sequence parts and evaluate the performance of the interviewers and the person being interviewed. For a more focused piece of writing, you could concentrate only on the person being interviewed.

"A Summary of 'How Low-Balling Works on Your Mind'"

9. In a reaction, apply the parts of this summary to a situation you have experienced. Automobile and real estate sales are often occasions for the low-balling scam experience.

GENERAL TOPICS

10. In a paragraph or an essay, explain how to perform a simple task at home (cleaning an oven), at school (dissecting a frog in a biology lab), or at work (building a display for a product).

11. Write a paragraph or an essay on one of the following topics. Although they are phrased as directive topics, each can be transformed into a how-it-was-done informative topic by personalizing it and explaining stage by stage how you, someone else, or a group did something. For example, you could write either a directive process analysis about how to deal with an obnoxious person or an informative process analysis about how you or someone else dealt with an obnoxious person. Keep in mind that the two types of process analysis are often blended, especially in the personal approach. Many of these topics will be more interesting to you and your readers if they are personalized.

    Most of the topics require some narrowing to be treated in a paragraph. For example, writing about playing baseball is too broad; writing about how to throw a curve ball may be manageable.

    a. How to end a relationship without hurting someone's feelings

    b. How to pass a test for a driver's license

    c. How to get a job at _____

    d. How to perform a magic trick

    e. How to repair _____

    f. How to assemble _____

    g. How to learn about another culture

    h. How to approach someone you would like to know better

CROSS-CURRICULAR TOPICS

12. Write a paragraph or an essay about a procedure you follow in your college work in a science (chemistry, biology, geology) lab. You may explain how to analyze a rock, how to dissect something, how to operate something, how to perform an experiment.

13. Write a paragraph or an essay about how to do something in an activity or performance class, such as drama, physical education, art, or music.

CAREER-RELATED TOPIC

14. Pretend you are going on vacation and your boss says there will be a replacement for you and you should write a paragraph or an essay about a particular

task (not a very complicated one) so that the temporary employee can do that part of your work. Imagine that the temp will not have seen your workstation, so you must explain in detail and perhaps even do a drawing to go with your writing. Now write that process analysis. Refer back to the instruction at the beginning of this chapter.

WRITER'S GUIDELINES Process Analysis

BRANDON BRIDGE

1. Decide whether your process analysis is mainly directive or informative, and be appropriately consistent in using pronouns and other designations.

Directive	**Informative**
I. Preparation	I. Background
A.	A.
B.	B.
II. Steps	II. Sequence
A.	A.
B.	B.
C.	C.

- For directive process analysis, use the second person, addressing the reader as *you*. The *you* may be understood, not written.
- For informative process analysis, use the first person, speaking as *I* or *we*, or the third person, speaking about the subject as *he*, *she*, *it*, or *they*, or by name.

2. Consider using these basic forms.

3. Listing is a useful prewriting activity for process analysis. Begin with the Roman-numeral headings indicated in number 2.

4. The order of a process analysis will usually be chronological (time based) in some sense. Certain transitional words are commonly used to promote coherence: *first, second, third, then, soon, now, next, finally, at last, therefore,* and *consequently*.

5. Career-related process analysis takes the same conventional form.

6. **Consider using the Writing Process Worksheet and the Brandon Guide for Revising and Editing for completing your assignment and the Revising and Editing Charts after your assignment is returned.**

Practicing the Brandon Guide for Revising and Editing

PATTERN: PROCESS ANALYSIS

Peruvian New Year, Miami Style
JULIO MONTEZ

(A) Last year in Miami, Florida, I helped a group of my people burn an effigy of an old man. (B) It wasn't an act of terrorism or protest. (C) It was part of a New Year's Eve ceremony my family brought with us from Peru. (D) This one was not quite the same as the ones we experienced in Peru. (E) It, nevertheless, gave us a good feeling. (F) In Peru we would have joined many neighbors, friends, and relatives to make a dummy, *el año Viejo,* the old year. (G) First, we would have dressed him in tattered rags and carried him to a barrio or a nearby plaza. (H) Then we would have run around him, singing, laughing, blowing whistles, shouting, and throwing firecrackers. (I) Next, we would have propped him up in a chair and begun reading the "old Year's testament." (J) It would be a funny reading, as people would come up with items for the dummy, items like a shoe for someone who always dressed well or a woman's wig for a bald man, and so on. (K) Meanwhile, people would be putting firewood around him. (L) Then, at exactly midnight, someone would set fire to the dummy. (M) All the revellers would throw there oldest clothes into the flames. (N) Finally, the bells from the churches would toll, the fire stations would turn on their sirens, and all the neighbors and visitors would hug and kiss each other and shout out, "happy New Year." (O) That was the old country history for last year when we held a scaled back version with about a dozen people present in the backyard of our hosts. (P) We made an effigy and we burned it. (Q) There was some changes in the ritual. (R) We didn't have the firecrackers, bells, and sirens. (S) We did have a blast. (T) We brought a little bit of Peru with us to our new country.

EXERCISE 12   Revise and Edit with the Brandon Guide

Revise with CLUESS **(pronounce as "clues" for easy memorization).**

1. **Coherence:** Connect your ideas. Circle the six transitional connectives that introduce some of the steps in this process.

2. **Language:** Use words appropriate for your purpose and audience. Cross out the slang expression and write in a better choice of words above it.

3. **Unity:** Stay on your topic. Underline the topic sentence and the closing sentence used for both unity and emphasis.

4. **Emphasis:** Call attention to your important ideas. Draw a box around the word *effigy* (10 altogether) and synonyms and pronouns referring to *effigy*. *Effigy* represents the old year that leads to the new year.

5. **Support:** Back up your controlling ideas with evidence and logic. In the left margin, number the six steps that are used in the process in Peru.

6. **Sentences:** Write correct, effective sentences with structural variety. Use *however* and the correct capitalization and punctuation to combine sentences R and S. Write the combined sentence above the crossed out parts.

Edit with CGPS **(pronounce as "see GPS" for easy memorization).**

7. **Capitalization:** One word that should begin with a capital letter is in lowercase. Make a line through that lowercase word and insert the capital letter above it.

8. **Grammar:** One sentence has a subject and verb agreement error. Cross out the verb and write the correct form above it.

9. **Punctuation:** One sentence has two instances of modifiers that function closely together and should be hyphenated. Insert the two hyphens.

10. **Spelling:** One word is misspelled. Cross it out and write the correct spelling above it.

11

Cause and Effect
Determining Reasons and Outcomes

Shallow men believe in luck or circumstance. Strong men believe in cause and effect.

— RALPH WALDO EMERSON

CHAPTER CONTENTS

BRANDON BRIDGE

When to Use Cause and Effect

FOR COLLEGE WRITING ASSIGNMENTS

- Cause-and-effect questions are at the center of scientific investigation. They are also commonplace in reading assignments, class discussion, reports, research papers, and tests. If you want to study for an examination or just to be prepared for class discussion, highlight any situation, event, or trend and list relevant causes and effects. Try that approach with these general topics: gang activity, high blood pressure, obesity, divorce rate, drug addiction, inflation, economic depression, drought, flood, political change, racism, foreign policy, earthquake, volcanic eruption, or tax increase.

IN CAREERS AND AT THE WORKPLACE

- Businesses and other institutions deal constantly with reasons and results. For the individual, the rise and fall of careers are usually tied to causes and effects. Businesses need to make money. Institutions need to function well. Helping them do so requires the use of cause-and-effect analysis in almost every measurable respect. Cause-and-effect issues are subjects of progress reports, performance reviews, memos, and proposals. Accountability, a key word in measuring effectiveness, is based on causes and effects. Being able to understand and explain cause and effect will make you indispensable in any vocational field.

CAUSE AND EFFECT IN A CARTOON

THE QUIGMANS   by Buddy Hickerson

The desert wedding is a greatly feared event, mostly because of the tossing of the bridal cactus.

Writing Cause and Effect

Causes and effects deal with reasons and results; they are sometimes discussed together and sometimes separately. Like other forms of writing that include explanations, writing about causes and effects is based on natural thought processes. The shortest, and arguably the most provocative, poem in the English language—"I/Why?"—is posed by an anonymous author about cause. Children are preoccupied with delightful and often exasperating "why" questions. Daily we encounter all kinds of causes and effects. The same subject may raise questions of both kinds.

The car won't start. Why? [*cause*]

The car won't start. What now? [*effect*]

At school, from the biology lab to the political science classroom, and at work, from improving workflows to analyzing sales data, causes and effects are everywhere.

EXPLORING AND ORGANIZING

One useful approach to developing a cause-and-effect analysis is *listing*. Write down the event, situation, or trend you are concerned about. Then on the left side, list the causes; on the right side, list the effects. From these lists you will select the main causes or effects for your paragraph or essay. Here is an example.

Causes	Event, Situation, or Trend	Effects
Poverty	Joining a gang	Protection and recognition
Low academic achievement		Violence
Lack of job opportunities		Criminal record
Fear or intimidation		Drug and alcohol addiction

As you use prewriting techniques to explore your ideas, you need to decide whether your topic should mainly inform or mainly persuade. If you intend to inform, your tone should be coolly objective. If you intend to persuade, your tone should be subjective. In either case, you should take into account the views of your audience as you phrase your ideas. You should also take into account how much your audience understands about your topic and develop your ideas accordingly.

COMPOSING A TOPIC SENTENCE OR A THESIS

Now that you have listed your ideas under causes and effects, you are ready to focus on the causes, on the effects, or, occasionally, on both.

Your controlling idea, the topic sentence or the thesis, might be one of the causes: "It is not just chance; people have reasons for joining gangs." Later, as you use the idea, you would rephrase it to make it less mechanical, allowing it to become part of the flow of your discussion. If you wanted to personalize the work—thereby probably making it more interesting—you could write about someone you know who joined a gang. You could use the same basic framework, the main causes, to indicate why this particular person joined a gang.

WRITING AN OUTLINE

Your selection of a controlling idea takes you to the next writing phase: completing an outline or outline alternative. There you need to

- consider kinds of causes and effects.
- evaluate the importance of sequence.
- introduce ideas and work with patterns.

In its most basic form, your outline, derived mainly from points in your listing, might look like one of the following:

Paragraph of causes

Topic sentence: It is not just chance; people have reasons for joining gangs.

 I. Poverty (cause 1)
 II. Low academic achievement (cause 2)
 III. Lack of job opportunities (cause 3)

Essay of effects

Thesis: There are consequences of gang membership.

 I. Violence (effect 1)
 II. Criminal record (effect 2)
 III. Drug and alcohol addiction (effect 3)

CONSIDERING KINDS OF CAUSES AND EFFECTS

Causes and effects can be primary or secondary, immediate or remote.

Primary or Secondary

Primary means "major," and **secondary** means "minor." A primary cause may be sufficient to bring about the situation (subject). For example, infidelity may be a primary (and possibly sufficient by itself) cause of divorce for some people but not for others, who regard it as secondary. Or, if country X is attacked by country Y, the attack itself, as a primary cause, may be sufficient to bring on a declaration of war. But a diplomatic blunder regarding visas for workers may be of secondary importance, and, though significant, it is certainly not enough to start a war over.

Immediate or Remote

Causes and effects often occur at a distance in time or place from the situation. The immediate effect of sulfur in the atmosphere may be atmospheric pollution, but the long-range, or remote, effect may be acid rain and the loss of species. The immediate cause of the greenhouse effect may be the depletion of the ozone layer, whereas the long-range, or remote, cause is the use of CFCs (chlorofluorocarbons, commonly called Freon, which are found in such items as Styrofoam cups). Even more remote, the ultimate cause may be the people who use the products containing Freon. Your purpose will determine the causes and effects that are appropriate to include in your essay.

EVALUATING THE IMPORTANCE OF SEQUENCE

The sequence in which events occur may or may not be significant. When you are considering several events that happen in a row, determine whether one event brings about another?

Consider this sequence of events: Joe gets bad grades on his report card, and then Joe joins a gang. We know that one reason for joining a gang is low academic achievement. Therefore, we may conclude that Joe joined the gang because of his lack of success at school. But if we do so, we maybe have reached a wrong conclusion because Joe's joining the gang after receiving bad grades does not necessarily mean the two events are related. It's possible that Joe joined the gang out of fear or intimidation, for example.

In each case, examine the connections. To assume that one event is *caused* by another just because it *follows* the other is a logical error called a **post hoc** ("**after this**") **fallacy**. An economic depression may occur after a president takes office, but that does not necessarily mean the depression was caused by the new administration. It might have occurred anyway, perhaps in an even more severe form.

Order

The order of the causes and effects you discuss in your paper may be based on time, space, emphasis, or a combination.

- *Time*: If one stage leads to another, as in a discussion of the causes and effects of upper atmospheric pollution, your paper would be organized best by time.
- *Space*: In some instances, causes and effects are best organized by their relation in space. For example, the causes of an economic recession could be discussed in terms of local factors, regional factors, national factors, and international factors.
- *Emphasis*: Some causes and effects may be more important than others. For instance, if some causes of divorce are primary (perhaps infidelity and physical abuse) and others are secondary (such as annoying habits and laziness), a paper about divorce could present the secondary causes first and then move on to primary causes to emphasize the latter as more important.

In some situations, two or more factors (such as time and emphasis) may be linked; in that case, select the order that best fits what you are trying to say, or combine orders.

Transitional Words

Consider using the following transitional words to improve coherence by connecting ideas with ideas, sentences with sentences, and paragraphs with paragraphs.

CAUSE: as, because, because of, due to, for, for the reason that, since, bring about, another cause, for this reason, one cause, a second cause, another cause, a final cause

EFFECT: accordingly, finally, consequently, hence, so, therefore, thus, as a consequence, as a result, resulting

FOR ALL PATTERNS OF WRITING: The HOTSHOT CAT words: However, Otherwise, Therefore, Similarly, Hence, On the other hand, Then, Consequently, Also, Thus

INTRODUCING IDEAS AND WORKING WITH PATTERNS

In presenting your controlling idea—probably near the beginning for a paragraph or in an introductory paragraph for an essay—you will almost certainly want to perform two functions:

1. *Discuss your subject.* For example, if you are writing about the causes or effects of divorce, begin with a statement about divorce as a subject.

2. *Indicate whether you will concentrate on causes or effects or a combination of both.* That indication should be made clear early in the paper. Concentrating on one—causes or effects—does not mean you will not mention the other; it only means you will emphasize one of them. You can bring attention to your main concern(s)—causes, effects, or a combination—by repeating key words such as *cause*, *reason*, *effect*, *result*, *consequence*, and *outcome*.

The most likely pattern for your work is one of those shown in Figure 11.1. These patterns may look familiar to you.

Figure 11.1

Patterns for Paragraph and Essay

For Paragraph

Subject and Topic Sentence

Cause or Effect 1

Cause or Effect 2

Cause or Effect 3

Reflection on Topic Sentence

For Essay

Subject and Thesis

Topic Sentence

Cause or Effect 1

Topic Sentence

Cause or Effect 2

Topic Sentence

Cause or Effect 3

Conclusion

FINDING PATTERNS IN PHOTOS

EXERCISE 1 An Image-Based Activity for Groups or Individuals

As we gaze at the photo of a glove and a baseball sharing space with syringes and vials, we may be disappointed at what "our national pastime" has become, but we are probably not shocked. After all, numerous well-known athletes have tested positive for illegal performance-enhancing drugs, while others have been charged with using those drugs at some time in their past career. Learning from the media about the drug-related charges, suspensions, lawsuits, testimonies, and confessions has prompted many of us to become more cynical about the purity of sports, to question sports ethics, and even to reexamine our own values.

Either as individuals or in groups, as directed by your instructor, make two lists—one for causes and the other for effects. First list the causes with the possible motives of players (the users), of the suppliers (personal trainers, pushers, manufacturers), of the teams (management and sponsors), and even of the fans. Then change your focus from causes to effects on the same entities: players, suppliers, teams, and fans.

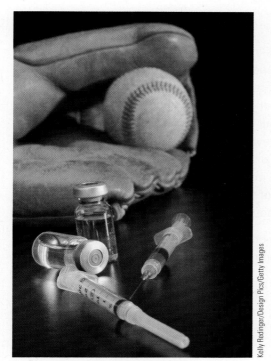

Kelly Redinger/Design Pics/Getty Images

Baseball glove with syringes and vials

Causes (why)	Trend	Effects (results)
	Athletes using illegal performance-enhancing drugs	
_____		_____
_____		_____
_____		_____
_____		_____
_____		_____
_____		_____
_____		_____

Possible Assignments (as directed by your instructor):

1. Class discussion of individual work

2. Class reports from group discussions

3. Writing assignment of a paragraph or an essay emphasizing either causes or effects on sports generally, a specific sport, or a specific player, with reference(s) to the photo

A SPECIFIC USE OF CAUSE AND EFFECT: THE SHORT STORY REVIEW

Short Story Review

A **short story** is a brief, imaginative narrative, with numerous functional elements (all of which can be analyzed): setting, conflict, characters, plot, theme, and point of view.

The overarching element of the short story is usually the plot. In the simplest terms, the plot begins when a character in a setting experiences (with or without being aware) a conflict. The plot develops as the character deals with the conflict in a single scene or sequence of scenes. All of this narrative is related from a first-person (*I*) or a third-person (*he*, *she*, *they*) point of view. The entire presentation has a theme, the underlying generalization or fictional point.

Short stories are fiction, meaning they are not a report of what has actually happened, though they may be based squarely on an author's experience.

Writing the Short Story Review

One theory about why we enjoy fiction—in print and film—is that we can analyze it. The events of our lives may often appear too complicated and close for us to figure out, but with fiction we can see connections more clearly. We can dissect fiction, examine the parts and their relationships, and speculate about what it all means. We can even relate fiction to our own experiences.

Like most writing, the short story review (analysis) is a combination of writing forms, but one form—analysis by division, comparison and contrast, cause and effect, or narration—may provide much of the pattern. For a short review, you will likely emphasize one aspect of the short story—setting, conflict, plot, character(s), theme, point of view—though you may touch on several.

- Develop your ideas by referring directly to the story; by explaining; and by using summaries, paraphrases, and quotations. Avoid the temptation to oversummarize.
- Use present tense in relating events in the story. For example, "Jude is trying to survive," not "Jude was trying to survive." Use quotation marks around the words you borrow and provide documentation if directed to do so by your instructor.
- Although a short story review is mainly analytical, it may include your speculation and call forth references to your personal experience.

Practicing Patterns of Cause and Effect

A detailed outline and your subsequent writing may include a combination of causes and effects, but almost always either causes *or* effects will be emphasized and will provide the main structure of your paper. Whether you are writing a basic outline for an assignment outside of class without a significant time constraint or you are writing in class under the pressure of time, you will always have a chance to jot down prewriting lists and a simple outline.

EXERCISE 2 Completing Patterns of Cause and Effect

Complete the following list on bullying. Then select three primary causes or three primary effects that could be used in writing a paragraph or an essay on this topic.

Causes   Effects

((Bullying))

Primary causes   Primary effects

1. _____   1. _____

2. _____   2. _____

3. _____   3. _____

EXERCISE 3 Completing Patterns of Cause and Effect

Complete the following list on air pollution. Then select three primary causes or three primary effects that could be used in writing a paragraph or an essay on this topic.

Causes   Effects

((Air Pollution))

Primary causes   Primary effects

1. _____   1. _____

2. _____   2. _____

3. _____   3. _____

EXERCISE 4 Completing Patterns of Cause and Effect

Complete the following list on getting enough sleep. Then select three primary causes or three primary effects that could be used in writing a paragraph or an essay on this topic.

Causes   Effects

((Getting Enough Sleep))

Primary causes

1. _____

2. _____

3. _____

Primary effects

1. _____

2. _____

3. _____

EXERCISE 5   Completing Patterns of Cause and Effect

Complete the following list on stress. Then select three primary causes or three primary effects that could be used in writing a paragraph or an essay on this topic.

Causes   Effects

Stress

Primary causes

1. _____

2. _____

3. _____

Primary effects

1. _____

2. _____

3. _____

EXERCISE 6   Completing a Pattern of Cause

Fill in the blanks to complete this outline of cause.

Causes for dropping out of high school

I. Financial pressures

II. _____

III. _____

IV. _____

EXERCISE 7   Completing a Pattern of Cause

Fill in the blanks to complete this outline of cause.

Causes for adopting a pet

I. To gain a loving companion

II. _____

III. _____

EXERCISE 8   Completing a Pattern of Effect

Fill in the blanks to complete this outline of effect.

Effects of practicing yoga

I. Increased flexibility

II. _____

III. _____

IV. _____

EXERCISE 9   Completing a Pattern of Effect

Fill in the blanks to complete this outline of effect.

Effects of becoming a parent

I. Increased responsibility

II. _____

III. _____

Readings for Critical Thinking, Discussion, and Writing

READING STRATEGIES AND OBJECTIVES

Underlining and annotating these reading selections will help you answer the questions that follow the selections, discuss the material in class, and prepare for reading-based writing assignments. As you underline and annotate, pay special attention to the author's writing skills, logic, and message, and consider the relevance of the material to your own experiences and values.

PARAGRAPH

Doing It for Money, Not Love*

ROY F. BAUMEISTER AND BRAD J. BUSHMAN

This paragraph is taken from the Second Edition of Social Psychology and Human Nature *by Roy F. Baumeister and Brad J. Bushman, published by Wadsworth Cengage Learning in 2011. Professor Baumeister teaches at Florida State University. Professor Bushman teaches at the University of Michigan and VU University, Amsterdam, the Netherlands.*

Topic sentence

Cause

One of the most important and dramatic instances of self-perception involves motivation. Early on, social psychologists learned to distinguish between intrinsic and extrinsic motivation. Intrinsic motivation refers to wanting to perform an activity for its own sake. The activity is an end in itself. Someone might be intrinsically

*From BAUMEISTER/BUSHMAN. *Social Psychology and Human Nature, Comprehensive Edition*, 2E. © 2011 Wadsworth, a part of Cengage Learning, Inc. Reproduced by permission. www.cengage .com/permissions

Cause

motivated to paint, for example, because he enjoys the process of dabbing colors onto a canvas and takes satisfaction in creating a beautiful or striking picture. Extrinsic motivation, in contrast, refers to performing an activity because of something that results from it. The activity is a means to some other end—it is pursued for what it accomplishes or leads to, rather than for the activity itself. A person who is extrinsically motivated to paint might paint in order to make money. This painter might be very motivated and might work very hard, even if she did not really like painting much at all. One test would be whether the person would choose to spend free time doing the activity, in the absence of external rewards or incentives. An intrinsically motivated painter might well spend a free Sunday afternoon painting, but an extrinsically motivated painter would not (unless there was money or some other incentive). Bill Russell, the former basketball star, said, "I remember that the game lost some of its magical qualities for me once I thought seriously about playing for a living."

EXERCISE 10   Discussion and Critical Thinking

1. What is the main difference between intrinsic motivation and extrinsic motivation?

2. What do the authors compare and contrast in this paragraph?

3. How did Bill Russell's motivations to play basketball change over time?

4. Consider your career goals. Are you more intrinsically or extrinsically motivated? Explain.

5. Is one kind of motivation more important than the other? Why or why not?

ESSAY

California Prisons Agree to Scale Back Solitary Confinement*

IAN LOVETT

This article about prison reform by reporter Ian Lovett appeared in The New York Times *on September 1, 2015.*

1   California has agreed to an overhaul of its use of solitary confinement in its prisons, including strict limits on the prolonged isolation of inmates, as part of a landmark legal settlement filed in federal court on Tuesday.

2   The settlement is expected to sharply reduce the number of inmates held in the state's isolation units, where inmates are often kept alone for more than 22 hours a day inside cells that sometimes have no windows, and cap the length of time prisoners can spend there.

3   Prison officials have used solitary confinement to separate prisoners who they say are too dangerous to house with the general population, either because they have been violent in prison or because they have been identified as gang members. Many such prisoners are left in solitary confinement indefinitely, with severe psychological effects; hundreds have spent more than a decade in isolation.

4   But a number of corrections officials across the country have increasingly come to see locking up inmates for years at a time as ineffective. Some human rights groups have assailed it as torture, and tens of thousands of inmates across California have participated in hunger strikes since 2011 to protest the state's use of solitary.

5   The California agreement, which settles a lawsuit brought by inmates held in isolation for at least 10 years at Pelican Bay State Prison near the Oregon border, marks a major shift in corrections practices in the state, one that prison reform advocates hope can serve as a model for other states.

6   Prisoners will no longer be sent to isolation indefinitely. And gang members will no longer be sent to solitary confinement based solely on their gang affiliation; only inmates found guilty of violating serious prison rules, like violence against other prisoners, weapons possession or escape, will be sent to isolation.

7   The state will create a new unit for prisoners who are deemed too dangerous to return to the general population, where they will have more privileges than in solitary, like more time out of their cells, small group leisure activities and some job opportunities and phone calls.

8   Gang members who have served their sentences in solitary, meanwhile, will enter a two-year program that will allow them some privileges—like phone calls— before they are placed back in the general prison population.

9   "This brings California in line with more modern national prison practices," said Jules Lobel, the president of the Center for Constitutional Right and a law professor at the University of Pittsburgh, who was the lead lawyer for the inmates in their suit against the state. "People have been kept in solitary confinement for outrageously long periods of time. That's one of the problems in the U.S.—people are ware-housed in these places, and now that's going to change."

10   Solitary confinement has come under increasing scrutiny across the country, as research has revealed the effects of long-term isolation on the psyche.

11   The suicide of Kalief Browder in June, after nearly two years in isolation at New York City's Rikers Island, brought renewed attention to young people in solitary confinement. That same month, Justice Anthony Kennedy of the Supreme Court seemed to invite a constitutional challenge to prolonged solitary confinement.

12   No state has housed more prisoners in solitary confinement, or kept them there for longer, than California, according to the Center for Constitutional Rights. As of Monday, 2,858 prisoners were in solitary housing units across the state. More than 1,100 were in Pelican Bay, the state's toughest prison, where the isolation cells do not have windows.

13   The lawsuit settled on Tuesday argued that the long-term isolation constituted a form of cruel and unusual punishment, and violated the prisoners' Eighth Amendment rights.

14   Since the hunger strikes began in 2011, inmates in long-term isolation had already won several concessions, like calendars for the walls in their cells. And the number of those held for over a decade in solitary confinement at Pelican Bay has dropped to 62 from more than 300 in 2012.

15   The settlement will probably push those numbers down even more, as the state moves away from policies that have used solitary confinement to help curb gangs.

16   All inmates who were sent to solitary confinement because of gang affiliations will have their cases reviewed within a year; unless they have committed another offense, they will be released to the general population. Prisoners who have been held in solitary for at least 10 years are expected to be released immediately with few exceptions, lawyers for the plaintiffs said.

17   And no one will be held in isolation units for more than 10 consecutive years, except in rare cases, which will be subject to review by a magistrate judge, the lawyers said.

18   "This settlement represents a monumental victory for prisoners and an important step toward our goal of ending solitary confinement in California, and across the country," the inmates who brought the lawsuit said in a written statement released by their lawyers. "The prisoners' human rights movement is awakening the conscience of the nation to recognize that we are fellow human beings."

EXERCISE 11   Vocabulary Highlights

Write a short definition of each word as it is used in the essay. (Paragraph numbers are given in parentheses.) Be prepared to use these words in sentences.

overhaul (1)	constituted (13)
indefinitely (3)	concessions (14)
assailed (4)	affiliations (16)
scrutiny (10)	consecutive (17)
psyche (10)	conscience (18)

EXERCISE 12   Discussion and Critical Thinking

1. What is solitary confinement?

2. Why have prison officials used solitary confinement?

3. What are the possible effects of long-term solitary confinement on inmates?

4. How did the death of Kalief Broder influence public opinion regarding the use of long-term solitary confinement in prisons?

5. What is the expected effect of the California settlement?

6. Before the settlement, how had the use of solitary confinement in California compared to the use of solitary confinement in other states?

7. What alternative practices will California officials use instead of solitary confinement?

8. The author quotes the inmates who initiated the lawsuit as saying that the California settlement is "one important step toward our goal." What is their ultimate goal?

9. Do you think that solitary confinement should be banned nationwide? Why or why not?

VIEWS ON VIOLENCE

Depending on the perspective of an individual, violence may be regarded in quite different ways. Here, in three essays, we have three different views.

- "The Ghetto Made Me Do It" makes a case for significantly taking into account the traumatic, violent childhood of those who go on to commit violent crimes.
- "Enough Is Enough" stresses the need for a perpetrator of violent crimes to accept personal responsibility without casting primary blame on society generally or family specifically. She says that most youngsters growing up in a difficult environment struggle to do what is right and do not play the "victim game."
- "From 'Kick Me' to 'Kiss Me'" is written by an inmate who was raised in an environment of violence, who learned to be violent, and who is now learning about herself.

The Ghetto Made Me Do It*

FRANCIS FLAHERTY

This essay by freelance author Francis Flaherty was first published in In These Times, *a magazine from Chicago.*

1   When Felicia "Lisa" Morgan was growing up, her parents would sit down to meals with guns next to their plates. They were defending themselves—against each other.

2   "This was Lisa's dinner," explains attorney Robin Shellow. "She was seven at the time."

3   If nothing else, Lisa Morgan's childhood in a poor, inner-city Milwaukee neighborhood starkly illustrates the tragic effects of omnipresent urban violence. "Mom shot dad," Shellow says. "And Mom shot boyfriend. . . . [Lisa's] uncle, who was actually her age, was murdered. Two days later, her other uncle was murdered. Her sister's boyfriend was paralyzed from the neck down by gunfire. Her brother was shot at and injured. Her mother once had set her father on fire."

4   If this weren't enough tragedy in one young life, Lisa Morgan's mother was a drug addict and Lisa was raped at age 12.

*Francis Flaherty, "The Ghetto Made Me Do It," In These Times, April 5, 1993. Reprinted by permission.

The "Ghetto Defense"

5   So perhaps it's not too surprising that Morgan, as a teenager, committed six armed robberies and one intentional homicide in the space of 17 minutes in October 1991. The victims were girls; the stolen objects were jewelry, shoes, and a coat. The dead girl was shot at point-blank range.

6   What *is* surprising—to the legal establishment, at least—is the approach Robin Shellow used in defending Morgan. In the girl's neighborhood and in her family, Shellow argued, violence is a *norm*, an occurrence so routine that Morgan's 17 years of exposure to it have rendered her not responsible for her actions.

7   This "ghetto defense" proved fruitless in Morgan's case. In court, the young woman was found both sane and guilty. Unless Shellow wins on appeal, Morgan will be behind bars well into [this] century.

8   But despite its failure for Morgan, Shellow's "cultural psychosis" or "psychosocial history" strategy has taken hold. "I've gotten hundreds of calls from interested attorneys," Shellow says. Already, the defense is being floated in courtrooms around the nation. It's eliciting both enthusiasm and outrage.

The Defense Is a Medical One

9   Technically, Shellow's defense is a medical one. She believes that Morgan suffers from post-traumatic stress disorder (PTSD) and other psychological ailments stemming from her lifelong exposure to violence.

10   Like other good lawyers, Shellow knows that the law abhors broadly applicable excuses, so she emphasizes the narrowness of her claim. Morgan belongs to a very small group of inner-city residents with "tremendous intra-familial violence," only some of whom might experience PTSD. She also stresses the unrevolutionary nature of the defense, medically and legally. PTSD has been recognized as a malady in standard diagnostic texts since 1980, she says, and it has been employed as a criminal defense for Vietnam veterans, battered wives, and many other trauma victims.

11   Despite Shellow's attempts to show that her defense is neither new nor broad, the case is ringing loud alarms. For, however viewed, her strategy sets up an inflammatory equation between inner-city conditions and criminal exculpation. The implication is that if you grew up in a poor, violent neighborhood and you commit a crime, you may go scot-free.

12   Yet why not a ghetto defense? After all, if a Vietnam veteran can claim PTSD from the shock of war, why shouldn't a similar defense be available for a young black reared in the embattled precincts of Bed-Stuy [Bedford-Stuyvesant neighborhood of New York City]? Sounds sensible, no? Isn't a ghetto like a battlefield?

Compare These Neighborhoods to War Zones

13   Alex Kotlowitz, who chronicled the lives of two Chicago black boys in *There Are No Children Here*, goes even further. He says the inner city can be worse than war. "You hear constant comparisons of these neighborhoods to war zones, but I think there are some pretty significant differences," he says. "In war, there's at least a sense that someday there will be a resolution, some vision that things could be different. That is not the case in the inner cities. There is no vision. And there's no sense of who's friend and who's foe."

14   There are other analogies that make the ghetto defense seem very legitimate. For instance, despite traditional self-defense principles, a battered wife in some jurisdictions can kill her sleeping husband and be legally excused for the homicide. The reason is the psychological harm she has sustained from her life of fear and violence.

15   Why not Lisa Morgan? Hasn't her life been debilitatingly violent and fearful?

16   These arguments make some lawyers hopeful about the future of Shellow's pioneering strategy. But most observers are pessimistic. "We'll get nowhere with it," says famous defense lawyer William Kunstler.

The Poor Instead of the Powerful

17   Why? One reason is that the American justice system often favors the powerful over the poor. For generations, for instance, the bloodiest crime in the nation—drunk driving—was punished with a relative wrist slap. By contrast, a recent federal law mandates that those convicted of the new crime of carjacking get socked with a minimum and mandatory 15-year sentence.

18   What explains these disparate approaches? Simple: protection of the affluent classes. Light penalties for drunk driving protect the affluent because they often drive drunk. Harsh carjacking penalties protect the affluent because they are the usual carjacking victims. "The middle class sees carjacking [laws] as protecting them from people coming out of some poor neighborhood and just showing up in their neighborhood and committing a crime in which they are at risk of dying," says Professor James Liebman of Columbia University School of Law.

19   Because the ghetto defense protects the poor instead of the powerful, Kunstler and others doubt it has a bright future. Other factors further dim the strategy's chances. Fear is a main one, says Professor Liebman. The ghetto defense brings a gulp from jurors because "their first thought is, 'If he's not responsible, then none of those people are,'" he reasons. And we all know what that means: riots, mayhem, Los Angeles.

20   Social guilt raises even higher the hurdles for the ghetto defense. To allow such a defense is a tacit admission that we—society—tolerate a situation so hobbling that its victims have become unaccountable for their actions. "If it ain't them who's guilty, it's us," says Michael Dowd, director of the Pace University Battered Women's Justice Center in New York. And "it's just too horrific for us to accept responsibility, too horrific to say, 'I'm responsible for what happened in L.A.' We will be able to accept the [ghetto] defense at the same moment that we are seriously moved to eradicate the realities behind that defense."

21   What are the biggest criticisms of the ghetto defense? One focuses on the victim's identity. Battered spouses and battered children are accused of killing precisely those who hurt them. This endows the crime with a certain rough justice. But in a ghetto defense case, the victim is usually an innocent stranger.

22   Others, like Kotlowitz, worry that the ghetto defense might dislodge the cornerstone of our justice system: personal responsibility. "We have to be careful not to view people growing up in neighborhoods completely as victims; they are both victims and actors," he warns. "We can't absolve them from responsibility."

23   Lisa Morgan "went up to someone she didn't know, stole a jacket from her, and then just blew her away," he says. "There's no way as a society that we can excuse that. We can understand it, but we can't excuse it."

24   He raises a fundamental question. Everyone can point to scars from the past—alcoholic parents, tragic love, etc.—and claim exculpation. And if all are excused, who is responsible?

25   Another worry is diminished standards. "[The ghetto defense] lowers expectations," Kotlowitz continues. "It says, 'OK, I understand what you've been through, so it's OK to go out and hurt somebody.' And once you lower your expectations, particularly with kids, they will meet only those lower expectations."

A Disease Is a Disease

26   It's only fair to note that other criminal defenses also have these weaknesses. For instance, the victim of a PTSD-afflicted veteran is often an innocent passerby, and the battered-spouse doctrine certainly raises questions about personal responsibility and lowered expectations.

27   And if, as seems likely, some ghetto residents do have PTSD largely as a result of their living conditions, it's hard to see why this ailment should be exculpatory for veterans, say, but not for ghetto residents. After all, a disease is a disease, and how you got it is irrelevant.

28   How deep go the wounds from the ghetto? Here are two incidents in Morgan's life: "When Felicia was about 11, her mother put a knife to her throat and threatened to kill her," according to a psychologist's report in the case. "Felicia escaped by running into the basement, where she 'busted the lights out with my hand' so that her mother could not see her." Then, when she was 12, the landlord attacked her. "Felicia fought him off by throwing hot grease onto him, but he finally subdued her, tied her hands to the bed, stuffed her mouth with a sock and raped her."

29   How does one live like this? Morgan gives a hint. "My ears be open," she told the psychologist, "even when I'm asleep."

30   This was a *child*. Society did nothing to stop these daily depredations upon her. While the legal propriety of the ghetto defense is an important question, the biggest question of all in this story has nothing to do with personal responsibility. It has to do with society's responsibility to poor children like Morgan. What does it say about our society that such a defense was conceived? How can things have come to this pass?

EXERCISE 13   Vocabulary Highlights

Write a short definition of each word as it is used in the essay. (Paragraph numbers are given in parentheses.) Be prepared to use these words in sentences.

omnipresent (3)	exculpation (11)
rendered (6)	sustained (14)
eliciting (8)	debilitatingly (15)
abhors (10)	tacit (20)
malady (10)	eradicate (20)

EXERCISE 14   Discussion and Critical Thinking

1. What writing pattern does Flaherty use in the first four paragraphs that serve as an introduction to her essay?

2. Which sentence in which paragraph contains the definition of "ghetto defense"?

3. What is post-traumatic stress disorder (PTSD)?

4. Does Shellow argue that all poor people living in the ghetto be granted excuses for any crimes they commit? If not, what is she arguing?

5. How is Morgan's case arguably similar to and different from those of battered spouses?

6. How is Morgan's case arguably similar to those of certain war veterans with PTSD who committed homicide?

7. According to Kotlowitz, how can the inner-city environment be worse than that of a war zone?

8. According to the ghetto defense, where does responsibility lie, with the person or with society?

9. What is your opinion of the ghetto defense? Explain your answer.

10. If the ghetto defense has validity, should the concept be extended to anyone who has had extremely violent experiences—"Everyone can point to scars from the past—alcoholic parents, tragic love, etc." (paragraph 24)? Why or why not?

11. Imagine you were a juror judging Morgan's case. How would you have voted and why?

Enough Is Enough

JUDY SHEINDLIN AND JOSH GETLIN

Judy Sheindlin is best known as the star of Judge Judy, *a top-rated American reality-based television court show. For twenty-five years prior to her media stardom, she served as a family court judge in New York. This commentary comes from a book written with Josh Getlin, titled* Don't Pee on My Leg and Tell Me It's Raining.

1   As a family court judge, I looked down daily on a pageant of dysfunction that would curl your hair. After twenty-four years on the bench, I came to realize that these are not legal problems. They mirror what is wrong with our society, reflecting just how far we have strayed from personal responsibility and old-fashioned discipline.

2   Most of the kids I prosecuted during my early years in court were involved in petty thefts, but as the 70s passed into the 80s, both the incidence and the ferocity of juvenile crime accelerated. A new breed of delinquents was born, and the system did not have a clue how to treat them. We still don't. . . .

3   I believe that you deal with these problems the way you would deal with any crisis in a family: by setting strict limits and by showing compassion. As the mother of five children, I know that you have to get tough at the same time that you show love. Family court should be no different. I think we should send a tough message to first-time offenders every chance we get, in the hopes that perhaps there will not be a second offense.

4   The primary obligation of any civilized society is to preserve the peace and protect its citizens. Only after that should you worry about the lawbreakers and their rehabilitation. This might be our last chance to do something about the future of these delinquents—and our own safety.

EXERCISE 15   Discussion and Critical Thinking

1. According to Judge Judy, what is wrong with our society?

2. How does she feel about showing compassion to first-time offenders?

3. Do you agree with Judge Judy's tough-love approach? Why or why not?

STUDENT ESSAY

From "Kick Me" to "Kiss Me"

SHANDRA BRYSON (PSEUDONYM)

Victims of abuse do not always feel sorry for themselves. They also do not always protect others who are being abused. These are shocking conclusions reached by Shandra Bryson, a victim who now looks at herself thoughtfully.

1   I can identify with people who were physically abused as children. I am one of them, and I've got all kinds of scars. In prison, I am surrounded by people with a background similar to mine. Like me, they are trying to leave a whole pattern of thinking and behavior behind. Here in prison, a woman I know filed a grievance against a guard who, she said, had struck her numerous times. When the Watch Commander read the statement, he said, "You didn't fill in this part that says, 'Action Requested'?" Her answer was immediate. "I want people to stop beating me unless I deserve it." A former victim of child abuse, she was taking an important step. The final one would occur when she stopped believing that she should be beaten for any reason. Some people might think that understanding is simple,

Thesis

but it isn't. First, one has to understand what happens to a person who gets beat on every day.

2   When I was a little kid, my father used to abuse me—in ways I don't want to describe just yet. Abuse was a normal part of my life. He especially liked to throw things such as ashtrays, books, the TV remote control, and beer cans (usually with beer in them). Then if he missed, he'd get even madder and chase me down and

Effect

pound me with his fists. Naturally I figured out it would be better to be hit with a flying object than to be pounded, so I learned to move toward whatever he threw. He never seemed to catch on. I'd lunge toward something like an ashtray, and it'd hit me—fleshy parts like my seat were the best targets—and then I'd cry, and he'd stop. Sometimes he'd say how sorry he was and how I got him all upset. It always was my fault.

Effect   3   Of course, I believed it was my fault. <u>Whenever he hit me, however he did it. I knew I deserved it, if not for the immediate mischief, for something else—I was wicked</u>. I always felt more guilt than anger. My life was full of guilt-producing incidents. I received bad grades in school. I embarrassed him in front of his friends. I got in his way around the house. The food I cooked was never as good as that cooked by my mother, who'd disappeared four years after I was born—which was another source of guilt because she probably didn't like me. There were plenty of reasons for me to feel guilty, and I didn't neglect any of them.

4   But I wasn't the only one around the house who felt guilty. <u>My little brother had his share of guilt feelings</u>. For him, it was not my father he had to watch out for.

Effect   My father thought Joey could do no wrong. <u>I was the one who beat Joey</u>. When my father was out, I slapped Joey around and threw things—ashtrays, books, hair brushes, whatever I had. Pretty soon I had me a little whiner to pick on, so I could feel better. I even had him apologizing, acting mousier than I ever did, and even cutting on himself.

5   Finally, when I went to school with bruises for the hundredth time, a teacher

Effect   took me to the principal, and I told all. <u>The result was juvenile hall, followed by a half-dozen foster homes and a pattern of beating by adults in all kinds of situations—even by men I lived with</u>.

Effects   6   Being abused is bad. <u>It made me feel guilty</u>. <u>It made me want to be abused. And it made me want to be an abuser</u>. Now I'm working on undoing the pattern of thinking that I've had all these years. I want to take the "Kick me" sign off my back and replace it with one that reads "Kiss me." But right now I'm all so mixed up in changing that if someone did kiss me, I don't know whether I'd kiss back or kick.

EXERCISE 16   Discussion and Critical Thinking

1. Does the author seem to understand her situation well in terms of causes and effects? Explain.

2. How would you relate the content of this essay to the two previous essays on the causes of violence?

3. If you were a judge in a case in which Shandra Bryson were the defendant, and you knew the story of her childhood, would you consider her family history in determining her incarceration or treatment? How do you think you might rule and what would you say to her?

STUDENT PARAGRAPH AND ESSAY

Responding to an assignment on a topic organized mainly around causes and effects, Richard Blaylock chose to write about the consequences of his becoming a college student. With much trepidation, at thirty-three he had enrolled in the evening program at a local community college. The reasons for his being there were multiple, and so, to his surprise, were the results.

Blaylock's Writing Process Worksheet shows how his writing evolved from idea to final draft. To conserve space here, the freewriting and the rough drafts marked for revision have been omitted. The balance of his worksheet has been lengthened for you to be able to see his other work in its entirety.

BRANDON BRIDGE

Writing Process Worksheet

Name Richard Blaylock   **Title** The Classroom and Beyond   **Due Date** Tuesday, May 8, noon

Use the back of this page or separate paper if you need more space.

Assignment

In the space below, write whatever you need to know about your assignment, including information about the topic, audience, pattern of writing, length, whether to include a rough draft or revised drafts, and whether your paper must be typed.

In a paragraph of 200 to 300 words, discuss the causes or effects of any new element in your life at any point. The element could be a relationship, death, health problem, marriage, college program, new job, or winning ticket in the lottery. Submit this completed worksheet, a rough draft marked for revision, and a typed final draft.

Stage One

Explore   Free write, brainstorm (list), cluster, or take notes as directed by your instructor.

Listing

Causes	Event, Situation, or Trend	Effects
Boss's suggestion	My going to college	Family pride
Company pays		Wife inspired
My desire		Personal growth
Family support		More competitive at work
		Better pay
		Work scholarship
		Tired
		School friendships

Stage Two

Organize   Write a topic sentence or thesis; label the subject and the focus parts.

My decision to enroll in college night school would offer more benefits than I could have imagined.

                     subject   focus

Write an outline or an outline alternative. For reading-based writing, include references and short quotations with page numbers as support in the outline.

I. Effects on family
   A. Wife inspired
   B. Family proud
II. Effects on me
   A. Learn usable skills
   B. More confident
   C. More curious
III. Effects at work
   A. In line for better pay
   B. Soon given new responsibilities
   C. Given new respect

Stage Three

Write   On separate paper, write and then revise your paragraph or essay as many times as necessary for **c**oherence, **l**anguage (usage, tone, and diction), **u**nity, **e**mphasis, **s**upport, and **s**entences (**CLUESS**). Read your work aloud to hear and correct any grammatical errors or awkward-sounding sentences.

Edit any problems in fundamentals, such as **c**apitalization, **g**rammar, **p**unctuation, and **s**pelling (**CGPS**).

Final Draft

THE CLASSROOM AND BEYOND
Richard Blaylock

"We think you would benefit from our work-study program," he said to me. He was not my high school counselor, and I wasn't 18. He was the division manager, and he had just offered to pay my expenses for attending a local community college. At 33, I was working for a large company in a dead-end job, dead-end because I was not qualified for any management positions. Naturally, I enrolled in college. More benefits than I expected were to follow. I had hardly started when the first response greeted me: my family was clearly proud. I heard my two kids in elementary school bragging about me to kids in the neighborhood. They even brought me some of their tough homework questions. My wife had lots of questions about college. We talked about taking a class together. Unlike me, she had been a good student in high school. Then I had had no interest in going on to college. Now I did, and one thing led to another. A geography class connected me with a geology class. A political science class moved me to subscribe to the *Los Angeles Times*. I became more curious about a variety of subjects, and I felt more confident in dealing with ideas. At work my supervisors started asking me to become more involved in ongoing projects and planning. By the time I had taken my second English class, I was writing reports with much more confidence and skill. Now, after receiving a good job review and being interviewed by my plant manager, I am in line for a promotion that I once thought was beyond my reach. At most, I had expected a classroom. I found much more.

EXERCISE 17   Discussion and Critical Thinking

1. Is this an essay mainly of causes or effects?

2. Circle the topic sentence.

3. Underline each effect.

READING-BASED WRITING: SHORT STORY REVIEW

The Use of Self-Analysis

GLORIA MENDEZ

This essay explains that the first-person point of view places the central character in "The Use of Force" in close focus, with all his strengths and weaknesses there on the surface for our analysis—and for his own. The underlinings and margin notes have been added to show how Mendez organized her final draft.

Thesis	1	One of the main thrusts in "The Use of Force" is point of view. <u>The narrator, a doctor, tells his own story, a story about his encounter with an uncooperative patient but also—and mostly—a story about the narrator's transformation from a mature, rational person to someone of a lower order who has lost considerable self-respect.</u> This transformation happens in stages of changes in attitude that occur during his arrival, his early attempt at obtaining cooperation, his loss of self-control, and his reflection on his behavior.
Parts of support		
Topic sentence	2	<u>When the doctor arrives at the small farmhouse, he feels like an outsider.</u> The family is self-conscious and not sure about how to act around a doctor. They are poor, and out of concern for the daughter, are spending some of their meager funds to get a diagnosis and possible treatment. The doctor sees that they are "all very nervous, eyeing me up and down distrustfully . . ." (330). They tell him very little, wanting to get their money's worth.
Causes		
Quotation and references		
Topic sentence	3	<u>The doctor initially follows standard procedure.</u> He sees that the daughter is feverish and panting. With concern about a local diphtheria epidemic, he asks the mother if she had looked at the girl's throat. In a foreshadowing that the doctor does not catch, the mother says, "I tried to . . . but I couldn't see." Moving to the hands-on stage, he asks the girl to open her mouth. "Nothing doing." He tries a gentle approach, shows her he has no concealed weapons by opening his hands. But her mother mentions the word "hurt," and the doctor grinds his "teeth in disgust" (330). He maintains his composure as he approaches her. She loses hers, as she tries to scratch his eyes out and succeeds in knocking his glasses to the floor.
Cause		
Quotations and references		
Causes		
Topic sentence	4	<u>Both his tact and his attitude change.</u> The parents are embarrassed; they apologize, threaten the daughter, and awkwardly try to help the doctor. He's disgusted with them, however; they've done all the wrong things. But he admires the girl, even saying he had "already fallen in love with the savage brat" (330). He knows that her anger is caused by her fear of him. He decides to use force—for her own good. The possibility that she has diphtheria is there. The girl's resistance builds: she screams and struggles. He uses a "wooden tongue depressor," and she chews it "into splinters" (331).
Effect		
Causes		
Quotations and references		

3. Decide whether to concentrate on causes, effects, or a combination of causes and effects. Most paragraphs will focus only on causes or only on effects. Many short essays will discuss causes and effects but will use one as the framework for the piece. A typical basic outline might look like this:

Topic sentence of paragraph or thesis of essay
 I. Cause or Effect 1
 II. Cause or Effect 2
 III. Cause or Effect 3

4. Do not conclude that something is an effect merely because it follows something else.

5. Emphasize your main concern(s)—causes, effects, or a combination—by repeating key words such as *cause*, *reason*, *effect*, *result*, *consequence*, and *outcome*.

6. Causes and effects can be primary or secondary, immediate or remote.

7. The order of causes and effects in your paper may be based on time, space, emphasis, or a combination.

8. The short story review is likely to include the following:

 * In a short paper, you would probably use one or more of the short story's elements: setting, conflict, characters, plot, point of view, theme.
 * Develop your ideas by referring directly to the story; by explaining; and by using summaries, paraphrases, and quotations.
 * Use the present tense in relating events in the story.

9. **Consider using the Writing Process Worksheet and the Brandon Guide for Revising and Editing for completing your assignment and the Revising and Editing Charts after your assignment is returned.**

Practicing the Brandon Guide for Revising and Editing

PATTERN: CAUSE AND EFFECT

Death by Gangbanging
ANNA GONZALES (PSEUDONYM)

(A) He was one of seventeen killed in one gangbanging weekend in a place called "the city of Angels." (B) Lying there in the baby blue casket with the white satin lining, he looked peaceful, but he left behind a world of vilence and turmoil. (C) His life cut short like the flowers on display around him that would wilt and die in hours. (D) Sorting out the causes of his becoming a gang member is not easy. (E) First, he got off to a bad start because his father was a gang member. (F) Once when a young teacher, with helpful intentions, tried to tell the father that his son might be a gang member, he said, "My kid's not a gang member. (G) He's just a wannabe, and I'm a gang member." (H) The young man idolized his father, and when his father was gunned down at a party, the family tradition of gang membership didn't die. (I) Then, a few years later, the young man would meet the stepfather who came into his home. (J) The stepfather soon decided it was time to dish out some *tough love,* but he left out the *love* part. (K) Next, fights started with the neighborhood gang, and the young man laughed and said, If you can't beat 'em, join 'em. (L) Finally, join 'em he did. (M) He said he found family and protection. (N) He wasn't bad. (O) Deep down he had a good heart, and he could be funny and warm. (P) He just had too much going against him. (Q) I should know. (R) I'm his mother.

EXERCISE 18   Revise and Edit with the Brandon Guide

Revise with CLUESS **(pronounce as "clues" for easy memorization).**

1. **C**oherence: Connect your ideas. Circle the four transitional connectives that introduce the causes and connect ideas.

2. **L**anguage: Use words appropriate for your purpose and audience. Draw a line through the slang phrase (two words) and insert a better word choice above it.

3. **U**nity: Stay on your topic. Underline the topic sentence that unites the paragraph.

4. **E**mphasis: Call attention to your important ideas. Make a box around the word and its related forms that are used most frequently.

5. **S**upport: Back up your controlling ideas with evidence and logic. In the left margin, annotate this narrative that provides a framework for the discussion of causes. Use these words: *situation, conflict, struggle, outcome, meaning.*

6. **Sentences**: Write correct, effective sentences with structural variety. Bring more impact to the statement by changing sentence G to two sentences. Just cross out one word and add a period.

Edit with C G P S **(pronounce as "see GPS" for easy memorization).**

7. **Capitalization**: One word is incorrectly capitalized; cross out the capital letter and write the lowercase letter above it.

8. **Grammar**: One sentence that is punctuated as a sentence is a fragment. By using a change in punctuation and capitalization, join that word group to the sentence that appears before it.

9. **Punctuation**: The quotation marks are missing from a quotation. Insert them.

10. **Spelling**: One word is misspelled. Cross it out and write the correct spelling above it.

12

Classification
Establishing Groups

 "Writing, to me, is simply thinking through my fingers."

—ISAAC ASIMOV

CHAPTER CONTENTS

BRANDON BRIDGE

When to Use Classification

FOR COLLEGE WRITING ASSIGNMENTS

If you are writing a statement of any length—sentence, paragraph, essay, or report—that is based on the phrase "different kinds—or classes—of [*your subject*]," you will use classification.

- In a literature course, you might write about different types of narrative forms or techniques.
- In a history course, you might write about different kinds of citizens, leaders, or governments.
- In an industrial design course, you might write about a variety of manufacturing processes.

Each of those classes will be formed according to a single principle that indicates your focus.

IN CAREERS AND AT THE WORKPLACE

Whether in preparation for a vocation or at the workplace, one deals critically with the formation of groups.

- Careers can be grouped according to common denominators of job descriptions, conditions, benefits, and requirements.
- Clients, products, and services are commonly grouped, or classified, in reports and by focus groups for analysis.

CLASSIFICATION IN A CARTOON

THE QUIGMANS   by Buddy Hickerson

THE MOST UNPLEASANT THING ABOUT BEING THE ONLY STUDENT IN THIS CLASS WILL BE WHEN I ASK YOU TO BREAK UP INTO GROUPS.

B. Hickerson, copyright Los Angeles Times Syndicate. Reprinted with permission

Writing Classification

To explain by classification, you put persons, places, things, or ideas into groups or classes based on their characteristics. Whereas analysis by division deals with the characteristics of just one unit, classification deals with more than one unit, so the subject is plural.

To classify efficiently, try following this procedure:

1. Select a plural subject.

2. Decide on a principle for grouping the units of your subject.

3. Establish the groups, or classes.

4. Write about the classes.

SELECTING A SUBJECT

When you say you have different kinds of neighbors, friends, teachers, bosses, or interests, you are classifying; that is, you are forming groups.

In naming the different kinds of people in your neighborhood, you might think of different groupings of your neighbors, the units. For example, some neighbors are friendly, some are meddlesome, and some are private. Some neighbors have yards like Japanese gardens, some have yards like neat-but-cozy parks, and some have yards like abandoned lots. Some neighbors are affluent, some are comfortable, and some are struggling. Each of these sets is a classification system and could be the focus of one paragraph in your essay.

USING A PRINCIPLE TO AVOID OVERLAPPING

All the sets in the preceding section are sound because each group is based on a single concern: neighborly involvement, appearance of the yard, or wealth. This one concern, or controlling idea, is called the **principle**. For example, the principle of neighborly involvement controls the grouping of neighbors into three classes: friendly, meddlesome, and private.

All the classes in any one group must adhere to the controlling principle for that group. You would not say, for example, that your neighbors can be classified as friendly, meddlesome, private, and affluent, because the first three classes relate to neighborly involvement, but the fourth, relating to wealth, refers to another principle. Any one of the first three—the friendly, meddlesome, and private—might also be affluent. The classes should not overlap in this way. Also, every member should fit into one of the available classes.

ESTABLISHING CLASSES

As you name your classes, rule out easy, unimaginative types such as *fast/medium/slow*, *good/average/bad*, and *beautiful/ordinary/ugly*. Look for creative, original phrases and unusual perspectives as shown in these simple forms.

Subject	Principle	Classes
neighbors	neighborhood involvement	friendly, meddlesome, private
neighbors	yard upkeep	immaculate, neat, messy
neighbors	wealth	affluent, comfortable, struggling

Complex classifications are based on one principle and then subgrouped by another related principle. The following example classifies neighbors by their neighborly involvement. It then subgroups the classes on the basis of motive.

I. Friendly
   A. Civic-minded
   B. Want to be accepted
   C. Chatty
II. Meddlesome
   A. Controlling
   B. Emotionally needy
   C. Suspicious of others
III. Private
   A. Shy
   B. Snobbish
   C. Secretive

Transitional Words

Consider using the following transitional words to improve coherence by connecting ideas with ideas, sentences with sentences, and paragraphs with paragraphs.

FOR CLASSIFICATION: classify, (to) group, categorize, the first class, the second class, the third class, another class, a subclass, another subclass

FOR ALL PATTERNS OF WRITING: The <u>HOTSHOT CAT</u> words: <u>H</u>owever, <u>O</u>therwise, <u>T</u>herefore, <u>S</u>imilarly, <u>H</u>ence, <u>O</u>n the other hand, <u>T</u>hen, <u>C</u>onsequently, <u>A</u>lso, <u>T</u>hus

DEVELOPING THE CLASSIFICATION

Here is an example of a student paragraph that demonstrates the steps for writing classification:

Subject: shoppers in a department store
Principle: reasons for shopping
Classes: looking, sales, special-item shoppers

I. Looking shoppers
II. Sales shoppers
III. Special-item shoppers

SORTING THEM OUT
José Morales

Transitional words

Class 1

Transitional words

Class 2

Transitional words

Class 3

I've had several kinds of customers at my job at Target. Specifically, I can <u>group</u> most of them into three classes: the looking shoppers, the sales shoppers, and the special-item shoppers. The <u>first</u> and largest <u>class</u> is the *looking shoppers*. One can see them wandering around all over the store as if they were lost or maybe out for exercise. They stop for discoveries here and there, but they don't want to be bothered by salespersons. They're pretty harmless, except sometimes they bump into each other. And quite infrequently they buy something. The <u>next class</u>, the *sales shoppers*, includes the ones who have read the advertisements. They may even be carrying an advertisement with them, matching pictures and numbers with items. If a salesperson can help them get to the merchandise before someone else does, they're grateful; otherwise, get out of their way. They are single-minded and ruthless. Beware of verbal assaults and vicious bodily contact at the sales tables. The <u>last group</u> is my favorite. It is the *special-item shoppers*. They know what they want, but they would like good quality and a good price. They are usually friendly, and they are appreciative of good service. On a given day, one person may move from one group to another, and when the person does, his or her behavior changes. After serving more than three thousand customers, I can identify and classify them almost immediately.

EXERCISE 1   Avoiding Overlapped Classes

Mark each set of classes as OK or OL (overlapping); circle the classes that overlap.

	Subject	Principle	Classes
	Example:		
OL	community college students	intentions	vocational academic transfer specialty needs (hardworking)
___	1. airline flights	passenger seating	first class business coach
___	2. country singers	clothing trademark	hat overalls decorative costume expensive
___	3. schools	ownership	private religious public

	4. faces	shape	round
			square
			oval
			beautiful
			broad
			long
	5. dates	behavior resembling aquatic animals	sharks
			clams
			jellyfish
			cute
			octopuses

FINDING PATTERNS IN PHOTOS

EXERCISE 2   An Image-Based Activity for Groups or Individuals

Yard sale

Imagine you are surrounded by clutter. Your loved ones are telling you it is time for a yard sale. It is an early Saturday morning. Traffic has not started to move much outside. You go through your house, your garage, and your toolshed, picking up items you need to lose. You put them on the lawn. You can bring more out later. You hastily make a sign, "Yard Sale," and are about to hang it on the back of your car parked curbside when it occurs to you that your items are jumbled. It is still early. Why not organize? You can classify the items according to their uses and place them in common areas marked with colored signs. You can have your own department store. Then when someone asks a question such as, "You got any old vinyl records?" you can point to a portion of the lawn that is marked "Entertainment."

Now it is time to classify. Come up with six or more phrases for groups of items that are commonly found at yard sales, and list some of the items you often see.

If your instructor directs, use your outline to write a paragraph or short essay of classification about this imagined preselling experience.

I. _____   II. _____
    A. _____   A. _____
    B. _____   B. _____
    C. _____   C. _____

III. _____   IV. _____
   A. _____   A. _____
   B. _____   B. _____
   C. _____   C. _____
V. _____   VI. _____
   A. _____   A. _____
   B. _____   B. _____
   C. _____   C. _____
VII. _____   VIII. _____
   A. _____   A. _____
   B. _____   B. _____
   C. _____   C. _____

Practicing Patterns of Classification

Because the basic pattern of classification consists of classes, the initial outline is predictable: It uses Roman-numeral headings for the classes, although some classes may be longer and more complex than others.

EXERCISE 3   Completing Patterns of Classification

Fill in the blanks to identify classes that could be discussed for each subject.

1. *Subject:* Professional athletes

   Principle: Why they participate in sports

   Classes:

   I. Glory
   II. _____
   III. _____

2. *Subject:* Pet owners

   Principle: Why they own pets

   Classes:
   I. Companionship
   II. _____
   III. _____

3. *Subject:* Dates or prospective spouses

   Principle: The way they can be compared to vehicles

   Classes:
   I. Economy (Taurus, Corolla, Civic)
      A. Low cost
      B. Low maintenance
      C. _____

    II. Minivans (Caravan, Quest, Odyssey)
        A. Practical
        B. _____
        C. _____
    III. Luxury (Porsche, BMW, Mercedes, Lexus)
        A. High cost
            1. Initial
            2. _____
        B. _____
        C. Impressive features
            1. _____
            2. Unnecessary

Readings for Critical Thinking, Discussion, and Writing

READING STRATEGIES AND OBJECTIVES

Underlining and annotating these reading selections will help you answer the questions that follow the selections, discuss the material in class, and prepare for reading-based writing assignments. As you underline and annotate, pay special attention to the author's writing skills, logic, and message, and consider the relevance of the material to your own experiences and values.

PARAGRAPH

Styles of Leadership

WILLIAM M. PRIDE, ROBERT J. HUGHES, AND JACK R. KAPOOR

Written by three business professors, this paragraph is excerpted from a college textbook. It refers mainly to business institutions and the workplace, but it also covers all social units that depend on leadership, from the family to nations.

For many years, leadership was viewed as a combination of personality traits, such as self-confidence, concern for people, intelligence, and dependability. Achieving a consensus on which traits were most important was difficult, however, and attention turned to styles of leadership behavior. In the last few decades, several styles of leadership have been identified: authoritarian, laissez-faire, and democratic. The **authoritarian leader** holds all authority and responsibility, with communication usually moving from top to bottom. This leader assigns workers to specific tasks and expects orderly, precise results. The leaders at United Parcel Service employ authoritarian leadership. At the other extreme is the **laissez-faire leader**, who gives authority to employees. With the laissez-faire style, subordinates are allowed to work as they choose with a minimum of interference. Communication flows horizontally among group members. Leaders at Apple Computer are known to employ a laissez-faire leadership style in order to give employees as much freedom as possible to develop new products. The **democratic leader** holds final responsibility but also delegates authority to others, who participate in determining work assignments. In this leadership style, communication is active both upward and downward. Employee commitment is high because of participation in the decision-making process. Managers for both Walmart and Saturn have used the democratic leadership style to encourage employees to become more than just rank-and-file workers.

EXERCISE 4   Discussion and Critical Thinking

1. Underline the topic sentence.

2. What is the subject of this paragraph?

3. What is the principle that divides the subject into classes?

4. This paragraph is concerned with explaining the different styles of leadership without showing favor. Do you have a preferred style? If so, what is your preference and why?

5. In the textbook *Business*, seventh edition, this paragraph is followed by another with this first sentence: "Today most management experts agree that no one 'best' managerial leadership style exists." How do you think the authors explain such a statement?

ESSAYS

Types of Rioters*

DAVID LOCHER

Written by a sociologist, this selection is excerpted from a textbook about collective behavior.

1   In March of 1992, Los Angeles was a city with a long history of conflict between racial groups. That year, a videotape of Rodney King being brutally beaten was shown over and over again on local, regional, and national television news reports. What almost no one realized at the time was that they were seeing an edited tape. KTLA, the Los Angeles television station that first acquired the videotape, edited out the first few seconds of the video because it was blurry. Most reporters, together with the public, saw only the edited, sixty-eight-second version of the video. They were not aware of the missing thirteen seconds, which apparently showed Rodney King charging at the police officers. The vast majority of Americans who saw the televised video believe that the beating had been totally

*LOCHER, DAVID A., *Collective Behavior*, 1st Edition, © 2002. Reprinted by permission of Pearson Education, Inc., New York, New York.

unprovoked and that the officers were therefore guilty. The untelevised thirteen seconds were enough to convince many jurors that the beating was at least partially provoked. Legally, they believed that the beating was excessive but not sufficient grounds for conviction in a court of law.

2   The video created a presumption throughout the country that the officers would be found guilty. When the not guilty verdict was announced, it led to the South-Central Los Angeles riot, which was the bloodiest, deadliest, most destructive riot in modern American history. At the time the riots were beginning, no one blamed the prosecutors; most blamed the jury and the system itself. The generalized belief throughout much of the country and shared by the rioters was that guilty verdicts could not have been reached, no matter what. Participants believed that legal justice was beyond their reach, but revenge was right at hand.

3   In all riots, there are categories of participants. Five categories can be labeled as ego-involved, concerned, insecure, curious spectators, and ego-detached exploiters. Each category of participant may be operating under a different generalized belief, and possibly even a different set of structural strains.

Ego-Involved

4   Ego-involved participants feel a deep connection to the concerns expressed. In Los Angeles, the ego-involved participants were the ones who felt most empathy for Rodney King, the most hatred for the LAPD, and the most outrage over the verdicts. They fully accepted the generalized beliefs and believed that it was up to them to do something. These individuals placed themselves into the position of responsibility. They threw bricks or started fires because they believed that doing so would produce real change and that their violent actions were the only way to produce that change. Ego-involved participants actually started the riot. Anger, outrage, and disappointment drove their actions. They believed that those actions were necessary, desirable, or unavoidable.

Concerned

5   Concerned riot participants are not so personally involved. They have a more general interest in the event. The concerned participants were those who took part in the rioting, but who focused their attention on following the lead of others. They accepted the generalized belief and engaged in riotous actions, but they did so as much out of empathy with the other rioters as empathy for Rodney King. These individuals helped the ego-involved start fires, break windows, and so on. Under only slightly different circumstances, they could just as easily have followed leaders in a peaceful march. In Los Angeles, the concerned participants were acting out of hatred of the system or of authority in general. They followed the lead of the ego-involved but did not choose the course of action themselves.

Insecure

6   Insecure participants just want to be part of something or are afraid of missing out. They may not have any understanding of the riot's causes. In this sense, they may get confused. They see others throwing objects and smashing windows, and they engage in the same behavior themselves. However, it could be that the ego-involved and concerned participants are all attacking a particular building because of what it represents, while the insecure simply smash whatever is handy. Insecure riot participants revel in the power that they feel by taking part, and they seek safety in numbers.

7   In the South-Central riot, the insecure participants went along with the actions of others because it made them feel powerful. They were standing up to authority,

spitting in the eye of society, and all from the relative safety of a large and anonymous crowd. Individuals who would never think of talking back to a police officer suddenly felt secure enough to throw rocks at them. The meek become powerful; the tame become dangerous. These participants turned the violence away from symbols of authority and toward anyone or anything that stood in the path of the crowd.

Spectators

8   In any form of collective behavior, there may be those who want to watch the actions of participants but do not wish to get directly involved. Photographs and videotaped segments of the Los Angeles riots frequently reveal more people standing around watching the action than participants. At one point during the riot, Reginald Denny, a truck driver who was passing through the area, was pulled out of his truck and nearly beaten to death by rioters. There were many more people watching the attack on Denny than there were actually hitting him. For spectators, the riot was simply an exciting form of entertainment.

9   Spectators are important for several reasons. In a deadly riot, they can frequently become targets for the hostile participants. They may also get caught up in the excitement and decide to join the action. They may take the side of the participants against police. Sometimes social control agents force them into action. Social control agents usually do not attempt to distinguish between spectators and active participants. Circumstances often make it impossible for them to do so. In Los Angeles, many spectators joined in the looting, and the police, soldiers, and guardsmen made no real attempt to distinguish between active participants and spectators. Everyone on the streets not wearing a uniform was perceived as a riot participant and treated accordingly. This sort of treatment sometimes outrages spectators to the extent that they become active in resisting social control.

Ego-Detached Exploiters

10   The ego-detached participant does not care about the issues that drive a riot. They do not accept the generalized belief shared by many other participants. They might not even know why the riot started in the first place. None of these issues matter to the ego-detached. They only want to exploit the conditions created by the riot for their own personal gain. An individual who throws a brick at a policeman might be driven by outrage over the verdicts (ego-involved), by a general hatred of the police (concerned), or by a sense of power and group identity (insecure). An individual who throws a brick at a store window to steal a television is driven by the desire for a free TV. Looting is an act of exploitation by those who are detached from the strain and generalized belief of a riot. Looters use the circumstances created by the riot to gather as many material goods as possible for themselves. No deep sense of outrage over a legal injustice drives an individual to steal a freezer. The exploiter uses the chaos, confusion, and temporary lack of social control to acquire commercial goods for free. They carry out their own personal agendas under cover of the collective episode.

11   The Los Angeles riot was literally taken over by exploiters. The pattern of destruction reveals that the targets changed within the first few hours. Rioters first attacked buildings that symbolized authority or individuals who, through their race, symbolized those with authority. By nightfall, however, they started attacking liquor stores. Before long, any business was fair game. If it could be moved, it was stolen. If it couldn't be moved, it was destroyed. The actions of the exploiters are not difficult to pick out in Los Angeles: They removed any object with any potential value before setting fire to each building. This is not the action of social revolutionaries; it is the action of greedy individuals looking to score. The passion

of the ego-involved and concerned participants may fade out with a brief period of time, but the greed of the exploiters does not go away. Only the return of effective social control or the absence of anything to steal ends looting.

12   By the time a riot as big as the South-Central riot has begun, the ego-involved participants may be dramatically outnumbered by those from other categories. This may make the entire event seem pointless or illogical to outside observers. "If they are so mad at the LAPD, why are they burning down their own houses?" was a common question asked by many Americans during the 1992 riot. These critics were overlooking the simple fact that many of the riot participants were not deeply concerned with the issues that caused the riot in the first place. Insecure participants blindly following the crowd and exploiters using the breakdown of social order for their own material gain can vastly outnumber those who actually care about the issues that caused the riot to begin in the first place. Spectators might outnumber all participants combined.

EXERCISE 5   Vocabulary Highlights

Write a short definition of each word as it is used in the essay. (Paragraph numbers are given in parentheses) Be prepared to use these words in sentences.

presumption (2)   revel (6)
ego-involved (3)   perceived (9)
categories (3)   agendas (10)
ego-detached (3)   potential (11)
empathy (4)   symbolized (11)

EXERCISE 6   Discussion and Critical Thinking

1. Identify the classification that David Locher outlines in the essay:

Subject: _____

Principle: _____

Classes: _____

_____

_____

_____

_____

2. The author does not explain his reason for presenting the classes in the order he chooses. What do you think is the reasoning behind the order of the classes?

3. How are the concerned riot participants similar to the ego-attached participants?

4. How are the insecure participants different from the ego-attached and concerned participants?

5. Why are the insecure participants sometimes unpredictable and dangerous?

6. Why do spectators attend riots?

7. Why are the ego-detached exploiters the most easily understood and, at the same time, the most despicable?

Kinds of Love and Relationships*

ROD PLOTNIK

In his textbook An Introduction to Psychology, *R od Plotnik discusses psychological research into the different forms of love. For a central framework for his discussion, he uses Robert Sternberg's famous theory about how love can be analyzed through classification. From there Plotnik presents research information concerning brain activity and the different kinds of love and relationships.*

Kinds of Love

1   *Which kind of love are you in?*   Previous researchers had thought love too mysterious for scientific study, but current researchers have begun to classify love according to various components. As a starting point, researchers distinguish between passionate and companionate love.

2   Passionate love involves continuously thinking about the loved one and is accompanied by warm sexual feelings and powerful emotional reactions.

3   Companionate love involves having trusting and tender feelings for someone whose life is closely bound up with one's own.

4   For example, when people fall madly in love, it's usually passionate love. When mature couples talk about enjoying each other's company, it's usually companionate love, which may or may not involve sexual behaviors. Thus, love is more complex than many think. One of the better known theories of love is Robert Sternberg's triangular theory of love.

5   The triangular theory of love has three components: passion, intimacy, and commitment. Passion is feeling physically aroused and attracted to someone. Intimacy is feeling close and connected to someone; it develops through sharing and communicating. Commitment is making a pledge to nourish the feelings of love and to actively maintain the relationship.

*From PLOTNIK, *Introduction to Psychology* (with InfoTrac®), 7E. © 2005 Cengage Learning.

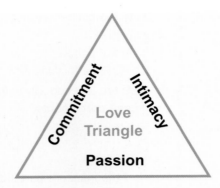

6   What makes you feel in love is the component of passion, which rises quickly and strongly influences biases and biases your judgment. What makes you want to share and offer emotional and material support is the component of intimacy. What makes you want to form a serious relationship, such as getting married and promising support through difficult times, is the component of commitment. Sternberg believes that the kind of love most of us strive for is complete or consummate love, which is a balanced combination of all three components—passion, intimacy, and commitment. Sternberg uses his triangular theory to answer some of the most commonly asked questions about love.

7   *Is there love at first sight?*   Love at first sight occurs when we are overwhelmed by passion, without any intimacy or commitment. Sternberg calls this infatuated love, which can arise in an instant, involves a great deal of physiological arousal, and lasts varying lengths of time. Because there is no intimacy or commitment, infatuated love is destined to fade away.

8   *Why do some people get married so quickly?*   Sternberg calls this Hollywood love, which is a combination of passion and commitment but without any intimacy. In Hollywood love, two people make a commitment but without any intimacy. In Hollywood love, two people make a commitment based on their passion for each other. Unless they develop intimacy over time, the relationship is likely to fail.

9   *Can there be love without sex?*   Sternberg calls love without sex companionate love, which is a combination of intimacy and commitment without any sexual passion. An example of companionate love is a married couple who are committed to each other and share their lives but whose physical attraction has waned.

10   *Why doesn't romantic love last?*   Romantic love, which is a combination of intimacy and passion usually doesn't last because there is no commitment. As soon as the passion dies and the intimacy fades, the individuals no longer feel in love and go their separate ways.

Brain in Love

11   Researchers took brain scans of college coeds who had been with their "one true love" for between 2 and 17 months and topped the charts on the passionate love (constantly think about their partners, can't sleep, feel euphoric). The brain's activity patterns were similar in men and women with one difference: An area in men's brains that is involved in penile erections also showed increased activity. In comparison, brain scans of partners who had been in longer relationships (average 2 years) indicated activity in additional emotional areas (insula, anterior cingulate). Researchers concluded that infatuated love primarily activates the brain's reward/pleasure center and the resulting euphoria lasts for a relatively limited time. In comparison, a more committed love activates additional emotional brain areas, which contributes to forming a longer-lasting relationship.

EXERCISE 7   Discussion and Critical Thinking

1. Of the three components of love,' according to Sternberg—passion, intimacy, and commitment—which one, if any, is most important? Explain your answer.

2. Sternberg believes that we strive for consummate, or complete, love. Do you believe it is possible to achieve that kind of love, or is it only a worth-while desire, like trying to perfectly balance a life with a high-pressure job, a demanding family, and a full-time load of college classes?

3. To what extent could Sternberg's system apply to an arranged marriage? Explain your answer.

4. What would you call a relationship that has intimacy and no other component?

5. Is it possible for one person in a couple relationship to have one set of compo-nents (from passion, intimacy, and commitment) in mind when the other person has a different set of components in mind? In other words, could one person be thinking in terms of Infatuated love or Romantic love while the other is think-ing of Hollywood love or Complete love? If so, what would that love be called?

6. If you were a marriage counselor, which kind of love-in-distress case would be more challenging for you to counsel—Romantic or Hollywood? Explain your answer.

7. Assuming that some couples move through several kinds of love during a long and healthy loving relationship, what would be a likely sequence if a couple experienced three kinds of love: A. Complete; B. Hollywood; C. Infatu-ated? Use the letters to place them in order.

Living Environments*

AVI FRIEDMAN

Avi Friedman, winner of the United Nations World Habitat Award and internationally acclaimed architect, is especially con-cerned with how the perimeter and interior of a house need to be expanded and changed to fit the space needs and bud-get of its owners. A professor at the McGill School of Architecture, Friedman wrote this essay for The Montreal Gazette.

1   When invited to design a home, I first like to know what kind of dwellers my clients are. In our first meeting, I ask them to take me on a guided tour of their current residence and describe how each room is used—when and by whom. Walking through hallways, scanning the interior of rooms, peeping into closets, looking at kitchen cupboards, and pausing at family photos have helped me devise several common categories of occupants.

*Avi Friedman, "Living Environments," originally appeared in *The Montreal Gazette*. Reprinted by permission of the author.

Class 1

2   <u>The "neat" household regards the house as a gallery</u>. The home is spotless. The placement of every item, be it hanging artwork, a memento on a shelf, or furniture, is highly choreographed. The color scheme is coordinated and the lighting superb. It feels as if one has walked into an *Architectural Digest* magazine spread. Recent trends, professional touches, and carefully selected pieces are the marks of the place.

Class 2

3   <u>The "utilitarian" family is very pragmatic</u>. They are minimalists, believing that they get only what they need. Environmental concerns play an important role in buying goods. The place, often painted in light tones, is sparsely decorated with very few well-selected items. Souvenirs from a recent trip are displayed and some photos or paintings are on the wall. They will resist excess consumption and will squeeze as much use as they can from each piece.

Class 3

4   <u>The home of the "collector" family is stuffed to the brim</u>. It is hard to find additional space for furniture or a wall area to hang a painting. Books, magazines, and weekend papers are everywhere. Newspaper cutouts and personal notes are crammed under magnets on the fridge door. The collector family seems to pay less attention to how things appear and more to comfort. Stress reduction is a motto. Being an excessively clean "show house" is not a concern. Placing dirty breakfast dishes in the sink and the morning paper in the rack before leaving home is not a priority as long as things are moving along.

5   Of course, these are only a few household types, but at the end of a house tour, I have a pretty good idea about my clients. More than the notes that I take during a meeting, these real-life images tell me all about my client's home life and desired domestic environment. When I began practicing, I quickly realized house design is about people more than architecture. As hard as I might try, I will never be able to tailor a new personality to someone by placing them in a trendy style, one that does not reflect who they really are. I can attempt to illustrate options other than their current life habits and decorating choices. But in the end, when they move into their new place, they will bring along their old habits.

6   My experience has taught me some homeowners have been trying hard to emulate lifestyles and décors that are really not theirs. The endless decorating shows on television and the many magazines that crowd supermarket racks provide a tempting opportunity to become someone else. Some homeowners are under constant pressure, it feels, to undergo extreme makeovers and borrow rather than mature into their natural selves. They search for a readymade packaged interior style rather than discovering their own.

7   I am often at a loss when clients ask me what style I subscribe to, or solicit advice on the style they are to adopt. I reply that styles are trendy and comfort is permanent, and that they should see beyond the first day of occupancy into everyday living. Sipping a freshly brewed coffee on the back porch on a summer Sunday and letting the morning paper litter the floor while watching a squirrel on the tree across the yard is a treasured moment. It will never be able to fit into a well-defined architectural style. Home design needs to create the backdrop for such opportunities. It is these types of moments that make us enjoy life.

8   If someone wants to read, why not have a wall of books? Does someone love listening to music? Then a music room or corner should be created, even if it is not trendy. Does someone want to interact with the children? He or she might add a hobby space, even if it is outdated and cannot be found in most magazines.

9   Referring to technological advances, the renowned French architect Le Corbusier once described the home as a "machine for living." It is partially true. Home is the site where mundane and utilitarian activities take place. It is also where special moments, uniquely ours, are created and treasured.

EXERCISE 8   Vocabulary Highlights

Write a short definition of each word as it is used in the essay. (Paragraph numbers are given in parentheses.) Be prepared to use these words in sentences.

choreographed (2)   solicit (7)

pragmatic (3)   technological (9)

minimalists (3)   mundane (9)

sparsely (3)   utilitarian (9)

emulate (6)   uniquely (9)

EXERCISE 9   Discussion and Critical Thinking

1. Underline the thesis.

2. Does Friedman's classification cover all lifestyles, or categories, of occupants? Explain.

3. Friedman specifies three categories of occupants—neat, utilitarian, collector. Does he seem to favor one or is he nonjudgmental? Explain.

4. How might one household type regard another? For example, how might the neat household type regard the collector household type, and vice versa?

5. What subdivisions do you see for some of Friedman's three household types? For example, are there degrees of a household being neat and a household being stuffed?

6. What is your personal evaluation of the three household types?

7. Evaluate this essay for the extent of the author's classification and the effectiveness of his development.

For all the years he could remember, Boris Belinsky has observed doctors from up close and at a distance. It was only natural, therefore, that, when asked to classify a group of people according to their behavior, he chose doctors.

His Writing Process Worksheet shows you how this writing evolved from idea to final draft. To conserve space here, the freewriting and two rough drafts have been omitted. The balance of his worksheet has been lengthened for you to be able to see his other work in its entirety.

BRANDON BRIDGE

Writing Process Worksheet

Name Boris Belinsky   **Title** Doctors Have Their Symptoms, Too   **Due Date** Friday, March 23, 8 a.m.

Use the back of this page or separate paper if you need more space.

Assignment

In the space below, write whatever you need to know about your assignment, including information about the topic, audience, pattern of writing, length, whether to include a rough draft or revised drafts, and whether your paper must be typed.

Write a paragraph of classification in which you group people according to their behavior in a particular vocation area. Your audience—your instructor and your peers—will be somewhat aware of the career field you select but will lack your insights. Submit a completed worksheet, a rough draft marked for revision, and a typed final draft of about 250 words.

Stage One

Explore Freewrite, brainstorm (list), cluster, or take notes as directed by your instructor.

Clustering

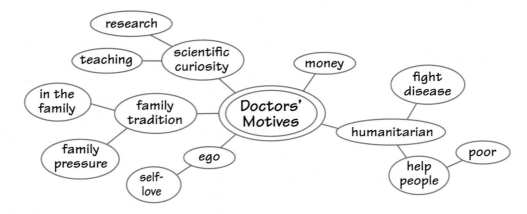

Stage Two

Organize Write a topic sentence or thesis; label the subject and the focus parts.

<u>Doctors</u> can be classified according to their motives for choosing their field of
subject   focus
<u>work</u>.

Write an outline or an outline alternative. For reading-based writing, include references and short quotations with page numbers as support in the outline.

    I. Motive: to make money
        A. Slow with patients
        B. Fast with bills
    II. Motive: to pursue scientific interests
        A. Work in labs
        B. Teach in medical schools
    III. Motive: to help people
        A. Spend much time with patients
        B. Have good standards
            1. May locate in poor areas
            2. Advocate preventative methods
            3. Do volunteer work

Stage Three

Write   On separate paper, write and then revise your paragraph or essay as many times as necessary for **c**oherence, **l**anguage (usage, tone, and diction), **u**nity, **e**mphasis, **s**upport, and **s**entences (**CLUESS**). Read your work aloud to hear and correct any grammatical errors or awkward-sounding sentences.

Edit any problems in fundamentals, such as **c**apitalization, **g**rammar, **p**unctuation, and **s**pelling (**CGPS**).

Final Draft

DOCTORS HAVE THEIR SYMPTOMS, TOO
Boris Belinsky

Topic sentence

    Because I come from a large family that unfortunately has had a lot of illnesses, I have learned to classify doctors according to why they became doctors. <u>As doctors can diagnose illnesses by the symptoms they identify, I can figure out doctors' motives by their symptoms, by which I mean behavior.</u> Some doctors have chosen the field of medicine because they want to make

Support (class)

<u>money</u>. They hurry to visit their patients (customers) waiting in multiple office spaces, answer few questions and never sit down. Although slow to respond to desperate phone calls, they are fast with the bills. The second class

Support (class)

is the group with <u>scientific</u> interests. Not as much concerned about money, they are often found in university hospitals, where they teach and work on special medical problems. They may be a bit remote and explain symptoms in technical terms. The third group is my favorite: those who became doctors to

Support (class)

<u>help people</u>. They spend much time with patients, often practice in areas that are not affluent, advocate preventative methods, and do volunteer work. <u>Not</u>

Concluding sentence

<u>all doctors easily fall into these three groups, but virtually every one has a tendency to do so.</u>

Community College Pressures

JOEL FOLLETTE

For an essay assignment in freshman composition, Joel Follette was asked to read the essay "College Pressures" and to apply its basic ideas to his experience at the community college he attends. Initially, he thought he was writing about two opposing worlds, Yale and Mt. San Antonio College, but then he found some similarities.

1   All college students have pressures. In his essay "College Pressures," William Zinsser describes the "modern undergraduate primarily as a driven creature," who is "fearful of risk" and "goal-obsessed." He says various harmful pressures exist "throughout American education" (78). Although he has some good insights, his focus is on Yale University, not a community college, such as the one I attend. The pressures he writes about—economic, parental, peer, and self-induced—do exist at Mt. San Antonio College in Southern California to some extent, but they take very different forms.

2   Zinsser says the Yale students feel economic pressure because they are looking for a "passport to security," and only good grades will get that for them (74). They are competing for slots in famous programs in law and medicine, such as the ones at Yale and Harvard. Other economic pressures come from the cost of education. He says some Yale students work part time during the school year and full time during the summer and still get loans. Students I know in the evening program at my school also have economic problems. I have a full-time job the year round in a company that makes cardboard boxes. I work overtime whenever I can get it without missing classes. I have a wife, who works part time, and two children in elementary school. I, too, have loans, but they are for a little house we bought last year and for a car that I first leased and then bought in a foolish transaction. Unlike Yale, my school only costs a few hundred dollars a year for the three classes I take in evening school each semester, but I passed on a job offer with a good salary because the new hours would have interfered with my class schedule.

3   Zinsser links economic pressure with parental pressure (75). The parents of most Yale students are paying for their education, and those parents expect results. They expect their offspring to do well in class and to major in a field that will pay well. He says the students want "to fulfill their parents' expectations." They often feel guilty if they do not do well and neglect their own preferences in what to study. Although that may exist to a lesser degree at my community college, usually the parents themselves do not have a college degree and now they are not paying all the college costs for their children, although a large percentage of students in day school still live at home. Most evening students work full time, and the family pressure comes from a spouse and maybe children. When I get home on class nights at ten-thirty and see my kids sleeping and my tired wife, I know why I am going to college, and I feel guilty if I do not do well. And, to some extent like the students at Yale, I am thinking about security, not so much about being a doctor but about having a better job.

4   The other two pressures discussed by Zinsser, the peer and self-induced (76), are also linked. Again, there are big differences between the students at Yale and Mt. San Antonio College. Zinsser says that Yale students are very competitive, and they often "do more than they are expected to do" in order to excel (77). He uses the term "grade fever" (77). I have a B average and I know I have to make some As to offset some Cs, but I don't feel I am competing with

my peers. We talk about grades, and usually ask each other about grades when we get tests or papers back. But I haven't seen a lot of competition. Of course, we have our pride, and we're embarrassed if we don't do well. Then we feel as if we have let ourselves and others down. According to my friend at UCLA, the students there are so grade conscious they hardly talk about their grades. Last semester one of his peers jumped to his death from a high-rise dorm room after finals. We do not jump here. I did see a guy kick a trash can one day after getting low marks on a research paper.

5   At all schools, pressures do exist. They may come from different sources and arrive in different degrees, but they are out there. Sometimes we do it to ourselves, and sometimes people do it to us. Pressures are the forces that may get in the way of our getting a good education, because we become too practical. But pressures are also what keep us going when we are dog-tired, sleepy, and cranky. I think Zinsser would say that if we did not have so many of these pressures that we might just sit down and read a good book—and that just might be the best education of it all.

Work Cited

Zinsser, William. "College Pressures." *Blair & Ketchum's Country Journal* 4 (April 1979): 72–78. Print.

EXERCISE 10   Discussion and Critical Thinking

1. Circle the thesis and underline all topic sentences.

2. What is the main pressure?

3. Which pressure differs to the greatest extent between Yale students and evening-division community college students? Explain.

4. Is Follette a typical community college student? Discuss.

5. Are your pressures different from the ones mentioned here?

Suggested Topics and Prompts for Writing Classification

READING-BASED WRITING

Reading-based writing requires you to read critically, write a reply that shows you understand what you have read, and give credit for ideas you borrow and words you quote. The form can be a summary, a reaction, or a two-part response (with separated summary and reaction). Documentation, in which you give credit for borrowed ideas and words, can be either formal (MLA style) or informal, as directed by your instructor. Definitions of the three forms follow. Any form can be used for any reading selection in this book.

Summary

- The summary is a statement written in response to a reading. It restates only the most important point and uses original wording instead of the author's language. It should not contain added information or personal opinions.
- Because summaries are intended to restate only the main points of a reading, they are typically much shorter than the original text. Often, they are approximately a third of the length.

Reaction

- In the reaction, the meaning of what you have read will be central to the topic sentence of your paragraph or to the thesis of your essay.
- Although the reaction is not a personal narrative by itself, it may include personal experience to explain elements of the text. For example, if your source is about driving styles, your own experiences as a driver or an observer of drivers could be relevant in your analysis of the text.
- The reaction may incorporate a summary to convey a broad view of what you have read, but your summary should never be the main part of your reaction.

Two-Part Response

- The two-part response separates the summary from the reaction.
- This form will give you practice in separating your objective summary in the first part from your more personal evaluation, interpretation, or application in the second part, the reaction.

READING–BASED WRITING TOPICS

"Styles of Leadership"

1. Write a reaction or two-part response. In the reaction part, explain why you think that one style is best or that each one has its advantages or disadvantages, depending on the situation.

"Types of Rioters"

2. Write a summary of the essay.

3. In his essay, Locher makes the following observation: "Insecure participants blindly following the crowd and exploiters using the breakdown of social order for their own material gain can vastly outnumber the issues that caused the riot in the first place." Write a response in which you consider another riot that you have learned about. Does Locher's observation hold true? Why or why not?

"Kinds of Love and Relationships"

4. Write a two-part response to this essay. First, summarize this essay. Then apply the main ideas to an expression (or expressions) of love presented in a reading elsewhere in this book. Or, summarize the essay; then discuss at least three loves you are familiar with.

13

Comparison and Contrast
Showing Similarities and Differences

 Mistakes are the portals of discovery.

—JAMES JOYCE

CHAPTER CONTENTS BRANDON BRIDGE

When to Use Comparison and Contrast
Writing Comparison and Contrast
Practicing Patterns of Comparison and Contrast
Readings for Critical Thinking, Discussion, and Writing
Suggested Topics and Prompts for Writing Comparison and Contrast
Writer's Guidelines
Practicing the Brandon Guide for Revising and Editing

When to Use Comparison and Contrast

FOR COLLEGE WRITING ASSIGNMENTS

- For good reasons, comparison and contrast topics for tests and special assignments are commonplace across the curriculum. They require the student to acquire, organize, and evaluate ideas. The sources on either side of a comparison and contrast may be abundant in the library and especially on the Internet, but usually the precise relationship of ideas must be established by the student writer.
- A comparison-and-contrast statement for a test or a special assignment will almost always be a paragraph or an essay.

IN CAREERS AND AT THE WORKPLACE

- At the workplace, employees prepare comparison-and-contrast studies in anticipation of modifying, acquiring, inventing, or discontinuing products, services, or procedures. The forms for such studies are likely to be standardized and computer-generated, but they employ many of the same principles used in this chapter.
- In determining career choice while still in college, you may use comparison and contrast to assess job descriptions, employment opportunities, and personal satisfaction in different fields.

COMPARISON AND CONTRAST IN A CARTOON

Evening with a flight attendant.

Writing Comparison and Contrast

DEFINING COMPARISON AND CONTRAST

Comparison and contrast is a method of showing similarities and differences between subjects. Comparison is concerned with organizing and developing points of similarity; contrast serves the same function for differences. In some instances, a writing assignment may require that you cover only similarities or only differences. Occasionally, an instructor may ask you to separate one from the other. Usually, you will combine them within the larger design of your paragraph or essay.

WORKING WITH THE 4 *Ps*

Regardless of the nature of your topic for writing, you will develop your ideas by using a procedure called the 4 *Ps*: purpose, points, patterns, and presentation.

PURPOSE

In most of your writing, the main purpose will be either to inform or to persuade.

Informative Writing

If you want to explain something about a topic by showing each subject in relationship with others, then your purpose is informative. For example, you might be comparing two composers, Beethoven and Mozart. Both were musical geniuses, so you might decide that it would be senseless to argue that one is superior to the other. Instead, you choose to reveal interesting information about both by showing them in relation to each other. The emphasis of your writing would be on insights into their characteristics, the insights heightened because the characteristics are placed alongside each other.

Persuasive Writing

If you want to show that one actor, one movie, one writer, one president, one product, or one idea is better than another, your purpose is persuasive. Your argument will take shape as you write, beginning with emphasis in the topic sentence or thesis and reinforcement by repetition throughout your paper, in each case indicating that one side is superior.

The extended example that follows is by student Judy Urbina. She chose to write a comparison-and-contrast dual paragraph-and-essay assignment arguing that Batman is more credible than Superman.

POINTS

Points are the phrases that will be applied somewhat equally to both sides of your comparison-and-contrast topic. They usually begin to emerge in freewriting, become more precise in brainstorming, and assume the major part of the framework in the outline. When writing an assigned topic based on lectures and reading, you will probably be able to select these points quickly. The subject material itself may dictate the points. For example, if you were comparing the governments of the United States and Canada, you would probably use these three points: executive, legislative, and judicial.

Listing is one of the most useful techniques for discovering points.

1. Make a list of points that can be applied to both sides of your topic. Judy Urbina listed points relating to Superman and Batman.

   Example:

   physical abilities   weapons they use   enemies
   motives for fighting crime company they keep   compassion
   helpers   upbringing   romantic interests

2. Then, select several of the strongest points as they relate to your controlling statement. Urbina selected the three most relevant points.

   Example:

   upbringing   motives   enemies

3. Finally, incorporate these points into your controlling idea: the topic sentence or thesis. (You may rewrite this controlling statement for your closing idea at the end of your composition.) Urbina composed this controlling statement.

   Example: Taking into account their upbringing, motives, and enemies, one can argue that Batman is more credible than Superman.

PATTERNS

Now you will choose between two basic patterns of organization: (1) subject-by-subject (opposing) or (2) point-by-point (alternating). In long papers you may mix the two patterns, but in most college assignments, you will probably select just one and make it your basic organizational plan.

In comparison and contrast, the outline works especially well in indicating relationships and sequence. As with most other writing forms we have worked with, the sequence of a comparison-and-contrast paragraph or essay can be based on time, space, or emphasis. Emphasis is the most likely order.

Figures 13-1 and 13-2 show the two patterns as Urbina applied them to both the paragraph (on the left) and the essay (on the right).

In the subject-by-subject approach, organize your material around the subjects—the sides of the comparative study, as shown in Figure 13.1. In the point-by-point approach, organize your paper mainly around the points that you apply to the two subjects, as shown in Figure 13.2.

PRESENTATION

The two patterns of organization—subject-by-subject and point-by-point—are equally valid, and each has its strengths for presentation of ideas.

As shown in Figure 13.1, the subject-by-subject pattern presents materials in large blocks, which means the reader can see two large, separate bodies of material. However, if the material is also complex, the reader has the burden of

Figure 13.1
Subject-by-Subject
Organization

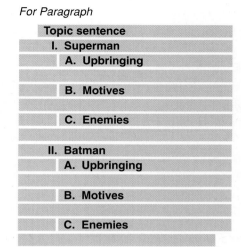

For Paragraph

Topic sentence
I. **Superman**
  A. **Upbringing**

  B. **Motives**

  C. **Enemies**

II. **Batman**
  A. **Upbringing**

  B. **Motives**

  C. **Enemies**

For Essay

Introduction with thesis

I. **Superman**
  A. **Upbringing**

  B. **Motives**

  C. **Enemies**

II. **Batman**
  A. **Upbringing**

  B. **Motives**

  C. **Enemies**

Conclusion

Figure 13.2
Point-by-Point
Organization

For Paragraph

Topic sentence
I. **Upbringing**
  A. **Superman**

  B. **Batman**

II. **Motives**
  A. **Superman**

  B. **Batman**

III. **Enemies**
  A. **Superman**

  B. **Batman**

For Essay

Introduction with thesis

I. **Upbringing**
  A. **Superman**

  B. **Batman**

II. **Motives**
  A. **Superman**

  B. **Batman**

III. **Enemies**
  A. **Superman**

  B. **Batman**

Conclusion

remembering ideas from one part to the next. Parallel development of ideas and cross-references in the second portion of the paragraph or essay can often offset that problem. Transitional words and phrases also help to establish coherence.

The point-by-point pattern shown in Figure 13.2 provides an immediate and direct relationship of points to subject. Therefore, it is especially useful in arguing that one side is superior to the other, in dealing with complex topics, and in working with longer compositions. But because of its systematic nature, if development is not sufficient, it can appear mechanical and monotonous. You can avoid that ping-pong effect by developing each idea thoroughly.

Some writers believe that the subject-by-subject form works better for short (paragraph-length) assignments and the point-by-point form works better for longer pieces (essays).

In the following examples, the topic of Superman and Batman is presented in the final draft stage of the paragraph form and then in the essay form. Note that the paragraph (often, as here, an essay in miniature) is expanded into an essay by developing the topic sentence, the supporting points, and the restated topic sentence into separate paragraphs: introduction, middle paragraph, middle paragraph, middle paragraph, and conclusion. Although both the paragraph and the essay make good observations and illustrate the use of the pattern, for this topic the full essay would probably be more suitable in fulfilling the writer's purpose. In both the paragraph and the essay, Urbina uses a point-by-point arrangement.

Here is the paragraph, followed by the essay.

SUPERMAN AND BATMAN (PARAGRAPH)

Topic sentence

I. Upbringing
*   A. Superman*

*   B. Batman*

II. Motives
*   A. Superman*

*   B. Batman*
III. Enemies
*   A. Superman*
*   B. Batman*

Concluding statement

<u>Both Superman and Batman are heroes, but only one is truly a superhero, and taking into account their upbringing, motives, and criminal targets, that is Batman.</u> Upbringing was not gentle for either. Superman came from Krypton, a planet that was about to self-destruct. His parents sent him as a baby on a spaceship to Earth. There he would be adopted by an ordinary farm family. His adoptive parents named him Clark Kent and reared him well. In the same generation, far away in Gotham, Bruce Wayne, the future Batman, was born to a contented, wealthy family. Tragically, his parents were killed in his presence during a mugging. He inherited the family wealth and was raised by his kindly butler. Those very different backgrounds provided Superman and Batman with powerful but different motives for fighting crime. Superman was programmed in his space capsule to know about the forces of good and evil on Earth and to fight the bad people. Unlike Superman, Batman learned from experience. Both have gone on to fight many bad people, but each one has a special enemy. For Superman, it is Lex Luthor, who has studied Superman and knows all about him, even his outstanding weakness—the mineral Kryptonite. For Batman, it is the Joker, who, as a wicked teenager, was the mugger-murderer of his parents. Many spectacular battles have ensued for both crime fighters, and one has reached the top in his profession. Superman offers overwhelming physical strength against crime, but Batman displays cunning and base passion. As he strikes fear in the hearts of the wicked, he's not just winning; he is getting even. Most people would cheer Superman on. However, they would identify more with Batman, and he is the superhero.

SUPERMAN AND BATMAN (ESSAY)

1   During the Depression in the 1930s, Superman and Batman were created as the first big comic-book heroes. More than two thousand similar but lesser characters were to follow. Both Superman and Batman have been enormously successful, but one seems to have more personality and is probably closer to most of us emotionally. Which hero wins out in this struggle for our hearts

Thesis

and minds? <u>Taking into account their upbringing, motives, and criminal targets, one can argue that it is Batman who is more credible.</u>

I. Upbringing
  A. Superman

  B. Batman

2   Neither came originally from a home environment we are likely to identify with completely. Superman was conceived on the planet Krypton by a highly intelligent couple. His life was threatened because Krypton was going to destruct. Superman's parents bundled him up in a kiddie spacecraft and launched him on a long journey to Earth to save his life. He was raised on a farm by Jonathan and Martha Kent, who adopted him and grew to love him as their own. Batman, however, had an upbringing that we can more easily imagine as a complete pattern. Really Bruce Wayne in disguise, Batman was left an orphan by his parents, who were killed in a mugging right in front of him. Fortunately for Bruce Wayne, his parents were rich, and he inherited millions when they died. He was raised by his butler, unlike Superman, who was nurtured by a conventional adoptive mom and dad. Obviously the upbringing of these two heroes had a lot to do with the kind of heroes they grew up to be.

II. Motives
  A. Superman

  B. Batman

3   Both comic book heroes had different motives for confronting killers and spoilers. Superman instinctively knew he was sent to Earth to fight crime. When his birth parents shipped him off to Earth as an infant, they programmed the spacecraft to educate him on the ways of the Earthlings. Superman's adoptive parents reinforced those lessons by teaching him that he had to hide his powers and use them for the well-being of the human race. To the contrary, Batman soon became a revenge-driven vigilante after his parents were killed in the mugging, so he decided to devote his life to fighting crime, with his butler as a domestic accomplice. To Batman no criminal is a good criminal. Although all of us citizens know we should not take the law into our own hands, nevertheless, we celebrate Superman and Batman as heroes, all the time identifying more with the guy in the fancy bat car.

III. Enemies
  A. Superman

  B. Batman

4   Like all superheroes, each of these two has an arch enemy. Superman's arch enemy is Lex Luthor, who has a brilliant criminal mind. Lex Luthor is always trying to destroy Superman. He knows everything about Superman, right down to his weakness—the mineral Kryptonite. Batman's main enemy is the Joker. As a teen, the Joker killed Batman's parents. Then Batman "accidentally" dropped the Joker into acid and permanently disfigured his face, so they are constantly getting into battles. More people are able to relate to Batman because most of us at least think about vengeance if someone has done us wrong. Superman just wants to fight for "truth, justice, and the American way," all worthwhile values, but they're abstract.

5   Superman does not offer love or self-knowledge as keys to a perfect world. He offers only physical strength. Displaying more cunning and base passion, Batman preys on fears and insecurities of criminals as keys to a perfect world. He wants to keep the bad men and women intimidated and on the run. His presence in Gotham strikes fear in the hearts of the wicked. Neither crime fighter is much concerned about rehabilitation. Mainly they knock heads. But Batman seems to enjoy his work more than Superman because Batman's getting even. The fact that we are in touch with that source of satisfaction says as much about us as it does about Batman.

CAREER-RELATED WRITING AS COMPARISON AND CONTRAST

Imagine you are on a career quest and you have narrowed the vocational fields to two. At that point you will naturally be thinking about comparing and contrasting to make the better choice. Or what if you are already at your workplace and you have to decide between two products, two services, two management styles, or two employees being considered for hiring, firing, or advancing? What pattern of thought does your mind shift to? Of course, again it is comparison and contrast.

If your mind just drifts around—going back and forth, up and down, sideways and other ways—then the ideas that come out of your mouth or computer will be jumbled. If, on the other hand, you have a system—say, the 4 *P*s: *p*urpose, *p*oints, *p*attern, and *p*resentation—you can move clearly and logically regardless of whether your comments will be written or spoken. If you need to make an oral presentation, maybe in PowerPoint, you can communicate with sense and continuity. You will just consider your audience, organize your thoughts, and proceed, following a simple outline.

In the example shown later in the chapter, student LaDonna Stallard compares and contrasts two careers: nursing and physical therapy. As for procedure in writing her essay, the subject could just as easily have been two ways of determining customer confidence, two locations for break rooms, two ride-sharing plans, or two software products used at the workplace. In her case, Stallard sets out to argue that one career is better for her by applying the points of working conditions, required education, and employment opportunities, before reaching a conclusion. Her essay was written for a college composition class. In a more objective comparison-and-contrast essay, she might have provided a less personal context, but she would have used the same flexible, adaptable system. After all, the 4 *P*s function well in college assignments and in workplace tasks.

Transitional Words

Consider using the following transitional words to improve coherence by connecting ideas with ideas, sentences with sentences, and paragraphs with paragraphs.

FOR COMPARISON AND CONTRAST:
Comparison: in the same way, similarly, likewise, also, by comparison, in a like manner, as, with, as though, both, like, just as
Contrast: but, by contrast, in contrast, despite, however, instead, nevertheless, on (to) the contrary, in spite of, still, yet, unlike, even so, rather than, otherwise

FOR ALL PATTERNS OF WRITING: The <u>HOTSHOT CAT</u> words: <u>H</u>owever, <u>O</u>therwise, <u>T</u>herefore, <u>S</u>imilarly, <u>H</u>ence, <u>O</u>n the other hand, <u>T</u>hen, <u>C</u>onsequently, <u>A</u>lso, <u>T</u>hus

FINDING PATTERNS IN PHOTOS

EXERCISE 1   An Image-Based Activity for Groups or Individuals

Your subject is lifestyles. Your specific subjects are two men. If you were to study these two individuals in a sociology class, with the intention of writing a paragraph or short essay of comparison and contrast, how might you use the 4 *P*s? First give the men names and then let the photo and your imagination do the talking.

Bill Varie/ Flirt/Corbis

Man with skateboard and executive

Purpose: Do you want to argue that one person is better than the other to explain their differences or, perhaps, to speculate about the workplace conditions each would prefer? Assume that both are successful at work.

Answer: _____

Points: Make a list of points—the phrases that could relate to the two subjects and could be main divisions of your outline for your writing. Some possibilities to consider, along with your own, are appearance, body language, equipment, passion (as in interests), success, goals, concerns, and influence.

List: _____   _____   _____

_____   _____   _____

_____   _____   _____

Pattern: Now select three or four points you could use for a paragraph or an essay and place them in a subject-by-subject or a point-by-point pattern.

Subject-by-subject

I. _____
   A. _____
   B. _____
   C. _____
II. _____
   A. _____
   B. _____
   C. _____

Point-by-point

I. _____
   A. _____
   B. _____
II. _____
   A. _____
   B. _____
III. _____
   A. _____
   B. _____

Presentation: If your instructor directs you to do so, write a paragraph or an essay using one of the patterns.

Practicing Patterns of Comparison and Contrast

Shorter compositions such as paragraphs are likely to be arranged subject-by-subject, and longer compositions such as essays are likely to be arranged point-by-point, although either pattern can work in either length. In longer works, especially in published writing, the two patterns may be mixed. Being able to organize your material quickly and effectively according to the pattern that is best for your material is important to your success as a writer. Even in a timed assignment, make a simple scratch outline that will guide you in writing a piece that is unified and coherent.

EXERCISE 2   Completing Patterns of Comparison and Contrast

Fill in the blanks to complete the following outlines.

A. Point-by-Point Outline

John: Before and after marriage

I. Way of talking (content and manner)

A. _____

B. John: After

II. _____

A. John: Before

B. John: After

III. _____

A. John: Before

B. _____

B. Subject-by-Subject Outline

Topic: Two jobs you have had (or another approved topic)

I. _____ (job)

A. _____ (point)

B. _____ (point)

C. _____ (point)

II. _____ (job)

A. _____ (point)

B. _____ (point)

C. _____ (point)

Readings for Critical Thinking, Discussion, and Writing

READING STRATEGIES AND OBJECTIVES

Underlining and annotating these reading selections will help you answer the questions that follow the selections, discuss the material in class, and prepare for reading-based writing assignments. As you underline and annotate, pay special attention to the author's writing skills, logic, and message, and consider the relevance of the material to your own experiences and values.

PARAGRAPHS

Blue as in *Boy*, Pink as in *Girl*

SHARON S. BREHM

This paragraph comes from "Stereotypes, Prejudices, and Discrimination," a chapter in Social Psychology, *a college textbook by Sharon S. Brehm. Comparing males and females, she maintains that discrimination based on gender begins at birth and never stops.*

When a baby is born, the first words uttered ring loud and clear: "It's a boy!" or "It's a girl!" In many hospitals, the newborn boy immediately is given a blue hat and the newborn girl a pink hat. The infant receives a gender-appropriate name and is showered with gender-appropriate gifts. Over the next few years, the typical boy is supplied with toy trucks, baseballs, pretend tools, toy guns, and chemistry sets; the typical girl is furnished with dolls, stuffed animals, pretend make-up kits, kitchen sets, and tea sets. As they enter school, many expect the boy to earn money by delivering newspapers and to enjoy math and computers, while they expect the girl to babysit and to enjoy crafts, music, and social activities. These distinctions persist in college, as more male students major in economics and the sciences and more female students in the arts, languages, and humanities. In the workforce, more men become doctors, construction workers, auto mechanics, airplane pilots, investment bankers and engineers. In contrast, more women become secretaries, schoolteachers, nurses, flight attendants, bank tellers, and housewives. Back on the home front, the life cycle begins again when a man and woman have their first baby and discover that "It's a girl!" or "It's a boy!" The traditional pinks and blues are not as distinct as they used to be. Many gender barriers of the past have been broken down, and the colors have somewhat blended together. Nevertheless, **sexism**—prejudice and discrimination based on a person's gender—still exists. Indeed, it begins with the fact that sex is the most conspicuous social category we use to identify ourselves and others.

EXERCISE 3   Discussion and Critical Thinking

1. Is Brehm trying mainly to inform or to persuade?

2. Is this paragraph more comparison or contrast?

3. What points does Brehm use?

4. Does Brehm use the alternating or opposing pattern?

5. Given a choice, would girls naturally choose dolls and boys trucks? In other words, are boys and girls just different by inclination genetically? Discuss.

6. Does your experience tell you that Brehm is right or wrong? If she is right, would you use the terms "prejudice" and "discrimination" to characterize the situation? Explain.

Public and Private

RICHARD RODRIGUEZ

Every person has a public life and a private life, and the character of each is colored by a variety of cultural forces. If the family in the United States includes parents born in Mexico, then the public life may be conducted mainly in English and the private life mainly in Spanish. In this passage from Private Language, Public Language, *Rodriguez says cultural contrast is natural and even complementary.*

For me there were none of the gradations between public and private society so normal to a maturing child. Outside the house was public society; inside the house was private. Just opening or closing the screen door behind me was an important experience. I'd rarely leave home all alone or without reluctance. Walking down the sidewalk, under the canopy of tall trees, I'd warily notice the—suddenly—silent neighborhood kids who stood warily watching me. Nervously, I'd arrive at the grocery store to hear there the sounds of the *gringo*—foreign to me—reminding me that in this world so big, I was a foreigner. But then I'd return. Walking back toward our house, climbing the steps from the sidewalk, when the front door was open in summer, I'd hear voices beyond the screen door talking in Spanish. For a second or two, I'd stay, linger there, listening. Smiling, I'd hear my mother call out, saying in Spanish (words), "Is that you, Richard?" all the while her sounds would assure me: *You are home now; come closer; inside. With us.*

EXERCISE 4   Discussion and Critical Thinking

1. What is the topic sentence of this paragraph?

2. What sounds especially remind Rodriguez of the separation between private or public society?

3. What part of the house separates public and private society?

4. Is the pattern used in this paragraph point-by-point or subject-by-subject?

ANALOGY

Analogy is a method of organizing and developing ideas by comparison. In an analogy, a writer explains or clarifies an unfamiliar subject by likening it to a familiar but strikingly different subject. Writers use analogy to make the new, the different, the complex, or the difficult more understandable for the reader. Analogy, therefore, explains, clarifies, illustrates, and simplifies; it does not prove anything.

The steps for writing the analogy are identical to those of writing comparison and contrast.

Heavenly Father, Divine Goalie

CHARLES PREBISH

Not many thinkers would connect sports with religion. Beginning with a basic idea from fellow writer Richard Lipsky about the religious overtones of games, Charles Prebish extended the comparison and produced an intriguing analogy.

In *How We Play the Game*, Richard Lipsky tells us (of baseball), "The game takes place in an atmosphere of piety. In many ways the ballplayers themselves can be seen as priests who represent us in a liturgy (game) that is part of a sacred tradition." Lipsky's comment reveals that far too little has been said about the role of the player in sport religion. In other words, we need to reflect on the actors in sport religion. It would be incorrect, though, to suggest that it is only the actual players who fulfill the role of religious participants in sport. We must include the coaches and officials as well, in their role as functionaries in the religious process. They are not untrained, either. Sport, no doubt, has its own seminaries and divinity schools in the various minor leagues and training camps that school the participants in all aspects of the tradition, from theology to ritual. The spectators, as video viewers, radio listeners, or game-going die-hards, form the congregation of sport religion. Their attendance is not required for all religious observances, but they do attend at specified times to share in religious rites. And they bear the religious symbols of their faith: the pennants, emblems, hats, coats, gloves, and whatever other objects the media geniuses can promote to signify the glory of sport in general and the home team in particular. The sport symbol may not be the cross, rosary, mezuzah, but it is no less valuable to the owner, and is likely considered to be just as powerful as its traditional counterpart, or more so.

EXERCISE 5   Discussion and Critical Thinking

1. What is the basis of the analogy?

2. What are the points of comparison?

ESSAYS

Are you fundamentally orderly or disorderly? We all have tendencies towards one or the other extreme. If we lean toward the disorderly, we may scoff at the opposite, referring to them as "uptight" or "anal retentive." If we are in the orderly camp, we may pity the disorderly for failures in work ethic, analytical power, or even personal hygiene.

As we read Suzanne Britt's essay, we are probably first surprised and then charmed by her wit and satirical jibes. She insists that the neat people are the bad guys and the sloppy people are the good guys. Moreover, to her, the distinction is not even close. She says, "Neat people are lazier and meaner than sloppy people." She doesn't use the term "neat freaks," but she makes it clear that the neat are twisted, self-centered individuals.

Joyce Gallagher, author of "The Messy are in Denial," is one of those people who she characterizes as the organized. Her group has a preordained mission—to save and sustain the less fortunate, the disorganized, the sloppy. A bemused and grudgingly forgiving participant (after all, the disorganized can't help themselves), she traces the history of the organized from a recent yard sale back to cave dwellers, saying that human nature hasn't changed much. The disorganized flounder, often in endearing ways, and the organized come to their rescue because of genetic imperative.

Neat People vs. Sloppy People*

SUZANNE BRITT

In this comparison-and-contrast essay from her book Show and Tell, *freelance author Suzanne Britt discusses two kinds of people. You are likely to agree or disagree strongly with her conclusion.*

1   I've finally figured out the difference between neat people and sloppy people. The distinction is, as always, moral. Neat people are lazier and meaner than sloppy people.

2   Sloppy people, you see, are not really sloppy. Their sloppiness is merely the unfortunate consequence of their extreme moral rectitude. Sloppy people carry in their mind's eye a heavenly vision, a precise plan, that is so stupendous, so perfect, it can't be achieved in this world or the next.

3   Sloppy people live in Never-Never Land. Someday is their métier. Someday they are planning to alphabetize all their books and set up home catalogs. Someday they will go through their wardrobes and mark certain items for tentative mending and certain items for passing on to relatives of similar shape and size. Someday sloppy people will make family scrapbooks into which they will put newspaper clippings, postcards, locks of hair, and the dried corsage from their senior prom. Someday they will file everything on the surface of their desk, including the cash receipts from coffee purchases at the snack shop. Someday they will sit down and read all the back issues of the *New Yorker*.

*Suzanne Britt, "Neat People vs. Sloppy People" from *Show and Tell*. By permission.

4   For all these noble reasons and more, sloppy people never get neat. They aim too high and wide. They save everything, planning someday to file, order, and straighten out the world. But while these ambitious plans take clearer and clearer shape in their heads, the books spill from the shelves onto the floor, the clothes pile up in the hamper and closet, the family mementos accumulate in every drawer, the surface of the desk is buried under mounds of paper and the unread magazines threaten to reach the ceiling.

5   Sloppy people can't bear to part with anything. They give loving attention to every detail. When sloppy people say they're going to tackle the surface of the desk, they really mean it. Not a paper will go unturned; not a rubber band will go unboxed. Four hours or two weeks into their excavation, the desk looks exactly the same, primarily because the sloppy person is meticulously creating new piles of papers with new headings and scrupulously stopping to read all the old book catalogs before he throws them away. A neat person would just bulldoze the desk.

6   Neat people are bums and clods at heart. They have cavalier attitudes toward possessions, including family heirlooms. Everything is just another dust-catcher to them. If anything collects dust, it's got to go and that's that. Neat people will toy with the idea of throwing the children out of the house just to cut down on the clutter.

7   Neat people don't care about process. They like results. What they want to do is get the whole thing over with so they can sit down and watch the rasslin' on TV. Neat people operate on two unvarying principles: Never handle any item twice, and throw everything away.

8   The only thing messy in a neat person's house is the trash can. The minute something comes to a neat person's hand, he will look at it, try to decide if it has immediate use and, finding none, throw it in the trash.

9   Neat people are especially vicious with mail. They never go through their mail unless they are standing directly over a trash can. If the trash can is beside the mailbox, even better. All ads, catalogs, pleas for charitable contributions, church bulletins and money-saving coupons go straight into the trash can without being opened. All letters from home, postcards from Europe, bills and paychecks are opened, immediately responded to, then dropped in the trash can. Neat people keep their receipts only for tax purposes. That's it. No sentimental salvaging of birthday cards or the last letter a dying relative ever wrote. Into the trash it goes.

10   Neat people place neatness above everything, even economics. They are incredibly wasteful. Neat people throw away several toys every time they walk through the den. I knew a neat person once who threw away a perfectly good dish drainer because it had mold on it. The drainer was too much trouble to wash. And neat people sell their furniture when they move. They will sell a La-Z-Boy recliner while you are reclining in it.

11   Neat people are no good to borrow from. Neat people buy everything in expensive little single portions. They get their flour and sugar in two-pound bags. They wouldn't consider clipping a coupon, saving a leftover, reusing plastic nondairy whipped cream containers or rinsing off tin foil and draping it over the unmoldy dish drainer. You can never borrow a neat person's newspaper to see what's playing at the movies. Neat people have the paper all wadded up and in the trash by 7:05 a.m.

12   Neat people cut a clean swath through the organic as well as the inorganic world. People, animals, and things are all one to them. They are so insensitive. After they've finished with the pantry, the medicine cabinet, and the attic, they will throw out the red geranium (too many leaves), sell the dog (too many fleas), and send the children off to boarding school (too many scuff marks on the hardwood floors).

EXERCISE 6   Vocabulary Highlights

Write a short definition of each word as it is used in the essay. (Paragraph numbers are given in parentheses.) Be prepared to use these words in sentences.

rectitude (2)	meticulously (5)
stupendous (2)	scrupulously (5)
métier (3)	cavalier (6)
tentative (3)	heirlooms (6)
excavation (5)	swath (12)

EXERCISE 7   Discussion and Critical Thinking

1. Is this essay mainly comparison or contrast?

2. Is Britt trying mainly to inform or to persuade?

3. What are the main points for this study?

4. Is the pattern mainly point-by-point or subject-by-subject?

5. What is the moral distinction between the neat and the sloppy?

6. Britt says that sloppy people are morally superior to neat people. How does that idea differ from common assumptions?

7. To what extent is Britt serious, and to what extent is she just being humorous?

8. It can be argued that Britt presents objectively the two extremes of neatness and sloppiness. Do you agree, or do you think she favors one side? Explain.

9. Of the two extremes of neatness and sloppiness, what qualities would a person in the middle have? Or, do most people tend decidedly toward an extreme?

The Messy Are in Denial

JOYCE GALLAGHER

Freelance journalist Joyce Gallagher gives us some insights into why the disorganized often marry the organized. She says it's all part of a design in Nature. Reasoning and her personal experience tell her so.

1   Others may see the disorganized as carefree, messy people wallowing happily in the cluttered chaos of their own making. I see their conduct for what is so obviously is—a crying out for help. If they are so contented, then why are so many of them latching onto and becoming entirely dependent on those of us who are organized? Complaining all the while about being controlled, they, nevertheless, behave as dependents. They're like mistletoe nailing itself to oaks, fleas colonizing St. Bernards, and funguses invading feet. All of this has nothing to do with sexual orientation; flip the male and female words and my hypothesis will stand.

2   The dependency is easy to document and understand. Anyone can see why the disorganized (the messy, the sloppy, the disorderly, the Pisces, the idealist, the daydreamer) needs the organized (the orderly, the systematic, the tidy, the Virgo, the neat, the realistic, the practical). But that leaves the more complicated question: Why would the organized even tolerate the disorganized? Or to use our figures of speech, why would oaks, St. Bernards, and feet be so passive and submissive? I say the answer to all such connections can be found in the phrase "balance of nature." Every creature-type occupies a niche or plunges into extinction. One role of those who are neat (while they are enjoying their own practical, philosophical, and artistic triumphs) is to provide a secure directive system so the sloppy can experience a measure of fulfillment. Like a stoical whale with a barnacle, it can't seem to shake loose, the organized hang in there while the disorganized hang on.

3   Of course, hanging on, or even hanging around, doesn't mean the disorganized are always complete parasites. Far from it. In fact, the disorganized are sometimes writers, musicians, pop philosophers, and lovable flakes. They may even be fun to be around, even get married to—even stayed married to, if you can get past their messiness.

4   If you will just listen, the disorganized will explain *ad nauseam their* lives as works in progress. And in a sense their lives are works in progress, not functioning in advanced stages of progress such as revision or editing, but stuck in freewriting, brainstorming, clustering. Without a thesis, they freewrite through the material world, not yet knowing what to keep or discard. Verily, they brainstorm through life, jumping from one acquisition to another, clustering their "treasures" in attics, work rooms, garages, and other handy, unprotected spaces. Finally, if not directed by an organized person, they run the risk of inundating themselves with their own worthless curios.

5   Fortunately, when Nature has its way, an organizer comes to the rescues—as a friend, a relative, or, perhaps, an official. In my situation, I'm the organized spouse, sometimes succumbing to my disorganized companion's pathetic romanticism, but more often saving him from himself.

6   I do what I can. As he busily accumulates, I busily distribute. The messy disorganized are siblings of hoarders. It's not easy for the organized like me. Toil as I might, I look around and see him effortlessly acquiring, like a tornado sucking in stuff faster than it disposes of it. I especially donate to thrift stores. Hapless children, the disabled of all kinds, and veterans of all wars

depend mightily on us organized people to provide merchandise to their benefactors. Unfortunately for the organized, the thrift industry also depends on the disorganized as customers to cart home items such as scratchy records, manual typewriters, vintage clothing, and myriad unspeakable artifacts called "collectibles."

7   And if it's not a thrift store providing a game preserve for the disorganized, it's a yard sale. Organized people conduct yard sales. The disorganized attend them. As slack-jawed, hollow-eyed hulks, they drive compulsively from one location to another, not knowing what they are looking for. I suppose it an ancient yearning for the hunt, even when the belly, larder, and garage are full. I've known my significant disorganized other to stake out a promising sale site a full hour before opening game time, peering through the windshield of his motorized blind, stalking the forlorn, unwanted inanimate prey. Way back in the distance, I shovel out the odds and ends, mostly odd with no end in sight, all the time knowing it is the burden of the neat to offset every shopping binge of the sloppy.

8   Despite my taking credit for rescuing and sustaining my disorganized mate, pride didn't prompt me to write this article. In fact, I don't particularly relish my lot as an organized person with a directive mission. My behavior is quite beyond my control. As mentioned previously, all of this is probably a product of our DNA. Tens of thousands of evolutionary years have made my opposite and me what we are.

9   My spouse's ancient counterpart was perhaps a daydreaming troglodyte, who decorated sandstone cave walls with drawings of hunts, imagining the glories of bringing down that mammoth with one club whomp. If so, there was a well-groomed organizer mate in the home cave, arranging his clubs all in a row and his life on an endless time line. If she hadn't done so, he couldn't have contributed to the diverse gene pool into which we now dip.

10   Reason tells me that's what happened to the Neanderthals—there was too much inbreeding among the disorganized. Look in your anthropology book and consider the artists' uniform depictions of these creatures, with grubby fingers and tousled hair, their privates barely concealed by scraps of moldy animal-fur clothing. It's no wonder science has failed to clearly establish kinship between them and the surviving relatively neat and tidy-looking *Homo sapiens*.

EXERCISE 8   Vocabulary Highlights

Write a short definition of each word as it is used in the essay. (Paragraph numbers are given in parentheses) Be prepared to use these words in sentences.

wallowing (1)	inanimate (7)
stoical (2)	sustaining (8)
parasites (3)	troglodyte (9)
ad nauseam (4)	Neanderthals (10)
artifacts (6)	Homo sapiens (10)

EXERCISE 9   Discussion and Critical Thinking

1. Is this essay mainly comparison or contrast?

2. Is Gallagher trying mainly to inform or persuade?

3. What points of contrasts does Gallagher apply to the disorderly and orderly?

4. According to Gallagher, why do orderly people tolerate the disorderly?

5. How much truth do you find in Gallagher's assessment of disorderly and orderly people? Explain.

EXERCISE 10   Discussion and Critical Thinking

1. Of the two authors, Britt and Gallagher, which one is more likely to say that a relationship between two messy people would work?

2. Britt says that neat people are lazy and mean. Does Gallagher say anything similarly harsh about the disorderly?

3. Which essay do you think most accurately represents the orderly and disorderly? Explain.

4. Which characterization of orderly or disorderly people do you most identify with, if at all?

STUDENT PARAGRAPH AND ESSAYS

Student Thung Tran takes us on an international journey to explore the different experiences of women in Vietnam and America. Born in Vietnam, Thung Tran emigrated to America as a young girl. After watching her mother make the unsteady transition from Vietnamese woman to American woman, Tran was well qualified to write this comparison-and-contrast paragraph. Her paragraph "Wives and Mothers in Vietnam and in America" immediately follows with a completed Writing Process Worksheet and her final draft. To conserve space here, the freewriting and rough drafts have been omitted.

Writing Process Worksheet

Name Thung Tran   **Title** Wives and Mothers in Vietnam and in America   **Due Date** Wednesday, February 15, 10 a.m.

Use the back of this page or separate paper if you need more space.

Assignment

In the space below, write whatever you need to know about your assignment, including information about the topic, audience, pattern of writing, length, whether to include a rough draft or revised drafts, and whether your paper must be typed.

Write a paragraph of comparison and contrast about two people or two types of people who are culturally different. Use the subject-by-subject pattern. Assume that your readers do not know your subjects well. Turn in this completed worksheet, one or more rough drafts, and a typed final draft.

Stage One

Explore Freewrite, brainstorm (list), cluster, or take notes as directed by your instructor.

Listing

cultural background

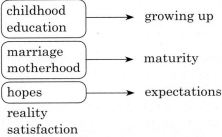

childhood
education   ⟶ growing up

marriage
motherhood   ⟶ maturity

hopes   ⟶ expectations

reality
satisfaction

Stage Two

Organize Write a topic sentence or thesis; label the subject and the focus parts.

Vietnamese immigrants discover just how American culture is different
                                        subject
from Vietnamese culture, especially for the women who become wives and
                                        focus
mothers.

Write an outline or an outline alternative. For reading-based writing, include references and short quotations with page numbers as support in the outline.

    I. Vietnam
        A. Growing up
        B. Maturity
        C. Expectations
    II. America
        A. Growing up
        B. Maturity
        C. Expectations

4. The sloppy people side: Using ideas and points from "Neat People vs. Sloppy People" (vision, action, dealing with clutter, attitudes toward saving items), discuss two people you have known to argue that Britt's view is correct. Refer to and quote from her essay.

5. The neat people side: Using ideas and points from "The Messy Are in Denial" (vision, action, dealing with clutter, attitudes toward saving items), discuss two people you have known to argue that Gallagher's view is correct. Refer to and quote from her essay.

6. Write a reading-based paragraph or essay to show how Britt or Gallagher uses exaggerations, imaginative examples, and colorful expressions to support her points of comparison and contrast. Use references and quotations.

7. In a reaction, compare and contrast Britt's sloppy person with Gallagher's disorganized person.

8. Write a two-part response to Britt's or Gallagher's essay.

GENERAL TOPICS

9. Write about two men or two women in two different societies, or cultures. Begin with whatever they have in common and then discuss how their experiences and behavior are different. You might want instead to consider different aspects of one society: city and suburb, male and female, straight and gay, young and old, and so on. As you compare and contrast, keep in mind that you are generalizing and that individuals differ within groups; avoid stereotyping. For a helpful model on a similar topic, review "Wives and Mothers in Vietnam and in America."

10. Compare and contrast one or more of the following topics. If you have had experience with the subject, consider personalizing your paragraph or essay by using examples from what you have done or observed.

    a. Two generations of college students

    b. Two types of (or specific) police officers, doctors, teachers, preachers, students, or athletes

    c. Living at college and living at home

    d. A small college and a large university or a four-year college and a community college

    e. Dating and being in a committed relationship, living together and being married, or a person before and after marriage

    f. Shopping malls and neighborhood stores

11. Select one of the following subjects to develop an analogy in a paragraph or an essay.

    a. Riding the merry-go-round and dating

    b. Juggling and paying bills

    c. Driving on the freeway and pursuing a career

   d. Going fishing and looking for a job

   e. Shopping in a supermarket and getting an education

   f. Caring for a child and caring for a dog

   g. Driving in traffic and fighting on a battlefield

   h. Sleeping and watching television

   i. Learning a new culture from an immigrant's viewpoint and learning an environment from an infant's viewpoint

   j. Looking for Elvis and looking for truth (or the Holy Grail, an honest person, a unicorn, the Loch Ness monster, Big Foot, or the Abominable Snowman)

CROSS-CURRICULAR TOPICS

12. In the fields of nutritional science and health, compare and contrast two diets, two exercise programs, or two pieces of exercise equipment.

13. Compare and contrast your field of study (or one aspect of it) as it existed some time ago (specify the years) and as it is now. Refer to new developments and discoveries, such as scientific breakthroughs and technological advances, cultural diversity, and changing cultural values.

CAREER-RELATED TOPICS

14. Select two careers that interest you and write a paragraph or an essay to show that one is better for you than the other. For your comparison and contrast, consider points such as your interest, your experience, educational requirements, opportunities, and salary. For an example of an essay on a similar topic, see "Is Nursing or Physical Therapy the Better Career for Me?

15. Compare and contrast two management styles or two working styles.

16. Compare and contrast two career fields to argue that one is better for you.

17. Compare and contrast a public school with a business.

WRITER'S GUIDELINES Comparison and Contrast

BRANDON BRIDGE

1. *Purpose*

   • During the exploration of your topic, define your purpose clearly.
   • Decide whether you are writing a work that is primarily comparison, primarily contrast, or balanced.
   • Determine whether your main purpose is to inform or to persuade.

2. *Points*

   • Indicate your points of comparison or contrast, perhaps by listing.
   • Eliminate irrelevant points.

3. *Patterns*

- Select the subject-by-subject or the point-by-point pattern after considering your topic and planned treatment. The point-by-point pattern is usually preferred in essays. Only in long papers is there likely to be a mixture of patterns.
- Compose an outline reflecting the pattern you select.
- Use this basic outline for the subject-by-subject pattern:

    I. Subject X
        A. Point 1
        B. Point 2
    II. Subject Y
        A. Point 1
        B. Point 2

- Use this basic outline for the point-by-point pattern:

    I. Point 1
        A. Subject X
        B. Subject Y
    II. Point 2
        A. Subject X
        B. Subject Y

4. *Presentation*

- Give each point more or less equal treatment. Attention to each part of the outline will usually ensure balanced development.
- Use transitional words and phrases to indicate comparison and contrast and to establish coherence.
- Use a carefully stated topic sentence for a paragraph and a clear thesis for an essay. Each developmental paragraph should have a topic sentence broad enough to embrace its content.

5. **Consider using the Writing Process Worksheet and the Brandon Guide for Revising and Editing for completing your assignment and the Revising and Editing Charts after your assignment is returned.**

Practicing the Brandon Guide for Revising and Editing

Showing Affection and Cultures

KAREN TRAN BAKER

(A) When an Asian American marries an American, it's not just two people getting married; it's two cultures. (B) As a Vietnamese immigrant, I married an American and discovered that both my husband and me had adjustments to make. (C) We married for love, and we are still in love. (D) Our love is the same deep down; however, our expression of it differs somewhat. (E) As for Americans, the majority seem to have no problem in showing affection for each other, whether in private or public. (F) When my husband comes home he sometimes wants to kiss me right there even if it is in front of the whole family. (G) In public, he may take my hand, or sometimes even kiss me in a place as open as a restaurant. (H) I am flattered by his affection and I know it is genuine, which makes me feel affectionate in return.

(I) I am sometimes self-conscious and uncomfortable. (J) In my culture, on the other hand, expressions of emotion such as kissing, touching, and hugging are done behind closed doors. (K) In my twenty-nine years, I don't recall the last time I hugged my Mother and Father. (L) I have never seen them hold hands or hug one another. (M) I don't want my husband to stop showing his affection in public, because it is his way. (N) Nevertheless, I do wish I could stop feeling embarassed when he bends over and gives me a big kiss in a restaurant.

EXERCISE 14   Revise and Edit with the Brandon Guide

Revise with C L U E S S **(pronounce as "clues" for easy memorization).**

1. **Coherence:** Connect your ideas. Circle the three transitional connectives that are used to show contrast between the cultures.

2. **Language:** Use words appropriate for your purpose and audience. The paragraph ends with the phrase *a restaurant*. To improve the word choice by adding something more colorful and specific, replace those two words with the name of a popular restaurant.

3. **Unity:** Stay on your topic. Underline the topic sentence and the two closing sentences. They unify the paragraph.

4. **Emphasis:** Call attention to your important ideas. Make boxes around the two words that are used most frequently, and their similar forms. Note how they promote emphasis.

5. **Support:** Back up your controlling ideas with evidence and logic. Annotate this paragraph of contrast by writing the word *contrast* to show the support for the topic sentence.

6. **Sentences:** Write correct, effective sentences with structural variety. Combine sentences K and L.

Edit with C G P S **(pronounce as "see GPS" for easy memorization).**

7. **Capitalization:** Two words should not begin with capital letters. Cross out the capital letters and write the lowercase letters above them.

8. **Grammar:** One sentence has an incorrect pronoun for a subject. Cross out that pronoun and write the correct pronoun above it. Reading the sentences aloud may help you find the pronoun.

9. **Punctuation:** One sentence begins with a long introductory modifier that is not followed by a comma. Find it and insert the comma.

10. **Spelling:** One word is misspelled. Cross it out and write the correct spelling above it.

14

Definition
Clarifying Terms

Language sets everyone the same traps; it is an immense network of easily accessible wrong turnings.

—LUDWIG WITTGENSTEIN

CHAPTER CONTENTS

BRANDON BRIDGE

When to Use Definition

FOR COLLEGE WRITING ASSIGNMENTS

- In all classes you will need to define both abstract and concrete terms in discussion and writing. Mastering techniques in defining can save you time and help you get credit for what you know. An identification item on a test requires only a sentence- or paragraph-long definition. An extended discussion of a term can require the bulk of an essay or a research paper.

IN CAREERS AND AT THE WORKPLACE

- Whether preparing for a vocation or performing at the workplace, you will encounter terms that are at the center of discussion and, often, debate.
- In career preparation, you will be expected to define your career and relate that definition to your value system. Just what is an accountant, a teacher, a nurse, an oceanographer, a coach, a physical therapist, or a pilot in the context of your anticipated life?
- At the workplace, you may ponder and have to explain terms as difficult as *business ethics or integrity* and as simple as a particular product or service.

DEFINITION IN A CARTOON

THE QUIGMANS   by Buddy Hickerson

B. Hickerson, copyright Los Angeles Times Syndicate. Reprinted with permission

Writing Definition

Most definitions are short; they consist of a **synonym** (a word or phrase that has about the same meaning as the term to be defined), a phrase, or a sentence. For example, we might say that a hypocrite is a person "professing beliefs or virtues he or she does not possess." Terms can also be defined by **etymology**, or word history. *Hypocrite* once meant "actor" (*hypocrites*) in Greek because an actor was pretending to be someone else. We may find this information interesting and revealing, but the history of a word may be of limited use because the meaning has changed drastically over the years. Sometimes definitions occupy a paragraph or an entire essay. The short definition is called a **simple definition**; the longer one is known as an **extended definition**.

TECHNIQUES FOR WRITING SIMPLE DEFINITIONS

If you want to define a term without being abrupt and mechanical, you have several alternatives. All of the following techniques allow you to blend the definition into your developing thought.

- *Basic dictionary meaning.* You can quote the dictionary's definition, but if you do, you are obliged to indicate your source, which you should do directly and explicitly. Always give the complete title of the dictionary, such as "*Merriam-Webster's Collegiate Dictionary* says." Do not write, "*Webster's* says." Dozens of dictionaries use the "*Webster's*" designation as part of their title.
- *Synonyms.* Although no two words have exactly the same meaning, synonyms often follow as if in parentheses.

  > He was guilty of the ancient sin of *hubris*, of excessive pride.

- *Direct explanation.* You can state the definition.

  > This spontaneous and loyal support of our preconception—this process of finding "good" reasons to justify our routine beliefs—is known to modern psychologists as *rationalizing*—clearly a new name for a very ancient thing.
  > (James Harvey Robinson, "On Various Kinds of Thinking")

- *Indirect explanation.* You can imply the definition.

  > Trance is a similar abnormality in our society. Even a mild mystic is *aberrant* in Western civilization.
  > (Ruth Benedict, *Patterns of Culture*)

- *Analytical or formal definition.* In using this method, you define by placing the term (the subject) in a class (genus) and then identifying it with characteristics that show how it differs from other members of the same class, as the following examples show:

Subject	Class	Characteristics
A democracy	is a form of government	in which voters elect representatives to manage society.
A wolf	is a dog-like mammal	that is large and carnivorous, with coarse fur; erect, pointed ears; and a bushy tail.
Jazz	is a style of music	that features improvisation and performance.

EXERCISE 1 Writing Simple Definitions

Complete the following formal definitions.

Subject	Class	Characteristics
1. A workaholic	is a person	
2. Dreadlocks	is a natural hairstyle	
3. A hawk		that has a short, hooked bill and strong claws.
4. Hay fever		affecting the mucous membranes of the upper respiratory tract and the eyes, causing sneezing, running nose, and itchy, watery eyes.
5. An antonym	is a word	
6. Bongos	are two connected drums	
7. A patriot		
8. A desert	is a large land area	
9. Jealousy	is a state of mind	
10. Sociology	is the study of human behavior	

Dictionary Entries—Which One to Use

Suppose that you do not know the meaning of the term in italics in the following sentence:

> That kind of cactus is *indigenous* to the Mojave Desert.

As you consider the term in context, you look at the dictionary definitions.

> in·dig·e·nous \ ĭn-dĭj´-ns \ *adj.* **1**. Originating and living or occurring naturally in an area or environment. See synonyms at **native**. **2**. Intrinsic; innate. [From Latin *indigena*, a native. See INDIGEN.]

> (*American Heritage Dictionary of the English Language*, 4th ed.)

The first definition seems to fit the context of *indigenous*. It is followed by a reference: "See synonyms at **native**." Then you look at the second set of definitions:

"Intrinsic; innate." The words are synonyms. You can see that only *native* fits. To provide more information for the reader, the dictionary also presents *native* with a special treatment of synonyms as indicated by the reference.

Looking under the word *native*, you find this definition:

> **Synonyms** *native, indigenous, endemic, autochthonous, aboriginal* These adjectives mean of, belonging to, or connected with a specific place or country by virtue of birth or origin. *Native* implies birth or origin in the specified place: *a native New Yorker*; *the native North American sugar maple*. *Indigenous* specifies that something or someone is native rather than coming or being brought in from elsewhere: *an indigenous crop*; *the Ainu, a people indigenous to the northernmost islands of Japan*. Something *endemic* is prevalent in or peculiar to a particular locality or people: *endemic disease*. *Autochthonous* applies to what is native and unchanged by outside sources: *autochthonous folk melodies*. *Aboriginal* describes what has existed from the beginning; it is often applied to the earliest known inhabitants of a place: *the aboriginal population*; *aboriginal nature*. See also synonyms at **crude**.

> **Usage Note** When used in reference to a member of an indigenous people, the noun *native*, like its synonym *aborigine*, can evoke unwelcome stereotypes of primitiveness or cultural backwardness that many people now seek to avoid. As is often the case with words that categorize people, the use of the noun is more problematic than the use of the corresponding adjective. Thus a phrase such as *the peoples native to northern Europe* or *the aboriginal inhabitants of the South Pacific* is generally much preferable to *the natives of northern Europe* or *the aborigines of the South Pacific*. · Despite its potentially negative connotations, *native* is enjoying increasing popularity in ethnonyms such as *native Australian* and *Alaska native*, perhaps due to the wide acceptance of *Native American* as a term of ethnic pride and respect. These compounds have the further benefit of being equally acceptable when used alone as nouns (*a native Australian*) or in an adjectival construction (*a member of a native Australian people*). Of terms formed on this model, those referring to peoples indigenous to the United States generally capitalize *native*, as in *Alaska Native* (or the less common *Native Alaskan*) and *Native Hawaiian*, while others usually style it lowercase.

> (*American Heritage Dictionary of the English Language*, 4th ed.)

In the synonyms at the close of the entry, did you observe the various shades of meaning, especially the meaning of *indigenous* and *native*? A dictionary is an invaluable aid to definition, but it must be used with care if you want to express yourself clearly and precisely. No two words have exactly the same meaning, and a word may have many meanings, some that extend to very different concepts.

Avoiding Common Problems

- Do not use the expression *is where* or *is when* in beginning the main part of a definition. The verb *is* (a linking verb) should be followed by a noun, a pronoun, or an adjective.

    Weak:　　A stadium is where they hold sports spectaculars.

    Better:　A stadium is a structure in which sports spectaculars are held.

    Weak:　　Socialism is when the ownership and operation of the means of production and distribution are vested in the community as a whole.

    Better:　Socialism is a theory or system of community organization that advocates that the ownership and control of the means of production, capital, land, and so forth, be vested in the community as a whole.

- Do not use the **circular definition**, a practice of defining a term with the term itself.

    Circular:　An aristocracy is a form of government based on rule by the aristocrats.

    Direct:　　An aristocracy is a form of government in which the power resides in the hands of the best individuals or a small privileged class.

- Do not define the subject in more complicated language than the original.

    Murky:　*Surreptitious* means "clandestine."

    Clear:　*Surreptitious* means "secret."

- Do not substitute the example for the definition; the example may be excellent for clarification, but it does not completely define.

    Weak:　　Political conservatives are people like John McCain and Sarah Palin.

    Better:　Political conservatives are people who are dedicated to preserving existing conditions. Examples of conservatives are John McCain and Sarah Palin.

TECHNIQUES FOR WRITING EXTENDED DEFINITIONS

Essays of definition can take many forms. Among the more common techniques for writing a paragraph or short essay of definition are the patterns we have worked with in previous chapters. Consider each of those patterns when you need to write an extended definition. For a particular term, some forms will be more useful than others; use the pattern or patterns that best fulfill your purpose.

Each of the following questions takes a pattern of writing and directs it toward definition.

- *Narration*: Can I tell an anecdote or a story to define this subject (such as *jerk*, *humanitarian*, or *citizen*)? This form may overlap with description and exemplification.
- *Description*: Can I describe this subject (such as *a whale* or *the moon*)?
- *Exemplification*: Can I give examples of this subject (such as naming individuals, to provide examples of *actors*, *diplomats*, or *satirists*)?
- *Analysis by division*: Can I divide this subject into parts (for example, the parts of *a heart*, *a cell*, or *a carburetor*)?
- *Process analysis*: Can I define this subject (such as *lasagna*, *tornado*, *hurricane*, *blood pressure*, or any number of scientific processes) by describing how to make it or how it occurs? (Common to the methodology of communicating in science, this approach is sometimes called the "operational definition.")
- *Cause and effect*: Can I define this subject (such as *a flood*, *a drought*, *a riot*, or *a cancer*) by its causes and effects?
- *Classification*: Can I group this subject (such as kinds of *families*, *cultures*, *religions*, or *governments*) into classes?

Subject	Class	Characteristics
A republic	is a form of government	in which power resides in the people (the electorate).

- *Comparison and contrast*: Can I define this subject (such as *extremist* or *patriot*) by explaining what it is similar to and different from? If you are defining *orangutan* to a person who has never heard of one but is familiar with the gorilla, then you could make comparison-and-contrast statements. If you want to define *patriot*, then you might want to stress what it is not (the contrast) before you explain what it is: a patriot is not a one-dimensional flag waver, not someone who hates "foreigners" because America is always right and always best.

When you use prewriting strategies to develop ideas for a definition, you can effectively consider all the patterns you have learned by using a modified clustering form (Figure 14.1). Put a double bubble around the subject to be defined. Then put a single bubble around each pattern and add appropriate words. If a pattern is not relevant to what you are defining, leave it blank. If you want to expand your range of information, you could add a bubble for a simple dictionary definition and another for an etymological definition.

Order

The organization of your extended definition is likely to be one of emphasis, but it may be space or time, depending on the subject material. You may use just one pattern of development for the overall sequence. If so, you would use the principles of organization discussed in previous chapters.

Figure 14.1 Bubble Cluster Showing How a Term Could Be Defined Using Different Essay Patterns

Transitional Words

Consider using the following transitional words to improve coherence by connecting ideas with ideas, sentences with sentences, and paragraphs with paragraphs.

FOR DEFINITION: originates from, means, derives from, refers to, for example, as a term, as a concept, label, similar to, different from, in a particular context, in common usage, in historical context.

FOR ALL PATTERNS OF WRITING: The HOTSHOT CAT words: However, Otherwise, Therefore, Similarly, Hence, On the other hand, Then, Consequently, Also, Thus

Introduction and Development

Consider these ways of introducing a definition: with a question, with a statement of what it is not, with a statement of what it originally meant, or with a discussion of why a clear definition is important. You may use a combination of these ways or all of them before you continue with your definition.

Development is likely to represent one or more of the patterns of narration, description, exposition (with its own subdivisions), and argumentation.

Whether you personalize a definition depends on your purpose and your audience. Your instructor may ask you to write about a word from a subjective or an objective viewpoint.

FINDING PATTERNS IN PHOTOS

EXERCISE 2   An Image-Based Activity for Groups or Individuals

American Indian veterans saluting during D-Day anniversary celebrations at Omaha Beach

Owen Franken/Corbis News/Corbis

At the center of arguments about patriotism is, of course, a definition of the word *patriotism*. These three photos—two veterans at a ceremony, protesters at a demonstration, and two people voting (with child)—show American citizens in public life. Do all three photos demonstrate parts of a comprehensive definition of democracy or would you exclude one or more? What other components should be added? Complete the outlines (altering them as needed) to show some main characteristics of your definition of patriotism in terms of what it is and is not. Include supporting information under the Roman-numeral headings if you like.

Patriotism is not

   I. _____

  II. _____

 III. _____

Patriotism is

   I. _____

  II. _____

 III. _____

Protestors rally against mass surveillance

If your instructor directs, write a paragraph or an essay of definition based on the outlines. Consider explaining some of the parts of your definition by using examples from your personal experience or your studies.

Texas: Voting polling place

Practicing Patterns of Definition

Doing the following exercise will help you remember the patterns of writing used in extended definitions.

EXERCISE 3   Completing Patterns of Definition

Fill in the double bubble with a term to be defined. You might want to define *culturally diverse society, educated person, leader, role model, friend, infatuation, true love, success,* or *intelligence.* Then complete a bubble on the right for each paragraph or essay pattern. If the pattern does not apply (that is, if it would not provide useful information for your definition), mark it NA ("not applicable").

A. Using Patterns in Definitions

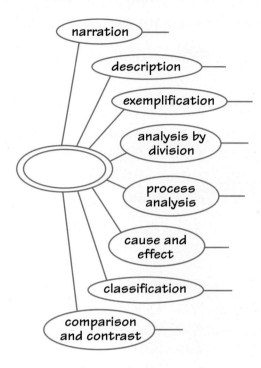

B. Using Patterns in Definitions

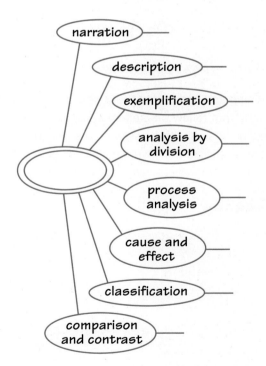

EXERCISE 4 Techniques for Introducing and Developing Definitions

Pick one of the topics you selected for Exercise 3: _____

A. Place an "X" beside each of the following techniques that might be useful in introducing the topic.

_____ A question calling for a definition.

_____ A statement about what the term does not mean.

_____ A statement about what the term meant originally (etymology).

_____ A statement about why a definition would help clarify an ongoing public debate.

B. Place an "X" beside each of the patterns that might be used in developing the topic.

_____ Exemplification

_____ Process analysis

_____ Analysis by division

_____ Cause and effect

_____ Comparison and contrast

Readings for Critical Thinking, Discussion, and Writing

READING STRATEGIES AND OBJECTIVES

Underlining and annotating these reading selections will help you answer the questions that follow the selections, discuss the material in class, and prepare for reading-based writing assignments. As you underline and annotate, pay special attention to the author's writing skills, logic, and message, and consider the relevance of the material to your own experiences and values.

PARAGRAPH

Burnout

GREGORY MOORHEAD AND RICKY W. GRIFFIN

Occupational sociologists Gregory Moorhead and Ricky W. Griffin provide the following definition of burnout *adapted from their book* Organizational Behavior *(2001). Their definition pertains mainly to vocational work, but burnout can occur in any organization—church, government, recreation, even marriage and family.*

Burnout, a consequence of stress, has clear implications for both people and organizations. Burnout is a general feeling of exhaustion that develops when a person simultaneously experiences too much pressure and has too few sources of satisfaction. Burnout usually develops in the following way. First, people with high aspirations and strong motivation to get things done are prime candidates for burnout under certain conditions. They are especially vulnerable when the organization suppresses or limits their initiative while constantly demanding that they serve the organization's own ends. In such a situation, the individual is likely to put too much of himself or herself into the job. In other words, the person may well keep trying to meet his or her own agenda while simultaneously trying to fulfill the organization's expectations. The most likely effects of this situation are prolonged stress, fatigue, frustration, and helplessness under the burden of overwhelming demands. The person literally exhausts his or her aspiration and motivation, much as a candle burns itself out. Loss of self-confidence and psychological withdrawal follow. Ultimately, burnout results. At this point, the individual may start dreading going to work in the morning, may put in longer hours but accomplish less than before, and may generally display mental and physical exhaustion.

EXERCISE 5 Discussion and Critical Thinking

1. Underline the sentence that best conveys the basic definition.

2. What other pattern—comparison and contrast, classification, cause and effect, or narration—provides structure for this definition?

3. If you were going to personalize this definition, what other pattern would you use?

ESSAYS

Soul Food at a Black American Family Reunion

SHEILA FERGUSON

Sheila Ferguson is the author of the enduring book Soul Food: Classic Cuisine from the Deep South.

1   Soul food is a legacy clearly steeped in tradition: a way of life that has been handed down from generation to generation, from one black family to another, by word of mouth and sleight of hand. It is rich in both history and variety of flavors. [Soul food] keeps you glued to your seat long after the meal is over and done with, enabling you to sit back, relax, and savor the gentle purrings of a well-satisfied stomach, feeling that all's right with the world....

2   To cook soul food, you must use all of your senses. You cook by instinct, but you also use smell, taste, touch, sight, and, particularly, sound. You learn to hear by the crackling sound when it's time to turn over the fried chicken, to smell when a pan of biscuits is just about to finish baking, and to feel when a pastry's just right to touch. You taste, rather than measure, the seasonings you treasure, and you use your eyes, not a clock, to judge when that cherry

3   pie has bubbled sweet and nice. These skills are hard to teach quickly. They must be felt, loving, and come straight from the heart.

3   It was down South that I went to my first family reunion. Now, I know I should be telling you that the highlight of this affair was the prayers that one member was chosen to deliver. But if I were to tell the gospel truth, and I think I'm a-gonna, it was definitely the dishes that everybody turned out. Oh, dear, I'm making myself sound like some kind of pagan, but all that food, spread out majestically, on a long banquet-sized picnic table, sure was one sight for a small girl to behold. The table at the farm on Blanton Street in Charlotte kind of sloped with the terrain, but that didn't stop us from keeping the food well balanced and from shooing the flies away from the pecan pies, stacked a mile high, I might add. With one long and narrow slice you had a hunk of pie big enough to last you for quite a spell.

4   I should explain, though, that a black American family reunion stands for a great deal more than just the sharing of a really fine meal. It is a testimonial both to the past and to what the future holds in store for the entire family. We gather to share all that is most precious to us, especially with those family members we don't get to see that often. We eat, we drink, and we pray, but also we encourage each other and lift our heads in praise of what our offspring have accomplished. We share in each other's joys and good fortunes and offer solace when the chips are down. We comfort each other and this enables us to retain a special kind of closeness, even when we're hundreds of miles apart.

EXERCISE 6 Discussion and Critical Thinking

1. How does one use all five senses to prepare soul food?

2. According to Ferguson, why is soul food, soul food?

3. What does a black American family reunion stand for?

4. What are Ferguson's standards in cooking?

5. In what ways is this similar to and different from reunions you have attended?

Loving People Who Love Themselves*

ROY F. BAUMEISTER AND BRAD J. BUSHMAN

This paragraph is taken from the Second Edition of Social Psychology and Human Nature *by Roy F. Baumeister and Brad J. Bushman, published by Wadsworth Cengage Learning in 2011. Professor Baumeister teaches at Florida State University. Professor Bushman teaches at the University of Michigan and VU University, Amsterdam, the Netherlands.*

1   Psychologist Erik Erikson said that people must resolve their identity crisis and know who they are before they are ready to start working on intimacy. He didn't say you had to love yourself—merely know yourself (and it is even questionable whether knowing yourself is prerequisite for having a good relationship).

2   Still, [that theory is no more than a theory]. What do the facts and findings say about loving yourself and loving others? The evidence is at best weak and inconsistent in terms of showing that loving yourself contributes to loving others. In some cases, people who love themselves lavishly are less likely to love anyone else.

3   Let us begin with self-esteem. People with low self-esteem engage in a variety of behaviors that can undermine a relationship. They are skeptical or distrustful when their partners express love or support, and sometimes they act as if they expect their partners to dump them. Still, these problematic behaviors do not seem to translate into breaking up faster. One possible reason is that people with high self-esteem do other, different things that are bad for relationships. When there are problems or conflicts in a relationship, people with high self-esteem are quicker to decide "I don't have to put up with this!" and to contemplate ending the relationship. Probably the different levels of self-esteem contribute to those different reactions. People with low self-esteem doubt that they are lovable, so they expect others to leave them. People with high self-esteem think they are lovable, so they think they can find a new partner relatively easily. The net result may be that high- and low-self-esteem people break up at about the same rate, but for different reasons. The other side of the coin is that people of all levels of self-esteem can have lasting, successful relationships.

4   The risk that self-love can present to relationship harmony is magnified if one looks at narcissism, which is a personality type based on very high self-love. Narcissists have high self-esteem and a strong though somewhat unstable self-love, but these qualities do not make for good relationships; indeed, their selfishness and other qualities may harm relationships. They approach relationships in a game-playing spirit of having fun or as a pragmatic way of getting what they want (including sex). They seek out successful, beautiful, admired people to date, because they think they are similar to them, and they believe that the glamour or prestige of their partners makes them look good.

5   Getting along with a narcissist is no picnic! Narcissists tend to hog the credit when things go well but blame their partners when things go badly, which can certainly put a strain on a relationship. In an observational study in which couples discussed problems that threatened their self-esteem, narcissists had fewer positive interactions with their spouses than other people did.

6   Ultimately, narcissists tend to be less committed to love relationships than other people are. Narcissists tend to keep an eye on the relationship but another eye out to see whether a better partner might come along. Narcissists think they are superior beings and overestimate how attractive they are; as a result, they think they can and should have the most desirable romantic partners. A narcissist may love you for the time being, but he or she will dump you as soon as a better prospect comes along.

7   If self-love leads to loving others, narcissists should be the best lovers, because they love themselves the most. The evidence suggests the opposite, however: In narcissists, at least, loving yourself detracts from loving others. Narcissists are interested in others mainly as a way of boosting their own inflated views of themselves. Hence their relationships tend to be prone to breakup. This may help explain why marriages among celebrities often end in divorce. Being a celebrity tends to push people to become more narcissistic (partly because they are widely admired and highly paid), and this leads to relationship problems, especially when new partners are constantly and readily available.

8   Although narcissism is one problematic extreme, some less extreme versions of self-love and self-esteem may be helpful for relationships. A more minimal form of self-love is self-acceptance, which means simply regarding yourself as being a reasonably good person as you are. The same study that found narcissism to be linked to few positive interactions with the spouse found that self-acceptance was linked to more positive interactions. These finds suggest that having a very negative, critical attitude toward yourself can interfere with the capacity to love. The best summary of current knowledge on this issue is to say that either extreme of self-love or self-hate is likely to be detrimental to intimacy. Conversely, someone with a simple and secure appreciation of self, without being conceited or overblown, will be the best romantic partner.

EXERCISE 7 Discussion and Critical Thinking

1. Draw a circle around the two sentences that contain the definition.

2. Is it possible for a person to be narcissistic in one relationship and not narcissistic in another?

3. Is narcissism a condition that can be treated, or is it just a curse that the narcissist thinks is a blessing?

4. Are narcissistic celebrities born or made? In other words, do they become celebrities because of their self-esteem and self-love or do they have high self-esteem and self-love because of their fame?

5. Of the two extremes of too much self-esteem and too little self-esteem, which is better? If you had to be one and you could choose, which one would you pick?

6. Underline at least six sentences or phrases that qualify the statements instead of suggesting that particular issues are always true; for example, "*Probably* the different levels of self-esteem contribute to those different reactions" (par. 3), "Narcissists *tend* to hog the credit when things go wrong" (par. 4), and "The evidence *suggests* the opposite" (par. 7).

Graffiti: Taking a Closer Look*

CHRISTOPHER GRANT

First published as a cover story in the FBI Law Enforcement Bulletin, *this article is included as general-interest material in* Info Trac, *a data service provider mainly for libraries. It offers a thorough analysis, but it also takes an argumentative position. See how it compares to your own views.*

1   Not long ago, the word *graffiti* conjured images of innocent messages, such as "Tom loves Jane," or "Class of '73." Such simple and innocuous scribblings, although occasionally still seen, have become essentially messages of the past. Most of the graffiti that mars contemporary American landscape—both urban and rural—contains messages of hatred, racism, and gang warfare. Public attitudes toward graffiti tend to fluctuate between indifference and intolerance. On a national level, the criminal justice system has yet to adopt a uniform response to graffiti and the individuals who create this so-called street art. While some jurisdictions combat the problem aggressively, others do very little or nothing at all to punish offenders or to deter the spread of graffiti.

2   To a large degree, society's inability to decide on a focused response to graffiti stems from the nature of the offense. It could be argued that graffiti falls into the grey area between crime and public nuisance. If graffiti is considered in a vacuum, such an argument could appear to have some credence. However, it is unrealistic, and ultimately foolhardy, to view such a public offense in a vacuum. There is a growing consensus in communities around the country that the problem of graffiti, if left unaddressed, creates an environment where other more serious crimes flourish and can quickly degrade once low-crime areas. At a time when law enforcement agencies nationwide are adopting more community-based policing philosophies, administrators are exploring ways to address the basic factors that lead to crime and neighborhood decline. The time has come to take a closer look at graffiti.

Wall Writing

3   **Graffiti** is a general term for wall writing, perhaps humankind's earliest art form. The crude wall writings of prehistoric times and the highly stylized street art of today's inner-city youths share one common feature: Each stems from a basic human need to communicate with others. For youths who may not be able to express themselves through other media, such as prose or music, graffiti represents an easily accessible and effective way to communicate with a large audience. Anyone can obtain a can of spray paint and "make their mark" on a highway overpass or the side of a building.

* Christopher Grant, "Graffiti: Taking a Closer Look" from *The FBI Law Enforcement Bulletin*, 1996.

4 Modern graffiti generally falls into one of three categories—junk graffiti, gang graffiti, and tagging. **Junk graffiti** messages are not gang-related but often involve obscene, racist, or threatening themes. The line separating gang graffiti and tagging has become blurred in recent years. **Tagging**, once seen as a nonviolent alternative to more threatening gang activities, is now considered an entry level offense that can lead to more serious crimes, including burglary and assault. In addition, tagging often results in direct gang affiliation. While all types of graffiti threaten the quality of life in affected areas, tagging and graffiti tied to gang activities represent the most widespread and formidable challenges to communities around the country.

Tagging

5 Tagging as a form of graffiti first appeared in the early 1980s and has grown immensely popular in many parts of the country, in both rural and urban areas. A tagger is someone who adopts a nickname, or tag, and then writes it on as many surfaces as possible, usually in highly visible locations. Although spray paint is the most common medium, taggers—sometimes referred to as "piecers," "writers," and "hip-hop artists"—also may use magic markers or etching tools to create their images.

6 The motivation behind tagging involves fame, artistic expression, power, and rebellion—all integral parts of what has been referred to as the hip-hop culture. Tagging may fill an even deeper void for youths without a strong sense of personal identity. Interviews with taggers reveal a deep desire simply to be known, to create an identity for themselves, and to communicate it to others. The thrill of risk taking also appears to be an underlying motivation for many taggers. While the images taggers create may not necessarily be gang-related, research shows that most taggers hope to join gangs and use tagging as a way to gain the attention of gang members. The more often their monikers appear in different locations, the more publicity they receive. Consequently, a small number of taggers can cause a disproportionate amount of property damage in a community. Tagging messages usually resemble handwriting, but may be difficult, if not impossible, to read. Taggers also have been known to invent their own letters or symbols, often adding to the confusion over the message and the author....

Communication and Territoriality

7 In an article about the increase in area gang violence, a local California newspaper accurately described graffiti as a "crude but effective way for gang members to communicate among themselves, with the community, and with rival gangs." Communication is an important attribute of graffiti that law enforcement and community leaders should understand as they attempt to address the problem. While neighborhood residents and police might see graffiti simply as a blight, gang members and many taggers view it not so much as property damage but as a means to send messages understood within the gang community.

8 The expressive value of graffiti also forms an important component of gang territoriality. Gangs, and potential gang members, use graffiti to identify and mark their territory. Although the traditional perception of gang territoriality has been altered by increased mobility via the automobile, research of a noted gang expert indicates that gangs continue to "mark, define, claim, protect, and

fight over their turf." In fact, territoriality among rival gangs continues to be a major source of gang violence. Graffiti as a primary form of communication and turf identification plays a direct part in feeding this violence.

True Impact of Graffiti

9   The threat posed by graffiti to neighborhoods and society in general goes much deeper than territorial gang violence. Community leaders need only to consider the reverberating effects of graffiti to understand how a seemingly low-grade misdemeanor can threaten or destroy the quality of life in an entire community. The monetary damages attributed to graffiti speak for themselves. In one year, the City of Los Angeles spent more than $15 million on graffiti eradication. This figure does not include the volunteer time devoted to graffiti cleanup or the estimated millions of dollars spent by private businesses taking care of the problem themselves. In addition, the Southern California Rapid Transit District spent $12 million on graffiti removal during the same year....

10   James Q. Wilson, UCLA criminologist and framer of the "broken windows" theory, states that signs of disorder in society—such as graffiti, abandoned cars, broken windows, and uncollected trash—frighten law-abiding citizens into avoiding public places. Those places are then left to criminals who further deface them, creating a downward spiral in which the fear of crime leads to an increase in criminal activity. The presence of graffiti discourages citizens from shopping or living in affected areas. As established businesses relocate or close, new businesses might be reluctant to move into areas where customers would feel unsafe. As property values decline and law-abiding citizens with resources move, once-thriving neighborhoods can quickly degrade into dangerous places. Thus, the seemingly trivial offense of graffiti ultimately can have devastating consequences for a community.

Response

11   Most experts agree that allowing graffiti to remain visible in a community sends a message that this type of behavior is acceptable to residents. Further, allowing graffiti in an area encourages other offenders to degrade the community with more graffiti or other acts of vandalism. As stated in a newspaper article, "... removing graffiti as soon as it appears is the best way to deter further vandalism."

12   Recognizing the serious threat posed by graffiti, a number of communities across the country have developed programs to respond to the problem. The City of Anaheim, California, is considered a leader in developing innovative programs dealing with taggers and the damage they cause. The city developed "Adopt-a-Block" and "Wipeout Graffiti" programs and also established a 24-hour graffiti hotline that encourages residents to report graffiti damage, as well as information about suspects. Information leading to an arrest and conviction can net the caller up to $500. The hotline has proven to be quite successful. To date, callers have received more than $16,500 for information provided about offenders. The courts sentence convicted taggers to perform community service that includes graffiti removal. Anaheim also adopted an antigraffiti ordinance that assigns responsibility for the cost of graffiti removal to taggers, prohibits possession of implements used to create graffiti, and requires merchants to keep aerosol spray cans or other implements used to create graffiti out of direct reach of the general public.... To enhance graffiti-related investigations, Orange County, California, uses a forensic scientist

specializing in handwriting analysis to help identify chronic offenders. Several other localities in California have passed ordinances calling for convicted taggers to perform up to 80 hours of graffiti removal as part of their sentences.

The Future

13   Although these approaches represent a step in the right direction, they are reactive measures and do little to address the causes of the graffiti problem. The causes lie deep within the roots of social structure; it will require much more than rollers and paint to correct the problem.

14   One of the first steps is to educate the public about graffiti—its meaning and its potential impact on a community. Citizens must understand that this type of behavior cannot be tolerated because its insidious nature threatens communities from within. To deter new graffiti, young people should be taught that their actions can have far-reaching consequences. Law enforcement agencies may consider augmenting drug- and gang-prevention efforts with lessons on graffiti. Students should be advised that damaging property with graffiti is a serious crime and offenders will be punished. As part of the lesson, instructors also may suggest and encourage alternative methods of self-expression.

Conclusion

15   Like prostitution and illegal gambling, people often view graffiti as a victimless crime. But as communities around the country have learned, there is no such thing as a victimless crime. In fact, crimes that do not produce a single, identifiable victim generally have more impact on the entire community. As a highly visible offense, graffiti represents a particularly menacing threat to the quality of life in a community. The residual effects of reduced property values, lost business, increased gang territoriality, and heightened fear of crime escalate the severity of graffiti-related offenses beyond their impact as visual pollution. Communities that do not develop measures to deter and prevent graffiti now may find themselves confronting more intractable problems in the future.

EXERCISE 8   Vocabulary Highlights

Write a short definition of each word as it is used in the essay. (Paragraph numbers are given in parentheses.) Be prepared to use these words in sentences.

fluctuate (1)	enhance (12)
consensus (2)	insidious (14)
disproportionate (6)	augmenting (14)
reverberating (9)	escalate (15)
innovative (12)	intractable (15)

EXERCISE 9 Discussion and Critical Thinking

1. Underline the sentence in paragraph 2 that indicates what the author is trying to do.

2. Underline the sentence in paragraph 4 that takes a clear position on graffiti and, therefore, can be called the proposition.

3. Draw vertical lines in the left margin to indicate the sentences in paragraphs 1 and 2 that tie this essay to an audience concerned with law enforcement.

4. According to Grant, what motivates taggers?

5. Why do many gang members do graffiti?

6. What is the "broken window" theory?

7. What form of writing is used in paragraph 10?

8. What is the best way to deter further graffiti?

9. What should be done to deal with the causes of graffiti problems?

10. Does the solution of educating young people about the problems caused by graffiti suggest that the writer has faith in human beings?

11. What parts of this essay do you agree and not agree with? Explain.

12. If you could add one more strong section (or strengthen one), what would it be? Discuss.

Americanization Is Tough on "Macho"*

ROSE DEL CASTILLO GUILBAULT

What does macho mean to you? If someone calls you or a person you respect "macho," are you pleased or offended? Or, are you perhaps unsure and listen on, reserving judgment and trying to determine what the speaker means. The fact is that macho has two distinctly different meanings.

1   What is *macho*? That depends on which side of the border you come from.

2   Although it's not unusual for words and expressions to lose their subtlety in translation, the negative connotations of *macho* in this country are troublesome to Hispanics.

**Rose Del Castillo Guilbault, "Americanization Is Tough on 'Macho'" from *This World*, 1989.*

3   Take the newspaper descriptions of alleged mass murderer Ramon Sal-cido. That an insensitive, insanely jealous, hard-drinking, violent Latin male is referred to as *macho* makes Hispanics cringe.

4   "*Es muy macho*," the women in my family nod approvingly, describing a man they respect. But in the United States, when women say, "He's so macho," it's with disdain.

5   The Hispanic *macho* is manly, responsible, hardworking, a man in charge, a patriarch. A man who expresses strength through silence. What the Yiddish language would call a *mensch*.

6   The American *macho* is a chauvinist, a brute, uncouth, selfish, loud, abrasive, capable of inflicting pain, and sexually promiscuous.

7   Quintessential *macho* models in this country are Sylvester Stallone, Arnold Schwarzenegger, and Charles Bronson. In their movies, they exude toughness, independence, masculinity. But a closer look reveals their machismo is really violence masquerading as courage, sullenness disguised as silence and irresponsibility camouflaged as independence.

8   If the Hispanic ideal of *macho* were translated to American screen roles, they might be Jimmy Stewart, Sean Connery, and Laurence Olivier.

9   In Spanish, *macho* ennobles Latin males. In English it devalues them. This pattern seems consistent with the conflicts ethnic minority males experience in this country. Typically the cultural traits other societies value don't translate as desirable characteristics in America.

10   I watched my own father struggle with these cultural ambiguities. He worked on a farm for twenty years. He laid down miles of irrigation pipe, carefully plowed long, neat rows in fields, hacked away at recalcitrant weeds and drove tractors through whirlpools of dust. He stoically worked twenty-hour days during harvest season, accepting the long hours as part of agricultural work. When the boss complained or upbraided him for minor mistakes, he kept quiet, even when it was obvious the boss had erred.

11   He handled the most menial tasks with pride. At home he was a good provider, helped out my mother's family in Mexico without complaint, and was indulgent with me. Arguments between my mother and him generally had to do with money, or with his stubborn reluctance to share his troubles. He tried to work them out in his own silence. He didn't want to trouble my mother—a course that backfired, because the imagined is always worse than the reality.

12   Americans regarded my father as decidedly un-*macho*. His character was interpreted as nonassertive, his loyalty, non-ambition, and his quietness, ignorance. I once overheard the boss's son blame him for plowing crooked rows in a field. My father merely smiled at the lie, knowing the boy had done it, but didn't refute it, confident his good work was well known. But the boss instead ridiculed him for being "stupid" and letting a kid get away with a lie. Seeing my embarrassment, my father dismissed the incident, saying "They're the dumb ones. Imagine, me fighting with a kid."

13   I tried not to look at him with American eyes because sometimes the reflection hurt.

14   Listening to my aunts' clucks of approval, my vision focused on the qualities America overlooked. "He's such a hard worker. So serious, so responsible." My aunts would secretly compliment my mother. The unspoken comparison was that he was not like some of their husbands, who drank and womanized. My uncles represented the darker side of *macho*.

15   In a patriarchal society, few challenge their roles. If men drink, it's because it's the manly thing to do. If they gamble, it's because it's how men relax. And if they fool around, well, it's because a man simply can't hold back so much

man! My aunts didn't exactly meekly sit back, but they put up with these transgressions because Mexican society dictated this was their lot in life.

16 In the United States, I believe it was the feminist movement of the early 1970s that changed *macho*'s meaning. Perhaps my generation of Latin women was in part responsible. I recall Chicanas complaining about the chauvinistic nature of Latin men and the notion they wanted their women barefoot, pregnant, and in the kitchen. The generalization that Latin men embodied chauvinistic traits led to this interesting twist of semantics. Suddenly a word that represented something positive in one culture became a negative prototype in another.

17 The problem with the use of *macho* today is that it's become an accepted stereotype of the Latin male. And like all stereotypes, it distorts the truth.

18 The impact of language in our society is undeniable. And the misuse of *macho* hints at a deeper cultural misunderstanding that extends beyond mere word definitions.

EXERCISE 10 Vocabulary Highlights

Write a short definition of each word as it is used in the essay. (Paragraph numbers are given in parentheses.) Be prepared to use these words in sentences.

subtlety (2)	recalcitrant (10)
connotations (2)	stoically (10)
alleged (3)	upbraided (10)
quintessential (7)	transgressions (15)
ambiguities (10)	embodied (16)

EXERCISE 11 Discussion and Critical Thinking

1. What is Hispanic *macho*?

2. What is American *macho*?

3. What other examples of the different definitions of *macho* can you provide?

4. The author's father worked "stoically." What does the word *stoical* imply about how a person looks at life with its many problems?

5. How does the author relate the word *macho* to the feminist movement?

6. Would the word *patriarch* be regarded differently by people with different cultural or political views?

7. What makes the author's view valuable?

8. To what kind of audience is this piece directed?

STUDENT PARAGRAPH AND ESSAY

Linda Wong looked at a list of abstract terms for her assignment to write an extended definition and almost immediately found one that intrigued her. She had often heard people say things such as "I just can't love him [or her] enough," and "It was too much of a good thing," and she connected those ideas with one of the terms: *extremist*.

Wong's Writing Process Worksheet shows you how her writing evolved from idea to final draft. To conserve space here, the freewriting and the rough drafts marked for revision have been omitted. The balance of the worksheet has been lengthened for you to be able to see her other work in its entirety.

BRANDON BRIDGE

Writing Process Worksheet

Name <u>Linda Wong</u>   **Title** <u>Going Too Far</u>   **Due Date** <u>Monday, December 3, 8 a.m.</u>

Use the back of this page or separate paper if you need more space.

Assignment

In the space below, write whatever you need to know about your assignment, including information about the topic, audience, pattern of writing, length, whether to include a rough draft or revised drafts, and whether your paper must be typed.

Write a paragraph that defines an abstract word. Use at least three patterns of writing in your extended definition. Keep in mind that members of your audience may use your term in different ways, so using examples and clear explanations will be helpful for clarification. Submit your completed worksheet, one or more rough drafts marked for revision, and a typed final draft of about 300 words.

Stage One   **Explore** Freewrite, brainstorm (list), cluster, or take notes as directed by your instructor.

Clustering

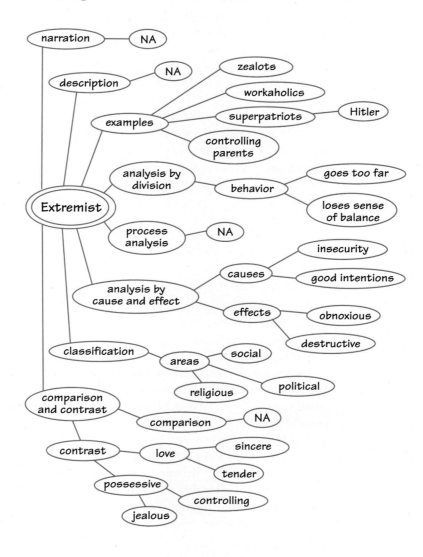

Stage Two   **Organize** Write a topic sentence or thesis; label the subject and the focus parts.

<u>Extremists</u> <u>are involved people who lose their sense of balance and go too far</u>
  subject   focus
<u>in concentrating on one thing</u>.

Write an outline or an outline alternative. For reading-based writing, include references and short quotations with page numbers as support in the outline.

    I. Going too far
       A. Become preoccupied with one thing
       B. Lose sense of balance

II. Produce bad effect
    A. Are unpleasant to be around
    B. Are often destructive

III. Become incomplete
    A. Are often thought of as one kind of person
        1. Workaholics
        2. Zealots
        3. Superpatriots
    B. Diminished by loss of perspective

Stage Three

Write On separate paper, write and then revise your paragraph or essay as many times as necessary for **c**oherence, **l**anguage (usage, tone, and diction), **u**nity, **e**mphasis, **s**upport, and **s**entences (**CLUESS**). Read your work aloud to hear and correct any grammatical errors or awkward-sounding sentences.

Edit any problems in fundamentals, such as **c**apitalization, **g**rammar, **p**unctuation, and **s**pelling (**CGPS**).

Final Draft

GOING TOO FAR
Linda Wong

What the term does not mean

Simple definition
Topic sentence

Example/contrast

Example/contrast

Example/contrast

Examples

Effect and concluding sentence

Some people believe that it is good to be an extremist in some areas, but those people are actually changing the meaning of the word. According to the *Random House Dictionary of the English Language*, the word *extremism* itself means "excessively biased ideas, intemperate conduct." The extremist goes too far; that means going too far in whatever the person is doing. I once heard someone say that it is good for people to be extremists in love. But that is not true. It is good to be enthusiastically and sincerely in love, but extremists in love love excessively and intemperately. People who love well may be tender and sensitive and attentive, but extremists are possessive or smothering. The same can be said of parents. We all want to be good parents, but parental extremists involve themselves too much in the lives of their children, who, in turn, may find it difficult to develop as individuals and become independent. Even in patriotism, good patriots are to be distinguished from extreme patriots. Good patriots love their country, but extreme patriots love their country so much that they think citizens from other countries are inferior and suspect. Extreme patriots may have Hitler-like tendencies. Just what is wrong with extremists then? It is the loss of perspective. The extremists are so preoccupied with one concern that they lose their sense of balance. They are the workaholics, the zealots, the superpatriots of the world. They may begin with a good objective, but they focus on it so much that they can become destructive, obnoxious, and often pitiful. The worst effect is that these extremists lose their completeness as human beings.

EXERCISE 12 Discussion and Critical Thinking

1. Wong says that extremists "can become destructive, obnoxious, and often pitiful." Can you think of any good effects from people who are extremists? For example, what about a scientist who works fifteen hours a day to find a cure for a horrible disease? Is it possible that the scientist may succeed in his or her profession and fail in his or her personal life? But what if the scientist does not want a personal life? Discuss.

2. Why does Wong use contrast so much?

3. According to Wong, is it bad for a person to be an extremist in religion? Discuss.

READING-BASED WRITING

My-graines

VINCENT SHEAHAN

The assignment was to read several essays related to health and write a reading-based, documented essay of extended definition about one health condition as it related to the student's experience. The final product would include at least two quotations and several paraphrases from the source, each to be formally identified. The source would be listed at the end, according to MLA style for an article in an anthology. (Your instructor may not ask you to formally document an essay based on a single textbook source.)

1   The aura set in like a suffocating stillness before a tropical storm. "This is going to be a bad one," I told myself as I shut off the lights, took my medication, lay down, and prepared for the inevitable—the relentless throbbing in my temple. About three hours of incapacitating agony later, I recovered, feeling strangely drained, and skimmed through my reading assignment for my college English class. What a coincidence! It included "In Bed," an essay about migraines by Joan Didion. Because I had only recently been diagnosed with migraines (although I had long suffered), I naturally had enormous curiosity about the subject, and now homework coincided with my private need for information. By closely comparing my family history, my triggers for attacks, and my personality with Joan Didion's, perhaps I could find some informed answers to my questions and be able to define *migraines* more precisely.

2   A year ago when I decided to seek medical help, the matter of family history was of immediate concern. At my first appointment, my neurologist informed me that, although no one knows why, migraines tend to run in families. I said the only person in my family who has migraines is my Uncle Joe, my father's brother. For Didion, the family connection is more apparent and pervasive: Both of her grandmothers, her father, and her mother all suffer from migraine headaches. But she does go on to explain, "One inherits, of course, only the predisposition" (59). Therefore, it is possible that everyone on my father's side has carried the gene for migraines, but only Uncle Joe has ever actually developed the headaches.

3   After the doctor asked his questions, I had one of my own: What actually causes migraine headaches? I was fearful that my job as an emergency
medical technician (E.M.T.), with its debilitating stress and irregular hours,
was the main reason. He explained that the exact causes are not completely
understood and that my fatigue and irregular sleep patterns are not the
causes of my migraines, because there are plenty of E.M.T.s who have the
same sleep patterns as I do yet do not have migraines. Nevertheless, the
fatigue and irregular sleep may trigger migraine headaches. For Didion, the
triggers are varied. She says, "Almost anything can trigger a specific attack
of migraine: stress, allergy, fatigue, an abrupt change in barometric pressure,
a contretemps over a parking ticket. A flashing light. A fire drill" (60). Yet she
explains that her headaches are not triggered at times when she needs to be
alert and thinking clearly, such as an emergency situation, but instead, they
are triggered when she is feeling overwhelmed or extremely stressed (60).

4   In addition to the exposure to these triggers, a migraine sufferer like me
usually has what is called a "migraine personality." Didion offers a good definition of that term, saying that she is typical, a perfectionist who is "ambitious,
inward, intolerant of error, rather rigidly organized" (60). But she points out
that not all perfectionists have migraines and not all people with migraines
are perfectionists. She says that she is a perfectionist about writing, not
housekeeping (60). And, as for me, I try—probably harder than most—to be
organized when it comes to my education, work, and personal life.

5   Like Joan Didion, I am intensely interested in migraines, and I am learning about them. We migraine sufferers have much in common, though each
of us has his or her own family history of migraines, triggers, and migraine
personality. Knowing that others go through what I do and having more information about my condition make it easier for me to deal with the pain of my
migraines. I will continue to do the same thing Joan Didion does when she has
an aura: I will not try to fight it. I will lie down and endure. When it is finally
over, I will count my blessings.

Work Cited

Didion, Joan. "In Bed." *Health Views*. Ed. Marjorie Ford and Jon Ford.
Boston: Houghton, 1998. 58–61. Print.

EXERCISE 13 Discussion and Critical Thinking

1. Circle the thesis and underline the topic sentences in the support
paragraphs.

2. Forms of writing other than definition are often used to define. Which form
provides structure for this extended definition?

3. How is Sheahan's introduction connected to his conclusion?

4. How do you explain Sheahan's change of verb tenses?

Suggested Topics and Prompts for Writing Definition

READING-BASED WRITING

Reading-based writing requires you to read critically, write a reply that shows you understand what you have read, and give credit for ideas you borrow and words you quote. The form can be a summary, a reaction, or a two-part response (with separated summary and reaction). Documentation, in which you give credit for borrowed ideas and words, can be either formal (MLA style) or informal, as directed by your instructor. All of the forms of reading-based writing and documentation are discussed with examples in Chapter 6. Definitions of the three forms follow. Any form can be used for any reading selection in this book.

Summary

- The summary is a statement written in response to a reading. It restates only the most important points and uses original wording instead of the author's language. It should not contain added information or personal opinions.
- Because summaries are intended to restate only the main points of a reading, they are typically much shorter than the original text. Often, they are approximately a third of the length.

Reaction

- In the reaction, the meaning of what you have read will be central to the topic sentence of your paragraph or to the thesis of your essay.
- Although the reaction is not a personal narrative by itself, it may include personal experience to explain elements of the text. For example, if your source is about driving styles, your own experiences as a driver or an observer of drivers could be relevant in your analysis of the text.
- The reaction may incorporate a summary to convey a broad view of what you have read, but your summary should never be the main part of your reaction.

Two-Part Response

- The two-part response separates the summary from the reaction.
- This form will give you practice in separating your objective summary in the first part from your more personal evaluation, interpretation, or application in the second part, the reaction.

READING-BASED WRITING TOPICS

"Burnout"

1. Borrow the definition from this paragraph and in a reaction develop it with an extended example of someone you know who is or was a burnout.

"Soul Food at a Black American Family Reunion"

2. Write a definition of a kind of reunion that you are familiar with and discuss how it is similar to and different from the one discussed by Ferguson. Refer to and quote from her essay in your reaction.

"Loving People Who Love Themselves"

3. Write a two-part response in which you summarize the essay and then analyze it according to how it relates to people you have met or know about and situations you know about or have encountered. Use quotations and references.

4. Some say that the current generation has a bad case of narcissism. Using the definitions and applications provided by Baumeister and Bushman, discuss an individual you have met or a relationship you have observed or been involved in that included narcissistic behavior. Use quotations and references. Consider renaming your subject(s).

5. Write a reaction in which you apply the definition and insights provided by Baumeister and Bushman to one or more sports, political, or entertainment celebrities you are familiar with.

"Graffiti: Taking a Closer Look"

6. Write a reaction to Grant's definition of *graffiti* in which you take issue with some of his views. Use quotations from and include references to his essay.

7. Write a reaction that is generally in agreement with Grant's view, using your own examples to refer to neighborhoods or towns damaged by graffiti.

8. If you know people who do or have done graffiti, interview them with questions framed around Grant's argument. Then write an essay that accepts or rejects their views. Use quotations from and include references to Grant's essay.

"Americanization Is Tough on 'Macho'"

9. Write a summary of this essay and underline the main idea and double-underline the parts of the definition, which takes the form of analysis by division.

10. Author Rose del Castillo Guilbault makes the point that there are two definitions of "macho"—the positive and the negative, essentially the Hispanic and the American. The qualities, or traits, of each are given in paragraphs 5 and 6. Relying on your familiarity with the term, write a reaction that focuses on either the positive or the negative as you would apply the term to someone you know, a character from the media, or a well-known public figure. Discuss at least three of the traits. Refer to and quote from the essay.

"Going Too Far"

11. Apply Wong's definition of *extremist* to a situation or situations with which you are familiar: an overprotective parent, a controlling companion, an over-controlling boss, a too-strict police officer or teacher, a too-virtuous friend or preacher, a too-clean housekeeper, a zealous patriot, a person fanatical about a diet, or a person concerned too much with good health or exercise. You might begin your paragraph or essay with the statement: "It is good to be _____, but when _____ is carried to the extreme, the result is _____."

GENERAL TOPICS

12. The following topics are appropriate for extended development of definitions; most of them will also serve well for writing simple definitions.

   a. Cult

   b. Workaholic

   c. Clotheshorse

   d. Educated

   e. Body language

   f. Hero

   g. Psychopath

   h. School spirit

   i. Jock

   j. Cool

CROSS-CURRICULAR TOPIC

13. Define one of the following terms in a paragraph or an essay.

   a. History and government: socialism, democracy, capitalism, communism

   b. Philosophy: existentialism, free will, determinism, ethics, stoicism

   c. Education: charter school, standardized test, MOOC (Massive Open Online Course), STEM (Science, Technology, Engineering, and Mathematics) majors, adaptive learning

   d. Music: symphony, sonata, orchestra, tonic systems

   e. Health science: autism, circulatory system, respiratory system, thyroid, cancer, herbal remedies, acupuncture

   f. Marketing: depression, digitalization, discretionary income, electronic commerce, globalization, marketing channel, free trade, telemarketing, warehouse clubs

CAREER-RELATED TOPICS

14. Define one of the following terms by using other patterns of development (such as exemplification, cause and effect, narration, comparison and

contrast): total quality management, quality control, business ethics, customer satisfaction, cost effectiveness, Internet, temporary worker, union, outsource, or downsize.

15. Define a good boss, good employee, good workplace, good employer, or good job. Analysis by division is a useful form.

16. Define a term from computer technology, such as Internet, World Wide Web, search engine, or chat room.

WRITER'S GUIDELINES Definition

BRANDON BRIDGE

Simple Definition

1. No two words have exactly the same meaning.

2. Several forms of simple definitions can be blended into your discussion: basic dictionary definitions, synonyms, direct explanations, indirect explanations, and analytical definitions.

3. For a formal or an analytical definition, specify the term, class, and characteristic(s).

<u>Capitalism</u> is an economic <u>system</u> <u>characterized by investment</u>
    term   class
<u>of money, private ownership, and free enterprise.</u>
                   characteristics

4. Avoid "is where" and "is when" definitions, circular definitions, and the use of words in the definition that are more difficult than the word being defined.

Extended Definition

1. Use clustering to consider other patterns of development that may be used to define your term.

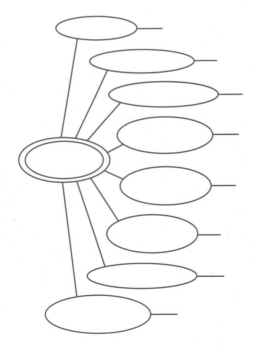

2. The organization of your extended definition is likely to be one of emphasis, but it may be space or time, depending on the subject material. You may use just one pattern of development for the overall organization.

3. Consider these ways of introducing a definition: with a question, with a statement of what it is not, with a statement of what it originally meant, or with a discussion of why a clear definition is important. You may use a combination of these ways before you continue with your definition.

4. Whether you personalize a definition depends on your purpose and your audience. Your instructor may ask you to write about a word within the context of your own experience or to write about it from a detached, clinical viewpoint.

5. **Consider using the Writing Process Worksheet and the Brandon Guide for Revising and Editing for completing your assignment and the Revising and Editing Charts after your assignment is returned.**

Practicing the Brandon Guide for Revising and Editing

PATTERN: DEFINITION

Feng Shui and Real Estate

JEAN CHEW

(A) My real estate client, Mrs. Wong, asked me, "Do you know about *feng shui?*" (B) I smiled and said, Of course. (C) Without that knowledge I could not function in my profession as a Real Estate agent. (D) Feng shui is the name for Chinese superstitions, especially those regarding the interrelationship of a person's birth chart and the home where he or she lives. (E) Thus, describing an ideal house to a client may be more a matter of listing examples of what it should not have instead of what it should have. (F) In fact, there is several negative characteristics other then those associated with personal charts. (G) At the entrance facing the front door, there should be no tree. (H) It may bring death or divorce. (I) The front door itself should not face the stairwell because all good fortune may roll right out of the house. (J) The back door should also not face the front door. (K) Such an arrangement may allow the money that comes in at the front door to go out the back and leave the family in poverty. (L) The house should sit on a lot that is square or rectangular;

sharp angles will bring very bad luck. (M) The land itself should be higher along the fence behind the house to hold in prosperity. (N) Moreover, the house must face the right direction according to the individual's time of birth, and the house location can affect a person's destiny. (O) Even the number of the house may be a factor. (P) For example, the number 4 has the same character as death. (Q) These kinds of rules of feng shui, along with the commonsense requirement of a bright and cheerful atmosphere and a functional floor plan, are points Mrs. Wong will consider in purchasing a home. (R) Because trying to follow all the rules of feng shui may keep people from finding an excellent house, my colleagues and I often advise clients not to take feng shui too seriously lest it make their life miserable.

EXERCISE 14   Revise and Edit with the Brandon Guide

Revise with **C L U E S S** (pronounce as "clues" for easy memorization).

1. **C**oherence: Connect your ideas. Circle the four transitional connectives that connect ideas.

2. **L**anguage: Use words appropriate for your purpose and audience. Make two lines under the words that are emotionally charged in stating the bad effects of feng shui.

3. **U**nity: Stay on your topic. Underline the topic sentence and the closing sentence that unify the paragraph.

4. **E**mphasis: Call attention to your important ideas. Draw a box around the most frequently used word and its related forms (six altogether) that promote emphasis and unity.

5. **S**upport: Back up your controlling ideas with evidence and logic. In the margin to the left, number the seven examples that support the topic sentence.

6. **S**entences: Write correct, effective sentences with structural variety. Combine Sentences G and H to show that one is the cause of another.

Edit with C G P S (pronounce as "see GPS" for easy memorization).

7. **C**apitalization: Two words are improperly capitalized. Cross out the capital letters and write the lowercase letters above them.

8. **G**rammar: One sentence has wrong subject and verb agreement. Cross out the verb and insert the correct verb above it.

9. **P**unctuation: The quotation marks are missing from a quotation near the beginning of the paragraph. Insert them.

10. **S**pelling: One word is misspelled. Cross out that misspelled word and write the correct spelling above it.

15

Argument
Writing to Persuade

“*People are never so likely to settle a question rightly as when they discuss it freely.*”

—ROBERT SOUTHEY

CHAPTER CONTENTS

BRANDON BRIDGE

When to Use Argument

FOR COLLEGE WRITING ASSIGNMENTS

• You will use argument and persuasion in all college writing—paragraphs, essays, tests, reports, and research papers—that requires you to discuss and support your views on topics about which others may disagree or reluctantly follow. You may argue that a theory in biology is sound, that a system in philosophy is inadequate, or that a short story in literature is flawed. You may persuade in nursing that a particular diet or exercise program is desirable.

IN CAREERS AND AT THE WORKPLACE

• Business and other institutions require persuasive and argumentative writing in memos to employers or fellow employees about team standards, in proposals to clients about projects, in promotional material about selling items and services, and in application letters about getting hired.

ARGUMENT IN A CARTOON

THE QUIGMANS   by Buddy Hickerson

"Looks like the work of that vampire from the Nursing Home."

B. Hickerson, copyright Los Angeles Times Syndicate. Reprinted with permission

Writing Argument

Persuasion is a broad term. When we persuade, we try to influence people to think in a certain way or to do something.

   Argument is persuasion on a topic about which reasonable people disagree. Argument involves controversy. Whereas exercising appropriately is probably not controversial because reasonable people do not dispute the idea, an issue such as gun control is controversial. In this chapter, we will be concerned mainly with the kind of persuasion that involves argument and uses evidence.

TECHNIQUES FOR DEVELOPING ARGUMENT

Statements of argument are informal or formal. An opinion column in a newspaper is likely to have little set structure, whereas an argument in college writing is likely to be tightly organized. Nevertheless, the opinion column and the college paper have much in common. Both provide a proposition, which is the main point of the argument, and both provide support, which is the evidence or the reasons that back up the proposition.

   For a well-structured college paragraph or essay, an organization plan is desirable. Consider these elements when you write an argument, and ask yourself the following questions as you develop your ideas:

Background: What is the historical or social context for this controversial issue?

Proposition (the thesis of the essay): What do I want my audience to believe or to do?

Qualification of proposition: Can I limit my proposition so that those who disagree cannot easily challenge me with exceptions? If, for example, I am in favor of using animals for scientific experimentation, am I concerned only with medical experiments or with any use, including experiments for the cosmetic industry?

Refutation (taking the opposing view into account, mainly to point out its fundamental weakness): What is the view on the other side, and why is it flawed in reasoning or evidence?

Support: In addition to sound reasoning, can I use appropriate facts, examples, statistics, and opinions of authorities?

The figure that follows shows the most commonly used pattern for an essay of argument, which is abbreviated for a paragraph.

   There are, of course, other variants, and there are also several methods of developing the material within each pattern. You may organize your support by a pro and con arrangement, presenting one side at a time or one issue at a time (discuss an issue favoring your position, then refute your opponent's claims). You may also develop the argument (or persuasive writing, in a broader sense) by a method such as cause and effect, definition, and comparison and contrast or by a combination of methods.

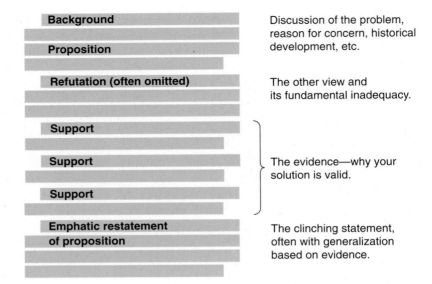

Background	Discussion of the problem, reason for concern, historical development, etc.
Proposition	
Refutation (often omitted)	The other view and its fundamental inadequacy.
Support	
Support	The evidence—why your solution is valid.
Support	
Emphatic restatement of proposition	The clinching statement, often with generalization based on evidence.

YOUR AUDIENCE

Your audience may be uninformed, informed, biased, hostile, receptive, apathetic, sympathetic, empathetic—any one, several, or something else. The point is that you should be acutely concerned about who will read your composition. If your readers are likely to be uninformed about the social and historical background of the issue, then you need to set the issue in context. The discussion of the background should lead to the problem for which you have a proposition or solution. If your readers are likely to be biased or even hostile to your view, take special care to refute the opposing side in a thoughtful way that does not further antagonize them. If your readers are already receptive and perhaps even sympathetic, and you wish to move them to action, then you might appeal to their conscience and the need for their commitment.

KINDS OF EVIDENCE

In addition to sound reasoning generally, you can use these kinds of evidence: facts, examples, statistics, and authorities.

First, you can offer facts. Martin Luther King Jr. was killed in Memphis, Tennessee, on April 4, 1968. Because an event that has happened is true and can be verified, this statement about King is a fact. But that James Earl Ray acted alone in killing King is, to some, questionable. That King was the greatest of all civil rights leaders is also opinion because it cannot be verified.

Some facts are readily accepted because they are general knowledge—you and your reader know them to be true, because they can be or have been verified. Other "facts" are based on personal observation and are reported in various publications but may be false or questionable. You should always be concerned about the reliability of the source for both the information you use and the information used by those with other viewpoints. Still other so-called facts are genuinely debatable because of their complexity or the incompleteness of the knowledge available.

Second, you can cite examples. Keep in mind that you must present a sufficient number of examples and that the examples must be relevant.

Third, you can present statistics. Statistics are numerical facts and data that are classified and tabulated to present significant information about a given subject.

Avoid presenting a long list of figures; select statistics carefully and relate them to things familiar to your reader. The millions of dollars spent on a war in a single week, for example, become more comprehensible when expressed in terms of what the money would purchase in education, highways, or urban renewal.

To test the validity of statistics, either yours or your opponent's, ask: Who gathered them? Under what conditions were they gathered? For what purpose are they used?

Fourth, you can cite evidence from, and opinions of, authorities. Most readers accept facts from recognized, reliable sources—governmental publications, standard reference works, and books and periodicals published by established firms. In addition, they will accept evidence and opinions from individuals who, because of their knowledge and experience, are recognized as experts.

In using authoritative sources as proof, keep these points in mind:

- Select authorities who are generally recognized as experts in their field.
- Use authorities who qualify in the field related to your argument.
- Select authorities whose views are not biased.
- Try to use several authorities.
- Identify the authority's qualifications clearly in your essay.

Transitional Words

Consider using the following transitional words to improve coherence by connecting ideas with ideas, sentences with sentences, and paragraphs with paragraphs.

FOR ARGUMENT: it follows that, as a result, causes taken collectively, as a concession, even though, of course, in the context of, in the light of, in the final analysis, following this, further, as additional support, moreover, consequently, according to, in support of, contrary to

FOR ALL PATTERNS OF WRITING: The <u>HOTSHOT CAT</u> words: <u>H</u>owever, <u>O</u>therwise, <u>T</u>herefore, <u>S</u>imilarly, <u>H</u>ence, <u>O</u>n the other hand, <u>T</u>hen, <u>C</u>onsequently, <u>A</u>lso, <u>T</u>hus

LOGICAL FALLACIES

Certain thought patterns are inherently flawed. Commonly called **logical fallacies**, these thought patterns are of primary concern in argument. You should be able to identify them in the arguments of those on the other side of an issue, and you should be sure to avoid them in your own writing.

Eight kinds of logical fallacies are very common.

1. ***Post hoc, ergo propter hoc*** ("after this, therefore because of this"): When one event precedes another in time, the first is assumed to cause the other. "If *A* comes before *B*, then *A* must be causing *B*."

"I knew I'd have a day like this when I saw that black cat run across my driveway this morning."

"What did I tell you? We elected him president, and now we have high inflation."

2. **False analogy**: False analogies ignore differences and stress similarities, often in an attempt to prove something.

"People have to get a driver's license because unqualified drivers could have bad effects on society. Therefore, couples should also have to get a license to bear children because unqualified parents can produce delinquent children."

"The leader of that country is a mad dog dictator, and you know what you do with a mad dog. You get a club and kill it."

3. **Hasty generalization**: This is a conclusion based on too few reliable instances.

"Everyone I met this morning is going to vote for Johnson, so I know Johnson is going to win."
"How many people did you meet?"
"Three."

4. **False dilemma**: This fallacy presents the reader with only two alternatives from which to choose. The solution may lie elsewhere.

"Now, only two things can be done with the savings and loan places. You either shut them down or let them go bankrupt."

"The way I see it, you either bomb them back into the Stone Age or let them keep on pushing us around."

5. ***Argumentum ad hominem*** ("argument against the person"): This is the practice of abusing and discrediting your opponent rather than keeping to the main issues of the argument.

"Who cares what he has to say? After all, he's a wild-eyed liberal who has been divorced twice."

"Let's put aside the legislative issue for a moment and talk about the person who proposed it. For one thing he's a Southerner. For another he's Catholic. Enough said."

6. **Begging the question**: This fallacy assumes something is true without proof. It occurs when a thinker assumes a position is right before offering proof.

"Those savages can never be civilized."

"I have one simple question. When is he going to stop ripping off his customers? Case closed."

7. **Circular reasoning**: This thought pattern asserts proof that is no more than a repetition of the initial assertion.

> "You can judge good art by reading what good critics say about it."
> "But who are good critics?"
> "The people who spend their time judging good art."

8. **Non sequitur**: This fallacy draws a conclusion that does not follow.

> "He's my first cousin, so of course you can trust him."

> "You can count on Gizmo computers; they were designed by native Californians."

EXERCISE 1   Identifying Logical Fallacies

Identify the logical fallacy (or fallacies) in the following sentences.

1. "If politicians can hire ghostwriters, why can't a little student like me be allowed to buy a research paper?"

2. "Stamp out dirty books, I say. Just look at all the crime we have since they started allowing this stuff."

3. "I was starting to have my doubts about the accuracy of newspapers until I read a newspaper editorial last week saying how reliable newspapers actually are."

4. "I can tell from listening to my family that the school bond issue will never pass."

5. "Blaming a company for making big profits is like blaming a cow for giving too much milk."

6. "Okay, so my spouse left me. Who cares? They're like buses; you miss one, and another one'll come along in a minute or two."

7. "I used to think Hemingway was a great writer until I read about his life. The guy was a self-centered, pompous jerk, and I'll never read any of his stuff again."

8. "I was really shocked until she told me it happened in New York, and then I just said, 'What's new?'"

9. "Like I say, you either fish or you cut bait. Will you marry me or won't you? Take your choice."

10. "Mark my words. If they start controllin' handguns, it's just a matter of time 'til we're back to defendin' ourselves with clubs and rocks against criminals with bazookas."

EXERCISE 2   Writing Examples of Logical Fallacies

Provide examples of the following logical fallacies. Work in a group or individually as directed by your instructor.

1. *Post hoc*: _____

_____

_____

2. False analogy: _____

_____

_____

3. Hasty generalization: _____

_____

_____

4. False dilemma: _____

_____

_____

5. *Argumentum ad hominem*: _____

_____

_____

6. Begging the question: _____

_____

_____

7. Circular reasoning: _____

_____

_____

8. Non sequitur: _____

_____

_____

PROPOSALS FOR THE WORKPLACE

In the workplace, the proposal is the purest expression of persuasion. Although it does not have a precise form, there are different kinds of proposals and different situations from which proposals arise. In this chapter, we will attempt to summarize the main forms and purposes of the proposal, but we will not try to teach how to write a long, complicated one that requires extensive research. Learning to work with the basic form will give you useful practice in this kind of writing. On the job, you will experience the many ways of framing proposals.

Notice the remarkable similarities between conventional college writing assignments and workplace proposals.

Paragraph or Essay of Persuasion (or Argument)	Proposal
Background (placing the issue into a social or historical perspective)	Background (indicating the problem or the need, emphasizing the urgency)
Proposition, with possible qualification	Solution to the problem, or need, stated concisely
Possible refutation	Possible explanation of why other solutions are inadequate
Support (reasoning and evidence)	In detail, what you can do
Support (reasoning and evidence)	How you can do it
Support (reasoning and evidence)	When you can do it
Support (reasoning and evidence)	What it will cost
Conclusion (clinching statement)	Conclusion (emphasizing the problem and solution)

The body of your proposal will usually have the parts shown in the proposal list. You will be able to determine what is necessary. For example, if you are proposing a change in procedure for an internal solution to a problem such as miscommunication, the cost may not be mentioned. As for order, the sequence shown in the list is common, but you can easily change the sequence to fit your needs.

Longer and highly technical proposals often begin with an executive summary, a statement that carries the major ideas but not the explanations. Such a component would be read by executives, who would depend on others to evaluate and report on the remaining parts of the extensively detailed proposal.

FINDING PATTERNS IN PHOTOS

EXERCISE 3   An Image-Based Activity for Groups or Individuals

Take a close look at the driver in the photo—listening to the Bluetooth in his ear, sipping coffee from a cup in his left hand, texting with his cell phone in his right hand, steering with his right wrist. What's your reaction? Would you wish to nominate him for the *Guinness Book of World Records* for multitasking? Or would you wish him off the road, signing an unsafe driving ticket just issued by the highway patrol?

Business person multitasking while driving

If your second wish were to be granted, you would have to select your place of residence carefully, for the cell-phone laws vary greatly from state to state. According to the Governors Highway Safety Association (as of this writing), fourteen states prohibit all drivers from the use of handheld cell phones while driving, thirty-eight states ban all cell phone use by novice drivers, twenty states ban school bus drivers from all cell phone use, forty-five states ban text messaging for all drivers, and forty-eight states ban text messaging for novice drivers.

Imagine you are a federal congressperson and you are on a committee studying the issue of whether to have a national law banning or partially banning the use of cell phones while driving. Trying to be objective, first list the reasons for not having restrictions on the use of cell phones while driving—the no restrictions, the con side. Then list the reasons for having a law with restrictions, the pro side.

Reasons for No Restrictions	Reasons for Restrictions
_____	_____
_____	_____
_____	_____
_____	_____
_____	_____
_____	_____

Now write a federal law that reads like the proposition, or thesis, in an argument in this chapter: one with a subject and a focus. Your proposed law should be specific and include any intended qualifications of key words, such as "all drivers," "novice drivers," "school bus drivers," "handheld cell phones," and "text messaging." Limit your statement to one or two (probably with semicolon) sentences.

If your instructor requires, write a paragraph or an essay on the proposition that you have proposed for a federal law. Use this basic form:

Proposition: _____

Support 1: _____

Support 2: _____

Support 3: _____

Practicing Patterns of Argument

The formal pattern of argument is not always followed in a set sequence, but the main components—the proposition and the support—are always included. You should also consider whether to qualify your proposition and whether to include a refutation.

EXERCISE 4   Completing Patterns of Argument

Fill in the blanks with supporting statements for each proposition. Each outline uses the following pattern:

Proposition

I. Support 1

II. Support 2

III. Support 3

A. Proposition: College athletes should be paid.

I. _____

II. They work long hours in practice and competition.

III. They have less time than many other students for study.

B. Proposition: Zoos are beneficial institutions.

I. _____

II. They preserve endangered species by captive breeding.

III. They study animal diseases and find cures.

EXERCISE 5   Writing Patterns of Argument

Complete the following outline. Use your own topic or write on the topic "There should be no curfew for teenagers" or "There should be a curfew for teenagers."

Proposition: _____

I. _____ (Support 1)

II. _____ (Support 2)

III. _____ (Support 3)

EXERCISE 6   Writing Patterns of Argument

Complete the following outline. Use your own topic or write on the topic "Known gang members should be prohibited from using public parks" or "Known gang members should not be prohibited from using public parks."

Proposition: _____

    I. _____ (Support 1)

    II. _____ (Support 2)

    III. _____ (Support 3)

Readings for Critical Thinking, Discussion, and Writing

READING STRATEGIES AND OBJECTIVES

Underlining and annotating these reading selections will help you answer the questions that follow the selections, discuss the material in class, and prepare for reading-based writing assignments. As you underline and annotate, pay special attention to the author's writing skills, logic, and message, and consider the relevance of the material to your own experiences and values.

ESSAYS

Pro/Con: How kids feel the swats of spanking; Do they hurt long after the initial sting, or will they be fine if it's done properly?*

JESSICA PAULINE OGILVIE

Jessica Pauline Ogilvie is a staff reporter for the Los Angeles Times.

1   When your 3-year-old is throwing a tantrum in the middle of the supermarket or has poured his milk all over the floor, the urge to spank may be overwhelming. If you've ever given in to that urge, you're not alone—research shows that up to 90% of parents spank their children, at least occasionally.

2   But does it work? And more importantly, is it harmful to kids? Once considered a fairly standard parenting practice, spanking is now opposed by the American Academy of Pediatrics and the American Psychological Assn. (The pediatricians' statement against the practice includes advice on what parents should do if they strike a child in the heat of the moment: apologize and explain why the spanking occurred.)

3   Corporal punishment in the home has been banned in 31 countries, including Spain, Israel, Kenya and Costa Rica. No such prohibition exists in the United States, although 32 states have laws forbidding teachers and administrators from striking students.

4   Those in favor of spanking say it is an effective method of discipline and hasn't been shown to damage children in the long run. Those against it argue that spanking can cause children to become violent later in life and may increase the chances that they will experience anxiety and depression. Besides, they add, there are better ways to deal with bad behavior.

* Jessica Pauline Ogilvie, "How kids feel the swats of spanking; Do they hurt long after the initial sting, or will they be fine if it's done properly?" from *Los Angele Times,* 2011. By permission.

Con

MURRAY STRAUS

Murray Straus is a professor of sociology and co-director of the Family Research Laboratory at the University of New Hampshire in Durham.

5   Spanking is dangerous to kids, puts them at risk for problems later in life and is no more effective than other methods of discipline. The research overwhelmingly shows that spanking is harmful to children. If you were to list all the things a parent wouldn't want their kid to be doing, you'd have the list of the harmful side effects of spanking. For instance, several studies have shown that the more parents spank, the more likely kids are to hit the parent. Kids who are spanked are also at a higher risk for committing juvenile crime, assaulting other kids, being depressed as an adult and hitting their dating or marital partner.

6   One explanation as to why spanking has these side effects is that the child is following the example of the parents hitting them. Another part of the explanation is that when parents spank, children miss out on instances of a conflict being resolved nonviolently and therefore have lower problem-solving skills. Another problem with spanking is that it undermines the relationship between parent and child. It's part of American mythology that spanking is not a big deal and that kids take it in stride, but that isn't what the research shows. Even among kids who say that parents have the right to spank—and most do—it's still a traumatic experience.

7   Spanking also violates a child's right to grow up free from being assaulted. Just imagine that someone twice or three times as big as you starts hitting you—that's the way kids describe it. It's fearful. Studies have shown that the more kids get spanked, the higher the child's score on a post-traumatic stress test.

8   People are very committed to the idea that spanking is necessary not because they want to hit their kids, but because they believe that it works when other things don't. But spanking doesn't eliminate bad behavior any more than other forms of discipline, such as explaining what the child is doing wrong or removing the child from the situation. In one study, 73% of mothers reported that their child repeated the same bad behavior even after being spanked for it.

9   Not all children will suffer negative consequences of spanking. The harm is in the form of a "dose-response." A small dose, like a rare occasional spank, is not going to make a difference most of the time, but sometimes it will. You don't know how spanking is going to affect your child, so the best thing is to avoid it. Instead, use the alternate medicine that works just as well, which is correction and control that doesn't involve hitting the child.

Pro

ROBERT LARZELERE

Robert Larzelere is a professor of research methodology and statistics in the Department of Human Development and Family Science at Oklahoma State University in Stillwater.

10   When used correctly, spanking is safe and effective, and can be an appropriate tool for parents. In reviewing all the literature that compares various kinds of punishment, there's one that leads to better outcomes, reduced defiance and reduced aggression in children, and that's what I call backup spanking.

11   In disciplining children, parents should do everything as kindly and gently as they can first. They should try to understand a child, make sure the child understands what is expected of them, use reasoning and find an adequate nonphysical consequence, like a "timeout" or taking away privileges. But if the child won't cooperate, some kids—at least some of the time—need something more forceful to back it up.

12   This is where backup spanking comes in. It involves two swats of an open hand to the rear end, and parents should affirm a love for the child afterward. Research finds this to be most effective with 2- to 6-year-olds.

13   In several studies, kids whose parents used a balance of love and limits, including backup spanking, were found to be doing much better 10 years later during adolescence than kids whose parents were overly punitive and did not show love in various ways to the child. They were also doing better than kids whose parents were permissive, emphasizing love and reasoning to the near-exclusion of any kind of negative consequences.

14   Just like any disciplinary tactic, the outcome with spanking depends on how it's used. It's important that the child understands that the parent is doing it out of concern—not out of rage or frustration, or to show who's the boss. Parents should not be out of control due to anger if they are spanking in this way.

15   In a study I published in the Clinical Child and Family Psychology Review in 2005, I found that when used correctly, spanking leads to lower defiance and lower aggression than 10 or 13 other disciplinary alternatives with which it has been compared. Spanking should be used with milder discipline tactics to enforce the idea that the parent and child need to work problems through verbally.

16   So as the child gets older, parents should be phasing out spanking and then using timeouts and privilege removal less and less so they can get to the point where they are resolving their differences in a mutually verbal way.

17   Opponents of spanking say that it has long-term negative consequences such as increased antisocial behavior. But in my research, I've found that those same consequences can be associated with nearly every other kind of nonphysical punishment. In comparative studies, spanking looked no better nor worse than grounding children, sending them to their room, or even getting them professional help. One likely reason for this is that children in these studies are more poorly behaved to begin with, and that's why they're being disciplined more. But it's naive to conclude that parents are causing kids to be more aggressive by using spanking when research does not support that notion.

EXERCISE 7   Discussion and Critical Thinking

1. According to Straus, spanking undermines the parent–child relationship. What does he mean by this?

2. What are some behavioral problems that have been linked to spanking?

3. Straus says that the harm of spanking relates to the concept of "dose response." What does he mean by this statement?

4. What alternative forms of discipline does Straus recommend?

5. What does Larzelere mean when he talks about "backup spanking"?

6. How does Larzelere address anti-spanking arguments?

7. Should the United States join the other 31 countries including Spain, Israel, and Kenya in banning spanking?

8. What are some points on which Ogilvie and Larzelere would agree?

Shouldn't Men Have "Choice" Too?*

MEGHAN DAUM

Meghan Daum is the author of The Quality of Life Report *and the essay collection* My Misspent Youth *and writes a weekly column for the* Los Angeles Times. *Known for her humor and acute cultural observations, she has inspired controversy over a range of topics, including social politics and class warfare.*

1   For pro-choicers like myself, Supreme Court nominee Samuel A. Alito Jr.'s position regarding spousal consent for abortion seems like one more loose rock in the ongoing erosion of Roe vs. Wade. Even those of us who are too young to remember the pre-Roe era often see any threat to abortion rights as a threat to our very destinies. We are, after all, the generation that grew up under Title IX, singing along to "Free to Be You and Me" (you know, the 1972 children's record where Marlo Thomas and Alan Alda remind us that mommies can be plumbers and boys can have dolls). When it comes to self-determination, we're as determined as it gets.

* Meghan Daum, "Shouldn't Men Have 'Choice' Too?" from *Los Angeles Times*, 2005. By permission.

2   But even though I was raised believing in the inviolability of a woman's right to choose, the older I get, the more I wonder if this idea of choice is being fairly applied. Most people now accept that women, especially teenagers, often make decisions regarding abortion based on educational and career goals and whether the father of the unborn child is someone they want to hang around with for the next few decades. The "choice" in this equation is not only a matter of whether to carry an individual fetus to term but a question of what kind of life the woman wishes to lead.

3   But what about the kind of life men want to lead? On December 1, Dalton Conley, director of the Center for Advanced Social Science Research at New York University, published an article on the Op-Ed page of the *New York Times* arguing that Alito's position on spousal consent did not go far enough. Describing his own experience with a girlfriend who terminated a pregnancy against his wishes, Conley took some brave steps down the slippery slope of this debate, suggesting that if a father is willing to assume full responsibility for a child not wanted by a mother, he should be able to obtain an injunction stopping her from having an abortion—and he should be able to do so regardless of whether or not he's married to her. Conley freely acknowledges the many obvious caveats in this position—the most salient being the fact that regardless of how "full" that male responsibility might be, the physical burden of pregnancy and childbirth will always put most of the onus on women. But as much as I shudder at the idea of a man, husband or not, obtaining an injunction telling me what I can or cannot do with my own body, I would argue that it is Conley who has not gone far enough.

4   Since we're throwing around radical ideas about abortion rights, let me raise this question: If abortion is to remain legal and relatively unrestricted—and I believe it should—why shouldn't men have the right during at least the first trimester of pregnancy to terminate their legal and financial rights and responsibilities to the child?

5   As Conley laments, the law does not currently allow for men to protect the futures of the fetuses they help create. What he doesn't mention—indeed, no one ever seems to—is the degree to which men also cannot protect their own futures. The way the law is now, a man who gets a woman pregnant is not only powerless to force her to terminate the pregnancy, he also has a complete legal obligation to support that child for at least 18 years. In other words, although women are able to take control of their futures by choosing from at least a small range of options—abortion, adoption or keeping the child—a man can be forced to be a father to a child he never wanted and cannot financially support. I even know of cases in which the woman absolves the man of responsibility, only to have the courts demand payment anyway. That takes the notion of "choice" very far from anything resembling equality.

6   I realize I've just alienated feminists (among whose ranks I generally count myself) as well as pro-lifers, neither of whom are always above platitudes such as "You should have kept your pants on." But that reasoning is by now as reductive as suggesting that a rape victim "asked for it." Yes, people often act irresponsibly and yes, abortion should be avoided whenever possible. But just as women should not be punished for choosing to terminate a pregnancy, men should not be punished when those women choose not to.

7   One problem, of course, is that the child is likely to bear the brunt of whatever punishment remains to be doled out. A father who terminates his rights, although not technically a deadbeat dad, has still helped create a kid who is not fully supported. And (in case you were wondering) there are dozens of other holes in my theory as well: What if a husband wants to terminate his

rights—should that be allowed? What if a father is underage and wants to terminate, but his parents forbid him? Should a father's decision-making time be limited to the first trimester? Should couples on first dates discuss their positions on the matter? Should Internet dating profiles let men check a box saying "will waive parental rights" next to the box indicating his astrological sign?

8   There's also the danger that my idea is not just a slippery slope but a major mudslide on the way to Conley's idea. If a man can legally dissociate himself from a pregnancy, some will argue, why couldn't he also bind himself to it and force it to term? That notion horrifies me, just as my plan probably horrifies others. But that doesn't mean these ideas aren't worth discussing. Though it may be hard to find an adult male who's sufficiently undiplomatic to admit out loud that he'd like to have the option I'm proposing, let alone potentially take it, I know more than a few parents of teenage boys who lose sleep over the prospect of their sons' landing in the kind of trouble from which they'll have no power to extricate themselves.

9   And although the notion of women "tricking" men into fatherhood now sounds arcane and sexist, we'd be blind not to recognize the extent to which some women are capable of tricking themselves into thinking men will stick around, despite all evidence to the contrary. Allowing men to legally (if not always gracefully) bow out of fatherhood would, at the very least, start a conversation for which we haven't yet found the right words.

10   Actually, there's one word we've had all along: choice. We just need to broaden its definition.

EXERCISE 8   Vocabulary Highlights

Write a short definition of each word as it is used in the essay. (Paragraph numbers are given in parentheses.) Be prepared to use these words in sentences.

erosion (1)	laments (5)
inviolability (2)	absolves (5)
injunction (3)	platitudes (6)
salient (3)	doled (7)
trimester (4)	extricate (8)

EXERCISE 9   Discussion and Critical Thinking

1. Which paragraph contains Daum's thesis?

2. How does Daum introduce her proposition?

3. What qualified support does she offer in paragraph 3?

4. Which paragraph contains the rebuttal?

5. If you were to support Daum's proposition, how would you answer the questions Daum poses in paragraph 7?

6. In paragraph 8, Daum says males might be reluctant to admit publicly that they agree with her proposition. How do you think most men would respond? Most women?

7. Daum has redefined the word *choice*. Use your own words to write her proposition.

8. Do you agree with Daum's proposition? Why or why not?

Indian Mascots—You're Out!*

JACK SHAKELY

Jack Shakely is president emeritus of the California Community Foundation in Los Angeles. His essays and opinion pieces have appeared in the Los Angeles Times, New York Times, Denver Post, *and many other newspapers. His two novels,* The Confederate War Bonnet, *and* POWs at Chigger Lake, *are both set in Oklahoma, Shakely's home state.* The Confederate War Bonnet *won the gold medal as best historical–military fiction and best mid-western fiction in the 2009 Independent Publishers Awards. Shakely is of Muscogee and Creek descent and was chair of the Los Angeles Native American Indian Commission from 1992 to 1996.*

1   I got my first lesson in Indians portrayed as sports team mascots in the early 1950s when my father took me to a Cleveland Indians–New York Yankees game. Dad gave me money to buy a baseball cap, and I was conflicted. I loved the Yankees, primarily because fellow Oklahoman Mickey Mantle had just come up and was being touted as rookie of the year. But being mixed-blood Muscogee/Creek, I felt a (misplaced) loyalty to the Indians. So I bought the Cleveland cap with the famous Chief Wahoo logo on it.

2   When we got back to Oklahoma, my mother took one look at the cap with its leering, big-nosed, buck-toothed redskin caricature just above the brim, jerked it off my head and threw it into the trash. She had been fighting against Indian stereotypes all her life, and I had just worn one home. I was only 10 years old, but the look of betrayal in my Creek mother's eyes is seared in my memory forever.

3   So maybe I shouldn't have been surprised when half a century later, a *Los Angeles Times* editorial about legislators in North Dakota struggling over whether the University of North Dakota should be forced to change its team name and mascot from the Fighting Sioux provoked such a strong reaction. It was an irritant, like a long-forgotten piece of shrapnel working its way to the surface.

4   Most stories about sports teams and their ethnic mascots are treated like tempests in a teacup. The *Times'* editorial writer, however, while noting that the solons probably had better things to do, understood the sensitivity and pain that can accompany such a seemingly trivial subject. It is a small matter, perhaps, but far from trivial.

5   Many of the fights over team names and mascots cover familiar territory. Usually the team name in question has been around so long as to lose a good

*Shakely, Jack. *Los Angeles Times*. 25 Aug 2011: A. 15. Reprinted with permission of the author.

bit of its meaning. The University of Illinois' Fighting Illini, for example, refers to an Indian nation, but now that its Chief Illiniwek mascot has been abandoned, few people make the connection. Nor do they think twice about what the Atlanta Braves or Edmonton Eskimos or Florida State Seminoles represent other than sports franchises. But that doesn't necessarily make the brands benign. And the irony that the football team in our nation's capital is called the Redskins is not lost on a single Native American.

6   The controversy over changing ethnocentric mascot names is not a simple matter of stodgy white alums holding onto college memories. Indians, too, are conflicted. In a 2002 study on the subject, *Sports Illustrated* reported that 84% of Native Americans polled had no problem with Indian team names or mascots. Although the methods used by the magazine to reach these figures were later criticized, that misses the point. If 16% of a population finds something offensive, that should be enough to signal deep concern. There are many things in this country that are subject to majority rule; dignity and respect are not among them.

7   And it is dignity and respect we are talking about. Since the creation of the National Coalition on Racism in Sports and Media in 1991, that group of Native American organizations has been protesting negative portrayals of Indians, hammering away at what's behind our discomfort with Indian sports mascots. Many of these mascots—maybe most of them—act like fools or savage cutthroats.

8   When I went to an Atlanta Braves game in the 1970s, the Braves name wasn't the biggest problem. It was that cringe-worthy Chief Noc-A-Homa who came stomping and war-dancing his way out of a tepee in center field every time the Braves hit a home run that got to me. He was dressed in a Plains Indian chief's eagle bonnet and acted like a village idiot. To their credit, the Braves retired Chief Noc-A-Homa and his girlfriend Princess Win-A-Lot in 1983, amid assertions by the Brave's home office that the protesters were over-dramatizing the issue.

9   Few people complain about Florida State University calling itself the Seminoles. But its war-painted and lance-threatening mascot Chief Osceola is intended to be menacing, and that's the take-away many children will have. Such casual stereotyping can breed callousness. In the "only good Indian" category, in 1999 the *New York Post* entitled an editorial about the pending New York–Cleveland baseball playoffs, "Take the Tribe and Scalp 'Em."

10   It isn't easy or inexpensive to remove ethnic and racial stereotypes from college and professional sports. When Stanford University changed from the Indians to the Cardinals in 1972, recriminations were bitter. Richard Lyman, a friend of mine, was president of Stanford at the time. He said the university lost millions of alumni dollars in the short run, but it was the right thing to do.

11   In 21st century America, to name a sports team after an African American, Asian or any other ethnic group is unthinkable. So why are Native Americans still fair game? As benign as monikers like Fighting Sioux and Redskins or mascots like Chief Osceola may seem, they should take their place with the Pekin, Ill., Chinks and the Atlanta Black Crackers in the dust bin of history. It is the right thing to do.

EXERCISE 10   Discussion and Critical Thinking

1. Did the author ever feel conflicted about an ethnic stereotype being used as a mascot? What were the circumstances?

2. How did most Native Americans feel about Native American sports mascots according to a study from 2002?

3. It's expensive to get rid of ethnic stereotypes from sports teams. Is it worth it?

4. Who was Chief Noc-A-Homa? Why was he offensive to the author?

5. A Native American mascot like Chief Osceola of the Florida State Seminoles has an unintended effect on children. What is that effect?

6. Do you think the author would be for getting rid of The Fightin' Irish mascot of the University of Notre Dame?

7. What is ironic about the mascot for the Washington Redskins?

STUDENT PARAGRAPH, ESSAY, AND PROPOSAL

After Angela DeSarro received a list of topics from which to select, she went to the library to obtain some information about the ones that interested her. One such topic was euthanasia. Her textbook contained an essay originally published in the *Journal of the American Medical Association* about a doctor who illegally assisted a suffering, terminally ill patient. DeSarro's mind and emotions came together on the issue and she had her topic.

DeSarro's Writing Process Worksheet shows how her writing evolved from idea to final draft. Notice how she turns her listing into an outline, which becomes the structure for her paragraph. To conserve space here, the freewriting and two rough drafts marked for revision and editing have been omitted. The balance of her worksheet has been lengthened for you to be able to see her other work in its entirety.

BRANDON BRIDGE

Writing Process Worksheet

Name Angela DeSarro   **Title** My Life to Live—or Not   **Due Date** Tuesday, October 16, 10 a.m.

Use the back of this page or separate paper if you need more space.

Assignment

In the space below, write whatever you need to know about your assignment, including information about the topic, audience, pattern of writing, length, whether to include a rough draft or revised drafts, and whether your paper must be typed.

Write a paragraph of 200 to 300 words in which you argue for a particular action or restraint. Include at least three supporting points. Keep in mind that some thoughtful readers will disagree with your proposition. Submit this completed worksheet, a rough draft marked for revision and editing, and a typed final draft.

Stage One

Explore Freewrite, brainstorm (list), cluster, or take notes as directed by your instructor.

Listing

Debbie's struggle	*Proposal*
(from *JAMA*)	—physician-assisted suicide
—terminally ill with cancer	—patient terminally ill, little
—nauseous, emaciated, suffering	time left
—wants to die with a bit of	—must be suffering
dignity intact	—must want suicide
—physician helps her	—physician can assist
—an illegal act	—must be regulated
—shouldn't be illegal	—should be national law, similar to
	the one in Oregon

Stage Two

Organize Write a topic sentence or thesis; label the subject and the focus parts.

The time has come for a national law legalizing <u>physician-assisted suicide for</u>

          subject   focus

<u>the terminally ill.</u>

Write an outline or an outline alternative. For reading-based writing, include references and short quotations with page numbers as support in the outline.

I. Person dying
   A. Pain
   B. Extreme discomfort
   C. Example: Debbie
II. Person desiring death with dignity
   A. Not wanting to wither away
   B. Not wanting to be alive on tubes and machines
   C. Example: Debbie
III. Person demanding choice in dying
   A. Of time
   B. Of method
   C. Example: Debbie
IV. A law that works
   A. Chosen by voters in Oregon
   B. Is not abused
V. Plea for a national law

Stage Three

Write On separate paper, write and then revise your paragraph or essay as many times as necessary for **c**oherence, **l**anguage (usage, tone, and diction), **u**nity, **e**mphasis, **s**upport, and **s**entences (**CLUESS**). Read your work aloud to hear and correct any grammatical errors or awkward-sounding sentences.

Edit any problems in fundamentals, such as **c**apitalization, **g**rammar, **p**unctuation, and **s**pelling (**CGPS**).

Final Draft

MY LIFE TO LIVE—OR NOT
Angela DeSarro

Debbie, 20, was dying of ovarian cancer. Racked with pain, nauseous, emaciated, she sought the ultimate relief and found it in euthanasia. A doctor administered a drug and she died. It was a hidden, secret act. It was also illegal in Debbie's state, but this case was written up in the *Journal of the American Medical Association*. <u>Surely the time has come for a nationwide law legalizing this practice under specific provisions and regulations</u>. Debbie had reached the point of not only enduring terrible pain but of vomiting constantly and not being able to sleep. Pain-killing medication no longer worked. She wanted to die with what she regarded as a degree of dignity. She had already become a withered, suffering human being with tubes coming out of her nose, throat, and urinary tract, and she was losing all self-control. She also believed that it should be up to her, under these conditions, to decide when and how she should die. Laws in most places prohibit terminally ill patients from choosing death and physicians from assisting them. One state, Oregon, has a law favoring physician-assisted suicide, at least in the limited cases of terminally ill people expected to live less than six months. In 1998, fifteen people benefited from that law; it was not abused. <u>It, or a similar form, should be enacted nationwide</u>.

Proposition

Support

Support

Concluding sentence as a restated proposition

EXERCISE 11   Discussion and Critical Thinking

1. What kinds of evidence does DeSarro use to support her argument?

2. What might be the objections to her reasoned argument?

3. Do you agree or disagree with DeSarro's argument? Why?

STUDENT ESSAY

A Battle in the Streets

MIRANDA WALKER

1   Some might not realize it yet, but a battle is being waged on the roadways of America. It's a David-and-Goliath struggle between the automobile and the bicycle. In response to the high expense and environmental impact of internal combustion–powered vehicles, many are taking to the roads on the latest high-tech vehicle—the bicycle.

2   Pilots of the new light-weight two-wheelers are fighting it out on the street against the reigning heavyweight champion of the commuting world—the automobile. Riding slowly in lanes previously the exclusive domain of cars, bicyclists—often costumed in skin-tight lycra spandex cycling togs—dare motorists to deny them their fair share of the road. Meanwhile, enraged drivers, slowed to a crawl by self-righteous peddlers, are powerless to escape the inevitable delay to their destinations. More than a few incidents of road rage leading to significant injury and even death of bicyclists at the hands of fed-up motorists have hit the news in the past few years.

3   In response to these clashes, and in preference for a cleaner and safer environment, some cities, such as Santa Monica, CA, have created car-free zones where bicyclists and pedestrians are kings. Other cities are creating more bike lanes, and some areas have enacted laws restricting motorists from passing too quickly or closely to bike riders. Redesigning urban landscapes to accommodate the bicycle might be the best solution to the problem, but it will take money—lots of money. And money is something the government must consider as it tries to figure out a way to encourage peaceful co-existence between these two groups.

4   Up to this point, bicyclists have gotten "a free ride" in terms of licensing and taxes. If people want to ride a bike, all they have to do is buy one and start riding, but on the dangerous and crowded roadways, this policy no longer works. Riders of vehicles sharing the streets with cars should be required to earn a license to operate their vehicles, just like motorcyclists and other motorists. Riding a bicycle alongside vehicles weighing two or three thousand pounds apiece requires skill, patience, and judgment—traits that should be encouraged and, yes, mandated by the state.

5   Better-educated riders should make for a safer road environment for all. Furthermore, the fees for issuing bike riding licenses along with increased sales tax on bicycle purchases could help fund the construction of more and better bicycle lanes along with increased police enforcement of rules to protect bicycle riders from unsafe motorists. Bicyclists have a right to use the roads, but they must pay for the privilege like anyone else.

EXERCISE 12   Discussion and Critical Thinking

1. Why are more people commuting on bicycles today?

2. Do you think bicycle commuters are "self-righteous"?

3. Should cities create more car-free zones? If so, why?

4. Do you think bicycle riders should have to pass exams—both written and riding—to operate a bicycle on the street?

5. How should increased funds from bicycle licensing and sales tax be used?

6. What would be arguments against licensing bicycle riders and taxing bike purchases?

7. Have you as a bicycle rider ever witnessed or experienced driver road rage? Explain.

READING-BASED WRITING

Schools as Political Combat Zones

ERIC HORNER

Student Eric Horner was required to write a reaction or a two-part response to one of the assigned professional essays in his textbook. He was to analyze the source he selected and provide documented references to and quotations from it. He chose to write a critical reaction to "Educators Declare War on Traditional Values" by Thomas Sowell.

Text thesis	1	According to Thomas Sowell in "Educators Declare War on Traditional Values," American society is involved in political combat with educators, and most citizens do not know that shots are being fired. The target, he says, is wholesome mainstream traditions and the parents who want to and should pass their values along to their children.
Topic sentence Logical fallacy Sowell position Short questions	2	His argument sticks to the image of warfare he mentions in his title. Instead of dealing with issues of sex education and personal counseling in a thoughtful way, he resorts to *argumentum ad hominem*. Educators are the "anointed" and the "zealots" (351) who "carry on unrelenting guerilla warfare against the traditional values of the society and against the very role of families in making decisions about their own children." They "camouflage what they are doing" on their "battlefields" in "an undeclared war" (352).
Topic sentence Transition Evidence Short quotation Sowell position Student reaction	3	Two examples of this warfare are his sole evidence, though he says they are typical of what is happening across this country. The first comes from a recent program in San Francisco, in which he says outside speakers "shocked and outraged" students and parents with tales of their sexual experiences. Sowell says it was just another instance of educators promising to teach biology and using that as a cover to replace traditional American values (352). He does not see that because of rampant pregnancy and sexually transmitted diseases among the young something must be done differently in schools. That is what people such as Sowell should be shocked and outraged about. Depending on parents talking to their children is

obviously far too often not enough. In that respect Sowell should offer some concrete suggestions.

4   His second example concerns a young female student who broke up with her boyfriend and said she "might as well be dead." Her boyfriend reported her statement to her mother and the school counselor. The counseling staff contacted the mother and daughter. Sowell saw this procedure as the school "busybodies … driving a wedge between parent and child" (351–52). He does not mention that schools have rules requiring counselors to take action when they hear that a student has talked about wanting to be dead. The rules were adopted because of the high rate of suicide among the young. Is it not better to risk interfering with the privacy, and even values, of a family if it is possible that in some instances doing so might save lives? In this instance the mother complained. What would the mother and Sowell have said if the daughter had not been counseled and had killed herself?

5   Public schools are just that—public—and, of course, people should be involved in what is and what should be taught. But it will take more than the two examples Sowell gives—one vague and one, I think, not typical—to support his views that devious educators are attacking virtuous families. At best he uses hasty generalizations. If he wants to make a case for the public schools being taken over by a counterculture, his argument would be better served by dealing with statistics and specific information and by going light on the name calling.

Margin annotations: Topic sentence · Evidence · Short quotation · Sowell position · Student reaction · Concluding student evaluation · Logical fallacy

Work Cited

Sowell, Thomas. "Educators Declare War on Traditional Values." *Paragraphs and Essays with Culturally Diverse Readings*. Ed. Lee Brandon. 7th ed. Boston: Houghton, 1998. 351–53. Print.

CAREER-RELATED WRITING: PROPOSAL

In writing career-related persuasion, you will write either an essay about some aspect of the workplace or a proposal. Each is a useful form. The essay about work will give you an opportunity to explore a topic and explain your view; a topic might be union membership, management style, or government regulation of business. The proposal can be about a student, a neighborhood, or a family issue, which is written in the form of a business proposal, or it can be about a business issue (to purchase an item, to modify a practice, to hire a certain kind of person, to discontinue or modify a product or service, or the like). Regardless of the topic, writing a form according to a format commonly used in the marketplace will give you practice for your future or continuing career.

Mandatory Tipping at BoBo's

ROBERTO BENTANCOURT

The assignment was for students to consider a problem they are encountering or have encountered at a job and to write a proposal to the appropriate manager who would have the authority to change a policy or practice. The assignment proposal would not have to be sent to that manager, but it should be generally accurate in the use of evidence. Students were asked to write the proposal as if they still worked at the establishment and to label the parts. Some of the suggested topics were working conditions, pay, uniforms, management style, parking, fringe benefits, worker behavior, worker appearance, cell-phone use, shifts, security, and safety. Bentancourt had recently worked as a shift manager at BoBo's Diner, a little restaurant near a large, urban community college. A favorite with student customers, it should have been a great place to work. But there was one problem that led to a rapid turnover of food servers. (The name of the restaurant has been changed to protect privacy.)

Background

1   Our student customers really like to eat at this restaurant. One can hear students say, "I'll meet you at BoBo's." Business is obviously good. But it could be better. When one hears a complaint, it is usually about service. The food servers are often inexperienced in dealing with multiple orders in a brief time and in separating work from friendly conversations. There is a reason for that. As you know, we have a high turnover in food servers. Some leave for personal reasons such as dropping out of school, moving, or getting married. Others obtain a job that is more closely related to their intended careers or a job that simply pays more or offers better hours or benefits. But the main reason for leaving work here at BoBo's is the low pay. The pay should not be an issue. You pay a dollar over minimum wage, and with tip money, that should be very rewarding. But it is not—because of the tips, or should I say, lack of tips.

2   Many of our customers eat light, drink as much as they can get with refills, and leave without tipping. That creates several problems. One, it makes the food servers unhappy and ultimately cynical, so many of them become unfriendly or cranky before they quit. And they usually do quit after a short period of time. Two, not getting tips has a double effect on food servers. They do not get the money and then when it is time to pay income tax, they have to pay 8 percent on total sales, so they are, in effect, being further penalized for not getting tips.

3   Of course, some students do tip. A few even tip generously. But far too many hardly tip at all, and the trend is getting worse. As I have said, when customers do not give tips, food servers may become surly and uncaring. When that happens, the customers may feel they have a reason for not tipping. The two problems feed on each other.

Solution to the Problem

4   The solution is to include a 10 percent tip in each bill.

Explanation of Why Other Solutions Are Unworkable

5   Other solutions that come to mind are not practical. Trying to educate customers on this issue will not work because they already know that argument. Paying the food servers more would not be a good idea because you are already selling food and drinks at a low percentage of profit.

What, How, and When Something Can Be Done

6   The addition of 10 percent to each check is a highly workable solution. The food server would automatically receive that tip. Customers could leave an additional amount if they like. Customers would continue to come to BoBo's. In fact, the food servers would be less inclined to leave to go down the street to work at a restaurant with more diverse clientele for better tips. Instead they would be more likely to stay, and they would be more cheerful and efficient, behavior that would bring in more business. Everyone would win. If you feel the food servers would not work hard if they already knew they would get the tip, then make out a receipt that says the customer, upon receiving poor service, could check a box and the tip would go to a charity such as the Salvation Army.

What It Will Cost

7   The cost of this change will be slight. You would need to insert a message inside the menu and post that message near the entrance and cash register. The message should include a brief explanation, with emphasis on the point that a food server who does not get a tip must pay additional income taxes on salary. You would also need to have new receipts printed to make a line for the new item.

Conclusion

8   As one of your shift managers and as a person who knows our customers from the college well, I would talk to individuals during the "breaking-in" period. I will also help you write a letter of explanation. I could even write a letter to the editor of the campus newspaper, explaining the new rule and the reason for the rule. Actually, as a little test, I have mentioned this idea to several of our customers, and they seemed very understanding. One even said that knowing everyone would be tipping at least 10 percent could make the customers happier because with the current practice, those who tipped sometimes felt they were being regarded as fools because other students were, in effect, paying less for their food.

EXERCISE 13   Discussion and Critical Thinking

1. If you were the manager, what would be your response?

2. How do you think nontipping customers would react?

3. Which section carries the thesis in this workplace version of persuasive writing?

4. Which section carries the refutation?

5. Which section carries the most support for this proposal?

Suggested Topics and Prompts for Writing Argument

READING-BASED WRITING

Reading-based writing requires you to read critically, write a reply that shows you understand what you have read, and give credit for ideas you borrow and words you quote. The form can be a summary, a reaction, or a two-part response (with separated summary and reaction). Documentation, in which you give credit for borrowed ideas and words, can be either formal (MLA style) or informal, as directed by your instructor. Definitions of the three forms follow. Any form can be used for any reading selection in this book.

Summary

- The summary is a statement written in response to a reading. It restates only the most important points and uses original wording instead of the author's language. It should not contain added information or personal opinions.
- Because summaries are intended to restate only the main points of a reading, they are typically much shorter than the original text. Often, they are approximately a third of the length.

Reaction

- In the reaction, the meaning of what you have read will be central to the topic sentence of your paragraph or to the thesis of your essay.
- Although the reaction is not a personal narrative by itself, it may include personal experience to explain elements of the text. For example, if your source is about driving styles, your own experiences as a driver or an observer of drivers could be relevant in your analysis of the text.
- The reaction may incorporate a summary to convey a broad view of what you have read, but your summary should never be the main part of your reaction.

Two-Part Response

- The two-part response separates the summary from the reaction.
- This form will give you practice in separating your objective summary in the first part from your more personal evaluation, interpretation, or application in the second part, the reaction.

READING-BASED WRITING TOPICS

"Pro/Con: How kids feel the swats of spanking; Do they hurt long after the initial sting, or will they be fine if it's done properly?"

1. Write a two-part response to Ogilvie's essay. Summarize both sides of the argument. Then, in your reaction, explain whether you think Straus or Larzelere argues his point more convincingly.

2. In a reaction, discuss your views on another issue relating to child-rearing or parenting.

"Shouldn't Men Have 'Choice' Too?"

3. Rely on what you have witnessed and experienced and what you believe to write a reaction to Daum's argument. Be sure to refer directly to her essay and use quotations. Your reaction should be an answer to the question posed in the essay title.

4. Write a two-part response in which you summarize Daum's view and then react with answers to the question in the title and the questions in paragraph 7.

5. Write a summary of Daum's essay, taking care to state her main points. Use references to and quotations from her essay; take care with your use of paraphrasing and use of quotation marks for words you borrow.

"Indian Mascots—You're Out!"

6. Write a summary of Shakely's essay.

7. Shakely asks a question at the end of his essay: "In 21st century America, to name a sports team after an African American, Asian, or any other ethnic group is unthinkable. So why are Native Americans still fair game?" In a response, explain why you think this might be the case.

8. In a reaction, write about a team mascot, a book, a movie, a product, a phrase or saying, or something else that you find offensive.

"My Life to Live—or Not"

9. Use the library or Internet sources to research the state law in Oregon that allows physicians to assist in suicides under certain conditions. In a two-part response, write a summary of that law in one paragraph and your reaction to the law in another. Print out a copy of the law you are summarizing if your instructor requires.

"A Battle in the Streets"

10. Write a summary of Walker's essay.

11. In a reaction, evaluate the strengths and weaknesses of the author's argument.

12. Walker proposes cycling licensing as a means of creating a safer road environment. In a reaction, propose another means to achieve the same result.

"Mandatory Tipping at BoBo's"

13. Write an argument from a customer's point of view in which you either agree or disagree with Bentancourt's view. Consider using your own examples from restaurants you have frequented. Discuss the effectiveness of Bentancourt's proposal. Use references and short quotations.

GENERAL TOPIC

14. The following are broad subject areas. You will have to limit your focus for a paragraph or an essay of argument. Modify the subject to correspond with your experiences and interests. Some of these subjects will benefit from research in the library or on the Internet. Some will overlap with subject material from classes you have taken and with studies you have made.

    a. School metal detectors
    b. Changing the juvenile justice system
    c. Endangered species legislation
    d. Advertising tobacco
    e. Jury reform
    f. Change in (your) college registration procedure
    g. Local public transportation
    h. Surveillance by video (on campus, in neighborhoods, or in shopping areas)
    i. Curfew for teenagers
    j. Laws keeping known gang members out of parks

CROSS-CURRICULAR TOPIC

15. From a class you are taking or have taken or from your major area of study, select an issue on which thoughtful people may disagree and write an essay of persuasion or argument. It could be an interpretation of an ambiguous piece of literature for an English class; a position on global warming, public land management, or the Endangered Species Act for a class in ecology; an argument about the effectiveness of a government program in a political science class; a view on a certain kind of diet in a food-science class; a preference for a particular worldview in a class on philosophy; or an assertion on the proper role of chiropractors as health-care practitioners in a health-science class.

CAREER-RELATED TOPIC

16. Write a proposal to solve a problem in your family, neighborhood, school, or workplace. The problem is likely to be the purchase or modification of something, the introduction or modification of a procedure, or the introduction of a service. For this assignment, use basically the same form regardless of the location or circumstances of the problem. You can use a basic pattern,

background, solution (as a proposition), support (how it can be done, when it can be done, what it will cost, if anything). The problem that you are proposing to alleviate or eliminate can be based on your experiences or it can be purely fictional. If you are suggesting the purchase of an item or items to solve a problem, the Internet can provide you with prices and specifications. Those data could be integrated into your proposal or photocopied and attached, with references. (See "Mandatory Tipping at BoBo's" for a student proposal.)

Following are a few specific topic suggestions:

a. *Home*: contracting with a gardener or a housekeeper, dividing the chores, respecting the privacy and space of others

b. *Neighborhood*: limiting noise; dealing with dogs—vicious, wandering, barking; parking recreational vehicles out front

c. *College*: parking, enrollment and registration, classroom procedures, safety

d. *Workplace*: doing your job (or part of it) at home rather than at the workplace, fringe benefits, evaluation procedures, staggering lunch hours and work breaks, communication between workers on different shifts

WRITER'S GUIDELINES Argument

BRANDON BRIDGE

1. Ask yourself the following questions; then consider which parts of the persuasive statement or argument you should include in your essay.

   • *Background*: What is the historical or social context for this controversial issue?

   • *Proposition* (the topic sentence of the paragraph or the thesis of the essay): What do I want my audience to believe or to do?

   • *Qualification of proposition*: Can I limit my assertion so that those who disagree cannot easily challenge me with exceptions?

   • *Refutation* (taking the opposing view into account, mainly to point out its fundamental weakness): What is the view on the other side, and why is it flawed in reasoning or evidence?

   • *Support*: In addition to sound reasoning, can I use appropriate facts, examples, statistics, and opinions of authorities?

2. The basic pattern of a paragraph or an essay of persuasion or argument is likely to be in this form:

   Proposition (the topic sentence of the paragraph or the thesis of the essay)

   I. Support 1
   II. Support 2
   III. Support 3

3. The proposal has the following parts, which can be adjusted to a particular need:

   • Background (indicating the problem or the need, emphasizing the urgency)
   • Solution to the problem, or need, stated concisely

- Possible explanation of why other solutions are inadequate
- In detail what you can do
- How you can do it
- When you can do it
- What it will cost
- Conclusion (emphasizing the problem and the solution)

4. **Consider using the Writing Process Worksheet and the Brandon Guide for Revising and Editing for completing your assignment and the Revising and Editing Charts after your assignment is returned.**

Practicing the Brandon Guide for Revising and Editing

PATTERN: ARGUMENT

When a Nanny State Is Necessary
LORETTA WILSON

(A) Some Americans say our country has become a nanny state. (B) They say their tired of laws that treat citizens like children being watched over by a nurse. (C) They complain about such things as a seat belt on anyone riding in an automobile and a helmet on anyone riding a motorcycle. (D) A new issue for nanny-bashers is the matter of not smoking tobacco products in cars when children are present. (E) A few states have passed legislation doing just that, and I say it s time to make it a Federal law. (F) Others believe that laws shouldn't ever interfere with parents' rights to raise their kids. (G) Some of the nanny-bashers are the same ones who didn't like the law about placing small children in car seats, which has been proven to protect children and saves lives. (H) That kind of protection should be in place for children in smoke-filled cars. (I) Proportionally, right now there is more children suffering from asthma and allergies than ever before. (J) If the kids in smoky cars were canaries, they'd all be dying or dead. (K) The opposition says, "Just roll down your windows." (L) However, doing that is not enough. (M) Besides, how many people would roll down windows during bad weather?

(N) Even if they did, the government health officials say that not all of the smoke would blow away. (O) In fact, it takes an hour to clear out second-hand smoke in a car after a window is rolled down. (P) Moreover, according to other health authorities, the upholstery and car lining soak up poisons from tobacco, which is released into the air as a third-hand poisonous tobacco product to be picked up through breathing or bodily contact. (Q) The results are all around us. (R) The people who don't know what's happening must be wearing blinders and ear plugs. (S) The smokers I know who smoke in cars in the presence of children are not wicked people; they just don't understand the issue. (T) Therefore, if we have to become a nanny state to get safe, relatively clean air to protect children then bring on the nanny. (U) The law won't solve all respiratory problems for all children because there are other sources of air pollution, but it would be helpful to many children and probably life-saving to some in the long run.

EXERCISE 14   Revise and Edit with the Brandon Guide

Revise with C L U E S S **(pronounce as "clues" for easy memorization).**

1. **C**oherence: Connect your ideas. Circle the five transitional words that connect ideas.

2. **L**anguage: Use words appropriate for your purpose and audience. Assume that the author is seeking a diverse audience and is trying to change the views of those who do not agree with her. If so, then there is a problem with tone. Draw a line through the most confrontational words and phrases and write milder, less belligerent choices above them.

3. **U**nity: Stay on your topic. Underline the topic sentence (proposition) that unifies the paragraph and the closing sentence that provides reflection and emphasis by its content and location.

4. **E**mphasis: Call attention to your important ideas. Draw a box around the word and its variations that is used the most times, promoting coherence, unity, and especially emphasis.

5. **S**upport: Back up your controlling ideas with evidence and logic. In the margin, label these parts of the argument: Background, Proposition (as topic sentence), Refutation, Support (for each part of support), Closing statement. If the support lacks documentation, include the letters *ND* (for *no documentation*) along with the word *support*.

6. **S**entences: Write correct, effective sentences with structural variety. Combine Sentences K and L.

Edit with C G P S **(pronounce as "see GPS" for easy memorization).**

7. **C**apitalization: Cross out the one word that should not be capitalized and write in the lowercase letter above it.

8. **G**rammar: Find the sentence with a subject and verb agreement problem, cross out the verb, and insert the correct verb above it.

9. **P**unctuation: Find the sentence that does not have a comma after a long introductory modifier and insert the comma.

10. **S**pelling: Cross out the two words that are spelled incorrectly and write in the correct spelling above each.

PART 4

USING SOURCES

Never before have students been able to access information so easily and swiftly. In little more than a decade, libraries have broadened searches from the shuffle of card catalogs to the click of the electronic keyboard. Cyberspace and electronic databases extend everywhere. They give us more as they require more from us as critical thinkers.

For the course you are now taking, connecting with sources, good sources, is essential. Your sources may help you understand yourself by providing you with information that will give you insights and challenge your views. Across the curriculum, your sources can connect you with a deeper understanding of the variety of subjects you study. In career-related writing, you can investigate vocational fields and workplace issues.

Some of these searches will take the form of research papers or other documented written assignments, usually moving away from personal writing. This part of the book will help you generate topics, do research in various ways, organize a paper, and write it in the appropriate form.

16

Writing the Research Paper

Research is formalized curiosity. It is poking and prying with a purpose.

—ZORA NEAL HURSTON

CHAPTER CONTENTS

BRANDON BRIDGE

The Research Paper Defined

The **research paper** is a long documented essay based on a thorough examination of your topic and supported by your explanations and by both references to and quotations from your sources. The traditional research paper in the style of the Modern Language Association, typically called "MLA style," includes a title page and an outline (if your instructor requires them), a thesis, a documented essay (text), and a list of sources (called "Works Cited," referring to the works used specifically in the essay—and if it's just one work, the list is called "Work Cited").

This chapter presents ten steps for writing a research paper. Don't be apprehensive; if you can write an effective essay, you can write an effective research paper. Pick a feasible topic and stay on schedule. (The two main problems for students working on research papers are [1] they select topics that are too broad or too narrow and [2] they fall behind schedule.) The form for documentation is shown in Step 3. Completing a research paper using the following ten steps will give you practice in finding sources in your school library and on the Internet, and it will give you experience in writing a longer, more complicated essay. It will help you master skills so that you can communicate better.

Although specific aims and methods may vary from one research activity to another, most nonexperimental, objective research tasks depend on ten basic steps. See the following explanation and then review the student work for illustration. A partial, annotated student final draft follows this discussion.

Ten Steps to Writing a Research Paper

STEP 1 SELECT A TOPIC

Select a topic and make a scratch outline. Then construct a thesis as you did for writing an essay by choosing what you intend to write about (subject) and by deciding how you will limit or narrow your subject (focus). Your purpose will be either to inform (explain) or to persuade (argue).

- Your topic should interest you and be appropriate in subject and scope for your assignment.
- Your topic should be researchable through library and other relevant sources, such as the Internet. Avoid topics that are too subjective or are so new that good source material is not available.

To write a focus for your subject, you may need to scan a general discussion of your topic area so that you can consider it in perspective and begin to see the parts or aspects on which you will want to concentrate. Relevant sections of encyclopedias and comprehensive books, such as textbooks, are often useful in establishing the initial overview. At this point, the closer you can come to a well-defined topic with a functional scratch outline of its divisions, the more likely you are to make a smooth, rapid, effective journey through the process. Try to divide your thesis into its functional parts.

Student Example:

Tentative thesis: Despite some valid criticism, <u>the zoo as an institution</u> will prob-
subject
<u>ably survive because of its roles in entertainment, education, and conservation.</u>
focus

   I. Entertainment
     A. Money
     B. Problems
  II. Education
     A. General public
     B. Students
 III. Conservation
     A. Science
     B. Breeding
 IV. Criticism
     A. Pro
     B. Con
  V. Zoos of future
     A. Education
     B. Conservation

STEP 2 FIND SOURCES

Find sources for your investigation. With your topic and its divisions in mind, use the resources and the electronic databases available in your library and on the Internet to identify books, articles, and other materials pertaining to your topic. The list of these items, called the **bibliography**, should be prepared on cards in the form appropriate for your assignment. Seek different kinds of materials, different types of source information (primary, meaning coming from direct study, participation, observation, involvement; and secondary, meaning coming from indirect means—usually reporting on what others have done, observed, or been involved in), and credible writers (authorities and relatively unbiased, reliable reporters on your topic).

The main parts of the library pertaining to most research papers are the book collection and the periodical collection. Books are arranged on shelves by subject according to the Library of Congress system or the Dewey Decimal system. Periodicals, including newspapers, are stored in a variety of ways: in unbound form (very recent editions), in bound form, on microfilm, in databases, and in online computer systems.

Books

Today most academic and municipal libraries provide information about books online, with databases accessible by author, title, subject, or other key words.

Usually a printout of sources is available. As with the Internet, selecting key words and their synonyms is crucial. A combination of words will help you focus your search. In the following sample printout on the topic *animal and conservation*, the user has keyed in the topic and then clicked to the title to check for location and availability:

```
BOOK - Record 1 of 20 Entries Found                    Brief View
------------------------------------------------------------------
   Title:            The atlas of endangered species
   Published:        New York : Macmillan : Toronto : Maxwell
                     Macmillan Canada, 1991.
   Subjects:         Endangered species.
                     Endangered plants.
                     Nature conservation.
                     Rare animals.
                     Rare plants.
                     Wildlife conservation.
                     Environmental protection.

                                            + Page 1 of 2
   ------------------------------------------------------      -----------

Search Request: ANIMAL? AND CONSERVATION MS<ENTER>-Book catalog
BOOK - Record 1 of 20 Entries Found                    Brief View
------------------------------------------------------------------
Title:         The atlas of endangered species
------------------------------------------------------------------
LOCATION:               CALL NUMBER          STATUS:
REFERENCE SHELVES       333.9516 At65        Not checked out
(Non-Circulating)
```

Printed Material Other Than Books

For the typical college research paper, the main printed nonbook sources are periodicals, such as newspapers, magazines, and journals. Various indexes will provide you with information for finding the source material you need. Depending on the library and the publication, periodicals are listed in indexes printed on paper or in electronic form. The most common index in bound volumes is the *Readers' Guide to Periodical Literature* (now also computerized). It indexes more than 200 popular magazines such as *Time* and *Newsweek*, which means it is useful for basic research but not for more scholarly studies. The *New York Times* and numerous other metropolitan newspapers are also covered by indexes. For more academic searches, check with a reference librarian for indexes in specific fields such as anthropology or art. Indexes are usually kept in one area of the reference section. The following figure shows three sample entries from the *Readers' Guide*.

A Personal Interview

Thomas, Carolyn. Personal interview. 5 Jan. 2009.

Films, Filmstrips, Slide Programs, and Videotapes

It's a Wonderful Life. Dir. Frank Capra. Perf. James Stewart,
  Donna Reed, Lionel Barrymore, and Thomas Mitchell. RKO, 1946.
  DVD.

Form for Electronic Sources

Formats vary widely in electronic media because of rapidly changing systems and terms. The information you provide in your bibliography and works cited will inform your reader about such matters as the subject of each source, who has worked on it, where it came from originally, when it was first written and last changed, when you found it, where you found it, and how you found it. Be sure that you give enough information. If you cannot find directions for citing a source, you should identify a form used for similar content as a model, improvise if necessary, and be as consistent as possible. Usually the URL is unnecessary.

Do not be intimidated by the length and seeming complexity of the citations. Every part is reasonable and every part is necessary. If you are not certain whether to include some information, you probably should. As you present an orderly sequence of parts in your entries, you must take great care in attending to detail, for a single keystroke can leave your source concealed in cyberspace with no electronic map for your reader.

The examples in this section follow latest MLA style. More details can be found at *www.mla.org.* Because the nature of electronic sources and references to them are constantly evolving, if you must include a URL, check each website for changes and updates.

This is the basic form for Internet and World Wide Web sources for your bibliography and Works Cited entries:

- Author's [editor's, compiler's, translator's, director's, narrator's, performer's] last name, first name, middle initial
- "Title of article or other short work" or *Title of Book*
- Title of the overall website
- Version or edition used
- Publisher or sponsor of the site
- Publication date
- Medium of publication
- Date of access to the source

Online Services—Library and Personal

Library Subscription Services (database with full texts)
Online library subscription services provide databases mainly of articles in journals, magazines, and newspapers. They are accessed either at a library terminal or by the student's computer. They often include hundreds of publications and

enable students to find and print out entire texts rapidly. Although most have complete printed versions, the illustrations are usually omitted, page numbers are changed or not given, and some material may be reformatted. For brief documented papers, instructors sometimes ask their students to include copies of the printouts with the final submission. Content ranges from works intended for the general reader to those written for scholarly purposes. Some are listed as "juried," which means that the selections have been evaluated for credible content by a group of experts in the field. Library online services include ProQuest Direct, LexisNexis, and EBSCOhost.

The basic form for citing sources is author, title, publication information, service company, library, medium of publication, and date of access. Include the URL of the service in angle brackets if the reader needs it to find the source.

Here are three examples.

> Meyer, Greg. "Answering Questions about the West Nile Virus."
> *Dayton Daily News* 11 July 2002: Z3-7. *LexisNexis*. Web. 17 Feb.
> 2003.
>
> Folks, Jeffrey J. "Crowd and Self: William Faulkner's Sources of
> Agency in *The Sound and the Fury*." *Southern Literary Journal*
> 34.2 (2002): 30+. *EBSCO*. Web. 6 June 2003.
>
> Taylor, Steven J. "Caught in the Continuum: A Critical Analy-
> sis of the Principle of the Least Restrictive Environment."
> *Research and Practice for Persons with Severe Disabilities*
> 29.4 (2004): 218-30. *ERIC*. Web. 3 Mar. 2009.

Personal Subscription Services (databases with full texts supplied by companies such as AOL)

Typically indicate author, title, publication information (if any), name of service, medium of publication, date of access, and the *Keyword* you used or the *Path* (sequence of topics) you followed in locating the source.

> "Cloning." BioTech's Life and Science Dictionary. 30 June 1998.
> Indiana U. America Online. Web. 4 July 1998. Path: Research
> and Learning; Science; Biology; Biotechnology Dictionary.
>
> "Tecumseh." Compton's Encyclopedia Online. Vers. 3.0. 1998.
> America Online. Web. 8 Apr. 2000. Keyword: Compton's.

Professional Site

> *The Purdue OWL Family of Sites*. The Writing Lab and OWL, at
> Purdue and Purdue U, 2008. Web. 9 Sept. 2009.

Personal Site

> Gladwell, Malcolm. Home page. N.p., 8 Mar. 2005. Web. 2 Mar.
> 2009.

Book Online

> Douglass, Frederick. *My Bondage and My Freedom*. Boston, 1855.
> *Google Book Search*. Web. 8 June 2005.

Poem Online

Hampl, Patricia. "Who We Will Love." *Woman Before an Aquarium.*
Pittsburgh: U of Pittsburgh P, 1978: 27–28. *A Poem a Week.*
Rice University. Web. 13 Mar. 1998.

Article in a Journal Online

DeKoven, Marianne. "Utopias Limited: Post-Sixties and Postmodern
American Fiction." *Modern Fiction Studies* 41.1 (1995): 75–97.
Web. 20 Jan. 2005.

Article in a Magazine Online

Keillor, Garrison. "Why Did They Ever Ban a Book This Bad?"
Salon.com. Salon Media Group, 13 Oct. 1997. Web. 14 Oct. 1997.

Article in a Newspaper Online

"Tornadoes Touch Down in S. Illinois." *New York Times.* New York
Times, 16 Apr. 1998. Web. 20 May 1998.

Newspaper Editorial Online

"The Proved and the Unproved." Editorial. *New York Times.* New
York Times, 13 July 1997. Web. 13 July 1997.

Review Online

Ebert, Roger. Rev. of *Star Wars: Episode I—The Phantom Menace,*
dir. George Lucas. *Chicago Sun-Times.* Digital Chicago, 8 June
2000. Web. 22 June 2000.

Government Publication Online

Cite an online government publication as you would cite a print version; end with
the information required for an electronic source.

United States. Dept. of Justice. Office of Justice Programs.
*Violence against Women: Estimates from the Redesigned National
Crime Victimization Survey.* By Ronet Bachman and Linda E.
Saltzman. Aug. 1995. *Bureau of Justice Statistics.* Web.
10 Jan. 2008.

Newspaper Article in a Library Database

Weeks, Linton. "History Repeating Itself; Instead of Describing
Our Country's Past, Two Famous Scholars Find Themselves
Examining Their Own." *Washington Post* 24 Mar. 2002: N. pag.
LexisNexis. Web. 3 Aug. 2005.

Journal or Magazine Articles in a Library Database

Fabel, Robin F. A. "The Other War of 1812: The Patriot War and
the American Invasion of Spanish East Florida." *Alabama Review*
57.4 (2004): 291–92. *ProQuest.* Web. 8 Mar. 2005.

```
Priest, Ann-Marie. "Between Being and Nothingness: The
     'Astonishing Precipice' of Virginia Woolf's Night and Day."
     Journal of Modern Literature 26.2 (2002–03): 66–80. InfoTrac.
     Web. 12 Jan. 2004.
Suggs, Welch. "A Hard Year in College Sports." Chronicle of
     Higher Education 19 Dec. 2003: 37. LexisNexis. Web. 17 July
     2004.
```

An Article in an Encyclopedia

Include the article's title, the title of the database (italicized), the version number (if available), the sponsor, the date of electronic publication, the publication medium, and the date of access.

```
"Hawthorne, Nathaniel." Encyclopaedia Britannica Online.
     Encyclopaedia Britannica. 2008. Web. 16 May 2008.
```

Personal E-Mail Message

```
Watkins, Jack. "Collaborative Projects." Message to Gabriel
     Mendoza. 12 Apr. 2009. E-mail.
```

EXERCISE 1   Form for Bibliography and Works Cited

Change the following items from printouts to MLA research-paper form.

1. A Book by One Author
   Printout Form
     Author: Colin Tudge
     Title: Last Animals at the Zoo: How Mass Extinction Can Be Stopped
     Publisher: Hutchinson Radius
     Place of Publication: London
     Date of Publication (or Copyright): 1991

   MLA ResearchPaper Form

2. A Work in an Anthology (May Be a Textbook)
   Printout Form
     Author of Work (Essay): Adam Goodheart
     Title of Essay: How to Paint a Fresco
     Title of Anthology: From Self to Sources: Essays and Documented Essays
     Editor of Anthology: Lee Brandon
     Publisher: Houghton Mifflin Company
     Place of Publication: Boston
     Date of Publication (or Copyright): 2003
     Page Numbers of Work (Essay): 262–264

References to Articles and Single-Volume Books

Articles and single-volume books are the two most common types of works you will be referring to most often in your research paper. When citing them, either mention the author's name in the text and note the appropriate page number in parentheses immediately after the citation or acknowledge both name and page number in the parenthetical reference, leaving a space between the two. If punctuation is needed, insert the mark outside the final parenthesis.

Author's Name Cited in Text: Marya Mannes has defined *euthanasia* as "the chosen alternative to the prolongation of a steadily waning mind and spirit by machines that will withhold death or to an existence that mocks life" (61).

Author's Name Cited in Parentheses: *Euthanasia* has been defined as "the chosen alternative to the prolongation of a steadily waning mind and spirit by machines that will withhold death or to an existence that mocks life" (Mannes 61).

Corresponding Works Cited Entry: Mannes, Marya. *Last Rights*. New York: Morrow, 1973. Print.

References to Works in an Anthology

When referring to a work in an anthology, either cite in the text the author's name and indicate in parentheses the page number in the anthology where the source is located, or acknowledge both name and page reference parenthetically.

Author's Name Cited in Text: One of the most widely recognized facts about James Joyce, in Lionel Trilling's view, is "his ambivalence toward Ireland, of which the hatred was as relentless as the love was unfailing" (153).

Author's Name Cited in Parentheses: One of the most widely recognized facts about James Joyce is "his ambivalence toward Ireland, of which the hatred was as relentless as the love was unfailing" (Trilling 153).

Corresponding Works Cited Entry: Trilling, Lionel. "James Joyce in His Letters." *Joyce: A Collection of Critical Essays*. Ed. William M. Chace. Englewood Cliffs: Prentice-Hall, 1974. 151–59. Print.

References to Works of Unknown Authorship

If you borrow information or ideas from an article or a book for which you cannot determine the name of the author, cite the title instead, either in the text of the paper or in parentheses, and include the page reference as well.

Title Cited in Text: According to an article titled "Going Back to Booze," surveys have shown that most adult alcoholics began drinking heavily as teenagers (42).

Title Cited in Parentheses: Surveys have shown that most adult alcoholics began drinking heavily as teenagers ("Going Back to Booze" 42).

Corresponding Work Cited Entry: "Going Back to Booze." *Time* 30 Nov. 1999: 41–46. Print.

References to Internet Material

Treat Internet material as you would other material. If the author's name is not available, give the title. Consider using page and paragraph numbers if they are available; usually they are not.

References in Block Quotations

Quotations longer than four typewritten lines are indented ten spaces or one inch without quotation marks, and their references are placed outside end punctuation.

> **Reference Cited after End Punctuation:** Implicit in the concept of Strange Loops is the concept of infinity, since what else is a loop but a way of representing an endless process in a finite way? And infinity plays a large role in many of Escher's drawings. Copies of one single theme often fit into each other, forming visual analogues to the canons of Bach. (Hofstadter 15)

> **Corresponding Works Cited Entry:** Hofstadter, Douglas. *Gödel, Escher, Bach: An Eternal Golden Braid*. New York: Vintage, 1980. Print.

EXERCISE 3   Giving Credit to Sources

Complete the parenthetical references and punctuation according to MLA style.

1. Quotation, taken from page 60 of the source, is introduced with the author's name (with only one source by this author in this paper).

   Schmidt reports that the Cincinnati Zoo Center for Reproduction of Endangered Wildlife has frozen "eggs from a rare female Sumatran rhino that died, hoping one day to obtain some sperm and learn how to make test-tube rhino embryos" _____.

2. Paraphrased information by James Rainey from an Internet source with no page numbers given (with only one source by this author in this paper).

   The Los Angeles Zoo faced similar opposition in 1994 when directors proposed a multimillion-dollar expansion of the education program rather than spending that money on facilities for animals popular with zoo-goers

   _____.

3. Quotation, from page 52 of the source, is introduced with the author's name. One other source by the same author is used in this paper. The title of this source is "Captive Audiences for Future Conservation."

   As Tudge points out, "Captive breeding is not an alternative to habitat protection. Increasingly, however, it is a vital backup" _____

   _____.

STEP 7 REVISE YOUR FIRST DRAFT

Evaluate your first draft and amend it as needed (perhaps researching an area not well covered for additional support material and adding or deleting sections of your outline to reflect the way your paper has grown).

Use the Brandon Guide for Revising and Editing as you would in writing any other essay:

- Write and then revise your paper as many times as necessary for **c**oherence, **l**anguage (usage, tone, and diction), **u**nity, **e**mphasis, **s**upport, and **s**entences (**CLUESS**).
- Correct problems in fundamentals such as **c**apitalization, **g**rammar, **p**unctuation, and **s**pelling (**CGPS**). Before writing the final draft, read your paper aloud to discover any errors or awkward-sounding sentence structure.

STEP 8 PREPARE YOUR WORKS CITED SECTION

Using the same form as in the preliminary bibliography, prepare a Works Cited section (a list of works you have referred to or quoted from and identified parenthetically in the text).

STEP 9 WRITE YOUR FINAL DRAFT

Write the final version of your research paper with care for effective writing and accurate documentation. The final draft will probably include the following parts:

1. Title page (sometimes omitted)

2. Thesis and outline (topical or sentence, as directed)

3. Documented essay (text)

4. List of sources used (Works Cited)

STEP 10 SUBMIT REQUIRED MATERIALS

Submit your research paper with any preliminary material required by your instructor. Consider using a checklist to make sure you have fulfilled all requirements. A comprehensive checklist might look like this:

Research Paper Checklist

❑ Title page (sometimes omitted, especially if the outline is not required)
❑ Thesis and outline
❑ Documented essay (text)
___ Approximate total number of words
___ Approximate number of words quoted (Usually, more than 20 percent quoted words would be excessive.)
❑ List of sources used (Works Cited)
___ Number of sources used

❑ Preliminary materials, such as preliminary bibliography, note cards, and rough draft, as required

❑ Double-spaced text, one-inch margins

Student Essay

The following material is an excerpt from a ten-page research paper by Michael Chung. Other parts of his assignment were shown in the ten-step approach. The material here includes a title page (which your instructor may not require), a full outline, the introduction, a sampling of body material, the conclusion, and a Works Cited section. The material is annotated to indicate form and technique in a well-written research paper.

Title page is optional; check with your instructor.

ZOOS—AN ENDANGERED SPECIES?

Michael Chung

Professor Lee Brandon

English 1A
8 January 2012

Double-space throughout (thesis and outline section is optional; check with your instructor).

Heading for all pages starting on the second page of the paper: last name, one space, page number (small Roman numerals for outline pages, Arabic for paper)

Align entries in columns

Chung ii

Thesis statement: Throughout the world, despite determined opposition, the modern zoo with a new image and compound purpose is taking shape.

I. Zoos as entertainment
   A. Attendance
   B. Income
   C. Customer preferences
      1. Favoring certain animals
      2. Favoring animals over education
II. Pandas for profit
   A. Criticism
   B. Benefits
      1. Money for zoo conservation projects
      2. Money back to natural habitat
III. Captive breeding success
   A. National
   B. International
IV. Scientific success
   A. Embryo transfers
   B. Artificial insemination
   C. Test-tube fertilization
   D. Storage of eggs, sperm, and tissue
      1. For use shortly
      2. Awaiting future development
   E. Computer projects
      1. Lab studies
      2. Animal tracking in field

Chung iii

    V. Education

        A. Purpose—change attitude

        B. Basic idea—show animals in ecosystem

        C. School applications

            1. Field trips

            2. Sleepovers

            3. Entire high school education in zoo

    VI. Different models of zoos

        A. Zoo/Park

        B. Safari park

        C. Regional zoo

    VII. Humane treatment of animals

        A. Problems without easy solution

            1. Unruly animals

            2. Animals with diseases

            3. Surplus animals

        B. Problems and solutions

            1. Providing better living areas

            2. Engaging animals in nature activities

    VIII. Response to critics

        A. Acknowledging contributions

        B. Pointing out flaws

            1. Zoos and support for wildlife linked

            2. Much habitat destruction inevitable and irreversible

½" from top

1" from top
Information here only
if you *do not* use a title page

Michael Chung
Professor Lee Brandon
English 1A
8 January 2012

[Introduction]

Title

Zoos—An Endangered Species?

Uses historical perspective for introduction

Early zoos were usually little more than crude holding pens where animals, often serving dually with circuses, died off and were replaced by a seemingly unlimited supply from the wilds. In the first seven decades of the twentieth century, zoos became institutions that offered some education, a little conservation of species, and mostly entertainment. Meanwhile, many vocal critics emerged, arguing for animal rights and questioning the effectiveness and appropriateness of zoo programs. They brought into focus the question, Are zoos necessary?

Basic thesis idea as question

[Excerpt from body]

In addition to the entertainment aspect of zoos is the captive breeding program. In one spectacular captive breeding success, the National Zoo in Washington, D.C., may have saved the endangered Komodo dragon from extinction by successfully incubating thirty eggs. This ten-foot, dangerous, ugly creature

Statistics

Chung 2

Paraphrased material
Citation

that resembles a dinosaur numbers only somewhere around 5,000–8,000 in the wild but soon will be represented in numerous zoos (Browne C1). Now that the incubation process is in place, the entire program offers an opportunity to restock the Komodo's habitat in Indonesia.

Not all captive breeding projects can end with a reintroduction of the species to the wild. For those species, the zoos have turned to science, which has been used in a variety of ways. In "Preserving the Genetic Legacies," Karen F. Schmidt says:

> Zoos are increasingly adapting the latest in human and agricultural reproductive technologies to aid beleaguered species by boosting their numbers, increasing gene variety in small populations and controlling inbreeding.... Although still in the early stages, embryo transfers, artificial insemination and even test-tube fertilization are seen by zoologists as having real or potential application in conserving endangered wildlife. (60)

These scientific activities began in the 1970s and now some of them are commonplace. Female apes are on the pill and surrogate mother tigers are receiving embryos. Schmidt reports that the Cincinnati Zoo Center for Reproduction of Endangered Wildlife has frozen "eggs from a rare female Sumatran rhino that died, hoping one day to obtain some sperm and learn how to make test-tube rhino embryos" (60). In many zoos, eggs, sperm, and skin for DNA storage have been frozen in zoo labs, awaiting scientific development by future generations.

Quotation introduced with title and author's name

Block-indented quotation, no quotation marks

Words omitted (ellipses)

Citation after period for long quotation

Reference introduced with author's name

Blended paraphrase and quotation

Citation after quotation marks for short quotation

Chung 3

[Conclusion]

The zoo of the future will almost surely be a projection of the contemporary model, one that teaches, conserves, explores, experiments, and entertains. Captive breeding cannot save thousands of creatures facing extinction but, as Tudge points out, "Captive breeding is not an alternative to habitat protection. Increasingly, however, it is a vital backup" ("Captive Audiences for Future Conservation" 51). Of course, the whole zoo operation must be monitored by those who know, appreciate, and understand animals. Nevertheless, zoos have demonstrated their value, and they have the potential to continue with their benefits.

Citation, author with two cited sources

Ends with emphasis on thesis

Works Cited

Browne, Malcolm W. "They're Back! Komodos Avoid Extinction." *New York Times* 1 Mar. 1994: C1, C4. Print.

Carpenter, Betsy. "Upsetting the Ark." *U.S. News & World Report* 24 Aug. 1992: 57–61. Print.

Cohn, Jeffrey. "Decisions at the Zoo." *Bioscience* Oct. 1992: 654–60. Print.

—. "The New Breeding Ground." *National Parks* Jan./Feb. 1997: 20–26. Print.

Diamond, Jared. "Playing God at the Zoo." *Discover* Mar. 1995: 78–86. Print.

Douglas-Hamilton, Ian and Oria Douglas-Hamilton. *Battle for the Elephants*. New York: Viking, 2002. Print.

Chung 4

Fravel, Laura. "Critics Question Zoo's Commitment to Conservation." *National Geographic News*. Web. 13 Nov. 2003.

"Not Endangered." *The Economist* 13 Apr. 1991: 55–56. Print.

"Project Technology." *Malaysian Elephant Satellite Tracking Project*. Web. 27 Apr. 1997.

Rainey, James. "Dogfight at the Zoo." *Los Angeles Times* 30 Jan. 1994: C1, C4. Web. 29 Apr. 1997.

Schmidt, Karen F. "Preserving the Genetic Legacies." *U.S. News & World Report* 24 Aug. 1992: 60. Print.

Tarpy, Cliff. "New Zoos." *National Geographic* July 1993: 6–37. Print.

Tudge, Colin. "Captive Audiences for Future Conservation." *New Scientist* 28 Jan. 1995: 51. Print.

—. *Last Animals at the Zoo: How Mass Extinction Can Be Stopped*. London: Hutchinson Radius, 1991. Print.

Rule: Capitalize words denoting family relationships when they are used before a name or substituted for a name.

> **Example:** I am grateful to Grandmother, Mother [words substituted for names], and Aunt [before a name] Julie.
> *but*
> **Example:** My mother, my grandmother, and my aunt [denote only relationships] bought me a car.

5. **Error:** Not capitalizing a title that comes before a name.

   Rule: Capitalize a title coming before a name.

   > **Example:** However, Professor Soto [before a name] teaches math.
   > *but*
   > **Example:** Gilberto Soto, a professor [not before the name], teaches math.

6. **Error:** Not capitalizing key words in titles.

   Rule: Capitalize titles of essays, paragraphs, movies, poems, and songs. However, do not capitalize prepositions or short conjunctions unless they come at the beginning or the end of the title.

   > **Example:** I read *The Last of the Mohicans* [preposition *of* inside the title].
   > *but*
   > **Example:** I also read *Of Mice and Men* [preposition *of* at the beginning of the title].

TOP 7
EDITING
ERRORS

Grammar

1. **Error:** Using the word *I*, *he*, *she*, *it*, or *they* as an object of a preposition.

   Rule: Prepositions are words (such as *to*, *at*, *in*, *of*, and *between*) that link their objects to the rest of the sentence in phrases: *to the game*, *at the store*, *in the car*, *of the issue*, and *between us*. The two main errors for objects of prepositions occur when the writer or speaker uses an object incorrectly in these ways: *between you and I* and *to you and I*.

   Solution: When you have prepositions (such as *between* and *to*) followed by two objects (such as *you and I*), just reverse the objects (*I and you*) and read them aloud and then try substituting *me* for *I*. The readings will reveal that *me* sounds better (more natural) than *I*. The correct forms are *between you and me* and *to you and me*.

2. **Error:** Changing verb tense without good reason.

   Rule: Verb tense should be consistent within a passage you are writing.

   Example of how to correct verb tense: I *left* for work, *drove* several hours in dense traffic, and *arrive* at my workplace late. The third verb, *arrive*, should be set in past tense as *arrived*: I *left* for work, *drove* several hours in dense traffic, and *arrived* at my workplace late.

3. **Error:** Mistaking the word *there* or *here* as a subject, causing a subject-verb agreement problem.

   Rule: A sentence filler is a word that is grammatically independent of other words in the sentence. The most common fillers are *there* and *here*. Even though a sentence filler precedes the verb, it should not be treated as the subject.

   > There *are* many *reasons* for his poor work. [The verb *are* agrees with the subject *reasons*.]

4. **Error:** Writing a fragment, which is an incomplete sentence.

   Rule: A sentence signals completeness with structure and punctuation. Structurally, a sentence must have a subject and a verb. The subject may be understood and not stated: "Take the dog outside." But a word group can have a subject and a verb and not be a sentence. If I say, "Because they arrived," *they* is a subject and *arrived* is a verb. However, it is not a sentence because of the word *because*, which subordinates the two words that follow; even if you placed a period after "Because they arrived," it would not signal completeness. So if you are not sure whether a word group is a sentence, consider whether it would signal completeness to your audience if you were to say, "Because they arrived." After hearing those words, unless you have asked a question, your audience would expect you to say something else because of the incompleteness of the structure. If you said, "They arrived," your audience would not necessarily expect more words; that word group is a complete sentence.

5. **Error:** Using *myself* instead of *I* or *me*.

   Rule: *Myself* (also the other *self* words—*himself, herself, themselves, itself*) is called a reflexive pronoun because it reflects back to the use of the word *I*, a personal pronoun.

   Correct: I myself am to blame.

   Incorrect: Only myself am to blame.

   Correct: Trixie and I had a great time at the beach.

   Incorrect: Trixie and myself had a great time at the beach.

6. **Error:** Needlessly repeating subjects with certain pronouns.

   Rule: A subject should not be repeated by using the nominative pronoun *she, it, we, he,* or *they* immediately after the subject.

   Incorrect: My father he is too strict.

   Correct: My father is too strict.

7. **Error:** Using double negatives.

   Rule: Avoid double negatives. Words such as *no, not, none, nothing, never, hardly, barely,* and *scarcely* should not be combined.

   Double Negative: I do *not* have *no* time for recreation. [incorrect]

   Single Negative: I have *no* time for recreation. [correct]

Double Negative: I have *hardly never* lied. [incorrect]

Single Negative: I have *hardly* ever lied. [correct]

TOP **6**
EDITING
ERRORS

Punctuation

1. **Error:** Not placing a comma after a long introductory modifier before the main part of the sentence.

   Rule: A group of four or more words that cannot stand alone and that appear at the beginning of a sentence should be set off with a comma. This group of words is usually a prepositional phrase (beginning with words such as *in*, *at*, *between*, and *over*) or a dependent, or adverbial, clause (beginning with words such as *because*, *when*, and *while*). One exception is the use of a group of words that become the subject of the sentence; for example: *That she is compassionate* is true.

   Correct: Before the ship sailed [introductory adverbial clause], the captain checked the weather report.

   Correct: In the middle of the night [long introductory prepositional phrase], the weather cleared.

2. **Error:** Writing a comma splice—two sentences with only a comma between them.

   Rule: The comma splice consists of independent clauses (actually two sentences) with only a comma between them.

   Example: The weather was disappointing, we canceled the picnic.

   Corrections: There are four common ways of correcting a comma splice.

   - Replace the first comma with a period and create two sentences. Begin the second sentence with a capital letter.

     Example: The weather was bad. *We* canceled the picnic.

   - Add a coordinating conjunction (FANBOYS—*for*, *and*, *nor*, *but*, *or*, *yet*, or *so*) after the comma.

     Example: The weather was bad*, and* we canceled the picnic. Or, The weather was bad, *so* we canceled the picnic.

   - Replace the comma with a semicolon, perhaps with a transitional connective such as those in HOTSHOT CAT: *however*, *otherwise*, *therefore*, *similarly*, *hence*, *on the other hand*, *then*, *consequently*, *accordingly*, and *thus*.

     Example without a Transitional Connective: The weather was bad*;* we canceled the picnic.

Example with a Transitional Connective: The weather was bad; *therefore*, we canceled the picnic.

- Use a subordinating conjunction.

    Incorrect: The weather was disappointing, we canceled the picnic. [comma splice]

    Correct: Because the weather was disappointing, we canceled the picnic.

    By inserting the subordinating conjunction *because*, you can transform the first independent clause into a dependent clause and correct the comma splice. Knowing the most common subordinating conjunctions, such as *because, after, that, when, although, since, how, than, until,* and *before*, will help you in writing sentences and correcting sentence problems.

3. **Error:** Writing a run-on sentence—two sentences with nothing joining them.

    Rule: The run-on differs from the comma splice in only one respect: It has no comma between the independent clauses (actually simple sentences). Therefore, the run-on is two independent clauses with *nothing* between them. It can be corrected in the same ways as the comma splice (see number 2), except there is no comma to replace.

4. **Error:** Not setting off parenthetical elements.

    Rule: Use commas to set off parenthetical elements such as mild interjections (*oh, well, yes, no,* and others), most conjunctive adverbs, or transitional connectives (*however, otherwise, therefore, similarly, hence, on the other hand,* and *consequently* but not *then, thus, soon, now,* and *also*), quotation indicators (*she said, he replied*), and special abbreviations (*etc., i.e., e.g.,* and others).

    Oh, what a silly question! [mild interjection]

    It is necessary, *of course,* to leave now. [sentence modifier]

    We left early; *however,* we missed the train anyway. [conjunctive adverb]

Especially for Reading-Based Writing:

5. **Error:** Including quoted sentence-long material without using quotation marks.

    Rule: Use quotation marks to indicate a sentence or sentences that are quoted directly; that is, the words were said, written, or thought.

    Elizabeth Wong writes: "I thought of myself as multicultural."

    [Note that the colon, which could have been a comma, is before the quotation marks and that the period is inside the quotation marks. Quotations of more than fifty words would be block indented and not enclosed in quotation marks.]

6. **Error:** Mixing paraphrased statements with short quotations of less than a sentence without setting the quotations off with quotation marks.

   Rule: Use quotation marks to blend quoted words of less than a sentence with words that you have paraphrased (put into your own words).

   She considered herself "multicultural." [Note that the word *multicultural* is enclosed in quotation marks and that there is no comma before or after the word *herself*.]

TOP **6**
EDITING
ERRORS

Spelling*

1. Confusing *you're* with *your*: *You're* is a contraction of *you are*, as in "*You're* the first to finish." *Your* is a possessive pronoun used as an adjective: Example: *Your* honesty is admirable.

   The simplest way to solve the spelling problem with contractions is to avoid using contractions.

2. Confusing *its* with *it's*: *It's* is a contraction of *it is*, as in "*It's* my turn." *It's* is a possessive pronoun that is an adjective, as in "The dog wagged *its* tail.

3. Confusing *they're*, *their*, and *there*. *They're* is a contraction of *they are*, as in "*They're* the winners." *Their* is a possessive pronoun used as an adjective: "*Their* word is *their* bond." *There* is an adverb that can be used in two ways: "Please drive *there* [adverb] and wait."

   There can also be a filler word (commonly called an adverb), as in "*There* is much to be said about politics."

4. Confusing *affect* with *effect*:

   Affect: Usually a verb meaning "change," as in "Ideas *affect* me."

   Effect: Usually a noun meaning "result," as in "That *effect* was surprising."

5. Confusing *accept* and *except*:

   Accept: A verb meaning "to receive" as in "I *accept* your apology."

   Except: A preposition meaning "to exclude," as in "I paid everyone *except* you."

6. Confusing *than* and *then*:

   Than: A conjunction, as in "He is taller *than* I."

   Then: An adverb, as in "*Then* she left town.

*The contractions among these spelling errors are also punctuation errors.

Other words that almost made the Top 6 List:

a lot, not one word
nowadays, not *now a days*
receive, not *recieve*
government, not *goverment*
environment, not *enviroment*
this and these (for students with Spanish as their first language)
embarrassment, not *embarassment*

EXERCISE A   Top 25 Editing Errors: C G P S

Underline the correct answers.

Capitalization

Grammar

Punctuation

Spelling

C **1.** *Green Eggs* (*And Ham/and Ham*) is both a fine book and a tasty breakfast.

C **2.** Passing (Basket Weaving 120/basket weaving 120) will allow you to play next year.

C **3.** Edward studied at the (University/university) in Oslo.

C **4.** Clifford struck out for the rich bottomland of the (South/south).

C **5.** Joline's (Uncle/uncle) can chunk a "punkin" over 120 feet.

G **6.** (The fisherman/the fisherman, he) brought home seven brown trout.

G **7.** After (him/he) and I left, the police arrived.

G **8.** I hit a line drive to left field; then we (score/scored).

G **9.** (Jogging around the lake./Jogging around the lake is pleasant.)

G **10.** Bonnie and (myself/I) will supply the masks for the play.

P **11.** (After lighting the fuse run!/After lighting the fuse, run!)

P **12.** The chocolate has set, take it out of the mold./The chocolate has set, so take it out of the mold.)

P **13.** (Airplanes are fast trains are romantic./Airplanes are fast, but trains are romantic.)

P **14.** (The Lorax says, I speak for the trees./The Lorax says, "I speak for the trees.")

P **15.** (What does Hamlet mean when he mentions a bare bodkin?/What does Hamlet mean when he mentions a "bare bodkin"?)

S **16.** Wherever you go, (their/there/they're) you are.

S 17. (It's/Its) time for me to learn how to use Twitter.

S 18. Of course, I will (accept/except) your apology.

S 19. For thousands of years, the pyramid has concealed (its/it's) secret passageways.

S 20. People have much respect for (your/you're) determination.

EXERCISE B   Top 25 Editing Errors: C G P S

Underline the correct answers.

Capitalization

Grammar

Punctuation

Spelling

C 1. (Scout Master/scout master) Ward was played by Edward Norton in *Moonrise Kingdom*.

C 2. Audiences lined up early to see *Avengers: Age (Of Ultron/of Ultron)*.

C 3. Beth was glad when she finally completed her senior year of (High School/high school).

C 4. Many people arrived in California by driving (west/West) on Highway 66.

C 5. Everyone gasped when (Cousin/cousin) Dewey began to open the bottle with his teeth.

G 6. (My teacher, she/My teacher) is an expert in origami.

G 7. Nobody on my team had (no/any) experience playing cricket.

G 8. This agreement is between you and (I/me).

G 9. The climber reached the summit; then he (took/takes) a picture of the view.

G 10. (When the race began./The race began.)

P 11. (After jumping on the bandwagon, smile./After jumping on the bandwagon smile.)

P 12. (The Ghostbusters are coming, they're ready to fight supernatural terrors./The Ghostbusters are coming; they're ready to fight supernatural terrors.)

P 13. (New cars are bland they are efficient./New cars are bland; on the other hand, they are efficient.)

P 14. (The baritone sang, "Nothing could be finer than dinner in the diner."/The baritone sang, Nothing could be finer than dinner in the diner.)

P 15. (The stranger rode into town and said, "Howdy, folks."/The stranger rode into town and said Howdy, folks.)

S **16.** Everyone knows (your/you're) going to get in trouble for street racing.

S **17.** My boss told me that (its/it's) not easy to launch a successful startup.

S **18.** Over the rainbow (there/their/they're) lies a pot of gold guarded by a leprechaun.

S **19.** Booing was not the (effect/affect) I had expected.

S **20.** (It's/Its) your only opportunity.

EXERCISE C   Top 25 Editing Errors: C G P S

TOP 25
EDITING
ERRORS

Underline the correct answers.

Capitalization

Grammar

Punctuation

Spelling

C **1.** I've heard that my (Doctor/doctor) received his degree online.

C **2.** (*To the Lighthouse*/*To The Lighthouse*) was written by Virginia Woolf.

C **3.** I would like to major in (Psychology/psychology).

C **4.** I am going to (college/College) to become a paralegal.

C **5.** To the coach's dismay, Johnny's curveball had gone (south/South) since June.

G **6.** Bubba and (herself/she) ran off to join the circus.

G **7.** The (interviewer he/interviewer) asked the star about unicorns.

G **8.** Many people hardly (never/ever) exercise.

G **9.** Soon after (him/he) moved, we left to find our fortunes in chinchilla ranching.

G **10.** I was lost, so I (asked/ask) for directions.

P **11.** (Before the semester was over I found a good job./Before the semester was over, I found a good job.)

P **12.** (The giant ants were attracted by sugar, fire was the only way to stop them./The giant ants were attracted by sugar; fire was the only way to stop them.)

P **13.** (The beast from the swamp stole my dog now I want revenge./The beast from the swamp stole my dog; now I want revenge.)

P **14.** (The Munchkins sang, We're off to see the wizard!/The Munchkins sang, "We're off to see the wizard!")

P **15.** (After doing something particularly stupid, G.O.B. would say, I've made a huge mistake./After doing something particularly stupid, G.O.B. would say, "I've made a huge mistake.")

S **16.** College teams must be careful that (there/their) athletes do not violate NCAA rules.

S **17.** One printing machine now does more work (than/then) fifteen human beings ten years ago.

S **18.** When presented the plastic trophy, the contestant said, ("Your/"You're) kidding, right?"

S **19.** (Its/It's) impossible to move faster than the speed of light—for now, anyway.

S **20.** When will (there/they're/their) be an affordable jet pack for the masses?

EXERCISE D   Top 25 Editing Errors: **C G P S**

Underline the correct answers.

Capitalization

Grammar

Punctuation

Spelling

C **1.** The part of (uncle/Uncle) Fester was originally played by Jackie Coogan.

C **2.** Students were assigned *The Moons (of Jupiter/Of Jupiter).*

C **3.** One of the languages spoken in Burkina Faso is (French/french).

C **4.** Junior (High School/high school) is a difficult time for many.

C **5.** My uncle is from the (Midwest/midwest).

G **6.** The dog running after a rabbit./The dog was running after a rabbit.)

G **7.** The rest of the juggling troupe and (myself/I) toured the mountain area.

G **8.** My company (boss he/boss) spoke grimly about the economy.

G **9.** No one had (never/ever) heard of *Bazooka Tooth*.

G **10.** The rude young man said, "After (I/me)," while slamming the door behind himself.

P **11.** (After eating a heap of nachos, Bob belched./After eating a heap of nachos Bob belched.)

P **12.** (The tuba is dark, the trumpet is bright./The tuba is dark, but the trumpet is bright.)

P **13.** (The P-51D fighter had an American airframe it had a British engine./The P-51D fighter had an American airframe; however, it had a British engine.)

P **14.** (Dylan Thomas writes that one should not go gentle into that good night./Dylan Thomas writes that one should not "go gentle into that good night.")

P 15. (Jackie Robinson said, "A life is not important except in the impact it has on other lives."/"Jackie Robinson said, A life is not important except in the impact it has on other lives.")

S 16. (Their/There) are many terrible diseases that have not been eradicated.

S 17. (It's/Its) never too late to be what you might have been.

S 18. In basketball it's unusual for a guard to be taller (than/then) a center.

S 19. More problems occurred in planning (than/then) in production.

S 20. Where do you intend to keep (you're/your) savings?

EXERCISE E   Top 25 Editing Errors: C G P S

Underline the correct answers.

Capitalization

Grammar

Punctuation

Spelling

C 1. I rode in the car with my nephew, aunt, and (cousin/Cousin) Dwight.

C 2. Olaf, the (king/King) of the Groats, proudly strode into the chamber.

C 3. Miranda is my favorite character in *Sex* (*in the City/In The City*).

C 4. Many could profit by taking (political science/Political Science) with Mr. Ramirez.

C 5. Our drummer graduated from the Covina (College/college) of Music.

G 6. So the guy gave me change, and then he (said/says), "Don't spend it all at once."

G 7. (While I was painting the garage door./While I was painting the garage door, I whistled.)

G 8. The team and (I/myself) will make the decision after the game is over.

G 9. The (dog it/dog) would not stop barking at the squirrels.

G 10. Nobody would (never/ever) buy a broken-down car like that.

P 11. (When pigs fly you may drive my car./When pigs fly, you may drive my car.)

P 12. (The corn dog is a meal in itself it may be your last./The corn dog is a meal in itself, but it may be your last.)

P 13. (The clown made a sacrificial gesture he threw himself onto the exploding cigar./The clown made a sacrificial gesture. He threw himself onto the exploding cigar.)

P 14. (Doctor Frankenfurter says, "In just seven days, I can make you a man."/
Doctor Frankenfurter says, In just seven days, I can make you a man.

P 15. (Doctor Frankenstein exclaimed, It's alive!/Doctor Frankenstein exclaimed,
"It's alive!")

S 16. Do you think (its/it's) funny when the clowns all get out of their tiny car?

S 17. (They're/There/Their) are many ways to skin a cat—none of them
palatable.

S 18. (There/Their) are very few car colors these days.

S 19. Will you (accept/except) the contract that cuts your salary but protects the
jobs of your fellow workers?

S 20. She is a happier person (than/then) I.

EXERCISE F   Top 25 Editing Errors: **C** **G** **P** **S**

Underline the correct answers.

Capitalization

Grammar

Punctuation

Spelling

C 1. Travel (North/north) on Interstate 5 to get to Sacramento.

C 2. I will never forget when (Grandpa/grandpa) taught me how to noodle for catfish.

C 3. Batman relies on the friendship of (Police Commissioner/police commissioner) Gordon.

C 4. *The Cabinet* (of Doctor Caligari/*Of Doctor Caligari*) is an early horror film.

C 5. Will (latin/Latin) count for my foreign language requirement?

G 6. The screenplay had been written by Harold and (she/her).

G 7. The cabbie gave me a wink; then he (drives/drove) away.

G 8. (She knew better./Although she knew better.)

G 9. He and (I/myself) will lead the meeting.

G 10. (There is many reasons/There are many reasons) that the Beatles replaced
Pete Best as drummer.

P 11. (Beyond the horizon about five miles, you will find a gas station./Beyond the
horizon about five miles you will find a gas station.)

P 12. (The band exploded with its hit song, the crowd roared./The band exploded
with its hit song, and the crowd roared.)

P   **13.** (Beginning drivers are usually overcautious they will learn to take more risks./Beginning drivers are usually overcautious, but they will learn to take more risks.)

P   **14.** (When the waiter left the table, her date still hadn't said Thank you./When the waiter left the table, her date still hadn't said, "Thank you.")

P   **15.** (I love the episode when Walter White demanded Say my name!/I love the episode when Walter White demanded, "Say my name!")

S   **16.** The teacher told her students not to use (there/their) cell phones.

S   **17.** When (you're/your) out of easy excuses, you will need to become responsible.

S   **18.** In the Mojave Desert, (its/it's) always a long, hot summer.

S   **19.** After (there/their) provisions ran out, the shipwrecked crew suffered.

S   **20.** (Your/you're) food today will be cooked by radio waves.

EXERCISE G   Top 25 Editing Errors: C G P S

TOP 25 EDITING ERRORS

Underline the correct answers.

Capitalization

Grammar

Punctuation

Spelling

C   **1.** The (eastern/Eastern) part of California has little population.

C   **2.** Vince, my (Uncle/uncle) from New Jersey, is an expert canasta player.

C   **3.** After watching *The Attack* (of the/Of The) *Clones*, he decided to watch the original trilogy.

C   **4.** It is a good idea to take (math/Math) before taking chemistry.

C   **5.** Jenny will be attending (Art School/art school) this fall.

G   **6.** The audience had (never/not never) seen a levitating elephant.

G   **7.** Between (they/them) and their enemies there was little difference.

G   **8.** She felt lost at her new job; then she (gains/gained) valuable experience and skills.

G   **9.** (Before stepping off the trail./Look before stepping off the trail.)

G   **10.** The lacrosse team and (she/herself) flew back to Boston.

P   **11.** (Before engaging in gator wrestling, put on goggles./Before engaging in gator wrestling put on goggles.)

P 12. (The Empire State Building is taller the Chrysler Building is more beautiful./The Empire State Building is taller; however, the Chrysler Building is more beautiful.)

P 13. After the hot front moves (in water/in, water) your lawn after dark.

P 14. (Blanche DuBois demurely tells Stanley I have always relied on the kindness of strangers./Blanche DuBois demurely tells Stanley, "I have always relied on the kindness of strangers.")

P 15. (Elvis always ended his concerts by saying Thank you, thank you very much./Elvis always ended his concerts by saying, "Thank you, thank you very much.")

S 16. Your phone may be newer (than/then) mine, but my plan is cheaper.

S 17. The athlete was more adept at collecting a salary (than/then) he was at promoting sports gear.

S 18. (There/Their) are many consumers who can't tell their needs from their desires.

S 19. If (your/you're) in the mood, we can play twenty questions.

S 20. (Its/It's) easy to do card tricks if you practice for many years.

EXERCISE H Top 25 Editing Errors: **C G P S**

TOP 25
EDITING
ERRORS

Underline the correct answers.

Capitalization

Grammar

Punctuation

Spelling

C 1. I plan to find a job by driving (westward/Westward) next year.

C 2. Your (Aunt/aunt) Mabel makes a delicious peach cobbler.

C 3. I believe the case should be given to (inspector/Inspector) Clouseau.

C 4. The book version of *The Fault* (in/*In*) *Our Stars* is better than the film.

C 5. Kaylee loves (philosophy/Philosophy) 101 with Professor Stevens.

G 6. The (author, she/author) signed her latest book for her adoring fans.

G 7. None of them had (never/ever) driven while blindfolded.

G 8. Beyond (him/he) lay the vast expanse of the Great Plains.

G 9. The mountain man killed the grizzly; then he (skins/skinned) the animal.

G 10. (After Magellan's ships circumnavigated the world./Magellan's ships circumnavigated the world.)

P 11. (After the commercial timeout was over Tomkins scored./After the commercial timeout was over, Tomkins scored.)

P 12. (Even when we managed to score, we could never gain the lead./Even when we managed to score we could never gain the lead.)

P 13. (No picnic is complete without ants and bikers however cole slaw makes things special./No picnic is complete without ants and bikers; however, cole slaw makes things special.)

P 14. (The Dodgers were often referred to as "Bums," the Yankees were known as the "Bombers."/The Dodgers were often referred to as "Bums." The Yankees were known as the "Bombers.")

P 15. (Darth Vader says, Luke, I am your father./Darth Vader says, "Luke, I am your father.")

S 16. The Martians took us to (there/their/they're) leader.

S 17. (You're/Your) lucky to have found affordable housing near the beach.

S 18. The doctor would not (accept/except) patients on Wednesday.

S 19. Every team member (except/accept) one refrained from using steroids.

S 20. The tumblers were more muscular (then/than) the tightrope walkers.

EXERCISE I   Top 25 Editing Errors: C G P S

TOP 25 EDITING ERRORS

Underline the correct answers.

Capitalization

Grammar

Punctuation

Spelling

C 1. Santa Ana (college/College) is at the corner of Bristol and Seventeenth.

C 2. A huge battle was fought at the wall in the (north/North) of the country.

C 3. Have you heard the story of Old (Mother/mother) Hubbard?

C 4. My friend is now the (Director/director) of human resources at his company.

C 5. (*Lord of the Flies/Lord Of The Flies*) is still assigned reading in most high schools.

G 6. Bill and (I/myself) hiked down to the beach before the others did.

G 7. The (pilot/pilot she) talked to the tower before making her final approach.

G 8. I haven't (ever/never) seen anything like it.

G 9. With (he/him) we could win the debate.

G 10. I drove away without my wallet; then I (ran/run) out of gas.

P 11. (Ahoy, matey! growled the pirate./"Ahoy, matey!" growled the pirate.)

P 12. (If you have tickets you can go on rides./If you have tickets, you can go on rides.)

P 13. (Led Zeppelin played rock and years later Public Enemy rapped. Led Zeppelin played rock, and years later Public Enemy rapped.)

P 14. (Mickey is a mouse and Bugs is a bunny nobody knows what a Goofy is./Mickey is a mouse and Bugs is a bunny; nobody knows what a Goofy is.)

P 15. (Porky always ends the cartoon by saying, That's all, folks!/Porky always ends the cartoon by saying, "That's all, folks!")

S 16. (Your/You're) the solution to your worst problems.

S 17. (Its/It's) in your best interest to study every day.

S 18. From here to (their/they're/there) is shorter than you think.

S 19. Math and science skills are more important (then/than) ever.

S 20. The storm had little (effect/affect) on the hay fields.

Parts of Speech

To classify a word as a part of speech, we observe two simple principles:

- The word must be in the context of communication, usually in a sentence.
- We must be able to identify the word with others that have similar characteristics—the eight parts of speech: nouns, pronouns, verbs, adjectives, adverbs, prepositions, conjunctions, or interjections.

The first principle is important because some words can be any of several parts of speech. The word *round*, for example, can function as five:

1. I watched the potter *round* the block of clay. [verb]

2. I saw her go *round* the corner. [preposition]

3. She has a *round* head. [adjective]

4. The astronauts watched the world go *round*. [adverb]

5. The champ knocked him out in one *round*. [noun]

NOUNS

- **Nouns** are naming words. Nouns may name persons, animals, plants, places, things, substances, qualities, or ideas—for example, *Bart, armadillo, Mayberry, tree, rock, cloud, love, ghost, music, virtue*.

- Nouns are often pointed out by noun indicators. These noun indicators—*the, a, an*—signal that a noun is ahead, although there may be words between the indicator and the noun itself.

the slime	*a* werewolf	*an* aardvark
the green slime	*a* hungry werewolf	*an* angry aardvark

PRONOUNS

A **pronoun** is a word that is used in place of a noun.

- Some pronouns may represent specific persons or things:

I	she	they	you
me	her	them	yourself
myself	herself	themselves	yourselves
it	he	we	who
itself	him	us	whom
that	himself	ourselves	

- Indefinite pronouns refer to nouns (persons, places, things) in a general way:

each	everyone	nobody	somebody

- Other pronouns point out particular things:

Singular	**Plural**
this, *that*	*these*, *those*
This is my treasure.	*These* are my jewels.
That is your prized possession.	*Those* are your trinkets.

- Still other pronouns introduce questions:

> *Which* is the best DVD player?
>
> *What* are the main ingredients of a Twinkie?

VERBS

Verbs show action or express being in relation to the subject of a sentence. They customarily occur in set positions in sentences.

- **Action verbs** are usually easy to identify:

> The aardvark *ate* the crisp, tasty ants. [action verb]
> The aardvark *washed* them down with a snoutful of water. [action verb]

- The *being* **verbs** are few in number and are also easy to identify. The most common *being* verbs are *is, was, were, are,* and *am*.

Gilligan *is* on an island in the South Pacific. [*being* verb]
I *am* his enthusiastic fan. [*being* verb]

* The form of a verb expresses its tense, that is, the time of the action or being. The time may be in the present or past.

    Rosea*nne sings* "The Star-Spangled Banner." [present]
    Roseanne *sang* "The Star-Spangled Banner." [past]

* One or more **helping verbs** may be used with the main verb to form other tenses. The combination is called a *verb phrase*.

    She *had sung* the song many times in the shower. [Helping verb and main verb indicate a time in the past.]
    She *will be singing* the song no more in San Diego. [Helping verbs and main verb indicate a time in the future.]

* Some helping verbs can be used alone as main verbs: *has, have, had, is, was, were, are, am*. Certain other helping verbs function only as helpers: *will, shall, should, could*.

The most common position for the verb is directly after the subject or after the subject and its modifiers.

    At high noon only two men [subject] *were* on Main Street.
    The man with the faster draw [subject and modifiers] *walked* away alone.

ADJECTIVES

Adjectives modify nouns and pronouns. Most adjectives answer the questions *What kind? Which one?* and *How many?*

* Adjectives answering the *What kind?* question are descriptive. They tell the quality, kind, or condition of the nouns or pronouns they modify.

red convertible	*dirty* fork
noisy muffler	*wild* roses
The rain is *gentle*.	Bob was *tired*.

* Adjectives answering the *Which one?* question narrow or restrict the meaning of a noun. Some of these are pronouns that become adjectives by function.

my money	*our* ideas	the *other* house
this reason	*these* apples	

- Adjectives answering the *How many?* question are, of course, numbering words.

some people	*each* pet	*few* goals
three dollars	*one* glove	

- The words *a*, *an*, and *the* are adjectives called *articles*. As "noun indicators," they point out persons, places, and things.

ADVERBS

Adverbs modify verbs, adjectives, and other adverbs. Adverbs answer the questions *How? Where? When?* and *To what degree?*

Modifying Verbs: They did their work quickly.
                                   v   adv

Modifying Adjectives: They were somewhat happy.
                                          adv   adj

- Adverbs that answer the *How?* question are concerned with manner or way:

  She ate the snails *hungrily*.
  He snored *noisily*.

- Adverbs that answer the *Where?* question show location:

  They drove *downtown*.
  He stayed *behind*.
  She climbed *upstairs*.

- Adverbs that answer the *When?* question indicate time:

  The ship sailed *yesterday*.
  I expect an answer *soon*.

- Adverbs that answer the *To what degree?* question express extent:

  She is *entire*ly correct.
  He was *some*what annoyed.

Most words ending in *-ly* are adverbs:

  He completed the task *skillfully*. [adverb]
  She answered him *courteously*. [adverb]

However, there are a few exceptions:

  The house provided a *lovely* view of the valley. [adjective]
  Your goblin mask is *ugly*. [adjective]

PREPOSITIONS

A **preposition** is a word or group of words that functions as a connective. The preposition connects its object(s) to some other word(s) in the sentence.

A preposition and its object(s)—usually a noun or pronoun—with modifiers make up a **prepositional phrase**, which will function as an adjective or adverb.

Bart worked <u>against</u> great <u>odds</u>.
prep   object
prepositional phrase

Everyone <u>in</u> his <u>household</u> cheered his effort.
prep   object
prepositional phrase

A storm is forming <u>on</u> the <u>horizon</u>.
prep   object
prepositional phrase modifying the verb phrase *is forming*, adverb

Some of the most common prepositions are the following:

about	before	but	into	past
above	behind	by	like	to
across	below	despite	near	toward
after	beneath	down	of	under
against	beside	for	off	until
among	between	from	on	upon
around	beyond	in	over	with

Some prepositions are composed of more than one word and are made from other parts of speech:

according to	as far as	because of	in spite of
ahead of	as well as	in back of	instead of
along with	aside from	in front of	together with

Caution: Do not confuse adverbs with prepositions.

I went *across* slowly. [without an object—adverb]
I went *across* the field. [with an object—preposition]
We walked *behind* silently. [without an object—adverb]
We walked *behind* the mall. [with an object—preposition]

CONJUNCTIONS

A **conjunction** connects and shows a relationship between words, phrases, or clauses. A phrase is two or more words acting as a part of speech. A clause is a group of words with a subject and a verb. An independent clause can stand by itself: *She plays bass guitar*. A dependent clause cannot stand by itself: *when she plays bass guitar*.

There are two kinds of conjunctions: coordinating and subordinating.

Coordinating conjunctions connect words, phrases, and clauses of equal rank: noun with noun, adjective with adjective, verb with verb, phrase with phrase, main clause with main clause, and subordinate clause with subordinate clause. The seven common coordinating conjunctions are *for*, *and*, *nor*, *but*, *or*, *yet*, and *so*. (An easy way to remember them is to think of the acronyn FANBOYS, which is made up of the first letter of each conjunction.)

Two Nouns: Bring a <u>pencil</u> <u>and</u> some <u>paper</u>.
　　　　　　　　　　 noun 　　 conj 　　　　　 noun

Two Phrases: Did she go <u>to the store</u> <u>or</u> <u>to the game</u>?
　　　　　　　　　　　　　 prep phrase 　 conj 　 prep phrase

Paired conjunctions such as *either/or*, *neither/nor*, or *both/and* are usually classed as coordinating conjunctions.

<u>Neither</u> the coach <u>nor</u> the manager was at fault.
　 conj 　　　　　　　　 conj

Subordinating conjunctions connect dependent clauses with main clauses. The most common subordinating conjunctions include the following:

after	because	provided	whenever
although	before	since	where
as	but that	so that	whereas
as if	if	till	wherever
as long as	in order that	until	
as soon as	notwithstanding	when	

Sometimes the dependent clause comes *before* the main clause, where it is set off by a comma.

<u>Although</u> <u>she</u> <u>was</u> in pain, she stayed in the game.
　 conj 　　 subj 　 v
　 └──────────────────┘
　　　　 dependent clause

Sometimes the dependent clause comes *after* the main clause, where it usually is *not* set off by a comma.

She stayed in the game <u>because</u> <u>she</u> <u>was</u> needed.
　　　　　　　　　　　 conj 　　 subj 　 v
　　　　　　　　　　　 └──────────────────┘
　　　　　　　　　　　　　　 dependent clause

Caution: Certain words can function as either conjunctions or prepositions. It is necessary to look ahead to see if the word introduces a clause with a subject and verb—conjunction function—or takes an object—preposition function. Some of the words with two functions are these: *after, for, since, until.*

After the concert was over, we went home. [clause follows—conjunction]
After the concert, we went home. [object follows—preposition]

INTERJECTIONS

An **interjection** conveys strong emotion or surprise. When an interjection appears alone, it is usually punctuated with an exclamation mark.

　　　Awesome!　　　　　Yikes!　　　　　Ouch!　　　　　Hey!

When it appears as part of a sentence, an interjection is usually followed by a comma.

　　　Oh, I did not consider that problem.

The interjection may sound exciting, but it is seldom appropriate for college writing.

EXERCISE 1   Identifying Parts of Speech

Identify the part of speech of each bold word or group of words by placing the appropriate abbreviations in the blanks:

n	noun	pro	pronoun
v	verb	adj	adjective
adv	adverb	prep	preposition
conj	conjunction		

1. I could **never** do **that** hard work at my age. _____ _____

2. We **must leave** for the seashore at once **before** the shower. _____ _____

3. **Until** Steve signs the checks, **we** must remain here. _____ _____

4. **These** men are anxiously awaiting your **instructions**. _____ _____

5. What is the **price** of those new **foreign** cars? _____ _____

6. Your **sister** is later than **you** this time. _____ _____

7. The coach is always **nervous before** the game begins. _____ _____

8. The **Norwegian** people protested the visit **of** the alleged terrorist. _____ _____

9. **I** shall have been absent a week **tomorrow**. _____ _____

10. That **reckless** driver hurt only **himself** in the accident. _____ _____

11. Her attitude **toward** the suspension of the students was **somewhat** reserved. _____ _____

12. We **found** the answer to those difficulties **since** he was last present. _____ _____

13. Joan is much **wiser** now, **and** she will never forget the lesson. _____ _____

14. We saw the ship **that** was in the **collision**. _____ _____

15. **Behind** the store is a **winding** road that leads to the farms. _____ _____

16. **If** you wish, I **will** take down his message for you. _____ _____

17. A **group** of students **asked** to see those new paintings earlier. _____ _____

18. When Kristin had finished talking, she came **over
    to my** side of the room.   _____   _____

19. **Certainly**, you may see **his** answers.   _____   _____

20. I will **not** agree to **your** criticism.   _____   _____

EXERCISE 2   Identifying Parts of Speech

**Identify the part of speech of each bold word or group of words by placing the
appropriate abbreviations in the blanks:**

n	noun	pro	pronoun
v	verb	adj	adjective
adv	adverb	prep	preposition
conj	conjunction		

1. **According to** legend, silk **was discovered**
   by Empress Hsi Ling-shi.   _____   _____

2. Empress Hsi Ling-shi **lived around** 2500 BCE.   _____   _____

3. **One** day while walking, **she** saw a mulberry tree
   covered with caterpillars.   _____   _____

4. The **caterpillars** were eating the **mulberry** leaves.   _____   _____

5. A few days **later** she saw the branches filled **with**
   the caterpillars' cocoons.   _____   _____

6. She plucked a cocoon **from** a branch and **took**
   it home.   _____   _____

7. **There** she placed **it** in a pot of water.   _____   _____

8. She **watched** as it loosened into a web.   _____   _____

9. She picked the **web apart**.   _____   _____

10. She discovered that **it** was a **long** thread of silk. _____   _____

11. The process of making silk **became** China's
    special secret.   _____   _____

12. The **secret lasted** for the next 3,000 years.   _____   _____

13. Foreign gold poured **into** China from the **silk** trade. _____   _____

14. To pass on the secret of silk-making **to** the
    outside world was forbidden.   _____   _____

15. Betraying the secret was punishable **by death**.   _____   _____

16. **Anyone** who has ever seen or worn a garment
    of pure silk knows why the Chinese had to guard
    their invention so jealously.   _____   _____

17. Silk is **petal** soft and lighter than the **sheerest** cotton.   _____   _____

18. It is **stronger** than **some** kinds of steel thread of equal thickness.   _____   _____

19. Silk **drapes** and flows **gracefully**.   _____   _____

20. It can be dyed to **richer** hues than any other natural **fabric**.   _____   _____

EXERCISE 3   Supplying and Identifying Words in Context

Luke and Lisa LaRue made a handsome couple at their wedding. Everyone had said so. But now, after seven years of marriage, they are not always happy with each other. After one heated argument, Lisa left, and Luke sat down with his guitar to write a song describing their situation.

Fill in the blanks with words that you think would fit the context of the song. Then identify the part of speech of each of your choices by placing the appropriate abbreviation in the blanks at the left. The lines from the songs have been converted to sentences and may seem a bit less lyrical than Luke's inspired original creation, "You Hurt My Feelings."

_____   You always burn my (1) _____ TV dinners.

_____   You (2) _____ my brand-new station-wagon car.

_____   You said (3) _____ didn't like to do housekeeping.

_____   By accident you broke my best (4) _____.

_____ _____   You went (5) _____ and spent my hard-earned (6) _____.

_____ _____   Then you (7) _____ a dozen bouncing (8) _____.

_____ _____   And then (9) _____ had to go and hurt my (10) _____

_____   when you ran (11) _____ with my best friend named Tex.

Chorus:

_____ _____   You (12) _____ my feelings, and I'm feeling (13) _____.

_____ _____   You hurt my (14) _____ (15) _____ I'm feeling sad.
You hurt my feelings, ran away with my friend.

_____ _____   (16) _____ hurt my feelings, and (17) _____ is the end.

_____   You went out drinking on my (18) _____.

_____ _____   Then you (19) _____ my mother is a (20) _____.

_____   You made (21) _____ of my special mustache.

_____   You (22) _____ it gives you a funny itch.

_____   You broke all my Dolly Parton (23) _____.

_____   Then you went (24) _____ dancing with your ex.

_____   And then you had to go and (25) _____ my feelings

_____   when you ran away with my best (26) _____ named Tex.

Chorus:

You hurt my feelings, and I'm feeling sad.

_____ _____   You hurt my (27) _____, and I'm feeling (28) _____.

_____   You (29) _____ my feelings, and I'm feeling sad

_____   because Tex was the best (30) _____ I ever had.

Scale for correctly labeled parts of speech (have your instructor check your answers):

0–10 = need help with grammar
11–20 = starting to catch on to parts of speech
21–25 = becoming highly capable with parts of speech
26–30 = excellent knowledge of parts of speech

Scale for correct answers (exact matches or close enough, as determined by your instructor) of word selections:

0–10 = need help with basic song writing
11–20 = ready for simple ditties
21–25 = becoming highly capable in dealing with sentimentality
26–30 = ready for advanced country song writing

Subjects and Verbs

The two most important parts of any sentence are the subject and the verb. The **subject** is who or what causes the action or expresses a state of being. The **verb** indicates what the subject is doing or is being. Many times the subject and verb taken together carry the meaning of the sentence. Consider this example:

The <u>woman</u> <u>left</u> for work.
　　　subject　verb

The subject *woman* and the verb *left* indicate the basic content of the sentence while providing structure.

SUBJECTS

The simple subject of a sentence is usually a single noun or pronoun.

The judge's <u>reputation</u> for order in the courtroom is well known.
　　　　　simple subject

The complete subject is the simple subject with all its modifiers—that is, with all the words that describe or qualify it.

The judge's reputation for order in the courtroom is well known.
complete subject

To more easily understand and identify simple subjects of sentences, you may want to review the following information about nouns and pronouns.

Nouns

Nouns are naming words. Nouns may name persons, animals, plants, places, things, substances, qualities, or ideas—for example, *Bart, armadillo, Mayberry, tree, rock, cloud, love, ghost, music, virtue*.

Pronouns

A **pronoun** is a word that is used in place of a noun.

- Pronouns that can be used as subjects of sentences may represent specific persons or things and are called **personal pronouns**:

I	we
you	you
he, she, it	they

  Example: They recommended my sister for the coaching position.
  subject
- **Indefinite pronouns** refer to nouns (persons, places, things) in a general way:

  each   everyone   nobody   somebody

  Example: Everyone wants a copy of that paragraph.
  subject
- Other pronouns point out particular things:

  Singular: *this, that*   **Plural:** *these, those*

  This is my treasure.   *These* are my jewels.

  That is your junk.   *Those* are your trinkets.
- Still other pronouns introduce questions:

  Which is the best iPhone?
  What are the main ingredients in a Twinkie?
  Who understands this computer command?

Note: To be the subject of a sentence, a pronoun must stand alone.

This is a treasure. [Subject is *this*; pronoun stands alone.]
This *treasure* is mine. [Subject is *treasure*. *This* is an adjective—a word that describes a noun; *This* describes *treasure*.]

Compound Subjects

A subject may be **compound**. That is, it may consist of two or more subjects, usually joined by *and* or *or*, that function together.

The *prosecutor* and the *attorney* for the defense made opening statements.
He and his *friends* listened carefully.
Steven, Juan, and *Alicia* attended the seminar. [Note the placement of commas for three or more subjects.]

Implied Subjects

A subject may be **implied** or understood. An **imperative sentence**—a sentence that gives a command—has *you* as the implied subject.

(You) Sit in that chair, please.
(You) Now take the oath.
(You) Please read the notes carefully.

Trouble Spot: Prepositional Phrases

A **prepositional phrase** is made up of a preposition (a word such as *at, in, of, to, with*) and one or more nouns or pronouns with their modifiers: *at the time, by the jury, in the courtroom, to the judge and the media, with controlled anger*. Be careful not to confuse the subject of a sentence with the noun or pronoun (known as the object of the preposition) in a prepositional phrase. The object of a preposition cannot be the subject of a sentence.

> The <u>car with the dents</u> is mine.
>   subject   prepositional
>   phrase

The subject of the sentence is *car*. The word *dents* is the object of the preposition *with* and cannot be the subject of the sentence.

> <u>Most of the pie</u> has been eaten.
> subject prepositional
>   phrase

> The <u>person in the middle of the crowd</u> has disappeared.
>   subject   prepositional   prepositional
>   phrase   phrase

Trouble Spot: The Words *Here* and *There*

The words *here* and *there* are adverbs (used as filler words) and cannot be subjects.

> There is no <u>problem.</u>
>   subject

> Here is the <u>issue.</u>
>   subject

VERBS

Verbs show action or express being in relation to the subject of a sentence.

Types of Verbs

Action verbs indicate movement or accomplishment in idea or deed. Someone can "consider the statement" or "hit the ball." Here are other examples:

She *sees* the arena.
He *bought* the book.
They *adopted* the child.
He *understood* her main theories.

***Being* verbs** indicate existence. Few in number, they include *is, was, were, am,* and *are*.

The movie *is* sad.
The book *was* comprehensive.
They *were* responsible.
I *am* concerned.
We *are* organized.

Verb Phrases

Verbs may occur as single words or as phrases. A **verb phrase** is made up of a main verb and one or more helping verbs such as the following:

is	was	can	have	do	may	shall
are	were	could	had	does	might	should
am		will	has	did	must	
		would				

Here are some sentences that contain verb phrases:

The judge *has presided* over many capital cases.
His rulings seldom are over*turned* on appeal.

Trouble Spot: Words Such as *Never, Not,* and *Hardly*

Never, not, hardly, seldom, and so on, are modifiers, not verbs.

The attorney could *not* win the case without key witnesses. [*Not* is an adverb. The verb phrase is *could win*.]
The jury could *hardly* hear the witness. [*Hardly* is an adverb; *could hear* is the verb phrase.]

Compound Verbs

Verbs that are joined by a word such as *and* or *or* are called **compound verbs**.

As a district attorney, Sumi *had presented* and *had won* famous cases.
She *prepared* carefully and *presented* her ideas with clarity.
We *will go* out for dinner or *skip* it entirely.

Trouble Spot: Verbals

Do not confuse verbs with verbals. **Verbals** are verblike words in certain respects, but they do not function as verbs. They function as other parts of speech. There are three kinds of verbals.

An **infinitive** is made up of the word *to* and a verb. An infinitive provides information, but, unlike the true verb, it is not tied to the subject of the sentence. It acts as a noun or describing unit.

He wanted *to get* a bachelor's degree.
To get a bachelor's degree was his main objective.

(In the first example, the word *wanted* is the verb for the subject *He*. The word *get* follows *to*; *to get* is an infinitive.)

A **gerund** is a verblike word ending in *-ing* that acts as a noun.

Retrieving her e-mail was always an exciting experience.
She thought about *retrieving* her e-mail.

Retrieving in each sentence acts as a noun.

A **participle** is a verblike word that usually has an *-ing* or an *-ed* ending.

Walking to town in the dark, he lost his way.
Wanted by the FBI, she was on the run.
The *starved* dog barked for food.

In the first example, the word *walking* answers the question *when*. In the second example, the word *wanted* answers the question *which one*. In the third example, *starved* describes the dog. *Walking, wanted,* and *starved* are describing words; they are not the true verbs in the sentences.

LOCATION OF SUBJECTS AND VERBS

Although the subject usually appears before the verb, it may follow the verb instead:

Into the court <u>stumbled</u> the <u>defendant</u>.
           verb   subject

From tiny acorns <u>grow</u> mighty <u>oaks</u>.
          verb   subject

There <u>was</u> little <u>support</u> for him in the audience.
    verb   subject

Here <u>are</u> your <u>books</u> and your <u>papers</u>.
   verb   subject   subject

Verb phrases are often broken up in a question. Do not overlook a part of the verb that is separated from another in a question such as "Where had the defendant gone on that fateful night?" If you have trouble finding the verb phrase, recast the question, making it into a statement: "The defendant *had gone* where on that fateful night." The result will not necessarily be a smooth or complete statement, but you will be able to see the basic elements more easily.

Can the defense lawyer *control* the direction of the trial?

Change the question to a statement to find the verb phrase:

The defense lawyer *can control* the direction of the trial.

EXERCISE 4   Finding Subjects and Verbs

Write the simple subject, without modifiers, in the first blank; write the verb in the second blank. Some sentences have compound subjects, compound verbs, or both; some sentences have an implied ("you") subject.

1. Every afternoon Joyce watches her favorite soap

   opera, *The Blameless and the Doomed.*   _____ _____

2. Never again will José order the mystery meat stew. _____ _____

3. Jack and Jill should have been more careful on that hill. _____ _____

4. Maybe you and I will learn to tango. _____ _____

5. Key West is the southernmost point of the United States. _____ _____

6. Several of the players are already stretching and warming up. _____ _____

7. Please knock three times on the window. _____ _____

8. Al Franken, a former *Saturday Night Live* comedian, was elected senator for Minnesota. _____ _____

9. Before long he will discover the sunken treasure and become famous. _____ _____

10. Whom can we persuade to clean the skunk's cage? _____ _____

11. There is plenty of borscht for everyone. _____ _____

12. How will you crack the code? _____ _____

13. The boxers, just before the fight, touched gloves and returned to their corners of the ring. _____ _____

14. In no time at all, Snow White had cleaned the whole cottage. _____ _____

15. Many of the ice skaters were injured during the last race. _____ _____

16. Has he ever wished upon a star? _____ _____

17. Please bring me flies for my Venus flytrap. _____ _____

18. His response to her marriage proposal was to ask if he would get a diamond ring. _____ _____

19. In the jar floats a lone pickled egg. _____ _____

20. Write your name on the paper. _____ _____

EXERCISE 5   Finding Subjects and Verbs

Write the simple subject, without modifiers, in the first blank; write the verb in the second blank. Some sentences have compound subjects, compound verbs, or both; some sentences have an implied ("you") subject.

1. The earliest evidence of Chinese writing comes from the Shang dynasty. _____ _____

2. Archaeologists have found and studied hundreds of animal bones and tortoise shells with written symbols on them.   _____   _____

3. These strange objects are known as oracle bones.   _____   _____

4. Priests used them in fortune telling.   _____   _____

5. People 3,500 years ago developed part of the culture existing in China today.   _____   _____

6. Some of the characters are very much like those in a modern Chinese newspaper.   _____   _____

7. In the Chinese method of writing, each character stands for an idea, not a sound.   _____   _____

8. On the other hand, many of the Egyptian hieroglyphs stood for sounds in their spoken language.   _____   _____

9. But there were practically no links between China's spoken language and its written language.   _____   _____

10. One might read Chinese and not speak it.   _____   _____

11. The Chinese system of writing had one great advantage.   _____   _____

12. People with different dialects in all parts of China could learn the same system of writing and communicate with it.   _____   _____

13. Thus, the Chinese written language aided the unification of a large and diverse land.   _____   _____

14. The disadvantage of the Chinese system is the enormous number of written characters.   _____   _____

15. A barely literate person needs at least 1,000 characters.   _____   _____

16. A true scholar needs about 10,000 characters.   _____   _____

17. For centuries, this requirement severely limited the number of literate, educated Chinese.   _____   _____

18. A noble's children learned to write.   _____   _____

19. A peasant's children did not.   _____   _____

20. Consider these ideas as a background to modern educational systems.   _____   _____

Kinds of Sentences

The four kinds of basic sentences in English are simple, compound, complex, and compound-complex. The terms may be new to you, but if you can recognize subjects and verbs, with a little instruction and practice you should be able to identify and write any of the four kinds of sentences. The only new idea to master is the concept of the *clause*.

CLAUSES

A **clause** is a group of words with a subject and a verb that functions as a part or all of a complete sentence. The two kinds of clauses are independent (main) and dependent (subordinate).

> **Independent Clause:**   I have the money.

> **Dependent Clause:**   When I have the money

Independent Clauses

An **independent (main) clause** is a group of words with a subject and a verb that can stand alone and make sense. An independent clause expresses a complete thought by itself and can be written as a separate sentence.

She plays the bass guitar.

The manager is not at fault.

Dependent Clauses

A **dependent clause** is a group of words with a subject and verb that depends on a main clause to give it meaning.

> since Shannon came home [no meaning alone]

> <u>Since Shannon came home</u>, <u>her mother has been happy</u>. [has meaning]
> dependent clause   independent clause

> because she was needed [no meaning alone]

> <u>She stayed in the game</u> <u>because she was needed</u>. [has meaning]
> independent clause   dependent clause

Relative Clauses

One type of dependent clause is called a relative clause. A **relative clause** begins with a relative pronoun, a pronoun such as *that*, *which*, or *who*. Relative pronouns *relate* the clause to another word in the sentence.

> that fell last night [no meaning alone]

> The snow <u>that fell last night</u> is nearly gone. [has meaning]
> dependent clause

In the sentence above, the relative pronoun *that* relates the dependent clause to the subject of the sentence, *snow*.

> who stayed in the game [no meaning alone]

> She was the only one who stayed in the game.
> <u>independent clause</u>   <u>dependent clause</u>

In the sentence above, the relative pronoun *who* relates the dependent clause to the word *one*.

Trouble Spot: Phrases

A **phrase** is a group of words that go together. It differs from a clause in that a phrase does not have a subject and a verb. In the previous section, we discussed prepositional phrases (*in the house, beyond the horizon*) and saw some verbal phrases (infinitive phrase: *to go home*; participial phrase: *disconnected from the printer*; and gerund phrase: *running the computer*).

TYPES OF SENTENCES

This section covers sentence types according to this principle: On the basis of the number and kinds of clauses it contains, a sentence may be classified as simple, compound, complex, or compound-complex. In the examples in the following list, the dependent clauses are italicized, and the independent clauses are underlined.

Type	Definition	Example
Simple	One independent clause	She did the work well.
Compound	Two or more independent clauses	She did the work well, and she was paid well.
Complex	One independent clause and one or more dependent clauses	*Because she did the work well,* she was paid well.
Compound complex	Two or more independent clauses and one or more dependent clauses	*Because she did the work well,* she was paid well, and she was satisfied.

Simple Sentences

A **simple sentence** consists of one independent clause and no dependent clauses. It may contain phrases and have more than one subject and/or verb.

> The *lake looks* beautiful in the moonlight. [one subject and one verb]
> The *Army, Navy,* and *Marines sent* troops to the disaster area. [three subjects and one verb]
> *We sang* the old songs and *danced* happily at their wedding. [one subject and two verbs]
> My *father, mother,* and *sister came* to the school play, *applauded* the performers, and *attended* the party afterward. [three subjects and three verbs]

EXERCISE 6 Writing Simple Sentences

Write six simple sentences. The first five have been started for you.

1. The mall _____

_____

2. The parking _____

_____

3. The sale _____

_____

4. After two hours _____

_____

5. Then _____

_____

6. _____

_____

Compound Sentences

A **compound sentence** consists of two or more independent clauses with no dependent clauses. Take, for example, the following two independent clauses:

He opened the drawer. He found his missing disk.

Here are two ways to join the independent clauses to form a compound sentence.

1. The two independent clauses can be joined by a connecting word called a coordinating conjunction. The coordinating conjunctions are *for*, *and*, *nor*, *but*, *or*, *yet*, *so*. (Remember the acronym FANBOYS.)

    He opened the drawer, *and* he found his missing disk.
    He opened the drawer, *so* he found his missing disk.

    Use a comma before the coordinating conjunction (FANBOYS) between two independent clauses (unless one of the clauses is extremely short).

2. Another way to join independent clauses to form a compound sentence is to put a semicolon between the clauses.

    He opened the drawer; he found his missing disk.

EXERCISE 7   Writing Compound Sentences

Write five compound sentences using coordinating conjunctions. The sentences have been started for you. Then write the same five compound sentences without the coordinating conjunctions. Use a semicolon to join the independent clauses.

1. It was the car of her dreams, _____

_____

2. She used the Internet to find the dealer's cost, _____

_____

3. She now was ready to bargain, _____

_____

4. Armed with facts, she went to the dealer, _____

_____

5. The dealer made an offer, _____

_____

6. _____

_____

7. _____

_____

8. _____

_____

9. _____

_____

10. _____

_____

Complex Sentences

A **complex sentence** consists of one independent clause and one or more dependent clauses. In the following sentences, the dependent clauses are italicized:

> *When lilacs are in bloom*, we love to visit friends in the country. [one dependent clause and one independent clause]
> *Although it rained last night*, we decided to take the path *that led through the woods*. [one independent clause and two dependent clauses]

Punctuation tip: Use a comma after a dependent clause that appears before the main clause.

> *When the bus arrived*, we quickly boarded.

A relative clause can be the dependent clause in a complex sentence.

> I knew the actress *who played that part in the 1980s*.

EXERCISE 8   Writing Complex Sentences

Write six complex sentences. The first four have been started for you.

1. Although the job paid well, _____
   _____

2. Before she went to work each day, _____
   _____

3. When she returned home each night, _____
   _____

4. Because her social life was suffering, _____
   _____

5. _____
   _____

6. _____
   _____

Compound-Complex Sentences

A **compound-complex sentence** consists of two or more independent clauses and one or more dependent clauses.

Compound-Complex Sentence:	Albert enlisted in the Army, and Jason, who was his older brother, joined him a day later.
Independent Clauses:	Albert enlisted in the Army Jason joined him a day later
Dependent Clause:	who was his older brother
Compound-Complex Sentence:	Because Mr. Sanchez was a talented teacher, he was voted teacher of the year, and his students prospered.
Independent Clauses:	he was voted teacher of the year his students prospered
Dependent Clause:	Because Mr. Sanchez was a talented teacher

EXERCISE 9   Writing Compound-Complex Sentences

Write six compound-complex sentences. The first five have been started for you.

1. When he began his research paper, he was confident, but _____
   _____

2. Although his library offered good traditional sources, he wanted some online sources, so _____

_____

3. After he found sources for background information, he focused on one issue, and then _____

_____

4. When he discovered that an expert in his study lived nearby, he _____

_____

5. After he wrote his final draft on his computer, he _____

6. _____

_____

EXERCISE 10   Identifying Types of Sentences

Indicate the kind of sentence by writing the appropriate letter(s) in the blank.

S	simple
CP	compound
CX	complex
CC	compound-complex

_____ 1. The *Titanic*, a British passenger liner, began its maiden voyage from England to New York on April 10, 1912.

_____ 2. It was the largest and most luxurious ship ever built, and it carried 2,227 passengers and crew members.

_____ 3. The ship was described as a floating palace, and because its hull included a complicated system of watertight compartments, it was also declared to be "practically unsinkable."

_____ 4. After three days of calm, clear weather at sea, the captain received seven warnings of ice in the area.

_____ 5. At 11:40 p.m. on April 14, lookouts in the ship's crow's nest saw an iceberg directly in the vessel's path, but it was too late to change course.

_____ 6. The *Titanic* struck the iceberg in the North Atlantic Ocean.

_____ 7. Because the ship was supposedly unsinkable, it carried only twenty lifeboats.

_____ 8. Women and children were first to board the lifeboats, which offered room for only about half of the people aboard.

_____ 9. Water poured into the ship, and by 1:15 a.m., its bow sank.

_____ 10. At 2:17 a.m., as the stern rose almost vertically into the air, the lights finally flickered and went out.

_____ 11. At 2:18 a.m. on April 15, the sinking ship broke in two, and at 2:20 a.m., it disappeared beneath the waves.

_____ 12. Those who did not drown froze to death in the icy water.

_____ 13. The disaster claimed 1,522 lives; 705 people were rescued.

_____ 14. After this tragedy occurred, new agreements revised lifeboat standards and created the International Ice Patrol in North Atlantic sea lanes.

_____ 15. Immediately, people began talking about ways to find the *Titanic* and raise it to the surface.

_____ 16. Not until 1985, though, did a team of U.S. and French researchers locate the wreck off the coast of Newfoundland at a depth of two and a half miles.

_____ 17. Several subsequent expeditions sent cameras, lights, and manned submarines down to the eerie scene, where they explored and photographed the rusted wreckage and collected artifacts from it.

_____ 18. The photos revealed that the iceberg ripped a hole in six of the watertight compartments; the ship might have survived if only four of its compartments had been ruptured.

_____ 19. In 1996, when researchers tried to salvage a section of the ship's hull by raising it to the surface with balloons, a storm caused the lines to break, and the piece fell back to the bottom of the sea.

_____ 20. The ship is deteriorating rapidly in its saltwater grave, and it will eventually melt into the floor of the sea.

EXERCISE 11 Identifying Types of Sentences

Indicate the kind of sentence by writing the appropriate letter(s) in the blank:

S   **simple**
CP   **compound**
CX   **complex**
CC   **compound-complex**

_____ 1. Throughout history there have been truth tests for the innocent and the guilty.

_____ 2. Many of these methods relied (unknowingly) on the basic physiological principles that also guided the creation of the polygraph.

_____ 3. For example, one method of lie detection involved giving the suspect a handful of raw rice to chew.

_____ 4. After the suspect chewed for some time, he or she was instructed to spit out the rice.

_____ 5. An innocent person was expected to do this easily, but a guilty person was expected to have grains of rice sticking to the roof of the mouth and tongue.

_____ 6. This technique relied on the increased sympathetic nervous system activity in the presumably fearful and guilty person.

_____ 7. This activity would result in the drying up of saliva.

_____ 8. That, in turn, would cause grains of rice to stick in the mouth.

_____ 9. A similar but more frightening technique involved placing a heated knife blade briefly against the tongue.

_____ 10. An innocent person would not be burned, but the guilty person would immediately feel pain, again because of the relative dryness of the mouth.

_____ 11. A more primitive but functional technique for detecting liars was supposedly used by a Persian king.

_____ 12. He was presumed to have a very special donkey, one that had the ability to tell an innocent person from a guilty one.

_____ 13. When a crime was committed, the suspects would be gathered in a hall next to the room that held the donkey.

_____ 14. According to directions, each suspect entered the room alone, found the donkey in the dark, and pulled its tail.

_____ 15. The donkey did the rest.

_____ 16. If an innocent person pulled the tail, the donkey was said to remain silent.

_____ 17. If a guilty person pulled the tail, the donkey would bray loudly.

_____ 18. In fact, the donkey's tail was dusted with graphite.

_____ 19. The guilty person emerged with clean hands because he or she wanted to avoid detection.

_____ 20. The king knew that the person with clean hands was guilty, and he proceeded with punishment.

Combining Sentences

The simple sentence, the most basic sentence in the English language, can be exceptionally useful and powerful. Some of the greatest statements in literature have been presented in the simple sentence. Its strength is in its singleness of purpose. However, a piece of writing made up of a long series of simple sentences is likely to be repetitive and boring. Moreover, the form may suggest a separateness of ideas that does not serve your purpose well. If your ideas are closely related, some equal in importance and some not, you can combine sentences to show the relationships between your ideas.

COORDINATION: THE COMPOUND SENTENCE

If you intend to communicate two equally important and closely related ideas, you certainly will want to place them close together, probably in a compound sentence.

Suppose we take two simple sentences that we want to combine:

> I am very tired. I worked very hard today.

We have already looked at coordinating conjunctions as a way of joining independent clauses to create compound sentences. Depending on which coordinating conjunction you use, you can show different kinds of relationships. (The following list is arranged according to the FANBOYS acronym discussed earlier. Only the first conjunction joins the original two sentences.)

For shows a reason:

> I am very tired, *for* I worked very hard today.

And shows equal ideas:

> I am very tired, *and* I want to rest for a few minutes.

Nor indicates a negative choice or alternative:

> I am not tired, *nor* am I hungry right now.

But shows contrast:

> I am very tired, *but* I have no time to rest now.

Or indicates a choice or an alternative:

> I will take a nap, *or* I will go out jogging.

Yet indicates contrast:

> I am tired, *yet* I am unable to relax.

So points to a result:

> I am tired, *so* I will take a nap.

Punctuation with Coordinating Conjunctions

When you combine two sentences by using a coordinating conjunction, drop the first period, change the capital letter that begins the second sentence to a small letter, and insert a comma before the coordinating conjunction.

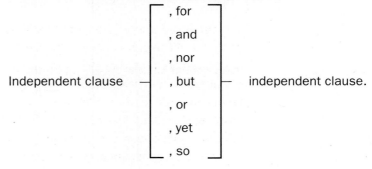

Independent clause — , for / , and / , nor / , but / , or / , yet / , so — independent clause.

Semicolons and Conjunctive Adverbs

In the previous section, we saw that a semicolon can join independent clauses to make a compound sentence. Here are two more simple sentences to combine:

> We were late. We missed the first act.

We can make one compound sentence out of them by joining the two clauses with a semicolon:

> We were late; we missed the first act.

We can also use words called conjunctive adverbs after semicolons to make the relationship between the two clauses clearer. Look at how the conjunctive adverb *therefore* adds the idea of "as a result."

> We were late; *therefore*, we missed the first act.

Conjunctive adverbs include the following words and phrases: *also, consequently, furthermore, hence, however, in fact, moreover, nevertheless, now, on the other hand, otherwise, soon, therefore, similarly, then, thus.*

Consider the meaning you want when you use a conjunctive adverb to coordinate ideas.

> As a result of: *therefore, consequently, hence, thus, then*

> To the contrary or with reservation: *however, nevertheless, otherwise, on the other hand*

> In addition to: *moreover, also*

> To emphasize or specify: *in fact, for example*

> To compare: *similarly*

Punctuation with Semicolons and Conjunctive Adverbs

When you combine two sentences by using a semicolon, replace the first period with a semicolon and change the capital letter that begins the second sentence to a small letter. If you wish to use a conjunctive adverb, insert it after the semicolon and put a comma after it. (However, usually no comma follows *then, now, thus,* and *soon*.) The first letters of ten common conjunctive adverbs make up the acronym HOTSHOT CAT.

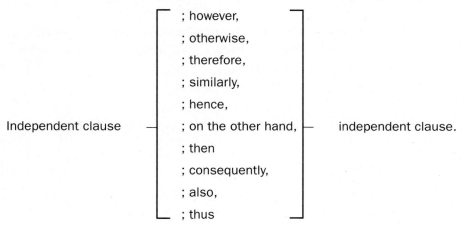

Independent clause
; however,
; otherwise,
; therefore,
; similarly,
; hence,
; on the other hand,
; then
; consequently,
; also,
; thus
independent clause.

SUBORDINATION: THE COMPLEX SENTENCE

Whereas a compound sentence contains independent clauses that are equally important and closely related, a complex sentence combines ideas of unequal value. The following two sentences can be combined as either a compound sentence or a complex sentence, depending on whether the writer thinks the ideas are of equal value:

> My neighbors are considerate. They never play loud music.

Combined as a compound sentence, suggesting that the ideas are of equal value, the new sentence looks like this:

> My neighbors are considerate, and they never play loud music.
>   independent clause   independent clause
>   (main idea)   (main idea)

Here are the same two ideas combined as a complex sentence, suggesting that the ideas are of unequal value:

> Because my neighbors are considerate, they never play loud music.
>   dependent clause   independent clause
>   (less important idea)   (main idea)

Although both the compound and the complex forms are correct, the complex form conveys the ideas more precisely in this sentence because one idea does seem to be more important—one idea depends on the other.

Thus if you have two sentences with closely related ideas and one is clearly more important than the other, consider combining them in a complex sentence. Compare these two paragraphs:

1. This version contains six simple sentences, implying that the ideas are of equal value:

   (1) I was very upset. (2) The Fourth of July fireworks were especially loud. (3) My dog ran away. (4) The animal control officer made his morning rounds. (5) He found my dog in another part of town. (6) I was relieved.

2. This version consists of two simple sentences and two complex sentences, showing that some ideas are more important than others:

   (1) I was very upset. (2) Because the Fourth of July fireworks were especially loud, my dog ran away. (3) When the animal control officer made his morning rounds, he found my dog in another part of town. (4) I was relieved.

You will probably consider Version 2 superior to Version 1. In Version 1, sentences 2 and 3 are closely related, but 3 is more important. Sentences 4 and 5 are closely related, but 5 is more important. In Version 2, the revision made each pair into a complex sentence.

Although you could combine sentences 1 and 2, the result would be illogical because the wrong idea would be conveyed:

Illogical Combination: I was very upset because the Fourth of July fireworks were especially loud.

The person was very upset because the dog ran away, not because the fireworks were especially loud.

Subordinating Conjunctions

As you learned in the previous section, a complex sentence is composed of one independent clause and one or more dependent clauses. In combining two independent clauses to write a complex sentence, your first step is to decide on a word that will best show the relationship between the clauses. Words that show the relationship of a dependent clause to an independent one are called **subordinating conjunctions**. The italicized words in the following sentences are subordinating conjunctions. Consider the meaning as well as the placement of each one.

Because the storm hit, the game was canceled.

After the storm passed, the dogs began to bark.

When she read her poem, they were moved to fits of hysterics.

He did not volunteer to work on the holiday, *although* the pay was good.

No one has visited her *since* she moved into town.

They decided to wait *until* the cows came home.

They refused to work *unless* they were allowed to wear chef's hats.

Before the session ended, all the "hep cats" blew some sweet sounds.

Other subordinating conjunctions include the following:

as	provided that	whereas
as if	rather than	wherever
even if	so that	whether
even though	than	while
if	whenever	
in order that	where	

Punctuation with Subordinating Conjunctions

If the dependent clause comes *before* the main clause, set it off with a comma.

Before Mike wrote his final draft, he looked over his outline.

If the dependent clause comes *after* or *within* the main clause, set it off only if the clause is not necessary to the meaning of the main clause or if the dependent clause begins with the word(s) *although*, *though*, or *even though*.

We went home *after* the concert had ended.

He continued painting, *although* he had repainted the cabinet twice.

Punctuation with Relative Pronouns

As you learned earlier, a relative clause begins with a relative pronoun, a pronoun such as *that*, *which*, or *who*.

The decision <u>that I made</u> is final.
relative clause

A student <u>who uses a computer</u> can save time in revising.
relative clause

Set off the dependent (relative) clause with commas when the clause is not necessary to the sentence. Do not set off the clause if it is necessary for the meaning of the sentence.

Everyone *who tries* will pass this class. [The dependent clause is necessary because one would not say, "Everyone will pass this class."]

Rachel, *who tries*, will pass this class. [The dependent clause is not necessary because one can say, "Rachel will pass this class."]

The relative pronoun *which* usually refers to things. The word *which* almost always indicates that a clause is not necessary for the meaning of the sentence. Therefore, a clause beginning with *which* is almost always set off by commas.

My car, *which* is ten years old, has a flat tire.

The relative pronoun *that* also usually refers to things. However, the word *that* almost always indicates that the clause *is* necessary for the meaning of the sentence. Therefore, a clause beginning with *that* is almost always *not* set off by commas.

The car *that* has a flat tire is ten years old.

The relative pronouns *who* and *whom*, as well as *whoever* and *whomever*, usually refer to people. Clauses that begin with those relative pronouns are not set off by commas if they are necessary for the meaning of the sentence; if they are not necessary, they are set off.

A person *who* has a way with words is often quoted. [necessary for the meaning of the sentence]

My uncle, *whom* I quote often, has a way with words. [not necessary for the meaning of the sentence]

COORDINATION AND SUBORDINATION: THE COMPOUND-COMPLEX SENTENCE

At times you may want to show the relationship of three or more ideas within one sentence. If that relationship involves two or more main ideas and one or more supporting ideas, the combination can be stated in a compound-complex sentence (two or more independent clauses and one or more dependent clauses).

<u>Before he learned how to operate a computer</u>,
dependent clause

<u>he had trouble with his typewritten assignments</u>,
independent clause

but now <u>he produces clean, attractive pages</u>.
independent clause

In our previous discussion of the complex sentence, we presented this group of six sentences:

> I was very upset. The Fourth of July fireworks were especially loud. My dog ran away. The animal control officer made his morning rounds. He found my dog in another part of town. I was relieved.

We then converted the group of six sentences to four:

> I was very upset. Because the Fourth of July fireworks were especially loud, my dog ran away. When the animal control officer made his morning rounds, he found my dog in another part of town. I was relieved.

But what if we wanted to show an even closer relationship of ideas? One solution would be to combine the two complex sentences in this way (the italicized sentence is compound-complex):

> I was very upset. *Because the Fourth of July fireworks were especially loud, my dog ran away; but when the animal control officer made his morning rounds, he found my dog in another part of town.* I was relieved.

Punctuation of Complicated Compound or Compound-Complex Sentences

If a compound or compound-complex sentence has one or more commas in the first clause, you may want to use a semicolon before the coordinating conjunction between the two clauses. Its purpose is to show the reader very clearly the division between the two independent clauses. The preceding example illustrates this use of the semicolon.

OTHER WAYS TO COMBINE IDEAS

1. Use an **appositive**, a noun or a noun phrase that immediately follows a noun or pronoun and renames it.

   > Garth Brooks claims Yukon, Oklahoma, as his hometown. He is a famous singer.

   > Garth Brooks, *a famous singer*, claims Yukon, Oklahoma, as his hometown.

2. Use a prepositional phrase, a preposition followed by a noun or pronoun object.

   > John Elway led the Denver Broncos to two Super Bowl victories. Both triumphs occurred in the 1990s.

   > John Elway led the Denver Broncos to two Super Bowl victories *in the 1990s*.

3. Drop the subject in the sentence that follows and combine the sentences.

   > Emily Dickinson's poetry went mostly unpublished during her lifetime. It was finally discovered and celebrated more than a half century later.

   > Emily Dickinson's poetry went mostly unpublished during her lifetime but was finally discovered and celebrated more than a half century later.

_____ 3. Credited with changing the king's role to include head of church.

_____ 4. However, Henry VIII's accomplishments are often overshadowed by the fact that he had six wives.

_____ 5. Many people believe that he executed all six, but that is not true.

_____ 6. He beheaded only two of them he divorced two of the others.

_____ 7. Of the other two, one died in childbirth, and one outlived him.

_____ 8. Wanting to divorce his first wife, Catherine of Aragon, who had not been able to give him an heir, and marry Anne Boleyn.

_____ 9. Unfortunately, the pope refusing to annul his marriage to Catherine.

_____ 10. Anne, already pregnant with Henry's daughter Elizabeth, who would eventually rule England as Queen Elizabeth I for forty-five years.

_____ 11. Henry was forced to take drastic measures he declared that he was head of the Church of England and would decide whether he was still married to Catherine.

_____ 12. But then Anne, Henry's second wife, failed to produce a male heir, she was unpopular and made many enemies, Henry became interested in Jane Seymour, one of Anne's attendants.

_____ 13. Henry had Anne arrested and charged with treason and infidelity she was beheaded in 1536.

_____ 14. Within 24 hours of Anne's execution, Henry was engaged to Jane Seymour, they wed two weeks later.

_____ 15. Jane gave birth to a son, but she died two weeks later.

_____ 16. For political reasons, Henry married Anne of Cleves next she was unattractive, and Henry was already smitten with young Kathryn Howard, cousin of Anne Boleyn.

_____ 17. Right after he annulled his marriage to Anne of Cleves, he married Kathryn.

_____ 18. She was nineteen, young, and vivacious, he was forty-nine, fat, and suffering from a painful leg ulcer.

_____ 19. Kathryn sought the company of handsome young men in 1542, she, too, was beheaded for infidelity.

_____ 20. Henry's last wife, Katherine Parr, who became his widow when he died in 1547.

EXERCISE 17   Correcting Fragments, Comma Splices, and Run-Ons

Write the appropriate identification in each blank. Correct the faulty sentences.

OK	**correct**
CS	**comma splice**
RO	**run-on**
FRAG	**fragment**

_____ 1. During the eighteenth and nineteenth centuries, many people developed an intense fear of being buried alive.

_____ 2. Doctors couldn't measure brainwaves and other vital signs, diagnosing death was an inexact science.

_____ 3. A person who was only in a coma could appear dead, lead poisoning, for example, led to a long state of unconciousness that mimicked death.

_____ 4. Premature burial was a real possibility people passed around hundreds of stories about re-opened caskets revealing lids with claw marks and corpses with bloodied fingers.

_____ 5. The horror stories of writer Edgar Allan Poe often included premature burials, in "The Fall of the House of Usher," a young woman breaks out of her tomb.

_____ 6. Poe's stories "The Premature Burial," "The Cask of Amontillado," and "The Black Cat."

_____ 7. Such stories contributed to the phobia, people developed customs designed to confirm that someone was actually dead.

_____ 8. The ceremony known as a "wake" allowed family and friends to sit with the deceased and give him or her time to wake up.

_____ 9. "Waiting mortuaries" were started in 1791 they were places where the deceased was kept for two weeks.

_____ 10. A system of cords and pulleys attached to the dead person's fingers, toes, and head that caused bells to ring if he or she made the slightest movement.

_____ 11. Although some people left instructions for their doctors to prod, poke, and pierce them in a variety of ways to confirm death.

_____ 12. In addition, numerous patents were issued for coffin escape devices.

_____ 13. One particular design gave the English language several phrases still in use today.

_____ 14. The deceased person's wrist was tied with a string attached to a bell above the ground, in the event of premature burial, he or she could ring the bell and be dug up by a person hired to keep watch.

_____ 15. Thus, the "dead ringer" "saved by the bell" by someone working the "graveyard shift."

_____ 16. An inventor named Herr Gusmuth, who invented a "security coffin" with a speaking tube.

_____ 17. Allowed the prematurely buried to yell for help.

_____ 18. The tube also permitted food and drink to be served to the awakened corpse while he or she was awaiting exhumation.

_____ 19. Some designs included flags or lights as signaling devices others were outfitted with heaters and stocked with food and beverages.

_____ 20. Today, of course, medical science is more advanced, we have more confidence in our doctors' abilities to recognize death.

EXERCISE 18   Correcting Fragments, Comma Splices, and Run-Ons

Write the appropriate identification in each blank. Correct the faulty sentences.

OK	**correct**
CS	**comma splice**
RO	**run-on**
FRAG	**fragment**

_____ 1. Piranhas live in freshwater streams and rivers of South America, they travel through the water in groups.

_____ 2. These ferocious-looking fish have a protruding lower jaw revealing a mouthful of sharp teeth.

_____ 3. Piranhas are meat-eaters they will eat just about any live or dead creature.

_____ 4. A school of piranhas consuming an animal the size of a pig in just minutes.

_____ 5. Like sharks, they are drawn toward the scent of blood in the water, movements such as splashing attract them, too.

_____ 6. When a school of piranhas is in a feeding frenzy.

_____ 7. The water appears to boil and become red with blood.

_____ 8. The piranha owes its savage reputation, in part, to adventurer Theodore Roosevelt.

_____ 9. Who wrote in a 1914 book that these ruthless predators would "devour alive any man or beast."

_____ 10. Roosevelt had heard of a man who went out alone on a mule, the mule returned to camp without its rider.

_____ 11. The man's skeleton was found in the water every bit of flesh had been stripped from his bones.

_____ 12. Still, Americans intrigued by stories bought piranhas for aquarium pets.

_____ 13. Fascinated by the fish's grisly reputation.

_____ 14. Perhaps admiring the silver body and bright red belly of this handsome creature.

_____ 15. As aquarium owners realized that their pets could be quite aggressive and dangerous.

_____ 16. Piranhas dumped into ponds, lakes, and reservoirs across the United States.

_____ 17. Fortunately, most of the waters were too cold for the piranhas to survive.

_____ 18. Truthfully, though, piranhas rarely attack humans, South Americans even bathe in piranha-infested waters.

_____ 19. South Americans also think piranhas are tasty and like to net, cook, and eat them.

_____ 20. However, U.S. officials are taking no chances, piranhas are illegal in many states.

Verbs

This section covers the use of standard verbs. To some, the word *standard* implies "correct." A more precise meaning is "that which is conventional among educated people." Therefore, a standard verb is the right choice in most school assignments, most published writing, and most important public-speaking situations. We all change our language when we move from these formal occasions to informal ones: We don't talk to our families in the same way we would speak at a large gathering in public; we don't write letters to friends the same way we write a history report. But even with informal language we would seldom change from standard to nonstandard usage.

REGULAR AND IRREGULAR VERBS

Verbs can be divided into two categories, called *regular* and *irregular*. Regular verbs are predictable, but irregular verbs—as the term suggests—follow no definite pattern.

Verbs always show time. **Present-tense verbs** show an action or a state of being that is occurring at the present time: I *like* your hat. He *is* at a hockey game right now. Present-tense verbs can also imply a continuation from the past into the future: She *drives* to work every day.

Past-tense verbs show an action or a state of being that occurred in the past: We *walked* to town yesterday. Tim *was* president of the club last year.

Regular Verbs

Present Tense

For *he*, *she*, and *it*, regular verbs in the present tense add an *-s* or an *-es* to the base word. The following chart shows the present tense of the base word *ask*, which is a regular verb:

	Singular	Plural
First Person:	I ask	we ask
Second Person:	you ask	you ask
Third Person:	he, she, it asks	they ask

If the verb ends in *-y*, you might have to drop the *-y* and add *-ies* for *he*, *she*, and *it:*

	Singular	Plural
First Person:	I try	we try
Second Person:	you try	you try
Third Person:	he, she, it tries	they try

Past Tense

For regular verbs in the past tense, add *-ed* to the base form:

Base Form (Present)	Past
walk	walked
answer	answered

If the base form already ends in *-e*, add just *-d*:

Base Form (Present)	Past
smile	smiled
decide	decided

If the base form ends in a consonant followed by *-y*, drop the *-y* and add *-ied*:

Base Form (Present)	Past
fry	fried
amplify	amplified

Regardless of how you form the past tense, regular verbs in the past tense do not change forms. The following chart shows the past tense of the base word *like*, which is a regular verb:

	Singular	Plural
First Person:	I liked	we liked
Second Person:	you liked	you liked
Third Person:	he, she, it liked	they liked

Past Participles

The past participle uses the helping verbs *has*, *have*, or *had* along with the past tense of the verb. For regular verbs, the past-participle form of the verb is the same as the past tense.

Base Form	Past	Past Participle
happen	happened	happened
hope	hoped	hoped
cry	cried	cried

Following is a list of some common regular verbs, showing the base form, the past tense, and the past participle. The base form can also be used with such helping verbs as *can*, *could*, *do*, *does*, *did*, *may*, *might*, *must*, *shall*, *should*, *will*, and *would*.

Regular Verbs

Base Form (Present)	Past	Past Participle
answer	answered	answered
ask	asked	asked
cry	cried	cried
decide	decided	decided
dive	dived (dove)	dived
finish	finished	finished
happen	happened	happened
learn	learned	learned
like	liked	liked
love	loved	loved
need	needed	needed
open	opened	opened
start	started	started
suppose	supposed	supposed
walk	walked	walked
want	wanted	wanted

Irregular Verbs

Irregular verbs do not follow any definite pattern.

Base Form (Present)	Past	Past Participle
shake	shook	shaken
make	made	made
begin	began	begun

Some irregular verbs that sound similar in the present tense don't follow the same pattern.

Base Form (Present)	Past	Past Participle
ring	rang	rung
swing	swung	swung
bring	brought	brought

Present Tense

For *he*, *she*, and *it*, irregular verbs in the present tense add an *-s* or an *-es* to the base word. The following chart shows the present tense of the base word *break*, which is an irregular verb:

	Singular	Plural
First Person:	I break	we break
Second Person:	you break	you break
Third Person:	he, she, it breaks	they break

If the irregular verb ends in *-y*, you might have to drop the *-y* and add *-ies* for *he*, *she*, and *it*:

	Singular	Plural
First Person:	I did	we did
Second Person:	you did	you did
Third Person:	he, she, it did	they did

Past Tense

Like past-tense regular verbs, past-tense irregular verbs do not change their forms. This chart shows the past tense of the irregular verb *do*:

	Singular	Plural
First Person:	I did	we did
Second Person:	you did	you did
Third Person:	he, she, it did	they did

The following list includes the past tense of many irregular verbs.

Past Participles

Use the past-participle form with the helping verbs *has*, *have*, or *had*.

Here is a list of some common irregular verbs, showing the base form (present), the past tense, and the past participle. Like regular verbs, the base forms can be used with such helping verbs as *can*, *could*, *do*, *does*, *did*, *may*, *might*, *must*, *shall*, *should*, *will*, and *would*.

Irregular Verbs

Base Form (Present)	Past	Past Participle
arise	arose	arisen
awake	awoke (awaked)	awoken (awaked)
be	was, were	been
become	became	become
begin	began	begun
bend	bent	bent
blow	blew	blown
break	broke	broken
burst	burst	burst

Base Form (Present)	Past	Past Participle
buy	bought	bought
catch	caught	caught
choose	chose	chosen
cling	clung	clung
come	came	come
cost	cost	cost
creep	crept	crept
deal	dealt	dealt
do	did	done
drink	drank	drunk
drive	drove	driven
eat	ate	eaten
feel	felt	felt
fight	fought	fought
fling	flung	flung
fly	flew	flown
forget	forgot	forgotten
freeze	froze	frozen
get	got	got (gotten)
go	went	gone
grow	grew	grown
hang	hung	hung
have	had	had
hit	hit	hit
know	knew	known
lead	led	led
leave	left	left
lose	lost	lost
make	made	made
mean	meant	meant
put	put	put
read	read	read
ride	rode	ridden
ring	rang	rung
see	saw	seen
shine	shone	shone
shoot	shot	shot
sing	sang	sung
sink	sank	sunk
sleep	slept	slept
slink	slunk	slunk
speak	spoke	spoken
spend	spent	spent

Base Form (Present)	Past	Past Participle
spread	spread	spread
steal	stole	stolen
stink	stank (stunk)	stunk
sweep	swept	swept
swim	swam	swum
swing	swung	swung
take	took	taken
teach	taught	taught
tear	tore	torn
think	thought	thought
throw	threw	thrown
thrust	thrust	thrust
wake	woke (waked)	woken (waked)
weep	wept	wept
write	wrote	written

EXERCISE 19   Selecting Verbs

Cross out the incorrect verb forms.

1. Mark (knew, knowed) he could not finish the term paper that semester.

2. They (dragged, drug, drugged) the cart into the back yard.

3. I was sure that I hadn't (ate, eaten) the lobster.

4. When we arrived, the windows were (broke, broked, broken).

5. Vanessa (dive, dived) from the high board and swam over to us.

6. Imelda had (spread, spreaded) the maps out on the table before the meeting.

7. Have they (began, begun) to gather that material this early?

8. Shawna (swimmed, swam, swum) that distance twice last week.

9. The water pipes have (burst, busted, bursted) again.

10. I (ran, runned) a 10K race this weekend.

"Problem" Verbs

The following pairs of verbs are especially troublesome and confusing: *lie* and *lay*, *sit* and *set*, and *rise* and *raise*. One way to tell them apart is to remember which word in each pair takes a direct object. A direct object answers the question *whom* or *what* in connection with a verb. The words *lay*, *raise*, and *set* take a direct object.

He *raised* the window. (He *raised* what?)

Lie, *rise*, and *sit*, however, cannot take a direct object. We cannot say, for example, "He rose the window." In the following examples, the italicized words are direct objects.

Present Tense	Meaning	Past Tense	Past Participle	Example
lie	to rest	lay	lain	I lay down to rest.
lay	to place something	laid	laid	We laid the *books* on the table.
rise	to go up	rose	risen	The smoke rose quickly.
raise	to lift, bring forth	raised	raised	She raised the *question*.
sit	to rest	sat	sat	He sat in the chair.
set	to place something	set	set	They set the *basket* on the floor.

EXERCISE 20   Selecting Verbs

Cross out the incorrect verb form.

1. The book is (lying, laying) on top of the bureau.
2. Will we (receive, received) your package soon?
3. His recent decision will certainly (change, changed) our policy.
4. When he heard Lenore call, he (rose, raised) and left the room.
5. That dog can (sit, set) in the yard for hours and bark constantly.
6. Marcia (done, did) many chores before she left for school.
7. Why are you (sitting, setting) those plants in the hot sun?
8. My mother (don't, doesn't) understand why Victor takes so long to come home from kindergarten.
9. A stray cat (drowned, drownded) in the river yesterday.
10. The spy (fool, fooled) his captor by disguising himself as a workman.
11. My cousins will (left, leave) Europe soon.
12. We (learn, learned) from his conversation that he did not wish to go again.
13. Kim hasn't been able to (taught, teach) her dog a new trick.
14. Have you (try, tried) to relax for a few minutes this evening?
15. The police officers could not (see, saw) us cross the bridge during the heavy rainstorm.

- Certain indefinite pronouns do not clearly express either a singular or plural number. Agreement, therefore, depends on the meaning of the sentence. These pronouns are *all*, *any*, *none*, and *some*.

  All the melon *was* good.

  All the melons *were* good.

  None of the pie *is* acceptable.

  None of the pies *are* acceptable.

4. Two or more subjects joined by *and* usually take a plural verb.

   The *captain* and the *sailors were* happy to be ashore.

   The *trees* and *shrubs need* more care.

- If the parts of a compound subject mean one and the same person or thing, the verb is singular; if the parts mean more than one, the verb is plural.

  The *secretary* and *treasurer is* not present. [one]

  The *secretary* and the *treasurer are* not present. [more than one]

- When *each* or *every* precedes singular subjects joined by *and*, the verb is singular.

  Each *boy* and each *girl brings* a donation.

  Each *woman* and *man has asked* the same questions.

5. Alternative subjects—that is, subjects joined by *or*, *nor*, *either/or*, *neither/nor*, *not only/but also*—should be handled in the following manner:

- If the subjects are both singular, the verb is singular.

  Rosa or *Alicia is* responsible.

- If the subjects are plural, the verb is plural.

  Neither the *students* nor the *teachers were* impressed by his comments.

- If one of the subjects is singular and the other subject is plural, the verb agrees with the nearer subject.

  Either the Garcia *boys* or their *father goes* to the hospital each day.

  Either their *father* or the Garcia *boys go* to the hospital each day.

6. Collective nouns—*team*, *family*, *group*, *crew*, *gang*, *class*, *faculty*, and the like—take a singular verb if the group is considered a unit, but they take a plural verb if the group is considered as a number of individuals.

   The *team is playing* well tonight.

   The *team are getting* dressed.

(In the second sentence the individuals are acting not as a unit but separately. If you don't like the way the sentence sounds, substitute "The members of the team are getting dressed.")

7. Titles of books, essays, short stories, and plays, a word spoken of as a word, and the names of businesses take a singular verb.

> *Harry Potter and the Deathly Hallows* was written by J. K. Rowling.
>
> *Ives is* my favorite name for a pet.
>
> *Markel Brothers has* a sale this week.

8. Sums of money, distances, and measurements are followed by a singular verb when a unit is meant. They are followed by a plural verb when the individual elements are considered separately.

> *Three dollars was* the price. [unit]
>
> *Three dollars were* lying there. [individual]
>
> *Five years is* a long time. [unit]
>
> The *first five years were* difficult ones. [individual]

9. Be careful of agreement with nouns ending in -s. Several nouns ending in -s take a singular verb—for example, *aeronautics, civics, economics, ethics, measles, mumps.*

> *Mumps is* an unpleasant disease.
>
> *Economics is* my major field of study.

10. Some nouns have only a plural form and so take only a plural verb—for example, *clothes, fireworks, scissors, pants.*

> His *pants are* badly wrinkled.
>
> Marv's *clothes were* stylish and expensive.

EXERCISE 24   Making Subjects and Verbs Agree

Underline the correct verb form.

1. There (is, are) very little remote wilderness left in the world.

2. Neither the oceans nor the desert (has, have) gone unexplored.

3. Mount Everest, the world's highest mountain, (is, are) no exception.

4. Before 1953, though, many a thrill-seeker (was, were) hoping to be the first to stand on its summit.

5. Everyone (know, knows) that George Mallory died trying in 1924.

6. Although we can never be sure, some of us (believe, believes) Mallory was the first to make it to the top.

7. According to the record books, Sir Edmund Hillary, along with his partner Tenzing Norgay, (was, were) the first to reach the highest place on Earth on May 29, 1953.

8. There (is, are) many reasons why someone would want to climb Mount Everest.

9. (Is, Are) personal satisfaction or prestige more important to today's climbers?

10. (Is, Are) mountaineers driven by passion or by sport?

11. Now, $65,000 (is, are) the price anyone can pay for a guided hike to the summit.

12. Trips to the top of Mount Everest (is, are) now routine.

13. A 64-year-old man, a legally blind person, and an amputee (has, have) successfully climbed the mountain.

14. A solo climber or a group (take, takes) about eleven hours to ascend.

15. Everest has been climbed thousands of times; however, not all attempts (was, were) successful.

16. Either falls or an avalanche (has, have) caused numerous deaths.

17. *Into Thin Air* (is, are) a riveting tale of one catastrophic expedition during which eight people died.

18. The majority of the 175 people who have died (is, are) still on the mountain.

19. The news (is, are) always bad when people make mistakes and lose their lives.

20. But adventurers like Sir Edmund Hillary (is, are) always willing to take the risk.

EXERCISE 25 Making Subjects and Verbs Agree

Underline the correct verb form.

1. Three varieties of poison ivy (grow, grows) in her garden.

2. Enrique, an executive with Sony Records, (is, are) looking for new talent.

3. Someone with psychic abilities (is, are) what you need.

4. My face, as well as my legs, (is, are) sunburned.

5. One B, not just A's, (was, were) on her report card.

6. (Is, Are) Bert and Ernie still roommates?

7. There (is, are) several skeletons in his particular closet.

8. Each of the bongo songs (sound, sounds) the same.

9. Neither of the girls (is, are) good at bagging groceries.

10. One of the Indians (shoot, shoots) better than the cowboys.

11. Some of the jelly (has, have) been stolen.

12. Some of the jelly beans (was, were) stuck together.

13. (Do, Does) your family or your friends know that you've joined the circus?

14. Neither the baton twirlers nor the band (like, likes) to march behind the horse-drawn carriages.

15. Every person, place, or thing (is, are) a noun.

16. My mentor and friend (advise, advises) me to read the *Wall Street Journal*.

17. *The Shell Seekers* (is, are) one of my favorite books.

18. McDonald's (stays, stay) open late.

19. My glasses (is, are) at the bottom of the pool.

20. Your thanks (is, are) much appreciated.

TOP **25**
EDITING
ERRORS

CONSISTENCY IN TENSE

Consider this paragraph:

> We (1) went downtown, and then we (2) watch a movie. Later we (3) met some friends from school, and we all (4) go to the mall. For most of the evening, we (5) play video games in arcades. It (6) was a typical but rather uneventful summer day.

Does the shifting verb tense bother you (to say nothing about the lack of development of ideas)? It should! The writer makes several unnecessary changes. Verbs 1, 3, and 6 are in the past tense, and verbs 2, 4, and 5 are in the present tense. Changing all verbs to past tense makes the paragraph much smoother.

> We went downtown, and then we watched a movie. Later we met some friends from school, and we all went to the mall. For most of the evening, we played video games in arcades. It was a typical but rather uneventful summer day.

In other instances you might want to maintain a consistent present tense. There are no inflexible rules about selecting a tense for certain kinds of writing, but you should be consistent, changing tense only for a good reason.

The present tense is ordinarily used in writing about literature, even if the literature was composed long in the past:

> *Moby Dick* is a novel about Captain Ahab's obsession with a great white whale. Ahab *sets* sail with a full crew of sailors who *think* they *are going* on merely another whaling voyage. Most of the crew *are* experienced seamen.

The past tense is likely to serve you best in writing about your personal experiences and about historical events (although the present tense can often be used effectively to establish the feeling of intimacy and immediacy):

> Hurricane Katrina *hit* the southern coast of the United States in the summer of 2005. It *was* a Category 5 storm. The levees and flood walls *failed* in New Orleans, which *caused* massive flooding in the area. FEMA *declared* the storm the "single most catastrophic natural disaster in U.S. history."

EXERCISE 26   Making Verbs Consistent in Tense

In each sentence, the last verb is in the wrong tense. Cross it out and write the correct form above it.

1. Ralph Waldo Emerson said that a success was defined as leaving the world a better place.

2. After Lou graduated from college, he joins the Peace Corps.

3. She lost the game because she wasn't sure where the Galapagos Islands were.

4. Joe was determined to shed twenty pounds before he goes to his high school reunion.

5. I'd like to fight you in the Tough Man contest, but I had a pedicure appointment.

6. After having dated only losers for fifteen years, Roxanne decides to remain single.

7. Not everyone who tries out got to play on the team next year.

8. She hopes to be a star some day, but she was not going to give up her day job.

9. The guest did not realize that caviar was fish eggs.

10. Albert Einstein said that imagination was more important than knowledge.

11. The lawyer answered all her questions; then he sends her a bill for $200.

12. She always claims to be on a diet, but she ordered dessert every time we go out to eat.

13. As Taloola cuts your hair, she gossiped about everyone in town.

14. Tanya takes her lunch to school because she disliked the smell of the cafeteria food.

15. When Rhonda pulled the gun from her purse, everyone in the room runs for cover.

16. Trixie wondered aloud if the 1930s were called the Great Depression because everyone is so depressed.

17. He did fifty sit-ups every morning before he takes a shower.

18. She regretted not telling him that she will always love him.

19. George thinks that he's in trouble when the police car pulled up behind him.

20. Last week Aaliyah bought her plane ticket and books her reservation at the hotel.

EXERCISE 27   Making Verbs Consistent in Tense

Change the verbs in the following paragraph as necessary to maintain a mostly consistent past tense.

(1) Tarzan spoke to Jane in simple language. (2) His most famous words were "Me Tarzan, you Jane." (3) Before the arrival of Jane, there are only jungle friends for Tarzan. (4) Those animals seldom used the full eight parts of speech. (5) For example, lions seldom utter verbs. (6) Elephants had no patience with prepositions. (7) Chimps condemn conjunctions. (8) Their punctuation was replaced largely by snarls, growls, and breast-beating. (9) Their language is well suited to Tarzan. (10) To him, jungle language was like swinging on a vine. (11) A one-syllable yell is a full oration. (12) Jane never ridiculed his grammar or even his yelling. (13) She holds back criticism of the king of the apes. (14) Despite their difference in language skills, they establish hut keeping. (15) They were very poor and wore simple garments made of skins. (16) Their main transportation is well-placed hanging vines. (17) Tarzan and Jane adopted a child. (18) They name him "Boy." (19) Fortunately, they did not have another male child. (20) Such an occurrence could have caused a language gridlock.

EXERCISE 28   Making Verbs Consistent in Tense

Change the verbs in the following paragraph as necessary to maintain a mostly consistent past tense.

(1) Once upon a time, a Professor Glen was very popular with his students.

(2) He kept long office hours and always speaks nicely to his students on campus.

(3) He even brought popcorn for them to munch on during tests. (4) Respecting their sensitivity, he marks with a soothing green ink instead of red. (5) He often told jokes and listened attentively to their complaints about assignments. (6) The leaders of student government elect him teacher of the century. (7) Who would not admire such a person? (8) Then late one semester, a strange and shocking thing happens. (9) Everywhere there were students in despair. (10) Professor Glen no longer speaks openly to students. (11) During his office hours, he locked his door and posted a pit bull. (12) He corrects student papers in flaming scarlet. (13) Instead of popcorn, he gave them hot scorn. (14) He told no more jokes and sneered at their complaints about assignments. (15) He sticks out his tongue at students on campus. (16) He offered good grades for cash. (17) Professor Glen even accepts Visa cards and validated parking. (18) One day the students heard a thumping sound in a classroom closet. (19) Looking inside, they find the true Professor Glen. (20) The other one was an evil twin professor.

ACTIVE AND PASSIVE VOICE

Which of these sentences sounds better?

> Andre Ethier slammed a home run.

> A home run was slammed by Andre Ethier.

Both sentences carry the same message, but the first expresses it more effectively. The subject (*Andre Ethier*) is the actor. The verb (*slammed*) is the action. The direct object (*home run*) is the receiver of the action. The second sentence lacks the vitality of the first because the receiver of the action is the subject; the one who performs the action is embedded in the prepositional phrase at the end of the sentence.

The first sentence demonstrates the active voice. It has an active verb (one that leads to the direct object), and the action moves from the beginning to the end of the sentence. The second exhibits the passive voice (with the action reflecting back on the subject). When given a choice, you should usually select the active voice. It promotes energy and directness.

The passive voice, though not usually the preferred form, does have its uses.

- When the doer of the action is unknown or unimportant:

> My car was stolen. [The doer, a thief, is unknown.]

- When the receiver of the action is more important than the doer:

  My neighbor was permanently disabled by an irresponsible drunk driver. [The neighbor's suffering, not the drunk driver, is the focus.]

As you can see, the passive construction places the doer at the end of a prepositional phrase (as in the second example) or does not include the doer in the statement at all (as in the first example). In the first example the receiver of the action (the car) is in the subject position. The verb is preceded by the *to be* helper *was*. Here is another example:

   Passive: The book was read by her.

   Active: She read the book.

Weak sentences often involve the unnecessary and ineffective use of the passive form; Exercise 29 gives you practice in identifying the passive voice and changing it to active.

EXERCISE 29   Using Active and Passive Voice

Rewrite these sentences to convert the verbs from passive to active voice.

1. A letter has been written by me to you.

2. An honest dollar was never made by his ancestors, and now he is following in their fingerprints.

3. The assignment was approved by the instructor.

4. The instructor was given a much-deserved medal of valor by the president of the student body.

5. Few people noticed that most of the work was done by the quiet students.

6. The performance was interrupted by the fire alarm.

7. The commotion at the apathy convention was caused by a person who attended.

8. The air was filled with speeches by him.

9. He doesn't have an enemy, but he is hated by all his friends.

10. His lips are never passed by a lie—he talks through his nose.

STRONG VERBS

Because the verb is an extremely important part of any sentence, it should be chosen with care. Some of the most widely used verbs are the *being* verbs: *is, was, were, are, am*. We couldn't get along in English without them, but writers often use them when more forceful and effective verbs are available. Consider these examples:

Verb:	He *is* the leader of the people.
Strong Verb:	He *leads* the people.
Weak Verb:	She *was* the first to finish.
Strong Verb:	She *finished* first.

EXERCISE 30   Using Strong Verbs

Rewrite the following sentences to strengthen the weak verbs.

1. He is the writer of that essay.

2. She was the driver of the speeding car.

3. He was the player of the guitar.

4. They were the leaders of the entire region in sales.

5. The medicine was a cure for the cold.

6. The last entertainer was the winner of the award.

7. The yowling cat was the cause of my waking up last night.

8. The mechanic is the fixer of my car.

9. He was in attendance at the computer seminar.

10. She is a car salesperson.

SUBJUNCTIVE MOOD

Mood refers to the intention of the verb. Three moods are relevant to our study: indicative, imperative, and subjunctive.

The **indicative mood** expresses a statement of fact.

> I considered the issue.

> I was tired.

The **imperative mood** expresses a command (and has a *you* understood subject).

> Go to the store.

The **subjunctive mood** expresses a statement as contrary to fact, conditional, desirable, possible, necessary, or doubtful. In current English the subjunctive form is distinguishable only in two forms: The verb *to be* uses *be* throughout the present tense and *were* throughout the past tense.

> He requires that we *be* [instead of *are*] on time.

> If she *were* [instead of *was*] the candidate, she would win.

In other verbs, the final -s is dropped in the third-person singular [*he*, *she*, *it*] of the present tense to make all forms the same in any one tense.

> I request that he *report* [instead of *reports*] today.

Here are examples of the common forms:

> If I *were* [instead of *was*] you, I wouldn't do that. [contrary to fact]

> She behaves as if she *were* [instead of *was*] not certain. [doubt]

> I wish I *were* [instead of *was*] in Texas. [wish]

EXERCISE 31   Selecting Subjunctive Verbs

Underline the subjunctive verbs.

1. If I (was, were) going to work, I would give you a ride.

2. I wish I (were, was) on the beach.

3. I demand that you (will return, return) the deposit.

4. They act as if they (are, were) rich.

5. I require that my workers (are, be) on time.

6. You may wish you (are, were) an adult, but you must show your ID.

7. You talk as if winning (was, were) possible.

8. My manager insists that I (be, am) tactful with clients.

9. Suppose, for sake of argument, your statement (was, were) true.

10. Sometimes I wish I (were, was) of the younger generation.

Pronouns

Should you say, "Between you and *I*" or "Between you and *me*"? What about "Let's you and *I* do this" or "Let's you and *me* do this"? Are you confused about when to use *who* and *whom*? Is it "Everyone should wear *their* coat [or *his* coat or *his or her* coat]"? Is there anything wrong with saying, "When *you* walk down the streets of Laredo"?

The examples in the first paragraph represent the most common problems people have with pronouns. This section will help you identify the standard forms and understand why they are correct. The result should be expertise and confidence.

PRONOUN CASE

Case is the form a pronoun takes as it fills a position in a sentence. Words such as *you* and *it* do not change, but others do, and they change in predictable ways. For example, *I* is a subject word and *me* is an object word. As you refer to yourself, you will select a pronoun that fits a certain part of sentence structure. You say, "*I* will write the paper," not "*Me* will write the paper," because *I* is in the subject position. But you say, "She will give the apple to *me*," not "She will give the apple to *I*," because *me* is in the object position. These are the pronouns that change:

Subject	Object
I	me
he	him
she	her
we	us
they	them
who, whoever	whom, whomever

Subjective Case

	Singular	Plural
First Person:	I	we
Second Person:	you	you
Third Person:	he she it	they
	who	

Subjective-case pronouns can fill two positions in a sentence.

1. Pronouns in the subjective case fill subject positions.

   a. Some will be easy to identify because they are at the beginning of the sentence.

I dance in the park.

He dances in the park.

She dances in the park.

We dance in the park.

They dance in the park.

Who is dancing in the park?

b. Others will be more difficult to identify because they are not at the beginning of a sentence and may not appear to be part of a clause. The words *than* and *as* are signals for these special arrangements, which can be called incompletely stated clauses.

He is taller t*han I (am).*

She is younger than we (are).

*We work as ha*rd as *they* (do).

The words *am*, *are*, and *do*, which complete the clauses, have been omitted. We are actually saying, "He is taller than *I am*," "She is younger than *we are*," and "We work as hard as *they do*." The italicized pronouns are subjects of "understood" verbs.

2. Pronouns in the subjective case refer back to the subject.

a. They follow a form of the verb *to be*, such as *was*, *were*, *am*, *is*, and *are*.

I believe it is he.

It was *she* who spoke.

The victims were *they*.

b. Some nouns and pronouns refer back to an earlier noun without referring back through the verb.

The leading candidates—Juan, Darnelle, Steve, Kimlieu, and *I*—made speeches.

Objective Case

	Singular	Plural
First Person:	me	we
Second Person:	you	you
Third Person:	him her it	them
	whom	

Objective-case pronouns can also fill two positions in sentences.

1. Pronouns in the objective case fill object positions.

   a. They may be objects after the verb.

      - A direct object answers the question *what* or *whom* in connection with the verb.

         We brought *it* to your house. [*What* did we bring? *It*]

         We saw *her* in the library. [*Whom* did we see? *Her*]

      - An indirect object answers the question *to whom* in connection with the verb.

         I gave *him* the message. [*To whom did* I give the message? *To him*]

         The doctor told us the test results. [*To whom* did the doctor tell the results? *To us*]

   b. Objective-case pronouns are objects after prepositions.

      The problem was clear to *us*.

      I went with Steve and *him*.

2. Objective-case pronouns may also refer back to object words.

   They had the costumes for us—Judy and *me*.

   The judge addressed the defendants—John and *her*.

Techniques for Determining Case

Here are three techniques that will help you decide which pronoun to use when the choice seems difficult.

1. If you have a compound element (such as a subject or an object of a preposition), consider only the pronoun part. The sound alone will probably tell you the answer.

   She gave the answer to Marie and (I, me).

   Marie and the pronoun make up a compound object of the preposition *to*. Disregard the noun, *Marie*, and ask yourself, "Would I say, 'She gave the answer *to me* or *to I*'?" The way the words sound would tell you the answer is *to me*. Of course, if you immediately notice that the pronoun is in an object position, you need not bother with sound.

2. If you are choosing between *who* (subject word) and *whom* (object word), look to the right to see if the next verb has a subject. If it does not, the pronoun probably *is* the subject, but if it does have a subject, the pronoun probably is an object.

   The person (*who*, whom) works hardest will win. [*Who* is the correct answer because it is the subject of the verb *works*.]

TOP 25
EDITING
ERRORS

The person (who, *whom*) we admire most is José. [*Whom* is the correct answer because the next verb, *admire*, already has a subject, *we*. *Whom* is an object.]

A related technique works the same way. If the next important word after *who* or *whom* in a statement is a noun or pronoun, the correct word will almost always be *whom*. However, if the next important word is not a noun or pronoun, the correct word will be *who*.

To apply this technique, you must disregard qualifier clauses such as "I think," "it seems," and "we hope."

Tyrone is a natural leader (*who*, whom) has charisma. [*Who* is the correct answer; it is followed by something other than a noun or pronoun.]

Tyrone is a natural leader (who, whom), we think, has charisma. [*Who* is the correct answer; it is followed by the qualifier clause *we think*, which is then followed by something other than a noun or pronoun.]

Tyrone is a natural leader (who, whom) we supported. [*Whom* is the correct answer; it is followed by a pronoun.]

3. *Let's* is made up of the words *let* and *us* and means "you *let us*"; therefore, when you select a pronoun to follow it, consider the two original words and select another object word—*me*.

Let's you and (I, *me*) take a trip to Westwood. [Think of "You let us, you and me, take a trip to Westwood." *Us* and *me* are object words.]

EXERCISE 32   Selecting Pronouns: Case

Underline the correct pronoun form.

Compounds

1. Sacagawea and (he, him) helped Lewis and Clark as they explored the West.

2. Did you and (she, her) practice throwing curve balls?

3. She insisted on setting up Roxanne and (them, they) with blind dates.

4. The fortune cookie revealed to (they, them) and me the truth.

Appositives

5. Let's you and (I, me) order the crawfish platter.

6. Two of the dancers—Cheyenne and (she, her)—couldn't high-kick very well.

7. She has narrowed her suitors down to three—you, Bob, and (he, him).

8. (We, Us) know-it-alls consider it our duty to correct those who are wrong.

9. They frowned upon (we, us) women showing off our tattoos.

Comparisons

10. My friend Raj is a better rapper than (I, me).

11. Lucy has more freckles than (she, her).

12. He makes a lot more money than (they, them).

13. The chimpanzee knew as many words as (he, him).

Who/Whom

14. (Who, Whom) did you invite to the luau?

15. She is a person (who, whom) we can trust.

16. (Who, Whom) leaked the information to the press?

17. She is now dating the fellow (who, whom) she accidently ran over last month.

18. (Who, Whom) do you predict will be our first female president?

Refer Back to Subject

19. Was it (I, me) you hoped to find?

20. It is (she, her) for whom he sold his soul.

EXERCISE 33   Selecting Pronouns: Case

Underline the correct pronoun form.

1. She did not realize that you and (I, me) would be asked to testify.

2. Give the award to (whoever, whomever) is voted most valuable player.

3. We need one person (who, whom) we can rely on.

4. Would you support (her, she) in the election?

5. Let's you and (I, me) take that trip next year.

6. Everybody but (he, him) was ready for the test.

7. Only two were chosen, Kathy and (he, him).

8. She thinks more clearly than (I, me).

9. Distribute the cards among John, Joe, and (he, him).

10. Gilligan knows the answer better than (we, us).

11. The person (whom, who) came will call on you again.

12. You know that much better than (I, me).

13. The police believed (they, them) to be us.

14. The court found (us, we) to be responsible.

15. (Whoever, Whomever) they choose will receive the promotion.

16. I would have taken (she, her) to the meeting.

17. Is it (I, me) you are looking for?

18. Just between you and (I, me), I think we should go.

19. It could have been (he, him) whom you saw.

20. The soldiers (who, whom) they trained were sent to the front.

PRONOUN-ANTECEDENT AGREEMENT

Every pronoun refers to an earlier noun, which is called the **antecedent** of the pronoun. The antecedent is the noun that the pronoun replaces. The pronoun brings the reader back to the earlier thought. Here are some examples:

> I tried to buy *tickets* for the concert, but *they* were all sold.

> *Roger* painted a *picture* of a pickup truck. *It* was so good that *he* entered *it* in an art show.

A **pronoun** agrees with its antecedent in person, number, and gender. **Person**—first, second, or third—indicates perspective, or point of view. **Number** indicates singular or plural. **Gender** indicates masculine, feminine, or neuter.

	Subject Words			**Object Words**	
	Singular	**Plural**		**Singular**	**Plural**
First Person:	I	we	**First Person:**	me	us
Second Person:	you	you	**Second Person:**	you	you
Third Person:	he, she, it	they	**Third Person:**	him, her, it	them
	who			whom	

Agreement in Person

Avoid needless shifting of person, which means shifting of point of view, such as from *I* to *you*. First person, second person, and third person indicate perspectives from which you can write. Select one point of view and maintain it, promoting continuity and consistency. Needless shifting of person, meaning changing perspectives without reasons important for your content and purpose, is distracting and awkward. Each point of view has its appropriate purposes.

First Person

Using the word *I* and its companion forms *we*, *me*, and *us*, the first-person point of view emphasizes the writer, who is an important part of the subject of the composition. Choose first person for friendly letters, accounts of personal experience, and, occasionally, business correspondence, such as a letter of application for a job, which requires self-analysis.

Observe the presence of the writer and the use of *I* in this example.

> *I* could tell that the wedding would not go well when the caterers started serving drinks before the ceremony and the bride began arguing with her future mother-in-law. After the sound system crashed, the band canceled and *I* wished *I* hadn't come.

Second Person

Using or implying the word *you*, the second-person point of view is fine for informal conversation, advice, and directions. Although it is occasionally found in academic writing, most instructors prefer that you use it only in process analysis, directions in how to do something.

In this example, note that the word *you* is sometimes understood and not stated.

> To juggle three balls, first *you* place two balls (A and B) in one hand and one ball (C) in the other. Then toss one of the two balls (A), and before *you* catch it with your other hand, toss the single ball (C) from that hand. Before that ball (C) lands in the other hand, toss the remaining inactive ball (B). Then pick up the balls and repeat the process until balls no longer fall to the ground.

Third Person

Referring to subject material, individuals, things, or ideas, the third-person point of view works best for most formal writing, be it academic or professional. Third-person pronouns include *he*, *she*, *it*, *they*, *him*, *her*, and *them*. Most of your college writing—essay exams, reports, compositions that explain and argue, critiques, and research papers—will be from this detached perspective with no references to yourself.

In this example, written in the third person, the name *Bartleby* is replaced by forms of *he*.

> *Bartleby*, one of Herman Melville's most memorable characters, has befuddled critics for more than a century. At a point in *his* life chosen for no obvious reason, *he* decides not to work, not to cooperate with others, and not to leave the premises of *his* employer because *he* "prefers not to." Most readers do not know what to make of *him*.

Correcting Problems of Agreement in Person

Most problems with pronoun agreement in person occur with the use of *you* in a passage that should have been written in the first or third person. If your composition is not one of advice or directions, the word *you* is probably not appropriate and should be replaced with a first- or third-person pronoun.

If you are giving advice or directions, use *you* throughout the passage, but, if you are not, replace each *you* with a first- or third-person pronoun that is consistent with the perspective, purpose, and content of the passage.

Inconsistent:	*I* love to travel, especially when *you* go to foreign countries.
Consistent:	*I* love to travel, especially when *I* go to foreign countries.
Inconsistent:	When *you* are about to merge with moving traffic on the freeway, *one* should not stop *his or her* car.
Consistent:	When *you* are about to merge with moving traffic on the freeway, *you* should not stop *your* car.
Consistent:	When *one* is about to merge with moving traffic on the freeway, *one* should not stop *his or her* car. [using third-person pronouns, including the indefinite pronoun *one*]
Consistent:	When *drivers* are about to merge with moving traffic on the freeway, *they* should not stop *their* car. [using third-person plural pronouns to match plural noun]

Agreement in Number

Most problems with pronoun-antecedent agreement involve **number**. The principles are simple: If the antecedent (the word the pronoun refers back to) is singular, use a singular pronoun. If the antecedent is plural, use a plural pronoun.

1. A singular antecedent requires a singular pronoun.

   Vincent forgot *his* notebook.

2. A plural antecedent requires a plural pronoun.

   Many *students* cast *their* votes today.

3. A singular indefinite pronoun as an antecedent takes a singular pronoun. Most indefinite pronouns are singular. The following are common indefinite singular pronouns: *anybody, anyone, each, either, everybody, everyone, no one, nobody, one, somebody, someone.*

   Each of the girls brought *her* book.

   When *one* makes a promise, *one* [or *he or she*] should keep it.

4. A plural indefinite pronoun as an antecedent takes a plural pronoun.
   Few knew *their* assignments.

5. Certain indefinite pronouns do not clearly express either a singular or plural number. Agreement, therefore, depends on the meaning of the sentence. These pronouns are *all, any, none,* and *some.*

   All the apple *was* wormy.

   All the apples were wormy.

   None of the cake *is* acceptable.

   None of the cakes *are* acceptable.

6. Two or more antecedents, singular or plural, take a plural pronoun. Such antecedents are usually joined by *and* or by commas and *and*.

Howard and his *parents* bought *their* presents early.

Students, instructors, and the *administration* pooled *their* ideas at the forum.

7. Alternative antecedents—that is, antecedents joined by *or, nor, whether/or, either/or, neither/nor, not only/but also*—require a pronoun that agrees with the nearer antecedent.

Neither Alex nor his *friends* lost *their* way.

Neither his friends nor *Alex* lost *his* way.

8. In a sentence with an expression such as *one of those* _____ *who*, the antecedent is usually the plural noun that follows the preposition *of*.

He is one of those *people who* want *their* money now.

9. In a sentence with the expression *the only one of those* _____ *who*, the antecedent is usually the singular word *one*.

She is the *only one* of the members *who* wants *her* money now.

10. When collective nouns such as *team, jury, committee,* and *band* are used as antecedents, they take a singular pronoun if they are considered as units.

The *jury* is doing *its* best.

When individual behavior is suggested, antecedents take a plural form.

The *jury* are putting on *their* coats.

11. The words *each, every,* and *many a(n)* before a noun make the noun singular.

Each child and *adult* was *his* or *her* own authority.

Each and *every person* doubted *himself* or *herself*.

Many a person is capable of knowing *himself* or *herself*.

Agreement in Gender

The pronoun should agree with its antecedent in gender, if the gender of the antecedent is specific. Masculine and feminine pronouns are gender-specific: *he, him, she, her*. Others are neuter: *I, we, me, us, it, they, them, who, whom, that, which*. The words *who* and *whom* refer to people. *That* can refer to ideas, things, and people, but usually does not refer to individuals. *Which* refers to ideas and things, but never to people.

My *girlfriend* gave me *her* best advice. [feminine]

Mighty *Casey* tried *his* best. [masculine]

The *people* with *whom* I work are loud. [neuter]

Indefinite singular pronouns used as antecedents require, of course, singular pronouns. Handling the gender of these singular pronouns is not as obvious; opinion is divided.

1. Traditionally, writers have used the masculine form of pronouns to refer to the indefinite singular pronouns when the gender is unknown.

   Everyone should work until *he* drops.

2. To avoid a perceived sex bias, use *he or she* or *his or her* instead of just *he* or *his*.

   Everyone should work until *he or she* drops.

3. Although option 1 is more direct, it is illogical to many listeners and readers, and option 2 used several times in a short passage can be awkward. To avoid those possible problems, writers often use plural forms.

   All people should work until *they* drop.

In any case, avoid using a plural pronoun with a singular indefinite pronoun; such usage violates the basic principle of number agreement.

Incorrect: *Everyone* should do *their* best.

Correct: *Everyone* should do *his or her* best.

Correct: *People* should do *their* best.

EXERCISE 34   Making Pronouns Agree

Underline the correct pronoun form.

1. When someone does a 'favor for you, (he or she, they) must be thanked.

2. The audience clapped and cheered to communicate (their, its) approval.

3. No one in the maze could find (his or her, their) way out.

4. The corporation has decided to move (its, their) headquarters to Hawaii.

5. Everyone wearing high heels knew that (she, they) had made a bad shoe choice.

6. Ricardo is one of those people who like to do everything (himself, themselves).

7. Lynn's name was on the list of people (that, who) still owed money.

8. The drill sergeant required perfection from everyone and everything (who, that, which) was part of his platoon.

9. Ellen is the only one in the whole class who can laugh at (himself or herself, themselves, herself) after making a mistake.

10. Both of my parents are careful about taking care of (his or her, **their**) health.

11. The team faces (**its**, their) toughest challenge this Friday.

12. Neither of the men wanted to carry (**his**, their) wife's purse while she shopped.

13. Either John or Ralph will win the contest and see (**his**, their) hard work pay off.

14. A parent should read to (you, **his or her**, their) child every day.

15. Either of the mothers will be willing to tell you (**her**, their) story.

16. The writer and the artist have joined forces to produce (his or her, **their**) next book.

17. Neither George nor his brothers have been able to locate (his, **their**) grand-mother's jewelry box.

18. Students must keep up with the reading if (he or she, **they**) want to pass the exam.

19. A babysitter should learn CPR in case (you, **he or she**, they) faces an emergency.

20. We assumed that everyone would take (**his or her**, their) time.

EXERCISE 35 Making Pronouns Agree

Underline the correct pronoun form.

1. I like to ride roller coasters, especially when (**I**, you) flip upside down.

2. He was the only one of the three judges who gave (**his**, their) honest opinion.

3. The music was lively and upbeat; (you, **one**) couldn't help tapping a foot in time with the rhythm.

4. Each of the men sucked in (**his**, their) stomach as the beautiful woman approached.

5. Neither Eric nor his brothers would take responsibility for (his, **their**) actions.

6. Todd is one of those people who like to get (his, **their**) own way all the time.

7. She is the only one of the cast who did not mess up (their, **her**) lines.

8. The members of the audience clapped (its, **their**) hands together.

9. Everybody should be treated as though (they, **he or she**) is a valued customer.

10. Only a few had brought (**their**, his or her) books to class.

11. Everyone likes to get discounts on (their, **his or her**) purchases.

12. To get ahead in life, (you need, one needs) a good education.

13. Too late, I realized that (you, one) should not eat a sloppy joe sandwich and drive at the same time.

14. Each of the rabbits had dug (its, his or her) way out of the pen.

15. She is the only one in her group of friends who is sure about (her, their) career path.

16. A fortune-teller should keep (his or her, their) crystal ball smudge-free and shiny.

17. Either of the tour guides will enlighten you with (his or her, their) vast knowledge.

18. The poet and the peasant declared (their, his) boundless love for her.

19. The committee submitted (their, its) recommendation to the president.

20. Every American must vote in order to do (his or her, their) civic duty.

PRONOUN REFERENCE

A pronoun must refer clearly to its antecedent. Because a pronoun is a substitute word, it can express meaning clearly and definitely only if its antecedent is easily identified.

In some sentence constructions, gender and number make the reference clear.

Kevin and Latisha discussed *his* absences and *her* good attendance. [gender]

If the three older boys in the *club* carry out those plans, *it* will break up. [number]

Avoid ambiguous reference. The following sentences illustrate the kind of confusion that results from structuring sentences with more than one possible antecedent for the pronoun:

Unclear: Tyler gave Walt *his* money and clothes.

Clear: Tyler gave his own money and clothes to Walt.

Unclear: Lynette told her sister that *her* car had a flat tire.

Clear: Lynette said to her sister, "Your car has a flat tire."

When using a pronoun to refer to a general idea, make sure that the reference is clear. The pronouns used frequently in this way are *this, that, which*, and *it*. The best solution may be to recast the sentence to omit the pronoun in question.

Unclear: She whistled the same tune over and over, which irritated me.

Clear: She whistled the same tune over and over, a *habit* that irritated me.

Recast: Her whistling the same tune over and over irritated me.

EXERCISE 36   Correcting Problems in Pronoun Reference

Some of the following sentences contain pronouns that are examples of faulty reference; cross out these pronouns and correct them. If the sentence is correct, write OK in the blank.

_____ 1. Tyrone said he would not be going on the trip, which worried his friends.

_____ 2. Yolanda criticized Monique because she was closed-minded and intolerant.

_____ 3. If that child doesn't get his own way, he has a temper tantrum.

_____ 4. During a recession, you find it harder to get a good job.

_____ 5. Fred told Barney that he may be laid off from his job at the quarry.

_____ 6. To cook sufficiently well, one must know how to read a cookbook.

_____ 7. That is Rachel's husband you met yesterday.

_____ 8. She loved to visit the Bahamas, but she did not want to live there.

_____ 9. In that state, they don't require motorists to wear seatbelts.

_____ 10. Dottie asked her mother if she could wear her high heels to the dance.

_____ 11. Jolene gave her daughter her dinner.

_____ 12. Rita told her boss that she was sorry.

_____ 13. It was one of those days that we'd like to forget.

_____ 14. Robert hinted that he would love a new watch.

_____ 15. Julio was able to get a discount, which pleased him.

_____ 16. Most Americans admit to speeding, eating while driving, and running yellow or even red lights. This is what causes accidents.

_____ 17. My father made a fortune by dealing in real estate. I want that, too.

_____ 18. If a victim catches on fire, you should stop, drop, and roll.

_____ 19. In this brochure, it says that the hotel's pool has a waterslide.

_____ 20. Paul listens to his mother and follows her advice.

EXERCISE 37   Correcting Problems in Pronoun Reference

The following sentences contain pronouns that are examples of faulty reference. Correct the sentences.

1. They treated him like a child and that angered him.

2. Noel talked while he was eating, which annoyed his companions.

3. You could disagree with the idea, but it would not be easy.

4. Marcus handed Jim his keys.

5. Jannis told Jannel that her hair was too long.

6. We installed mud flaps, but some of it still got on the fenders.

7. The instructor told the student that his deadline was tomorrow.

8. This is my sister's house, whom you met yesterday.

9. They say unemployment is causing social problems.

10. Timothy never looked at me when he talked, which made me distrust him.

11. He often interrupted other people, which I found annoying.

12. They regarded him as incompetent, which embarrassed him.

13. You could come to her aid, but would it be appreciated?

14. Franklin told Jeff that his car needed to be repaired."

15. They say that the big bands are coming back.

16. In prison, you have little freedom.

17. This is my uncle's dog, who has a hundred-acre farm.

18. You could build a baseball field, but would it be worth the bother?

19. They say on television that anyone can buy a new car.

20. Hans put his finger into a hole in the dike at the edge of the ocean, but some of it still came in.

Adjectives and Adverbs

Adjectives modify (describe) nouns and pronouns and answer the questions *Which one? What kind?* and *How many?*

> *Which one?* The <u>new</u> <u>car</u> is mine.
>   adj n
>
> *What kind?* <u>Mexican</u> <u>food</u> is my favorite.
>   adj   n
>
> *How many?* A <u>few</u> <u>friends</u> are all one needs.
>   adj   n

Adverbs modify verbs, adjectives, or other adverbs and answer the questions *How? Where? When?* and *To what degree?* Most words ending in *-ly* are adverbs.

> *Where?* The cuckoo <u>flew</u> <u>south</u>.
>   v   adv
>
> *When?* The cuckoo <u>flew</u> <u>yesterday</u>.
>   v   adv
>
> *Why?* The cuckoo <u>flew</u> <u>because of the cold weather</u>.
>   v   adv phrase

How? The cuckoo <u>flew</u> <u>swiftly</u>.
               v   adv

<u>Without adjectives and adverbs</u>, <u>even</u> John Steinbeck, the <u>famous</u>
       adv phrase   adv   adj

<u>Nobel Prize–winning</u> author, <u>surely</u> could <u>not</u> have described the
     adj   adv   adv

<u>crafty</u> octopus <u>very</u> <u>well</u>.
 adj   adv   adv

We have two concerns regarding the use of adjectives and adverbs (modifiers) in writing. One is a matter of diction, or word choice—in this case, selecting adjectives and adverbs that will strengthen the writing. The other is how to identify and correct problems with modifiers.

SELECTING ADJECTIVES AND ADVERBS

If you want to finish the sentence "She was a(n) _____ speaker," you have many adjectives to select from, including these:

distinguished	dependable	effective	sly
influential	impressive	polished	astute
adequate	boring	abrasive	humorous

If you want to finish the sentence "She danced _____," you have another large selection, this time of adverbs such as the following:

bewitchingly	angelically	quaintly	zestfully
gracefully	grotesquely	carnally	smoothly
divinely	picturesquely	serenely	unevenly

Adjectives and adverbs can be used to enhance communication. If you have a thought, you know what it is, but when you deliver that thought to someone else, you may not say or write what you mean. Your thought may be eloquent and your word choice weak. Keep in mind that no two words mean exactly the same thing. Further, some words are vague and general. If you settle for a common word such as *good* or a slang word such as *neat* to characterize something that you like, you will be limiting your communication. Of course, those who know you best may understand fairly well; after all, certain people who are really close may be able to convey ideas using only grunts and gestures.

But what if you want to write to someone you hardly know to explain how you feel about an important issue? In that case, the more precise the word, the better the communication. By using modifiers, you may be able to add significant information. Keep in mind, however, that anything can be overdone; therefore, use adjectives and adverbs wisely and economically.

Your first resource in searching for more effective adjectives should be your own vocabulary storehouse. Another resource is a good thesaurus (book of synonyms), either in print form or on a computer.

Supply the appropriate modifiers in the following exercises, using a dictionary, a thesaurus, or the resources designated by your instructor.

EXERCISE 38 Supplying Adjectives

Provide adjectives to modify these nouns. Use only single words, not adjective phrases.

1. A(n) _____ cat

2. A(n) _____ politician

3. A(n) _____ echo

4. A(n) _____ friend

5. A(n) _____ waiter

6. A(n) _____ conference

7. A(n) _____ goal

8. A(n) _____ street

9. A(n) _____ school

10. A(n) _____ vacation

EXERCISE 39 Supplying Adverbs

Provide adverbs to modify these verbs. Use only single words, not adverb phrases.

1. stare _____

2. flee _____

3. yell _____

4. approach _____

5. taste _____

6. smile _____

7. look _____

8. leave _____

9. cry _____

10. eat _____

COMPARATIVE AND SUPERLATIVE FORMS

For making comparisons, most adjectives and adverbs have three different forms: the positive (one), the comparative (comparing two), and the superlative (comparing three or more).

Adjectives

1. Some adjectives follow a regular pattern:

Positive (one)	Comparative (two)	Superlative (three or more)
nice	nicer	nicest
rich	richer	richest
big	bigger	biggest
tall	taller	tallest
lonely	lonelier	loneliest
terrible	more terrible	most terrible
beautiful	more beautiful	most beautiful

These are the general rules:

a. Add *-er* (or *-r*) to short adjectives (one or two syllables) to rank units of two.

Julian is *nicer* than Sam.

b. Add *-est* (or *-st*) to short adjectives (one or two syllables) to rank units of three or more.

Of the fifty people I know, Julian is the *kindest*.

c. Add the word *more* before long adjectives (three or more syllables) to rank units of two.

My hometown is *more beautiful* than yours.

d. Add the word *most* before long adjectives (three or more syllables) to rank units of three or more.

My hometown is the *most beautiful* in all America.

2. Some adjectives are irregular in the way they change to show comparison:

Positive (one)	Comparative (two)	Superlative (three or more)
good	better	best
bad	worse	worst

Adverbs

1. Some adverbs follow a regular pattern:

Positive (one)	Comparative (two)	Superlative (three or more)
clearly	more clearly	most clearly
quickly	more quickly	most quickly
carefully	more carefully	most carefully
thoughtfully	more thoughtfully	most thoughtfully

a. Add *-er* to some one-syllable adverbs for the comparative form and add *-est* for the superlative form.

My piglet runs *fast*. [positive]

My piglet runs *faster* than your piglet. [comparative]

My piglet runs *fastest* of all known piglets. [superlative]

b. Add the word *more* before longer adverbs for the comparison form and *most* before longer adverbs for the superlative form.

Judy reacted *happily* to the marriage proposal. [positive]

Judy reacted *more happily* to the marriage proposal than Nancy. [comparison]

Of all the women Clem proposed to, Judy reacted *most happily*. [superlative]

c. In some cases, the word *less* may be substituted for *more*, and *least* for *most*.

Mort's views were presented *less effectively* than Craig's. [comparative]

Of all the opinions that were shared, Mort's views were presented *least effectively*. [superlative]

2. Some adverbs are irregular in the way they change to show comparisons:

Positive (one)	Comparative (two)	Superlative (three or more)
well	better	best
far	farther (distance)	farthest (distance)
	further	furthest
badly	worse	worst

USING ADJECTIVES AND ADVERBS CORRECTLY

1. Avoid double negatives. Words such as *no, not, none, nothing, never, hardly, barely,* and *scarcely* should not be combined.

Double Negative: I do *not* have *no* time for recreation. [incorrect]

Single Negative: I have *no* time for recreation. [correct]

Double Negative: I have *hardly never* lied. [incorrect]

Single Negative: I have *hardly* ever lied. [correct]

2. Do not confuse adjectives with adverbs. Among the most commonly confused adjectives and adverbs are *good/well, bad/badly,* and *real/really*. The words *good, bad,* and *real* are always adjectives. *Well* is sometimes an adjective. The words *badly* and *really* are always adverbs. *Well* is usually an adverb.

To distinguish these words, consider what is being modified. Remember that adjectives modify nouns and pronouns and that adverbs modify verbs, adjectives, and other adverbs.

Incorrect: I feel *badly* today. [We're concerned with the condition of *I*.]

Correct: I feel *bad* today. [The adjective *bad* modifies the pronoun *I*.]

Incorrect: She feels *well* about that choice. [We're concerned with the condition of *she*.]

Correct: She feels *good* about that choice. [The adjective *good* modifies the pronoun *she*.]

Incorrect: Lazarro plays the piano *good*. [The adjective *good* modifies the verb *plays*, but adjectives should not modify verbs.]

Correct: Lazarro plays the piano *well*. [The adverb *well* modifies the verb *plays*.]

Incorrect: He did *real* well. [Here the adjective *real* modifies the adverb *well*, but adjectives should not modify adverbs.]

Correct: He did *really* well. [The adverb *really* modifies the adverb *well*.]

3. Do not use an adverb such as *very*, *more*, or *most* before adjectives such as *perfect*, *round*, *unique*, *square*, and *straight*.

Incorrect: It is *more* round.

Correct: It is round.

Correct: It is *more nearly* round.

4. Do not double forms, such as *more lonelier* or *most loneliest*.

Incorrect: Julie was *more nicer* than Jake.

Correct: Julie was *nicer* than Jake.

5. Do not confuse standard and nonstandard forms of adjectives and adverbs.

- **Accidently.** This is a substandard form of *accidentally*.
- **All ready, already.** *All ready* means "completely prepared." *Already* means "previously."

We are *all ready* to give the signal to move out. [prepared]

When he arrived at the station, we had *already* left. [previously]

- **All right, alright.** *All right* (two words) means "correct," "yes," "fine," "certainly." *Alright* is a substandard spelling of "all right."

Yes, I am *all right* now.

- **All together, altogether.** *All together* means "in a group." *Altogether* means "completely," "wholly," "entirely."

The boys were *all together* at the end of the field.

The manuscript is *altogether* too confusing.

Be careful to place such words as *also*, *almost*, *even*, *just*, *hardly*, *merely*, *only*, and *today* in the right position to convey the intended meaning. As these words change position in the sentence, they may also change the meaning of the sentence.

I *only* advised him to act cautiously.
I advised *only* him to act cautiously.
Only I advised him to act cautiously.
I advised him *only* to act cautiously.

EXERCISE 40   Selecting Adjectives and Adverbs

Cross out the mistake in each sentence and write in the correction above it.

1. Ping-Sim thought his teacher had a most unique method of lecturing.

2. Some jobs are done easier by blind people than by those with sight.

3. It was up to the parents to decide if this kind of movie is real bad for children.

4. The adventure of life is too impossible to discuss.

5. Oscar felt badly about rejection slips but worse about his bank account.

6. Victor was not the stronger of the pair, but he was the best boxer.

7. The whole class thought Kyoka's sunglasses the most perfect they had seen.

8. The suspect became violenter as the police drew nearer.

9. Of all the potential winners, the judges agreed that Miss Idaho was more beautiful.

10. The United States has no central educational authority, but overall it does good.

11. An unambiguous word only can mean one thing.

12. It is real easy to forget that "liquor" used to mean "liquid."

13. Hurtful experiences in childhood don't fade out easy.

14. She said he had all ready ruined his reputation by making her buy her own flowers.

15. A trembling voice may indicate that the speaker does not feel alright.

16. Julian had two ways of starting a speech: One way was with a definition, but the easiest way was with a joke.

17. Sherman choked as if the very words tasted badly to him.

18. Natasha made a real good decision.

19. Erika didn't say the food was terrible; only she said it was bad.

20. On controversial topics, he was all together too easily offended.

EXERCISE 41   Selecting Adjectives and Adverbs

Cross out the mistake in each sentence and write in the correction above it.

1. I remember one real good experience.

2. It left me feeling alright.

3. Of the two cars I have owned, the '90 Mazda Miata was best.

4. It was also the beautifulest car I have ever seen.

5. When I drove it, I felt like the most rich person in town.

6. For a year I didn't have no time for anything except polishing my car.

7. I had it painted lightning blue so that it was real handsome.

8. My name for it was the "Bolt," and when people gave me glances as I drove it, I felt well.

9. I hardly never abused that vehicle.

10. When I finally traded it in, I didn't never look back for fear I would cry.

11. All I can say is that it was most perfect.

12. Later I went back to the dealer, but I was all ready too late.

13. The Bolt had been bought by a young man who thought it was the better of all the cars on the lot.

14. He said he couldn't find no better car anywhere.

15. I could see he felt real good.

16. He and his family were standing altogether.

17. It was no time for me to feel badly.

18. In fact, as I said, I felt alright about the transaction.

19. I didn't shed no tears.

20. That experience is a real happy memory for me.

DANGLING AND MISPLACED MODIFIERS

Modifiers should clearly relate to the word or words they modify.

1. A modifier that fails to modify a word or group of words already in the sentence is called a **dangling modifier**.

Dangling:	*Walking down the street*, a snake startled him. [Who was walking down the street? The person isn't mentioned in the sentence.]
Correct:	*Walking down the street*, Don was startled by a snake.
Correct:	*As Don walked down the street*, he was startled by a snake.
Dangling:	*At the age of six*, my uncle died. [Who was six years old? The person isn't mentioned in the sentence.]
Correct:	*When I was six*, my uncle died.

2. A modifier that is placed so that it modifies the wrong word or words is called a **misplaced modifier**. The term also applies to words that are positioned to unnecessarily divide closely related parts of sentences such as infinitives (*to* plus verb) or subjects and verbs.

Misplaced:	The sick man went to a doctor *with a high fever*.
Correct:	The sick man *with a high fever* went to the doctor.
Misplaced:	I saw a great movie *sitting in my pickup*.
Correct:	*Sitting in my pickup*, I saw a great movie.
Misplaced:	Kim found many new graves *walking through the cemetery*.
Correct:	*Walking through the cemetery*, Kim found many new graves.
Misplaced:	I forgot all about my sick dog *kissing my girlfriend*.
Correct:	*Kissing my girlfriend*, I forgot all about my sick dog.
Misplaced:	They tried to *earnestly and sincerely* complete the task. [splitting of the infinitive *to complete*]
Correct:	They tried *earnestly and sincerely* to complete the task.
Misplaced:	My neighbor, *while walking to the store*, was mugged. [unnecessarily dividing the subject and verb]
Correct:	*While walking to the store*, my neighbor was mugged.

Try the following procedure in working through Exercises 42 and 43.

1. Circle the modifier.

2. Draw an arrow from the modifier to the word or words it modifies.

3. If the modifier does not relate directly to anything in the sentence, it is dangling, and you must recast the sentence.

4. If the modifier does not modify the nearest word or words, or if it interrupts related sentence parts, it is misplaced and you need to reposition it.

EXERCISE 42   Correcting Dangling and Misplaced Modifiers

In the blank, write D for dangling modifier, M for misplaced modifier, and OK for correct sentences. Correct the sentences with modifier problems.

_____ 1. Late again, there was no time for breakfast.

_____ 2. Racking up points, the video-game player was close to setting a new record.

_____ 3. Bathed, clipped, and perfumed, she allowed the dog to enter the house again.

_____ 4. We guessed approximately that the jar contained 3,000 jelly beans.

_____ 5. Filling out the form, my pen ran out of ink.

_____ 6. With grim determination, the mountain had been conquered.

_____ 7. Rudely, the interrupting child burst into the room without knocking.

_____ 8. The student made an appointment to see the teacher with a complaint.

_____ 9. By brushing and flossing every day, cavities can be avoided.

_____ 10. Sitting in the back row, the speaker was hard to hear.

_____ 11. He asked her to marry him yesterday.

_____ 12. Right after buying it, the popcorn was spilled all over the floor.

_____ 13. Strolling through the garden, the hot sun beat down.

_____ 14. I only have one objection to your devious plan.

_____ 15. To be healthy, smoking must be given up.

_____ 16. To find the gold, the map was followed by the treasure hunters.

_____ 17. When I was two years old, my mother enrolled me in swimming lessons.

_____ 18. I only signed up for one class.

_____ 19. Bill tried to slowly and persistently worm his way into her heart.

_____ 20. As the mother of six children, her grocery bill is always high.

EXERCISE 43   Correcting Dangling and Misplaced Modifiers

In the blank, write D for dangling modifier, M for misplaced modifier, and OK for correct sentences. Correct the sentences with modifier problems.

_____ 1. When I was in the third grade, my family moved to Texas.

_____ 2. When ten years old, my father won the lottery.

_____ 3. During the summer, I worked at the mall.

_____ 4. Raynelle went after the game was over, to the banquet.

_____ 5. Traveling over the mountain road, the inn was reached.

_____ 6. To be a successful runner, one needs strength and stamina.

_____ 7. Driving through the forest, many deer were seen from our car.

_____ 8. After studying it for many weeks, the plan was discontinued.

_____ 9. Searching the computer screen, we found the answer.

_____ 10. After driving the car for ten years, it was sold.

_____ 11. After three hours of walking, they rested.

_____ 12. The ring sparkled on her hand, which she had bought in Italy.

_____ 13. Climbing the mountain, we stopped to admire the view.

_____ 14. Ms. Prank wanted to buy a car for her husband with a large trunk.

_____ 15. He found a wallet in the park that didn't belong to him.

_____ 16. Standing on top of the hill, we could see Catalina Island.

_____ 17. Ginny took, to miss the construction, a detour.

_____ 18. To play basketball well, good coordination is needed.

_____ 19. After playing all the game, the coach knew that Jean was tired.

_____ 20. It is desirable to usually avoid splitting an infinitive.

Balancing Sentence Parts

We are surrounded by balance. Watch a colorful cross-frame, or diamond, kite as it soars in the sky. If you draw an imaginary line from the top to the bottom of the kite, you will see corresponding parts on either side. If you were to replace one of the sides with a loose-fitting fabric, the kite would never fly. A similar lack of balance can also cause a sentence to crash.

Consider these statements:

> "_To be or not to be_—that is the question." [dash added]

This line from *Hamlet*, by William Shakespeare, is one of the most famous lines in literature. Compare it to the well-balanced kite in a strong wind. Its parts are parallel and it "flies" well.

> *"To be or not being—that is the question."*

It still vaguely resembles the sleek kite, but now the second phrase causes it to dip like an unbalanced kite. Lurching, the line begins to lose altitude.

> *"To be or death is the other alternative—that is the question."*

The line slams to the floor. Words scatter across the carpet. We return to the revision board.

The first sentence is forceful and easy to read. The second is more difficult to follow. The third is almost impossible to understand. We understand it only because we know what it should look like from having read the original. The point is that perceptive readers are as critical of sentences as kite-watchers are of kites.

BASIC PRINCIPLES OF PARALLELISM

Parallelism as it relates to sentence structure is usually achieved by joining words with similar words: nouns with nouns, adjectives (words that describe nouns and pronouns) with adjectives, adverbs (words that describe verbs, adjectives, and other adverbs) with adverbs, and so forth.

> *Men, women*, and *children* enjoy the show. [nouns]

> The players are *excited*, *eager*, and *enthusiastic*. [adjectives]

> The author wrote *skillfully* and *quickly*. [adverbs]

You can create parallel structure by joining groups of words with similar groups of words: prepositional phrase with prepositional phrase, clause with clause, sentence with sentence.

> She fell *in love* and *out of love* in a few minutes. [prepositional phrases]

> *Who he was* and *where he came from* did not matter. [clauses]

> *He came in a hurry. He left in a hurry.* [sentences]

Parallelism means balancing one structure with another of the same kind. Faulty parallel structure is awkward and draws unfavorable attention to what is being said.

Nonparallel: Gary Payton's reputation is based on his ability in *passing, shooting*, and *he is good at rebounds*.

Parallel: Gary Payton's reputation is based on his ability in *passing, shooting*, and *rebounding*.

In the nonparallel sentence, the words *passing* and *shooting* are of the same kind (verblike words used as nouns), but the rest of the sentence is different. You do not have to know terms to realize that there is a problem in smoothness and emphasis. Just read the material aloud. Then compare it with the parallel statement; *he is good at rebounds* is changed to *rebounding* to make a sentence that's easy on the eye and ear.

SIGNAL WORDS

Some words signal parallel structure. If you use *and*, the items joined by *and* should almost always be parallel. If they are not, then *and* is probably inappropriate.

> The weather is hot *and* humid. [*and* joins adjectives]

> The car *and* the trailer are parked in front of the house. [*and* joins nouns]

The same principle is true for *but*, although it implies a direct contrast. Where contrasts are being drawn, parallel structure is essential to clarify those contrasts.

> He *purchased a Dodger Dog, but* I *chose the Stadium Peanuts*. [*but* joins contrasting clauses]

> She *earned* an A in math *but failed* her art class. [*but* joins contrasting verbs]

You should regard all the coordinating conjunctions (FANBOYS: *for*, *and*, *nor*, *but*, *or*, *yet*, *so*) as signals for parallel structure.

COMBINATION SIGNAL WORDS

The words *and* and *but* are the most common individual signal words used with parallel constructions. Sometimes, however, **combination words** signal the need for parallelism or balance. The most common ones are *either/or*, *neither/nor*, *not only/but also*, *both/and*, and *whether/or*. Now consider this faulty sentence and two possible corrections:

> **Nonparallel:** *Either we will* win this game, *or let's* go out fighting.

> **Parallel:** *Either we will* win this game, *or we will* go out fighting.

The correction is made by changing *let's* to *we will* to parallel the *we will* in the first part of the sentence. The same construction should follow the *either* and the *or*.

> **Nonparallel:** Flour is used *not only* to bake cakes *but also* in paste.

> **Parallel:** Flour is used *not only to bake* cakes *but also to make* paste.

The correction is made by changing *in* (a preposition) to *make* (an infinitive). Now an infinitive follows both *not only* and *but also*.

EXERCISE 44 Correcting Faulty Parallelism

Mark each sentence as P for parallel or NP for nonparallel. Correct the sentences with nonparallel structure.

_____ 1. Jacques Cousteau was an adventurer, explorer, and educated people.

_____ 2. He will be remembered not only as a pioneer but also he was an environmentalist of great influence.

and between the adjectives. If it fits naturally, the adjectives are coordinate; if it does not, they are not, and you do not need a comma.

> She is a kind, beautiful person.

> kind and beautiful [natural, hence the comma]

> I built a red brick wall.

> red *and* brick wall [not natural, no comma]

7. Use a comma to separate sentence elements that might be misread.

> Inside the dog scratched his fleas.

> *Inside*, the dog scratched his fleas.

Without benefit of the comma, the reader might initially misunderstand the relationship among the first three words.

Commas to Set Off

1. Use commas to set off (enclose) adjectives in pairs that follow a noun.

> The scouts, *tired and hungry*, marched back to camp.

2. Use commas to set off nonessential (unnecessary for meaning of the sentence) words, phrases, and clauses.

> My brother, *a student at Ohio State University*, is visiting me. [If you drop the phrase, the basic meaning of the sentence remains intact.]

> Marla, *who studied hard*, will pass. [The clause is not essential to the basic meaning of the sentence.]

> All students *who studied hard* will pass. [Here the clause *is* essential. If you remove it, you would have *All students will pass*, which is not necessarily true.]

> I shall not stop searching *until I find the treasure*. [A dependent clause at the end of a sentence is usually not set off with a comma. However, a clause beginning with the word *though* or *although* will be set off regardless of where it is located.]

> I felt unsatisfied, *though we had won the game*.

3. Use commas to set off parenthetical elements such as mild interjections (*oh*, *well*, *yes*, *no*, and others), most conjunctive adverbs (*however*, *otherwise*, *therefore*, *similarly*, *hence*, *on the other hand*, and *consequently* but not *then*, *thus*, *soon*, *now*, and *also*), quotation indicators, and special abbreviations (*etc.*, *i.e.*, *e.g.*, and others).

> *Oh*, what a silly question! [mild interjection]

> It is necessary, *of course*, to leave now. [sentence modifier]

> We left early; *however*, we missed the train anyway. [conjunctive adverb]

TOP 25 EDITING ERRORS

"When I was in school," *he said*, "I read widely." [quotation indicators]

Books, papers, pens, *etc.*, were scattered on the floor. [The abbreviation *etc.* should be used sparingly, however.]

4. Use commas to set off nouns used as direct address.

Play it again, *Sam*.

Please tell us the answer, *Jane*, so we can discuss it.

5. Use commas to separate the numbers in a date.

June 4, *1965*, is a day I will remember.

6. Do not use commas if the day of the month is not specified, or if the day is given before the month.

June 1965 was my favorite time.

One day I will never forget is 4 June 1965.

7. Use commas to separate the city from the state. No comma is used between the state and the ZIP code.

Walnut, CA 91789

8. Use a comma after both the city and the state when they are used together in a sentence.

Our family visited Anchorage, *Alaska*, last summer.

9. Use a comma following the salutation of a friendly letter and the complimentary closing in any letter.

Dear John,

Sincerely,

10. Use a comma in numbers to set off groups of three digits. However, omit the comma in dates, serial numbers, page numbers, years, and street numbers.

The total assets were *$2,000,000*.

I look forward to the year *2050*.

EXERCISE 46   Using Commas

Insert all necessary commas in the following sentences.

1. Commas are used to separate words phrases and clauses in a series.

2. A strong assertive comma separates coordinate adjectives.

3. After long introductory modifiers a comma is used.

4. A comma is used between independent clauses and a period is usually found at the end of a sentence.

5. After all the meaning of the sentence is often clarified by a comma.

6. Inside the car smelled new and clean.

7. In the beginning of the game there was nothing but noise and chaos.

8. The crazy-looking car was painted pink black green and lavender.

9. Cherise worked at her desk all night but the job was not finished in time.

10. The sharp burning rays of the sun would soon be hidden by the trees.

11. Having finished the banquet the diners moved to the living room.

12. Bach and Handel both born in 1685 were the two greatest baroque composers.

13. Motor racing not horse racing is the more popular sport.

14. "When I was a boy" Arturo said "one dollar a week was enough!"

15. Dwight Jones the salesperson will take your order now.

16. Well that's the way it's going to be!

17. The new car all sleek and shiny was nowhere to be found.

18. He arrived in Tribbey Oklahoma on February 21 1934.

19. The old boxer was only down not out.

20. The Eiffel Tower which is located in Paris is no longer the highest tower in the world.

EXERCISE 47   Using Commas

Insert all necessary commas in the following sentences.

1. Before most people were superstitious.

2. People now know that superstitions are silly but many of these beliefs are still alive and well.

3. I know you believe dear friend that blowing out all the candles on your birthday cake will make your wish come true.

4. Do you knock on wood say "bless you" when someone sneezes and avoid opening your umbrella indoors?

5. When you knock on wood you're calling upon the good spirits that live in trees to protect you.

6. Pope Gregory passed a law requiring people of the sixth century to bless a sneezer who had probably contracted the deadly plague.

7. If you break a mirror you face seven years of bad luck.

8. The bird which had flown into the house was an omen of death.

9. Brides must wear something old something new something borrowed and something blue.

10. It is however bad luck for the groom to see his bride before the wedding.

11. "Don't step on a crack or you'll break your mother's back."

12. You've heard I'm sure that pulling out a gray hair causes ten more to grow back.

13. The young guy well schooled in superstition waited beneath the mistletoe for the object of his affection to happen by.

14. If you take a test with the same pencil you used when you studied the pencil will remember the answers.

15. He carried at all times a rabbit's foot a four-leaf clover and a horseshoe.

16. Throw a coin into the fountain and make a wish.

17. Edmund Burke said "Superstition is the religion of feeble minds."

18. But Johann Wolfgang von Goethe a German novelist said that "superstition is the poetry of life."

19. The wishbone clean and dry was ready to be pulled in two.

20. Don't harm a cricket or a ladybug for they both bring good luck.

SEMICOLONS

The **semicolon** indicates a stronger division than the comma. It is used principally to separate independent clauses within a sentence.

1. Use a semicolon to separate independent clauses not joined by a coordinating conjunction.

   You must buy that car today; tomorrow will be too late.

2. Use a semicolon between two independent clauses joined by a conjunctive adverb such as one of the HOTSHOT CAT words (*however, otherwise, therefore, similarly, hence, on the other hand, then, consequently, accordingly, thus*).

   It was very late; therefore, I remained at the hotel.

3. Use a semicolon to separate main clauses joined by a coordinating conjunction if one or both of the clauses contain distracting commas.

   Byron, the famous English poet, was buried in Greece; and Shelley, who was his friend and fellow poet, was interred in Italy.

4. Use a semicolon in a series between items that themselves contain commas.

   He has lived in Covina, California; Reno, Nevada; Prague, Oklahoma; and Bangor, Maine.

EXERCISE 48   Using Commas and Semicolons

Each sentence needs one or more semicolons or commas. Insert the appropriate marks.

1. Each year many species of birds fly south for the winter for example ducks and geese migrate to warmer areas to find more abundant food.

2. Most insects cannot fly the distances that these birds can fly instead they time their development so that they are in eggs or cocoons during the winter.

3. There is one exception however the Monarch butterfly is different from other insects.

4. Birds avoid lethal cold by getting away from it the Monarch butterfly does the same thing.

5. The long, hot days begin to grow shorter the temperatures grow colder and the beautiful, black and orange Monarch butterflies know that it's time to make their amazing journey.

6. These butterflies have tiny insect brains however, those brains somehow guide them over thousands of miles they've never seen before.

7. On their way to central Mexico, eastern Monarch butterflies stop in places like San Angelo, Texas Bracketville, Texas and Eagle Pass, Texas.

8. Thousands of them travel together in the same "flyways" to see all of them flying together at once is truly awesome.

9. They don't mind crowds as a matter of fact a 10-acre colony can contain five to six million butterflies per acre.

10. Biologists estimate that 15,000 to 20,000 butterflies perch on a single tree bough as a result the trees appear to be covered with bright autumn leaves.

11. They arrive in their winter home in November and they remain until March of the next year.

12. The Monarch butterfly breeds four or five times per year in a cycle each generation migrates either north or south.

13. The generation of butterflies that migrates to Mexico returns to the Gulf Coast states of the South and this generation lays eggs on milkweed plants.

14. The next generation lives only four to six weeks its mission is to get to the northern states and southern Canada.

15. Milkweed is plentiful at north latitudes so the butterflies spend their summer there eating and increasing their numbers.

16. Milkweed is the only thing these butterflies eat and this plant has one additional benefit.

17. Milkweed contains toxins therefore the butterflies become poisonous to predators when they ingest these toxins.

18. These butterflies need no camouflage for their bright colors signal poison to animals looking for a snack.

19. The generation that makes the journey to Mexico is rewarded for its hard work with a longer life those butterflies live eight months instead of two.

20. The Monarch butterfly is a fascinating creature and its travels are one of the world's biological wonders.

EXERCISE 49   Using Commas and Semicolons

Each sentence needs one or more semicolons or commas. Insert the appropriate marks.

1. The oldest science is the study of the stars and planets even ancient peoples looked up at the night sky with wonder and awe.

2. Early scientists plotted the positions and changing brightness of the stars and people worshipped the Sun and the Moon as gods.

3. Modern scientific discoveries have led to new knowledge about our solar system but astronomers continue to gather more information every day.

4. We've learned that our Sun is a star it radiates heat and light because of nuclear reactions inside its core.

5. The mass of the universe including our bodies is made up of elements from stars that exploded billions of years ago therefore humans are the stuff of stars.

6. A galaxy is a huge collection of stars bound together by gravity our Sun and its satellites are part of the spiral-shaped Milky Way Galaxy.

7. The universe is unbelievably vast astronomers estimate that there are at least one *billion* different galaxies close enough to photograph.

8. Our own solar system is so big that it could take up to twelve years to journey from Earth to the outermost planet yet it occupies only a tiny area of this vast universe.

9. There are two types of planets Earth and the three planets like it (Mercury Venus and Mars) are known as the terrestrial planets.

10. The other group consists of the planets that resemble Jupiter these Jovian planets include Jupiter Saturn Uranus and Neptune.

11. Pluto a dwarf planet does not resemble either Earth or Jupiter so some astronomers suggest that it be classified as an asteroid rather than a planet.

12. The farthest planet from the Sun is Pluto it orbits the Sun only once every 248 years.

13. Pluto is the only planet that has not been visited by a probe from Earth but scientists hope to launch one in the near future.

14. Venus is the closest planet to Earth as a result it is the brightest object in our nighttime sky.

15. Jupiter is the largest planet of our solar system also it has sixteen moons more than any other planet.

16. One of Jupiter's moons Europa may have an ocean of liquid water if it does it could contain life.

17. Saturn is distinctive because of its rings they are believed to be composed of ice and rocks.

18. Many scientists believe that Mars may have once supported life for a Martian asteroid contains what looks like fossils of tiny organisms.

19. Neptune and Uranus are twins both have rings like Saturn and a similar composition.

20. Mercury is closest to the Sun thus its average surface temperature is 350 degrees Fahrenheit during the day.

QUOTATION MARKS

Quotation marks are used principally to set off direct quotations. A direct quotation consists of material taken from the written work or the direct speech of others; it is set off by double quotation marks. Single quotation marks are used to set off a quotation within a quotation.

> **Double Quotation Marks:**   He said, "I don't remember."
>
> **Single Quotation Marks:**   He said, "I don't remember if she said, 'Wait for me.'"

1. Use double quotation marks to set off direct quotations.

   Erin said, "Give me the book."

   As Edward McNeil writes of the Greek achievement: "To an extent never before realized, mind was supreme over faith."

2. Use double quotation marks to set off titles of shorter pieces of writing such as magazine articles, essays, short stories, short poems, one-act plays, chapters in books, songs, and separate pieces of writing published as part of a larger work.

   The book *Literature: Structure, Sound, and Sense* contains a deeply moving poem titled "On Wenlock Edge."

   Have you read "The Use of Force," a short story by William Carlos Williams?

   My favorite Elvis song is "Don't Be Cruel."

3. Use double quotation marks to set off slang, technical terms, and special words.

> There are many aristocrats, but Elvis is the only true "King." [special word]

> The "platoon system" changed the game of football. [technical term]

4. Use double quotation marks in writing dialogue (conversation). Write each speech unit as a separate paragraph and set it off with double quotation marks.

> "Will you go with me?" he asked.

> "Yes," she replied. "Are you ready now?"

5. Use single quotation marks to set off a quotation within a quotation.

> Professor Baxter said, "You should remember Shakespeare's words, 'Nothing will come of nothing.'"

6. Do *not* use quotation marks for indirect quotations.

> **Incorrect:**   He said that "he would bring the supplies."

> **Correct:**   He said that he would bring the supplies.

7. Do *not* use quotation marks for the title on your own written work. If you refer to that title in another piece of writing, however, you need the quotation marks.

PUNCTUATION WITH QUOTATION MARKS

1. A period or comma is always placed *inside* the quotation marks.

> Our assignment for Monday was to read Poe's poem "The Raven."

> "I will read you the story," he said. "It is a good one."

2. A semicolon or colon is always placed *outside* the quotation marks.

> He read Robert Frost's poem "Design"; then he gave the examination.

> He quoted Frost's "Stopping by Woods on a Snowy Evening": "But I have promises to keep."

3. A question mark, an exclamation point, or a dash is placed *outside* the quotation marks when it applies to the entire sentence and *inside* the quotation marks when it applies to the material in quotation marks.

> He asked, "Am I responsible for everything?" [quoted question within a statement]

> Did you hear him say, "I have the answer"? [statement within a question]

> Did she say, "Are you ready?" [question within a question]

> She shouted, "Impossible!" [exclamation]

Roy screamed, "I'll flunk if I don't read Poe's short story 'The Black Cat'!" [exclamation belongs to the material inside the quotation marks]

"I hope—that is, I—" he began. [dash]

"Accept responsibility"—those were his words. [dash that does not belong to the material inside the quotation marks]

4. A single question mark is used in sentence constructions that contain a double question—that is, a quoted question following a question.

Mr. Martin said, "Did he say, 'Are you going?'"

ITALICS

Italics (slanting type) is used to call special attention to certain words or groups of words. In handwriting, such words are <u>underlined</u>; however, computers provide italics.

1. Italicize (underline) foreign words and phrases that are still listed in the dictionary as foreign.

c'est *la vie*

*nic*ht wahr

2. Italicize (underline) titles of books (except the Bible); long poems; plays; magazines; motion pictures; musical compositions; newspapers; works of art; names of aircraft and ships; and letters, figures, and words.

I think Hemingway's best novel is *A Farewell to Arms*.

His source material was taken from *Time*, *Newsweek*, and the Los Angeles *Times*. [Sometimes the name of the city in titles of newspapers is italicized—for example, the *New York Times*.]

The Mon*a Lisa* is my favorite painting.

3. Italicize (underline) the names of ships, airplanes, spacecraft, and trains.

Ships: *Queen Mary   Lurline   Stockholm*

Spacecraft: *Challenger   Voyager 2*

4. Italicize (underline) to distinguish letters, figures, and words when they refer to themselves rather than to the ideas or things they usually represent.

Do not leave the o out of *sophomore*.

Your 3's look like 5's.

DASHES

The dash is used when a stronger break than the comma is needed. The dash may be typed as two hyphens with no space before or after them (- -).

1. Use a dash to indicate a sudden change in sentence construction or an abrupt break in thought.

Here is the true reason—but maybe you don't care.

2. Use a dash after an introductory list. The words *these*, *those*, *all*, and occasionally *such* introduce the summarizing statement.

> English, French, history—these are the subjects I like.

COLONS

The colon is a formal mark of punctuation used chiefly to introduce something that is to follow, such as a list, a quotation, or an explanation.

1. Use a colon after a main clause to introduce a formal list, an emphatic or long restatement (appositive), an explanation, an emphatic statement, or a summary.

> The following cars were in the General Motors show: Cadillac, Chevrolet, Buick, Oldsmobile, and Pontiac. [list]
>
> He worked toward one objective: a degree. [restatement or appositive]
>
> Let me emphasize one point: I do not accept late papers. [emphatic statement]

2. Use a colon to introduce a formal quotation or a formal question.

> Shakespeare's Polonius said: "Neither a borrower nor a lender be." [formal quotation]
>
> The question is this: Shall we surrender? [formal question]

3. Use a colon in the following conventional ways: to separate a title and subtitle, a chapter and verse in the Bible, and hours and minutes; after the salutation in a formal business letter; and between the act and the scene of a play.

> Title and subtitle: *Korea: A Country Divided*
> Chapter and verse: Genesis 4:12
> Hour and minutes: 8:25 p.m.
> Salutation: Dear Ms. Johnson:
> Act and scene: *Hamlet* III:ii

PARENTHESES

Parentheses are used to set off material that is of relatively little importance to the main thought of the sentence. Such material—numbers, supplementary material, and sometimes explanatory details—merely amplifies the main thought.

1. Use parentheses to set off material that is not part of the main sentence but is too relevant to omit altogether. This category includes numbers that designate items in a series, amplifying references, explanations, directions, and qualifications.

> Jay offered two reasons for his losing: (1) he was tired, and (2) he was out of condition. [numbers]

Review the chapters on the Civil War (6, 7, and 8) for the next class meeting. [references]

Her husband (she had been married about a year) died last week. [explanation]

2. Use a comma, semicolon, or colon after the parentheses when the sentence punctuation requires their use.

Although I have not lived here long (I arrived in 2014), this place feels like my only true home.

3. Use the period, question mark, and exclamation point in appropriate positions depending on whether they go with the material within the parentheses or with the entire sentence.

The greatest English poet of the seventeenth century was John Milton (1608–1674).

The greatest English poet of the seventeenth century was John Milton. (Some might not agree; I myself favor Andrew Marvell.)

BRACKETS

Brackets are used within a quotation to set off editorial additions or corrections made by the person who is quoting.

Churchill said: "It [the Yalta Agreement] contained many mistakes."

APOSTROPHES

The **apostrophe** is used with nouns and indefinite pronouns to show possession; to show the omission of letters and figures in contractions; and to form the plurals of letters, figures, and words referred to as words.

1. A possessive shows that something is owned by someone. Use an apostrophe and s to form the possessive of a noun, singular or plural, that does not end in s.

man's coat   women's suits

2. Use an apostrophe alone to form the possessive of a plural noun ending in s.

girls' clothes   the Browns' house

3. Use an apostrophe and s or the apostrophe alone to form the possessive of singular nouns ending in s. Use the apostrophe and s only when you would pronounce the s.

James' hat *or* (if you would pronounce the s) James's hat

4. Use an apostrophe and s to form the possessive of certain indefinite pronouns.

everybody's idea   one's meat   another's poison

5. Use an apostrophe to indicate that letters or figures have been omitted.

o'clock (short for *of the clock*) in the '90s (short for *1990s*)

6. Use an apostrophe with pronouns only when you are making a contraction. A contraction is a combination of two words. The apostrophe in a contraction indicates where a letter (or letters) has been omitted.

it is	=	it's
she has	=	she's
you are	=	you're

If no letters have been left out, do not use an apostrophe.

Incorrect: The dog bit it's tail.

Correct: The dog bit its tail. [not a contraction]

Incorrect: Whose the leader now?

Correct: Who's the leader now? [a contraction of *who is*]

Incorrect: Its a big problem.

Correct: It's a big problem. [a contraction of *it is*]

7. Use an apostrophe to indicate the plural of letters, figures, and words used as words.

Dot your *i*'s.   five *8*'s   *and*'s

Note that the letters, figures, and words are italicized, but the apostrophe and *s* are not.

HYPHENS

The **hyphen** brings two or more words together into a single compound word. Correct hyphenation, therefore, is essentially a spelling problem rather than one of punctuation. Because the hyphen is not used with any degree of consistency, consult your dictionary for current usage. Study the following as a beginning guide:

1. Use a hyphen to separate the parts of many compound words.

brother-in-law   go-between

2. Use a hyphen between prefixes and proper names.

all-American   mid-Atlantic

3. Use a hyphen to join two or more words used as a single adjective modifier before a noun.

bluish-gray eyes   first-class service

4. Use a hyphen with spelled-out compound numbers up to ninety-nine and with fractions.

twenty-six   two-thirds

Note: Dates, street addresses, numbers requiring more than two words, chapter and page numbers, time followed directly by a.m. or p.m., and figures after a dollar sign or before measurement abbreviations are usually written as figures, not words.

CAPITALIZATION

Following are some of the many conventions concerning the use of capital letters in English.

1. Capitalize the first word of a sentence.

2. Capitalize proper nouns and adjectives derived from proper nouns.

Names of persons
Edward Jones

Adjectives derived from proper nouns
a Shakespearean sonnet   a Miltonic sonnet

Countries, nationalities, races, languages
Germany   English   Spanish   Chinese

States, regions, localities, other geographical divisions
California   the Far East   the South (but not directions, as in *I am going west.*)

Oceans, lakes, mountains, deserts, streets, parks
Lake Superior   Sahara Desert   Fifth Avenue

Educational institutions, schools, courses
Santa Ana College   Joe Hill School   Rowland High School   Spanish 3

Organizations and their members
Boston Red Sox   Audubon Society   Boy Scouts

Corporations, governmental agencies or departments, trade names
U.S. Steel Corporation   Treasury Department
Coca-Cola   White Memorial Library

Calendar references such as holidays, days of the week, months
Easter   Tuesday   January

Historic eras, periods, documents, laws
Romantic Age   First Crusade
Declaration of Independence   Geneva Convention

3. Capitalize words denoting family relationships when they are used before a name or substituted for a name.

He walked with his nephew and Aunt Grace.

but

TOP 25 EDITING ERRORS

He walked with his nephew and his aunt.

Grandmother and Mother are away on vacation.

but

My grandmother and my mother are away on vacation.

4. Capitalize abbreviations after names.

    Henry White Jr.   Juan Gomez, M.D.

5. Capitalize titles of essays, books, plays, movies, poems, magazines, newspapers, musical compositions, songs, and works of art. Do not capitalize prepositions or short conjunctions unless they come at the beginning or the end of the title.

Desire under the Elms	*Terminator*
The Last of the Mohicans	*Of Mice and Men*
"Blueberry Hill"	

6. Capitalize any title preceding a name or used as a substitute for a name. Do not capitalize a title following a name.

Judge Wong	Alfred Wong, a judge
General Clark	Raymond Clark, a general
Professor Fuentes	Harry Fuentes, the biology professor

EXERCISE 50   Using Punctuation and Capitalization

One punctuation mark, a capital letter, or italic type is omitted in each of the following sentences. Insert them as needed. Pairs of quotation marks, parentheses, or dashes are considered one unit.

1. The Odyssey is a famous epic poem of Greek mythology.

2. The professor said, The poem tells of the wanderings and sufferings of Odysseus, who is also known as Ulysses.

3. This poem is a great classic of literature; its famous for its beautiful poetry as well as its exciting tales of adventure.

4. The author was Homer, who wrote this poem and the equally well-known Iliad in the ninth century BCE.

5. The story begins at the end of the Trojan war as Odysseus and his band of Greeks prepare to sail back to their home in Ithaca.

6. It would take Odysseus if you can believe it ten years to get back.

7. He and his companions encounter many obstacles people, creatures, and gods who seek to kill them.

8. A one-eyed giant called the Cyclops eats several of Odysseus men and imprisons the rest in his cave.

9. Odysseus blinds the giant, and his men must sneak out of the cave by tying themselves under the bellies of the Cyclops sheep.

10. The sea-god Poseidon the Cyclops' father tries to sink the Greek ships in a storm.

11. Many of Odysseus' sailors are eaten by cannibals called lestrigonians.

12. For a year, Odysseus and his men remain captives of the beautiful sorceress circe on her enchanted island.

13. Circe turns Odysseus' twenty two companions into pigs but finally lets them go.

14. The Sirens half women and half birds enticed sailors to their doom with their sweet songs.

15. Odysseus evades their charms by putting wax in his men s ears and lashing himself to the mast of the ship, where he can enjoy the songs but resist temptation.

16. Next, he manages to get past two more monsters Scylla and Charybdis.

17. Scylla is a six headed female monster, with six mouths containing three rows of sharp teeth.

18. Did you know that Charybdis caused a dangerous whirlpool.

19. This is a great story! exclaimed the students.

20. It's amazing that a poem so old can be so action packed.

EXERCISE 51   Using Punctuation and Capitalization

Twenty punctuation marks are needed in the following paragraph; the locations are indicated by the numbers. Pairs such as quotation marks and parentheses are considered one unit. Insert the marks as needed.

Shakespeares age was like ours it was full of change and turmoil" the old gentleman said. New ideas were not confined exclusively to one social class one religion or one political party. Outer space stirred the imaginations of most of the people not just the astronomers. They went to see Hamlet for fun and they bought all the books available on the strange customs of other cultures. And whos to say that when Hamlets father says I am thy fathers spirit he is any less visible than the ghosts some people say they see today. There wasnt much Shakespeare didnt know about us. Thats why we still quarrel about the meaning of his plays we are still discovering the truth about ourselves in them.

Spelling

SPELLING TIPS

The following tips will help you become a better speller.

1. Do not omit letters.

Many errors occur because certain letters are omitted when the word is pronounced or spelled. Observe the omissions in the following words. Then concentrate on learning the correct spellings.

Incorrect	Correct	Incorrect	Correct
aquaintance	acquaintance	irigation	irrigation
ajourned	adjourned	libary	library
agravate	aggravate	paralell	parallel
aproved	approved	parlament	parliament
artic	arctic	paticulaly	particularly
comodity	commodity	readly	readily
efficent	efficient	sophmore	sophomore
envirnment	environment	stricly	strictly
familar	familiar	unconsious	unconscious

2. Do not add letters.

Incorrect	Correct	Incorrect	Correct
athelete	athlete	ommission	omission
comming	coming	pasttime	pastime
drownded	drowned	priviledge	privilege
folkes	folks	similiar	similar
occassionally	occasionally	tradgedy	tragedy

3. Do not substitute incorrect letters for correct letters.

Incorrect	Correct	Incorrect	Correct
benefisial	beneficial	offence	offense
bullitins	bulletins	peculier	peculiar
sensus	census	resitation	recitation
discription	description	screach	screech
desease	disease	substansial	substantial
dissention	dissension	surprize	surprise
itims	items	technacal	technical

4. **Do not transpose letters.**

Incorrect	Correct	Incorrect	Correct
alu*nm*i	alu*mn*i	p*reh*aps	p*erh*aps
child*er*n	child*re*n	p*erf*er	p*ref*er
dup*il*cate	dup*li*cate	p*ers*cription	p*res*cription
irreve*la*nt	irre*lev*ant	princip*els*	princip*les*
kind*el*	kind*le*	y*ei*ld	y*ie*ld

Note: Whenever you notice other words that fall into any one of these categories, add them to the list.

5. **Apply the spelling rules for spelling ei and ie words correctly.**
   Remember this poem?

> Use *i* before *e*
> Except after *c*
> Or when sounded like *a*
> As in *neighbor* and *weigh*.

i **before** *e*

achieve	chief	niece	relieve
belief	field	piece	shield
believe	grief	pierce	siege
brief	hygiene	relief	variety

Except after **c**

ceiling	conceive	deceive	receipt
conceit	deceit	perceive	receive

Exceptions: either, financier, height, leisure, neither, seize, species, weird

When sounded like **a**

deign	freight	neighbor	sleigh
eight	heinous	rein	veil
feign	heir	reign	vein
feint	neigh	skein	weigh

6. **Apply the rules for dropping the final *e* or retaining the final *e* when a suffix is added.**
   Words ending in a silent *e* usually drop the *e* before a suffix beginning with a vowel; for example, *accuse* + *-ing* = *accusing*. Here are some common suffixes beginning with a vowel: *-able, -age, -al, -ary, -ation, -ence, -ing, -ion, -ous, -ure*.

admire + *-able* = admirable	imagine + *-ary* = imaginary
arrive + *-al* = arrival	locate + *-ion* = location
come + *-ing* = coming	please + *-ure* = pleasure
explore + *-ation* = exploration	plume + *-age* = plumage
fame + *-ous* = famous	precede + *-ence* = precedence

Exceptions: *dye* + *-ing* = *dyeing* (to distinguish it from *dying*), *acreage, mileage*.

Words ending in a silent *e* usually retain the *e* before a suffix beginning with a consonant; for example: *arrange* + *-ment* = *arrangement*. Here are some common suffixes beginning with a consonant: *-craft, -ful, -less, -ly, -mate, -ment, -ness, -ty*.

entire + *-ty* = entirety	manage + *-ment* = management
hate + *-ful* = hateful	safe + *-ly* = safely
hope + *-less* = hopeless	stale + *-mate* = stalemate
like + *-ness* = likeness	state + *-craft* = statecraft

Exceptions: Some words taking the *-ful* or *-ly* suffixes drop the final **e**:

awe + *-ful* = awful	true + *-ly* = truly
due + *-ly* = duly	whole + *-ly* = wholly

Some words taking the suffix *-ment* drop the final *e*; for example:

acknowledgment   argument   judgment

Words ending in silent *e* after *c* or *g* retain the *e* when the suffix begins with the vowel *a* or *o*. The final *e* is retained to keep the *c* or *g* soft before the suffixes.

advantageous	noticeable
courageous	peaceable

7. **Apply the rules for doubling a final consonant before a suffix beginning with a vowel.**

Words of one syllable:

blot	blotted	get	getting	rob	robbed
brag	bragging	hop	hopped	run	running
cut	cutting	hot	hottest	sit	sitting
drag	dragged	man	mannish	stop	stopped
drop	dropped	plan	planned	swim	swimming

Words accented on the last syllable:

acquit	acquitted	equip	equipped
admit	admittance	occur	occurrence
allot	allotted	omit	omitting
begin	beginning	prefer	preferred
commit	committee	refer	referred
concur	concurring	submit	submitted
confer	conferring	transfer	transferred
defer	deferring		

Words that are not accented on the last syllable and words that do not end in a single consonant preceded by a vowel do not double the final consonant (regardless of whether the suffix begins with a vowel).

FREQUENTLY MISSPELLED WORDS

a lot	eliminate	meant	sense
absence	embarrassed	medicine	separate
across	environment	neither	severely
actually	especially	ninety	shining
all right	etc.	ninth	significant
among	exaggerate	nuclear	similar
analyze	excellent	occasionally	sincerely
appearance	exercise	opinion	sophomore
appreciate	existence	opportunity	speech
argument	experience	parallel	straight
athlete	explanation	particular	studying
athletics	extremely	persuade	succeed
awkward	familiar	physically	success
becoming	February	planned	suggest
beginning	finally	pleasant	surprise
belief	foreign	possible	thoroughly
benefit	government	practical	though
buried	grammar	preferred	tragedy
business	grateful	prejudice	tried
certain	guarantee	privilege	tries
college	guard	probably	truly
coming	guidance	professor	unfortunately
committee	height	prove	unnecessary
competition	hoping	psychology	until
complete	humorous	pursue	unusual
consider	immediately	receipt	using
criticism	independent	receive	usually
definitely	intelligence	recommend	Wednesday
dependent	interest	reference	writing
develop	interfere	relieve	written
development	involved	religious	
difference	knowledge	repetition	
disastrous	laboratory	rhythm	
discipline	leisure	ridiculous	
discussed	length	sacrifice	
disease	library	safety	
divide	likely	scene	
dying	lying	schedule	
eighth	marriage	secretary	
eligible	mathematics	senior	

CONFUSED SPELLING AND CONFUSING WORDS

The following are more words that are commonly misspelled or confused with one another. Some have similar sounds, some are often mispronounced, and some are only misunderstood.

a	An adjective (called an article) used before a word beginning with a consonant or a consonant sound, as in "I ate *a* donut."
an	An adjective (called an article) used before a word beginning with a vowel (*a, e, i, o, u*) or with a silent *h*, as in "I ate *an* artichoke."
and	A coordinating conjunction, as in "Sara *and* I like Alison Krauss."
accept	A verb meaning "to receive," as in "I *accept* your explanation."
except	A preposition meaning "to exclude," as in "I paid everyone *except* you."
advice	A noun meaning "guidance," as in "Thanks for the *advice*."
advise	A verb meaning "to give guidance," as in "Will you please *advise* me of my rights?"
all right	An adjective meaning "correct" or "acceptable," as in "It's *all right* to cry."
alright	Not used in formal writing.
all ready	An adjective that can be used interchangeably with *ready*, as in "I am *all ready* to go to town."
already	An adverb meaning "before," which cannot be used in place of *ready*, as in "I have *already* finished."
a lot	An adverb meaning "much," as in "She liked him *a lot*," or a noun meaning "several," as in "I had *a lot* of suggestions."
altogether	An adverb meaning "completely," as in "He is *altogether* happy."
all together	An adverb meaning "as one," which can be used interchangeably with *together*, as in "The group left *all together*."
choose	A present-tense verb meaning "to select," as in "Do whatever you *choose*."
chose	The past-tense form of the verb *choose*, as in "They *chose* to take action yesterday."
could of	A misspelled phrase caused by confusing *could've*, meaning *could have*, with *could of*.
could have	Correctly spelled phrase, as in "I *could have* left."
could've	Correctly spelled contraction of *could have*, as in "He *could've* succeeded."

affect	Usually a verb meaning "change," as in "Ideas *affect* me."
effect	Usually a noun meaning "result," as in "That *effect* was unexpected."
hear	A verb indicating the receiving of sound, as in "I *hear* thunder."
here	An adverb meaning "present location," as in "I live *here*."
it's	A contraction of *it is*, as in "*It's* time to dance."
its	Possessive pronoun, as in "Each dog has *its* day."
know	A verb usually meaning "to comprehend" or "to recognize," as in "I *know* the answer."
no	An adjective meaning "negative," as in "I have *no* potatoes."
lead	A present-tense verb, as in "I *lead* a stable life now," or a noun referring to a substance, such as "I sharpened the *lead* in my pencil."
led	The past-tense form of the verb *lead*, as in "I *led* a wild life in my youth."
loose	An adjective meaning "without restraint," as in "He is a *loose* cannon."
lose	A present-tense verb from the pattern *lose*, *lost*, *lost*, as in "I thought I would *lose* my senses."
paid	The past tense form of *pay*, as in "He *paid* his dues."
payed	Misspelling.
passed	The past-tense form of the verb *pass*, meaning "went by," as in "He *passed* me on the curve."
past	An adjective meaning "former," as in "That's *past* history," or a noun, meaning "a time gone by," as in "He lived in the *past*."
patience	A noun meaning "willingness to wait," as in "Job was a man of much *patience*."
patients	A noun meaning "people under care," as in "The doctor had fifty *patients*."
peace	A noun meaning "a quality of calmness" or "absence of strife," as in "The guru was at *peace* with the world."
piece	A noun meaning "part," as in "I gave him a *piece* of my mind."
quiet	An adjective meaning "silent," as in "She was a *quiet* child."
quit	A verb meaning "to cease" or "to withdraw," as in "I *quit* my job."
quite	An adverb meaning "very," as in "The clam is *quite* happy."

(Second "TOP 25 EDITING ERRORS" marker appears beside *it's* / *its*.)

receive	A verb meaning "to accept," as in "I will *receive* visitors now."
recieve	Misspelling.
stationary	An adjective meaning "not moving," as in "Try to avoid running into *stationary* objects."
stationery	A noun meaning "paper material to write on," as in "I bought a box of *stationery* for Sue's birthday present."
than	A conjunction, as in "He is taller *than* I am."
then	An adverb, as in "She *then* left town."
their	An adjective (possessive pronoun), as in "They read *their* books."
there	An adverb, as in "He left it *there*," or a filler word, as in "*There* is no time left."
they're	A contraction of *they are*, as in "*They're* happy."
thorough	An adjective, as in "He did a *thorough* job."
through	A preposition, as in "She went *through* the yard."
to	A preposition, as in "I went *to* town."
too	An adverb meaning "exceeding or going beyond what is acceptable," as in "You are *too* late to qualify for the discount," or "also," as in "I have feelings, *too*."
two	An adjective of number, as in "I have *two* jobs."
truely	Misspelling.
truly	An adverb meaning "sincerely" or "completely," as in "He was *truly* happy."
weather	A noun meaning "condition of the atmosphere," as in "The *weather* is pleasant today."
whether	A conjunction, as in "*Whether* he would go was of no consequence."
write	A present-tense verb, as in "Watch me as I *write* this letter."
writen	Misspelling.
written	A past participle verb, as in "I have *written* the letter."
you're	A contraction of *you are*, as in "*You're* my friend."
your	A possessive pronoun, as in "I like *your* looks."

YOUR SPELL CHECKER

Your computer spell checker is an important tool with many benefits and some limitations. With about 100,000 words in a typical database, the spell checker alerts you to problem words in your text that should be verified. If you agree that the spelling of a word should be checked, you can then select from a list of words with similar spellings. A likely substitute word will be highlighted. With a keystroke, you can correct a problem, add your own word to the database, or ignore the alert.

With a few more keystrokes, you can type in your own correction, and you can add an unusual spelling or word to the database. You will be amazed at how many times your computer will catch misspellings that your eye did not see.

However, the spell checker has limitations. If you intended to type *he* and instead typed *me*, the spell checker will not alert you to a possible problem because the word you typed is spelled correctly. If you use the wrong word, such as *herd* instead of *heard*, the spell checker will not detect a problem. Thus you should always proofread your writing after you have spell checked it.

Avoiding Wordy Phrases

Certain phrases clutter sentences, consuming our time in writing and our readers' time in reading. Watch for wordy phrases as you revise and edit.

Wordy: *Due to the fact that* he was unemployed, he had to use public transportation.

Concise: *Because* he was unemployed, he had to use public transportation.

Wordy: *Deep down inside* he believed that the Red Sox would win.

Concise: He believed that the Red Sox would win.

Wordy	Concise
at the present time	now
basic essentials	essentials
blend together	blend
it is clear that	(delete)
due to the fact that	because
for the reason that	because
I felt inside	I felt
in most cases	usually
as a matter of fact	in fact
in the event that	if
until such time as	until
I personally feel	I feel
in this modern world	today
in order to	to
most of the people	most people
along the lines of	like
past experience	experience
at that point in time	then
in the final analysis	finally
in the near future	soon
have a need for	need
in this day and age	now

EXERCISE 52   Wordy Phrasing

Circle the wordy phrases and revise them to form concise phrases.

1. Past experience tells me I should read the fine print.

2. In the final analysis, I feel inside that the college courses will blend together.

3. It is clear that most of the people can be fooled.

4. For the reason that I am too young, I must say no to your marriage proposal.

5. In most cases I would agree with you.

6. I am learning the basic essentials in this class.

7. In the near future I will have some investment money.

8. I personally feel that success is within my grasp.

9. I have no other comment at the present time.

10. I don't have a need for a pocket tool kit.

Brief Guide for ESL Students

If you came to this country knowing little English, you probably acquired vocabulary first. Then you began using that vocabulary within the basic patterns of your own language. If your native language had no articles, you probably used no articles; if your language had no verb tenses, you probably used no verb tenses, and so on. Using the grammar of your own language with your new vocabulary may initially have enabled you to make longer and more complex statements in English, but eventually you learned that your native grammar and your adopted grammar were different. You may even have learned that no two grammars are the same, and that English has a bewildering set of rules and an even longer set of exceptions to those rules. This Handbook presents grammar (the way we put words together) and rhetoric (the way we use language effectively) that can be applied to your writing. The following are some definitions, rules, and references that are of special help to writers who are learning English as a second language (ESL).

USING ARTICLES IN RELATION TO NOUNS

Articles

Articles are either indefinite (*an, a*) or definite (*the*). Because they point out nouns, they are often called *noun determiners*.

Nouns

Nouns can be either singular (*book*) or plural (*books*) and are either count nouns (things that can be counted, such as "book") or noncount nouns (things that cannot be counted, such as "homework"). If you are not certain whether a noun is a count noun or a noncount noun, try placing the word *much* before the word. You can say, "much homework," so *homework* is a noncount noun.

Rules

- **Use an indefinite article (a or an) before singular count nouns and not before noncount nouns. The indefinite article means "one," so you would not use it before plural count nouns.**

Correct:	I saw a book. [count noun]
Correct:	I ate an apple. [count noun]
Incorrect:	I fell in a love. [noncount noun]
Correct:	I fell in love. [noncount noun]
Incorrect:	I was in a good health. [noncount noun]
Correct:	I was in good health. [noncount noun]

- **Use the definite article (the) before both singular and plural count nouns that have specific reference.**

Correct:	I read the book. [a specific one]
Correct:	I read the books. [specific ones]
Correct:	I like to read a good book. [nonspecific, therefore the indefinite article]
Correct:	A student who works hard will pass. [any student, therefore nonspecific]
Correct:	The student on my left is falling asleep. [a specific student]

- **Use the definite article with noncount nouns only when they are specifically identified.**

Correct:	Honesty (as an idea) is a rare commodity.
Correct:	The honesty of my friend has inspired me. [specifically identified]
Incorrect:	I was in trouble and needed the assistance. [not specifically identified]
Correct:	The assistance offered by the paramedics was appreciated. [specifically identified]

- **Place the definite article before proper nouns (names) of the following:**

  oceans, rivers, and deserts (for example, *the* Pacific Ocean and *the* Red River)
  countries, if the first part of the name indicates a division (*the* United States of America)
  regions (*the* South)
  plural islands (*the* Hawaiian Islands)

museums and libraries (*the* Los Angeles County Museum)
colleges and universities when the word *college* or *university* comes before the
    name (*the* University of Oklahoma)

These are the main rules. For a more detailed account of rules for articles, see a comprehensive ESL book in your library.

SENTENCE PATTERNS

The Kinds of Sentences section in this Handbook defines and illustrates the patterns of English sentences. Some languages include patterns not used in standard English. The following principles are well worth remembering:

- **The conventional English sentence is based on one or more clauses, each of which must have a subject (sometimes the implied "you") and a verb.**

    Incorrect: Saw the book. [subject needed even if it is obvious]

    Correct: I saw the book.

- **English does not repeat a subject, even for emphasis**.

    Incorrect: The book that I read it was interesting.

    Correct: The book that I read was interesting.

VERB ENDINGS

- **English indicates time through verbs**. Learn the different forms of verb tenses and the combinations of main verbs and helping verbs.

    Incorrect: He watching the game. [A verblike word ending in *-ing* cannot be a verb all by itself.]

    Correct: He is watching the game. [Note that a helping verb such as *is*, *has*, *has been*, *will*, or *will be* always occurs before a main verb ending in *-ing*.]

- **Take special care in maintaining consistency in tense**.

    Incorrect: I went to the mall. I watch a movie there. [verb tenses inconsistent]

    Correct: I went to the mall. I watched a movie there.

All twelve verb tenses are covered with explanations, examples, and exercises in the Verbs section of the Handbook.

IDIOMS

Some of your initial problems with writing English are likely to arise from trying to adjust to a different and difficult grammar. If the English language used an entirely systematic grammar, your learning would be easier, but English has patterns that are both complex and irregular. Among them are idioms, word groups that often defy grammatical rules and mean something other than what they appear to mean on the surface.

The expression "He kicked the bucket" does not mean that someone struck a cylindrical container with his foot; instead, it means that someone died. That example is one kind of idiom. Because the expression suggests a certain irreverence, it would not be the choice of most people who want to make a statement about death; but if it is used, it must be used with its own precise wording, not "He struck the long cylindrical container with his foot," or "He did some bucket-kicking." Like other languages, the English language has thousands of these idioms. Expressions such as "the more the merrier" and "on the outs" are ungrammatical. They are also very informal expressions and therefore seldom used in college writing, although they are an indispensable part of a flexible, effective, all-purpose vocabulary. Because of their twisted meanings and illogic, idioms are likely to be among the last parts of language that a new speaker learns well. A speaker must know the culture thoroughly to understand when, where, and how to use slang and other idiomatic expressions.

If you listen carefully and read extensively, you will learn English idioms. Your library will have dictionaries that explain them.

MORE SUGGESTIONS FOR ESL WRITERS

1. Read your material aloud and try to detect inconsistencies and awkward phrasing.

2. Have others read your material aloud for the same purposes.

3. If you have severe problems with grammatical awkwardness, try composing shorter, more direct sentences until you become more proficient in phrasing.

4. On your Self-Evaluation Chart, list the problems you have (such as with articles, verb endings, clause patterns), review relevant parts of the Handbook, and concentrate on your own problem areas as you draft, revise, and edit.

EXERCISE 53   Correcting ESL Problems

Make corrections in the use of articles, verbs, and phrasing.

GEORGE WASHINGTON AT TRENTON

One of most famous battles during the War of Independence occur at Trenton, New Jersey, on Christmas Eve of the 1776. The colonists outmatched in supplies and finances and were outnumbered in troop strength. Most observers in other countries think rebellion would be put down soon. British overconfident and believe there would be no more battles until spring. But George

Washington decide to fight one more time. That Christmas, while large army of Britishers having party and thinking about the holiday season, Americans set out for surprise raid. They loaded onto boats used for carrying ore and rowed across Delaware River. George Washington stood tall in lead boat. According to legend, drummer boy floated across river on his drum, pulled by rope tied to boat. Because British did not feel threatened by the ragtag colonist forces, they unprepared to do battle. The colonists stormed living quarters and the general assembly hall and achieved victory. It was good for the colonists' morale, something they needed, for they would endure long, hard winter before fighting again.

Brandon Text Credit Lines

This page constitutes an extension of the copyright page. We have made every effort to trace the ownership of all copyrighted material and to secure permission from copyright holders. In the event of any question arising as to the use of any material, we will be pleased to make the necessary corrections in future printings. Thanks are due to the following authors, publishers, and agents for permission to use the material indicated.

Chapter 4. 59: Eric Hoffer, "A Time for Juveniles." **59–60:** James Maurer, "Adobe: Mud for Castles and Hovels."

Chapter 6. 90: S. Feshback and B. Weiner, "Total Institutions" from *Personality*, 1991. **91–92:** (Adapted from Scot Ober, *Contemporary Business Communication*).

Chapter 7. 125–126: Sandy Banks, "Teacher's protest of tasteless T-shirt creates a teachable moment," September 9, 2014, *LA Times*. Copyright 2015 by Los Angeles Times. **127–129:** From the *New York Times*, February 25, 2007, © 2007 The New York Times. All rights reserved. Used by permission and protected by the Copyright Laws of the United States. The printing, copying, redistribution, or retransmission of this Content without express written permission is prohibited.

Chapter 8. 157–158: From *USA Today*, February 17, 2012 © 2012 Gannett. All rights reserved. Used by permission and protected by the Copyright Laws of the United States. The printing, copying, redistribution, or retransmission of this Content without express written permission is prohibited. **160–161:** Adair Lara, "Who's Cheap?" from *San Francisco Chronicle*. By permission. **162–163:** Luis Torres, "Dreaming Together on the Day of the Dead."

Chapter 9. 185–186: "A Partial Remembrance of a Puerto Rican Childhood" is reprinted with permission from the publisher of "Silent Dancing: A Partial Remembrance of a Puerto Rican Childhood" by Judith Ortiz Cofer (© 1999 Arte Publico Press–University of Houston). **187–190:** Excerpt from pp. 8–14 from MEN ARE FROM MARS, WOMEN ARE FROM VENUS by JOHN GRAY. Copyright © 1992 by John Gray. Reprinted by permission of HarperCollins Publishers.

Chapter 10. 217–219: Shara Tonn/Wired; © Conde Nast. **220–222:** Reprinted with the permission of Scribner, a Division of Simon & Schuster, Inc. and Prairie Home Productions, LLC, from "Attitude," *The New Yorker*, August 27, 1979, as included in HAPPY TO BE

HERE by Garrison Keillor. Copyright © 1979 by Garrison Keillor. All rights reserved. **223–225:** C. Edward Good and William Fitzpatrick, "A Successful Interview," 1993. By permission.

Chapter 11. 247–248: From BAUMEISTER/BUSHMAN. *Social Psychology and Human Nature, Comprehensive Edition*, 2E. © 2011 Wadsworth, a part of Cengage Learning, Inc. Reproduced by permission. www.cengage.com/permissions. **248–250:** From *The New York Times,* September 1, 2015 © 2015 The New York Times. All rights reserved. Used by permission and protected by the Copyright Laws of the United States. The printing, copying, redistribution, or retransmission of this Content without express written permission is prohibited. **251–254:** Francis Flaherty, "The Ghetto Made Me Do It," *In These Times*, April 5, 1993. Reprinted by permission.

Chapter 12. 277–280: LOCHER, DAVID A., *Collective Behavior*, 1st Edition, © 2002. Reprinted by permission of Pearson Education, Inc., New York, New York. **281–282:** From PLOTNIK, *Introduction to Psychology* (with InfoTrac®), 7E. © 2005 Cengage Learning. **283–284:** Friedman, "Living Environments," originally appeared in *The Montreal Gazette*. Reprinted by permission of the author.

Chapter 13. 308–309: Suzanne Britt, "Neat People vs. Sloppy People" from *Show and Tell*. By permission.

Chapter 14. 330–331: (American Heritage Dictionary of the English Language, 4th ed.). **339–340:** Sheila Ferguson is the author of the enduring book *Soul Food: Classic Cuisine from the Deep South*. **341–342:** From Baumeister/Bushman, *Social Psychology and Human Nature, Comprehensive Edition*, 2E. © 2011 Cengage Learning. **343–346:** Christopher Grant, "Graffiti: Taking a Closer Look" from *The FBI Law Enforcement Bulletin*, 1996. **347–349:** Rose Del Castillo Guilbault, "Americanization Is Tough on 'Macho'" from *This World*, 1989.

Chapter 15. 374: Jessica Pauline Ogilvie, "How kids feel the swats of spanking; Do they hurt long after the initial sting, or will they be fine if it's done properly?" from *Los Angele Times*, 2011. By permission. **377–379:** Meghan Daum, "Shouldn't Men Have 'Choice' Too?" from *Los Angeles Times*, 2005. By permission. **380–381:** Source: Shakely, Jack. *Los Angeles Times*. 25 Aug 2011: A. 15. Reprinted with permission of the author.

Author/Title Index

Subject Index

575